Sports in Chicago

Sport and Society

Series Editors
Benjamin G. Rader
Randy Roberts

*A list of books in the series
appears at the end of this book.*

SPORTS
IN CHICAGO

Edited by
ELLIOTT J. GORN

UNIVERSITY OF ILLINOIS PRESS
Urbana and Chicago

Published in cooperation
with the Chicago History Museum

Robin F. Bachin, "Baseball Palace of the
World: Commercial Recreation and the
Building of Comiskey Park," first appeared
in Robin F. Bachin, *Building the South Side:
Urban Space and Civic Culture in Chicago,
1890–1919,* © 2004 by the University of
Chicago Press.

L. J. D. Wacquant, "The Social Logic of
Boxing in Black Chicago: Toward a Sociology
of Pugilism," first appeared in *Sociology of
Sport,* 9 (1992): 221–54, © 1992 by Human
Kinetics Publishers, Inc. Reprinted with
permission from Human Kinetics, Inc.
(Champaign, Ill.).

Library of Congress Cataloging-in-Publication Data
Sports in Chicago / edited by Elliott J. Gorn.
p.   cm. — (Sport and society)
Includes bibliographical references and index.
ISBN 978-0-252-03317-9 (cloth : alk. paper)
ISBN 978-0-252-07523-0 (pbk. : alk. paper)
1. Sports—Illinois—Chicago—Miscellanea.
I. Gorn, Elliott J.
GV584.5.C4G67   2008
796.'0977311—dc22   2008002233

Contents

Preface

ELLIOTT J. GORN

On the opening day of the Chicago Historical Society exhibit, "Chicago Sports! You Shoulda' Been There," a teenaged visitor strolled through the gallery, looking at objects and reading the stories. When he got to the glass case containing all six Chicago Bulls championship trophies, won during the glorious 1990s of Michael Jordan, the kid dropped to his knees and crossed himself.

Every real Chicago sports fan understands—not just Catholics in this most Catholic of American big cities, but Protestants and Jews, Hindus, Muslims, and atheists. Those trophies are genuine relics of our faith, evidence that once we were filled with the spirit, testimony that saints and miracles graced our city, proof that righteous days will return. We hope.

"Chicago Sports: You Shoulda' Been There," which was on display at the Chicago Historical Society between March 2003 and January 2004, chronicled some of the biggest stories from the city's sporting past. More, we tried to show how play, games, and leisure functioned within the city, sometimes dividing us, sometimes uniting us. Chicago grew rapidly during the late nineteenth and early twentieth centuries, doubling, then doubling again over the decades. The town was full of new arrivals from the countryside and from overseas. Before the First World War, over two-thirds of Chicago's population was made up of immigrants and the children of immigrants. When Congress slammed the doors shut on immigration in the 1920s, new groups, such as African Americans and white southerners, began pouring in. Overseas immigration opened up again in the 1960s, and today there are new communities of Indians in Rogers Park, South East Asians in Uptown (more Asians now live in

Chicago than Honolulu), and Latinos (Chicago holds America's second largest Hispanic population) in several neighborhoods. More, Chicago's explosive growth shifted to the suburbs after World War II, and today those same ethnic groups, along with Russians, Poles, and Serbians, not to mention a range of African, Asian, and Middle Eastern peoples, have established new communities in the "collar counties."

From the late nineteenth century, sport has been one way for newcomers to find a place in the city. But the process has not always been smooth and harmonious. Baseball's Negro leagues—the most successful and long-lasting of which was founded in Chicago—provide an obvious example of a group being oppressed, excluded, and forced to develop its own "parallel institution," to use a sociologist's term. Yet less than a century later, the very face of Chicago was that of a black man, Michael Jordan, a fact that would have been unthinkable a few decades earlier.

Sports at their best are about belonging. Going to Wrigley Field, or joining a Chicago Park District team, or playing a high school sport all reinforce our sense of being part of something larger than ourselves. Cities are held together by water supplies, sewage systems, rail lines, and power grids. But equally important, they are made whole by citizens' shared experiences and memories. Sport in the past hundred years or so has become a vital part of culture—and it is culture as much as technology or government that cements individual identity to nations, cities, and communities. Memories of Super Bowl XXV in 1986, of the 1919 Black Sox scandal, of the Cubs' collapse in 1969, of the 1990s Bulls' six championships, and countless other events, great and small, give us shared experiences, a common life.

The following essays cover a range of topics in the history of Chicago sports. We have not aimed for comprehensive coverage but for a series of interesting case studies. The first piece, however, surveys the broad contours of how Chicagoans played. Gerald Gems's opening essay demonstrates how themes of identity—ethnic, racial, religious, gender—have been woven into the fabric of our games from the beginning. His survey is followed by chapters arranged roughly by chronology. The first group of these concern Chicago during its era of heroic growth and change. Gabe Logan goes back to the late nineteenth century to uncover an early example of an ethnic group bringing their games to America, in this case, British migrants who began some of the earliest soccer leagues. Steven Riess's "Closing Down the Open City" discusses the movement at the beginning of the twentieth century to end boxing and horse racing in Chicago; he argues that ending gambling and brutal spectacles was not at the fringe of American politics, but squarely in the middle of that era's vaunted progressive reforms. In "Jewish Women, Sports, and

Chicago History," Linda Borish discusses how, from the beginning of the twentieth century, one of the city's new ethnic groups built its own institutions and then sent its daughters out to seek athletic excellence. Robin Bachin's "Baseball Palace of the World" explores the building of Comiskey Park on the South Side in 1910 in the context of urban development in America's fastest-growing city. Bachin reveals how the ballpark embodied civic ideals, although those ideals were not uniformly agreed upon, nor were their blessings equally shared.

The next group of essays takes a little darker tone. Like Borish's essay, Peter Alter's "Serbs, Sports, and Whiteness" explores the process of Americanization for immigrants and their children, but he finds race— more specifically, the need for ethnics to think of themselves as white and to be seen as white—the key to understanding the process of becoming American. Here assimilation is less a story of triumphal accomplishment than an ambivalent tale of groups setting themselves off from each other. The saga of Charles Comiskey and his White Sox that Robin Bachin introduced continues in Dan Nathan's "A Dirty Rotten Shame," but once again, we hear the story in a lower register, because Nathan recounts the 1919 Chicago Black Sox scandal. More than just telling how the World Series was thrown to gamblers, Nathan discusses how we remember the event and its importance to Chicago's image. The act of remembering is also central to the next essay. In his autobiographically based piece on the legendary Chicago Bears running back Bronko Nagurski, Timothy Spears explores the boundary between sport and folklore. He too muses on youth and aging, and on the meanings of sports across generations. The great running back was first coached by Spears's grandfather, and playing college football bound the men of the Spears family across generations.

The final group of essays carries us toward the present. Timothy Neary's "An Inalienable Right to Play" discusses one of the nation's most important movements in spreading the gospel of sports, focusing on Chicago's Catholic Youth Organization and its early commitment to racially integrated athletics. While segregation remained the national norm, the CYO began the process of breaking down sports' Jim Crow barriers. If the Black Sox scandal represented a stain that could not be washed away, the Cubs are about perennially dashed hopes. In "An Athlete Dying Young," Richard Kimball recounts the tragic story of Kenny Hubbs, the Cubs' promising second baseman, who died in a plane crash shortly after his rookie season. Kimball explores the cultural connections in America between youth, hope, and tragedy. Loic Wacquant's classic essay, "The Social Logic of Boxing in Black Chicago," with its careful ethnographic exploration of the culture of the ring, provides striking contrast to Kimball's piece. "Recent Stadium Development Projects in

Chicago" by Costas Spirou and Larry Bennett, returns us to the question of sports and public space, for it examines the relationship between business, the city, and neighborhoods in the building of Chicago's newest stadiums. How, the authors ask, can development coexist with neighborhood needs? Our last chapter takes us back to the exhibit out of which this book came. John Russick, who curated "Chicago Sports! You Shoulda' Been There," describes how the exhibit evolved, how we decided on the themes we wished to develop, and why we chose to emphasize certain stories and objects over others. Finally, the epilogue explores the futility of being a Cubs fan; the Cubs are the city's oldest athletic organization, and arguably—after one hundred years without a championship—the least successful sports franchise in American history.

The Chicago Historical Society (which changed its name to the Chicago History Museum in 2006) provided a fine home for the exhibit, and the University of Illinois Press offered an equally fine home for this book. Above all, I would like to thank John Russick, Rosemary Adams, and Lonnie Bunch for their aid and advice.

1

Sports and Identity in Chicago

GERALD GEMS

Chicago was one of the wonders of the nineteenth century. Within a single lifetime, it exploded from a frontier outpost to a city of more than a million inhabitants. More, it was a remarkably diverse town, containing dozens of racial, ethnic, and religious groups, each with its own interests and values. Their communities, often near workplaces, provided jobs, leisure, and recreational opportunities. Despite conflicts between these groups, sports provided a common interest. Though groups often shunned contact in other spheres of life, sports came to serve as a visible social bond among a host of factions, eventually culminating in a measure of accommodation between them.

Even before Europeans established their residence in Chicago, the southwest corner of Lake Michigan served as the crossroads for nine major Native American tribes. By the seventeenth century, French-Catholic explorers, missionaries, and fur trappers had intruded upon their space; but that comparative handful of men managed to coexist with the natives in a relatively harmonious fashion, often intermarrying and adopting indigenous customs. The process of cultural transformation changed more abruptly as British colonists moved westward. Anglos assumed a cultural superiority and rationalized their conquest of the frontier as part of their manifest destiny.

Once the Europeans had settled their own differences in the so-called French and Indian War and the American colonials' Revolutionary War for independence, the new republic set about extending its boundaries and influence. The intrusive construction of Fort Dearborn on the shore of Lake Michigan in 1803, the subsequent Anglo perception of a "massacre" of its inhabitants in 1812, and consequent resettling of a garrison in 1816 signaled the violent transformation of society. The federal occupation of the site and its advantageous location for western trade encouraged settlement by New England entrepreneurs in the 1830s. Chicago declared itself a town in 1833, the native peoples moved farther westward, and the white settlers established their laws, governing agencies, and civic services. By 1837, Chicago fancied itself a city.[1]

The New Englanders were joined by European immigrants in the 1840s. Germans, some fleeing a failed revolution, and Irish escaping the potato famine, soon landed in Chicago. Not only their Catholic religion set them apart but their leisure habits differed from the Protestant New Englanders'. Moral issues, primarily beer drinking in German saloons and Anglo attempts to prohibit it, resulted in the Lager Beer Riot of 1855. Protestants attempted to enforce Sabbath days filled with churchgoing, not drinking or traditional recreations. Tavern closings and increased license fees erupted in violence, and the dispute over liquor was only the first of many that centered on different values and sensibilities based on religion and ethnicity. Still, the growing numbers and strength of the immigrant communities eventually led to repeal of nativist legislation.

As the city grew exponentially during the Civil War era, one of the activities that brought Chicagoans together was baseball. Employers praised and promoted it as a wholesome alternative to leisure time spent in the saloon. They felt that the game instilled a strong work ethic, cooperative teamwork, and self-sacrifice, qualities beneficial to an efficient, productive, industrial workforce, and businessmen willingly sponsored clubs. Baseball games against local rivals fostered company camaraderie that employers hoped would transfer to the workforce. Those rivalries extended to other midwestern cities, as they contested for the lucrative hinterland trade engendered by continuing westward settlement. Cincinnati had already formed the first fully professional team in 1869, and its undefeated national tour brought publicity and prestige to that city. Chicago's business leaders formed their own pro team in response, and thousands of city residents welcomed the White Stockings (renamed the Cubs thirty years later) home after its 157–1 defeat of Memphis. A national league of professional teams followed, with Chicagoans presiding over the association.[2]

Baseball did not, however, unite all Chicagoans. Large numbers of southern and eastern European immigrants, who flooded into the city after 1880 and provided a ready workforce, were often troubled by a capitalist system that did not meet their expectations of opportunity, freedom, and democracy. Long hours, low pay, and even less job security favored employers rather than employees, and Chicago emerged as headquarters for socialist and anarchist movements in the 1880s. Labor strikes, armed conflict, and the Haymarket riot became synonymous with the city. Among the participants were the German Turnvereins, gymnastic clubs dedicated to maintaining their European culture, and for some, a socialistic vision at odds with American capitalism. Other ethnics, especially the Polish Falcons and Czech *sokol* clubs, fostered similar nationalistic sentiments that differed from nativists' conceptions of American loyalty and patriotism.

George Pullman, a prominent Chicago industrialist, moved to rectify some of the class differences as early as 1880, when he constructed his company town south of the city, complete with workers' housing and services, a comprehensive athletic program with magnificent facilities, but no saloon available to employees. Athletic events, such as rowing, cycling, and track meets brought national attention and positive publicity to the town of Pullman. Other businesses around the country soon copied Pullman's model as they sought greater harmony with their employees. That temporary peace ended with the Pullman Strike of 1894, when the employer-landlord slashed salaries and working hours but maintained high rents during an economic depression. The strike required federal troops to quell it. Pullman soon died, and the city of Chicago annexed his town; but the workers maintained their athletic teams.[3]

Sports provided the working class with an alternative means to social mobility, one more conducive to their cherished value of physical prowess. Professional teams offered working-class men a greater measure of wealth and recognition than industrial labor. The growth of enormous corporations turned independent craftsmen into "wage slaves," many workers charged. But playing ball, or even wagering large sums on the outcome of sporting events, could augment a family's weekly wages.

Chicago entrepreneurs found in the sports boom a means to profitable business ventures. John Brunswick moved his billiard table business to Chicago in 1884 and soon expanded his operations to include bowling equipment and elaborate bars, all mainstays of the saloon trade. Albert Spalding parlayed his career as a star pitcher for the Chicago White Stockings into the club presidency and a sporting goods firm of international magnitude that brought him millionaire status and celebrity. Other promoters formed corporate groups to cultivate sports as a business. Wealthy subscribers to the Washington Park Jockey Club, with General Philip Sheridan as president, built a racetrack that served as the site of the American Derby, the premier horseracing event of the 1880s. There, socialites dressed, preened, and pranced to show their status, while gamblers and prostitutes plied their trades, and commoners wagered in pursuit of their American dream. Sports thus provided one area of common interest that crossed class lines.

Sports also produced athletic heroes who crossed both class and ethnic boundaries. Irish American Mike "King" Kelly, star of the White Stockings teams and darling of the Chicago fans, thrilled spectators with both his play and his antics throughout the 1880s. His drinking caused Albert Spalding to sell him to Boston for the then phenomenal sum of $10,000 in 1887.[4] Colorful characters like Kelly brought both interest and disrepute to sports. In the 1890s, for example, Bill Lange, a Chicago outfielder, had to temporarily forsake the game because his future father-in-law forbade his daughter to marry a ballplayer.

Baseball became an indoor game in 1887, when George Hancock and friends gathered at the Farragut Boat Club for telegraphic reports of a major football game between eastern schools. During a lull, one listener threw a rolled up boxing glove at another, who swatted it with a broomstick. Indoor baseball, or softball as it came to be called, was soon organized into leagues as a winter pastime. It became integral to assimilation efforts when reformers adapted it to playground use as a means to Americanize ethnic youth. The 16" version of the game remains a Chicago hallmark played throughout the summer months with thousands of neighborhood, tavern, and corporate teams vying in the city's parks.

Parks, playgrounds, settlement houses, and schools all employed teachers and coaches who used "American" sports, such as baseball, football, and basketball to teach particular values to immigrant children, many of whom did not speak English. From the 1880s through the 1930s, such educators urged the children of immigrants to adopt, or at least adapt, their prescribed Anglo, commercial values. Sports were the high road to Americanism. Competition taught the basics of capitalism; teamwork and self-sacrifice taught democracy; and deference to authority in the form of a coach or referee countered radical notions. Such lessons often contradicted the values learned at home, but sports were merely part of a larger process by which parents lost control of their offspring, as the state, for example, enacted child labor laws that forbade early employment, and mandatory education laws required school attendance.

Students at both high schools and colleges formed their own athletic leagues outside the jurisdiction of adult authorities. The new University

1. *Hull-House Basketball.* Just a few years after basketball's 1891 invention in Springfield, Massachusetts, Jane Addams sponsored playgrounds and teams in Chicago. Pictured here, the Hull-House men's team in 1910. (Courtesy of the Chicago History Museum.)

of Chicago, following Ivy League schools back east in recognizing the importance of sports for creating a student culture, but also for promoting its national image, hired Amos Alonzo Stagg in 1892. The Yale All American became the first coach given faculty status, and Chicago's athletic teams soon became national powers, traveling cross country and as far as Japan. Chicago's football team even challenged the Ivy League. Sports became one prominent way that the university promoted a revived sense of regional pride in the Midwest and the city fancied itself poised to overtake New York as the nation's cultural leader. That power play further expressed itself in a series of regional football challenges at the high school level. New Yorkers, still featuring the mass plays popular in the East, traveled to Chicago, where the Midwest displayed a faster, "open" game of end runs and reverses. To the dismay of the New Yorkers,

Hyde Park High School defeated Brooklyn Poly 105–0 in 1902. When New Yorkers demanded a rematch in their city the following year, Chicago's North Division High School piled up a 75–0 lead before darkness ended the game.[5]

The commercialization of school athletics, with thousands of paying customers eager for victory, led to recruiting violations, eligibility issues, and downright cheating. Adults moved to take greater control of students' extracurricular activities and forestall the worst abuses. Faculty at midwestern colleges formed the Western Conference (later the Big Ten) in 1895 and high school administrators took over full control of the loosely organized Cook County Athletic League in 1913.

Few working-class boys attended high school during these years, and neighborhood youth found their own uses for sports. Good community or company teams became semiprofessional by hiring players, charging admissions, betting on the side, and distributing profits. The Roseland Eclipse team even scavenged enough railroad construction material to

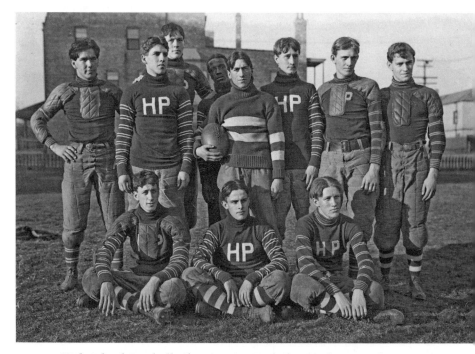

2. *High School Football.* The University of Chicago dominated America's college football scene during the first decade of the twentieth century, and Hyde Park High School's team, shown here in 1901, dominated the South Side. (Courtesy of the Chicago History Museum.)

3. *Football Powerhouse.* Amos Alonzo Stagg, pictured here in 1914, shaped the University of Chicago into one of the greatest football powers in the country. He also coached championship basketball and baseball teams. (Courtesy of the Chicago History Museum.)

build its own stadium. Others, like the Chicago Cardinals football team, started as a club team using a public park. Under the guidance of Chris O'Brien, they evolved into a fully professional contingent with charter membership in the American Professional Football Association in 1920 (later renamed the National Football League). George Halas, son of Czech immigrants to Chicago, represented the Staley Starch Company of Decatur, which also became a member. Halas had honed his playing skills in Chicago schools and parks and he soon transferred the Decatur Staleys to his hometown, where they became the beloved Bears.

Ethnic entrepreneurs like O'Brien and Halas brought previously disparate factions together to produce winning teams and attract fans. The off-the-field animosity of the Cubs' famed infielders, Joe Tinker and Johnny Evers, did not carry over to the diamond, as the Cubs won four National League pennants between 1906 and 1910, but lost the 1906 World Series to the White Sox, known as the Hitless Wonders. The Cubs rebounded for a Series victory in 1908, as Chicagoans basked in the glow of national superiority.

The city also provided a venue for the hopes of African Americans, who began streaming north. Rube Foster played for the Leland Giants, then the American Giants, in the Chicago City League before embarking on his own dream. He founded the Negro National League in an era when blacks were denied entry to the top level of organized baseball. Another Chicago resident, Jack Johnson, proved even more challenging to the white power structure. As heavyweight champion from 1908 to 1915, Johnson defied the notion of Social Darwinism that assumed white superiority, and he flaunted social mores by cohabiting with white women and refusing to cater to white whims. The consequent search for a "Great White Hope" kept Johnson and Chicago in the limelight throughout the era.[6]

Sports allowed not only African Americans but also women to challenge the prescribed norms. Chicago hosted the first women's national archery championship in 1879, and women took up tennis in the following decade. Some also engaged in pedestrianism, a form of long-distance racing. It was the cycling craze of the 1890s, however, that brought even greater change to society. Cycling became popular for several reasons, the fascination with speed and technology among them. But the activity also allowed courting couples to elude the required chaperone, thereby circumventing the Victorian prohibitions that had endured throughout the century. Cycling had other implications for gender roles. Women wore bloomers or pants to cycle because the long dresses of the era got caught in the spokes, and some women even defeated men in distance races. Cycling signaled a transition to the more independent "new woman," who not only sought greater activity, but education and voting rights too.[7]

Women quickly embraced the new game of basketball in the 1890s, and Chicago high school girls were among the first to form a league. Wealthier young women also took up golf, and Chicagoan Margaret Abbott became the first female gold medalist in the modern Olympic Games when she won the golf competition in Paris in 1900. Still, female sports remained contested ground. Many male physicians and female physical educators declared highly competitive and strenuous sports to be inappropriate for women. But in the playgrounds, parks, industrial recreation programs, and athletic clubs, many Chicago women and girls engaged in competitive sports. The Illinois Women's Athletic Club (IWAC), founded in 1918, recruited the best schoolgirls and working women as members. Sybil Bauer, an Olympic swimmer in 1924, had even broken the men's world record in the backstroke. Numerous other Chicago women earned berths on the Olympic track team and IWAC members held many of the early world records in track and field, as the club won two national track championships.

Not only women, but many members of ethnic gymnastic clubs participated in sports, and such inclusion brought previously marginalized groups closer to the mainstream culture.[8] For example, the Chicago He-

4. *Cycling*. A bicycling craze swept America in the 1890s, and Chicago responded with countless wheel clubs. (Courtesy of the Chicago History Museum.)

brew Institute, founded in 1903 by German Jews for the purpose of assimilating their eastern European brethren, did so largely through sports. The institute fielded championship teams and its athletes won numerous individual awards, including national titles. Such prowess helped to dispel the stereotype of Jews as physically weak, and Gentile groups soon sought to use the institute's facilities. Its sponsorship of athletic events brought greater contact between Jews, Catholics, and Protestants throughout the city.[9]

As such previously disparate and divergent groups began to coalesce around the common interest in sports, the city suffered the collective shame of the Black Sox scandal of 1919. Eight White Sox players conspired with gamblers to throw the World Series to the Cincinnati Reds, allegedly to spite Charles Comiskey, the team's miserly owner. Their ruse was discovered a year later, and although a Chicago jury acquitted them of any wrongdoing, the newly appointed baseball commissioner,

5. *Club Sports.* Luddy Malina played for the Western Electric Hawthorne Works Women's Basketball Club in 1924. Many industries supported teams as part of "welfare capitalism," the effort to build good relations with workers while staving off unions. (Courtesy of the Chicago History Museum.)

Judge Kenesaw Mountain Landis, discarded the ruling by banning each of the players for life, despite varying degrees of complicity.

The city rebounded and resurrected its athletic reputation in the 1920s. Johnny Weissmuller became a swimming sensation and Olympic hero in 1924, and starred as Tarzan in Hollywood films thereafter. In addition to the championship teams of the Illinois Women's Athletic Club, the Taylor Trunks, a Chicago company team, won the national women's championship in both bowling and basketball. Chicago also produced top-flight African American basketball teams, as the Chicago Roamers and the Olivet Baptist Church squads challenged the Trunks for local honors. Isadore Channels, star of the Roamers team, later won the championship at the national black tennis tournament. Chicago also yielded the Savoy 5, a spectacular team of African American players who adopted the name of "the Harlem Globetrotters" as a mark of racial pride. Under Abe Saperstein, their Jewish booking agent and eventual owner, the team achieved international acclaim, but they continued to draw their players from Chicago hardcourts for years. The 1920s also witnessed Chicago's first entry in a professional basketball league when George Halas started the Chicago Bruins. Also in 1921, the Chicago Blackhawks entered the professional hockey league (they won their first Stanley Cup in 1934).[10]

Soldier Field opened in 1924, providing the site that tied Chicago sporting events to patriotism, as it memorialized the veterans of World War I. In the ensuing years, Soldier Field served as a communal gathering place that hosted athletic spectacles of local and national significance. The Army-Navy football game of 1927 drew more than 110,000 fans; and the famous "long-count" fight between Jack Dempsey and Gene Tunney that same year attracted more than 120,000 spectators. A similar number witnessed the Prep Bowl football game between the Catholic and public high school league champions for city supremacy a decade later. That game featured Bill DeCorrevont, the high school sensation who led the nation in scoring.[11]

Boxing proved among the most popular sports during the 1930s. The *Tribune* initiated its Golden Gloves rivalry with New York in 1927, and Chicago's Catholic Youth Organization (CYO) started its comprehensive athletic program in 1931. The CYO claimed the largest basketball league in the world, but boxing remained at the organization's core and provided the bulk of its funding. Bishop Sheil, founder and chief administrator of the CYO, allied with Arch Ward, sports editor of the *Chicago Tribune*, to the mutual benefit of each. They produced highly successful national and international boxing teams that promoted the *Tribune*, the Catholic Church, and the city of Chicago. Both tournaments often shared the same competitors, and in the process they generated working-class heroes from Chicago's ethnic neighborhoods. Many Golden Gloves and CYO boxers developed into professional fighters, several of whom became world champions.

Arch Ward proved equally adept at promoting baseball and football. In 1933, he initiated the first major league baseball all-star game between the American and National League stars, held at Comiskey Park. The following year, Ward organized the College Football All-Star Game in Soldier Field, in which the collegians played the professional champions. Both affairs became annual classics.[12] Jay Berwanger, a University of

Chicago halfback, brought the city more football acclaim when he won the very first Heisman Trophy after the 1935 season.

Throughout the 1930s, women's basketball teams decreased in number, but women's interest in softball escalated as the parks, churches, and industrial teams vied for local and national honors. The Windy City Softball League, started in 1934, provided similar opportunities for men; gambling on softball games even enabled some of them to get through the Depression. The *Chicago Evening American* newspaper attracted more than a million spectators to its 4,800-game tournament and thirty thousand fans appeared at the 1935 championship game alone. Tavern owners and small-time gamblers ran neighborhood leagues that kept money circulating within the community.

Even more popular than softball, bowling gained ascendance in German saloons as early as the late nineteenth century. The American Bowling Congress was organized in 1895, and Chicagoans controlled its executive council for decades afterward. The Woman's (*sic*) International Bowling Congress (WIBC) formed in 1916; twenty years later, more than fifteen thousand Chicago women were members. In 1935, the city hosted its national tournament, with $15,000 in prize money, and Marie Warmbier, a local favorite, won two titles. By 1938, there were nine hundred bowling leagues, nine thousand teams, and five hundred thousand bowlers in the city. The large Polish population had a particular attraction to the sport; the Polish National Alliance sponsored sixty men's and sixteen women's teams. Casimir Wronski owned the bowling alleys that hosted the state tournament, while Frank Kafora and Felix Gajewski became city champs. Indeed, Alderman George Rozczynialski first came to fame when he won a national bowling championship. Sports thus provided social mobility for some and perpetuated the hopes of others, as it drew insular groups into the larger popular culture.

Czechs favored baseball and soccer, in addition to their beloved gymnastics. Czech baseball players appeared on local diamonds by the 1890s, and they counted at least three of their own in the professional leagues by 1901. Anton Cermak, a Czech politician, won favor with some of his constituents by providing playing fields and sponsoring teams. (Cermak won election to numerous offices, including mayor of Chicago, a post that ended with his assassination in 1933). Czechs often settled their internecine squabbles on the athletic fields. In addition to the numerous *sokol* clubs that competed within the community, soccer clubs challenged other ethnic teams, and the Sparta Club adopted the Czech national colors to honor its heritage. Czechs also battled each other as they divided between the Reds and Blues, colors that represented the free-thinking atheists and

6. *Bowling.* Bowling always held special appeal for Chicagoans, especially in neighborhood, ethnic, and industrial leagues. Here, the American Bowling Tournament gets underway at the Chicago Coliseum. (Courtesy of the Chicago History Museum.)

the more traditional Catholics. All Czechs took pride in the 1938 Sparta team, which won the national championship.

Other Chicago teams won major titles during this era. The Globetrotters defeated the Chicago Bruins for the 1940 professional basketball championship. That same year, the Bears overwhelmed Washington with a 73–0 victory in the NFL showdown. In 1945, DePaul University won collegiate basketball laurels with its victory in the National Invitational Tournament, then considered the premier event. Its star player, 6' 10" George Mikan, revolutionized the game, as big men assumed a dominant role. DePaul's coach, Ray Meyer, dribbled his way to legendary status within the city and in the national coaching ranks.

The Chicago Stadium increasingly served as the scene for nationally prominent athletic events. Barney Ross, a Chicagoan, enjoyed a home-crowd advantage for his national championship boxing matches of the 1930s. The CYO contests regularly filled the stadium to capacity, but it drew further national attention when it hosted one of the historic bouts between Tony Zale and Rocky Graziano in 1947. Chicago witnessed numerous title fights in the ensuing decade, as Sugar Ray Robinson battled Jake LaMotta, Gene Fullmer, and Carmen Basilio.

Hockey fans, too, braved winter winds to get to the Stadium, particularly after Bobby Hull joined the Blackhawks as an eighteen year old in 1957. He soon reached the sport's pinnacle by scoring fifty goals in the 1961–62 season, and led the team to numerous play-off berths. Other new heroes to the Chicago sports scene also arrived in the 1950s. Cuban born Minnie Minoso joined the White Sox as their first black player in 1951. Ernie Banks became a Cub two years later. On his way to a long, Hall-of-Fame career, Banks never enjoyed a World Series appearance, though his heroics on the field and jubilant spirit off it earned him the title "Mr. Cub" and endeared him to a generation of Chicagoans.

Chicagoans enjoyed a banner year in 1963, when Loyola University won a dramatic overtime victory over Cincinnati to gain the national collegiate basketball championship, and the Bears took the NFL crown in a close 14–10 win over the New York Giants. For a while, at least, Chicagoans could disregard the appellation of "second city." Though the Bears team fortunes declined in subsequent years, the arrival of Gale Sayers and Dick Butkus in 1965 produced weekly thrills for football fans. Sayers scored six touchdowns in one game to cap his rookie season, and Butkus became one of the most feared linebackers to ever play the game.

Their stellar play stood in stark contrast to the 1969 Cubs, whose monumental collapse at the end of a league-leading season broke northsiders' hearts. Yet the "bleacher bums" and play-by-play announcer Jack Brickhouse remained loyal year after year. Harry Caray, another broad-

7. *Black Ball.* Coach Jim Brown and his DuSable High School Basketball team, 1954. DuSable was the first all-black team to play for the Illinois State Championship. (Courtesy of the Chicago History Museum.)

casting legend and eventual Chicago icon, arrived as announcer for the White Sox in 1971. He left before the infamous Disco Demolition night and the ensuing riot at Comiskey Park in 1979, which forced the cancellation and subsequent forfeit of the second game of a scheduled doubleheader. Caray crossed town to replace Jack Brickhouse with the Cubs in 1982, and secured his place in the hearts of Chicagoans.

The 1970s brought more milestones to the city, with the first Chicago marathon in 1977. The following year the town hosted a franchise known as the Chicago Hustle in the first women's professional basketball league. The enterprise lasted for three seasons. In 1975, Walter Payton made his first appearance for the Chicago Bears in a phenomenal career that lasted thirteen years. Payton led his team to the 1986 Super Bowl, where their 43–10 triumph over the Buffalo Bills sent their fans into jubilation. An estimated three hundred thousand attended the team's victory celebration, and coaches Mike Ditka and Buddy Ryan were established as civic heroes. In a city often torn by ethnic, racial, and political strife, the ongoing celebration may have presented the greatest display of cultural unity in over a century, as Chicagoans reveled in the national spotlight.

Other Chicago teams sandwiched championships around the Bears' outstanding season, though none matched the exuberance of that occasion. The Chicago Sting won the North American Soccer League title in 1981, and again in 1984. The White Sox and the Cubs won divisional titles in 1983 and 1984 respectively, and the Cubs won another in 1989, but both teams floundered in the play-offs. In each case these successes failed to achieve the unifying heights of the Bears' conquest. Soccer gained new followers in the 1990s with the Chicago Fire team, which won the national professional championship, and when the city hosted five second-round World Cup games at Soldier Field in 1994. The United States women's team garnered legions of fans with their World and Olympic titles.

The final decade of the twentieth century provided an ongoing celebration of athletic achievement in Chicago. Michael Jordan, drafted by the Bulls in 1984, led the team to continual play-off appearances thereafter, and six national championships during the 1990s. Ably assisted by all-star Scottie Pippen, and a revolving cast of other Bulls players, Jordan led the league in scoring, and his leaping ability and astonishing kinesthetic sense provided nightly highlights for Chicagoans. An astute businessman, marketed as a corporate spokesman by the advertising media, Jordan became an international celebrity, as children around the world donned his facsimile jerseys and gym shoes to "be like Mike."

With Jordan's retirement, Sammy Sosa, a native of the Dominican Republic, emerged as a hero in both his native land and Chicago. Formerly a White Sox player, Sosa became a star after being traded to the Cubs. His home-run barrages throughout the 1998 and 1999 seasons, and the parallel duel with Mark McGwire to break the single season home-run record, captivated not only Chicago, but the entire nation.

The twentieth century ended on a bittersweet note for Chicagoans with the death of the beloved Walter Payton. The city united in its grief in a final tribute to the football star, businessman, and charitable benefactor who had brought joy to so many in his various endeavors. Payton symbolized the positive possibilities of sports and life that had allowed disparate groups and individuals to pursue their own dreams as they established communal identity, self-esteem, and confidence. Though the city's residents have always disagreed on numerous issues, sports provided a place where class, ethnic, racial, religious, and gender differences momentarily merged into our pride as Chicagoans.[13]

Notes

1. The rapid transition of the 1830s can be traced in the Medore Beaubien Papers at the Chicago Historical Society (CHS.)

2. On early baseball in Chicago, see Stephen Freedman, "The Baseball Fad in Chicago, 1865–1870; An Exploration of the Role of Sport in the Nineteenth Century City," *Journal of Sport History*, 5 (Summer 1978): 42–64; and Peter Levine, *A. G. Spalding and the Rise of Baseball* (New York: Oxford University Press, 1985).

3. On Pullman, see Stanley Buder, *Pullman: An Experiment in Industrial Order and Community Planning, 1880–1930* (New York: Oxford University Press, 1968); and Wilma J. Pesavento, "Sport and Recreation in the Pullman Experiment, 1880–1900," *Journal of Sport History*, 9:12 (Summer 1982): 38–62.

4. Kelly's problems with the Chicago club are detailed in the *Chicago Tribune*, February 10, 1887 and March 6, 1887; his career and brief life are covered by Marty Appel, *Slide, Kelly, Slide: The Wild Life and Times of Mike "King" Kelly, Baseball's First Superstar* (Lanham, Md.: Scarecrow, 1996).

5. The Amos Alonzo Stagg Papers are housed in the Special Collections at the University of Chicago. Robin Lester, *Stagg's University: The Rise, Decline, and Fall of Big-Time Football at Chicago* (Urbana: University of Illinois Press, 1995), covers his long career in comprehensive fashion. The *New York Times*, December 7, 1902, November 21, 1903, November 29, 1903, and *Chicago Tribune*, December 2, 1902, December 7, 1902, November 29, 1903, December 1, 1903, provide accounts of the high school games.

6. Randy Roberts, *Papa Jack: Jack Johnson and the Era of White Hopes* (New York: Free Press, 1983).

7. Richard Harmond, "Progress and Flight: An Interpretation of the American Cycle Craze of the 1890s," *Journal of Social History*, 5 (Winter 1971): 235–37; George D. Bushnell, "When Chicago Was Wheel Crazy," *Chicago History*, 4:3 (Fall 1975): 167–75; Henry J. Garrigues, "Women and the Bicycle," *Forum* (January 1896): 576–87.

8. Bertha Severin Papers, Chicago Historical Society. Mrs. Severin founded the Illinois Women's Athletic Club. For detailed coverage of the ethnic clubs, see Gerald R. Gems, "Sport and the Americanization of Ethnic Women in Chicago," in *Ethnicity and Sport in North American History and Culture*, ed. George Eisen and David Wiggins (Westport, Conn.: Praeger, 1994), 177–200.

9. Gerald R. Gems, "Sport and the Forging of a Jewish American Culture: The Chicago Hebrew Institute," *Journal of American Jewish History*, 83:1 (March 1995): 15–62.

10. Gerald R. Gems, "Blocked Shot: The Development of Basketball in the African American Community of Chicago," *Journal of Sport History*, 22:2 (Summer 1995): 135–48.

11. See Elliott J. Gorn, "The Manassa Mauler and the Fighting Marine: An Interpretation of the Dempsey-Tunney Fights," *Journal of American Studies*, 19 (1985): 22–47; and Gerald R. Gems, "The Prep Bowl: Sport, Religion, and Americanization in Chicago," *Journal of Sport History*, 23:3 (Fall 1996): 284–302, for the cultural significance of each.

12. Thomas B. Littlewood, *Arch: A Promoter, Not a Port: The Story of Arch Ward* (Ames: Iowa State University Press, 1990).

13. This process is described and analyzed in Gerald R. Gems, *Windy City Wars: Labor, Leisure, and Sport in the Making of Chicago* (Lanham, Md.: Scarecrow, 1997). A chronology of Chicago sporting events is available in Richard C. Lindberg and Biart Williams, *The Armchair Companion to Chicago Sports* (Nashville, Tenn.: Cumberland House, 1997).

2

The Rise of Early Chicago Soccer

GABE LOGAN

An examination of soccer in turn-of-the-twentieth-century Chicago reveals the ethnic origins of that sport. Immigrant organizations, such as the German Turnerbunds, the Polish and Slavic *sokols,* and the Nordic skiing and shooting clubs, perpetuated Old World sporting traditions. Similarly, the English, Welsh, and Scots enthusiastically maintained and supported soccer. As with the sports of other immigrant groups, soccer became a basis for asserting kinship, providing mutual aid, and marking community boundaries.

Chicago soccer developed in the city's athletic clubs, industrial workplaces, and ethnic communities. These venues served as incubators for the soccer traditions British players brought with them to the city. Of course, Chicago soccer was not as professionalized as that played back in Britain, but the game provided significant opportunities for a handful of players.

Like much of the United States, Chicago in the 1890s had a love affair with sports. Historian Benjamin Rader has noted that many sports organizations began in ethnic clubs, then converged with the mainstream society. Rader argues that Caledonian clubs (started by Scots to keep alive the Highland games, which included track and field events) and cricket clubs functioned as distinctive ethnic enclaves, but evaporated as members assimilated into the larger society.[1] Rader's conclusion supports the assumption that the British easily melded into America. Specifically, Rader notes how the Caledonian games were readily taken up by wealthy "old stock" American clubs, whose members likewise organized track and field games. Eventually, Caledonian track and field clubs merged with or simply lost membership to the national organizations. This phenomenon also occurred with English cricket clubs. Following the Civil War, cricket began to lose popularity as baseball became more prominent.[2] At the same time, national athletic clubs embraced and promoted cricket, which steadily lost out to baseball.

In addition to participating in track and field, cricket, and baseball, the wealthy urban upper class competed in sports that required costly facilities and equipment. Rader contends that this helped to construct a privileged sub-community; sports, in other words, helped define social status.[3] By the 1890s, athletic clubs tended to draw members from elite men's organizations and university alumni. This disproportionately empowered the athletic clubs to lure the top athletes, while supporting the sport-minded upper class. One reason the athletic clubs prospered was their policy of compensating athletes. Athletes who garnered the most victories naturally brought fame to the team, so professionalization was a way to promote the whole organization.

Historian Stephen Riess affirms the significance of indigenous sports organizations among immigrants—the German Turnvereins and Irish Gaelic Association, for example. But Riess suggests that the "new" immigrants, like the Italians and the Bohemians, who came after 1870, did not bring their own sporting traditions to any major degree, but rather, embraced U.S. or "Yankee" sports such as baseball. However, the newcomers did in fact develop significant sports.[4]

Often unnoticed by sport historians, soccer flourished in late-nineteenth-century Chicago, and it was a sport that was brought in by outsiders. The game was played primarily by Welsh, Scottish, and English immigrants in ethnic communities, on industrial ballfields, and in their own athletic clubs. To better understand the development of the game and the organizers who brought soccer to Chicago, a brief review of turn-of-the-century British football is in order.

Tony Mason's study of English soccer and society offers several points that relate to Chicago. Soccer developed out of village games that had existed long before the Victorian and Edwardian periods. Peasants ignored royal bans against the kicking sport, and slowly, multitudes of customs were codified into formal rules. Mason argues that soccer likewise developed with the working class and evolved into recreational matches on workers' holidays, such as "Shrove Tuesday" (a day of celebration for apprentices), and on religious holidays, such as Christmas and Easter, when games were played.[5]

The next important venue for soccer's development was the English schools. Early informal games of the eighteenth century were retrofitted to the new ideals of "muscular Christianity," or a healthy mind in a healthy body. Many nineteenth-century clergymen came to see in sports in general and soccer in particular a way to reach young scholars. Spiritual leaders discovered that soccer served as an excellent way to induce lads to play under religious supervision. These developments naturally carried into the universities and seminaries, which promoted soccer through athletic clubs and rectory leagues.[6] In cities, public school alumni formed soccer clubs, while church and chapel teams often developed in the rural areas (Mason points out that these rural teams usually became independent of the church and evolved into secular football clubs).

In addition to the schools and parishes, public houses and workplaces also sponsored soccer. Taverns took an especially keen interest in the game. Pub owners frequently employed the telegraph during the mid to late nineteenth century to report scores to enthusiastic patrons who chose to drink at the local public house rather than walk across town to a rival pitch.[7]

Industrial sponsorship was more complex. Mason notes that scholars seldom indicate how much or how little businesses supported factory soccer clubs. However, he does suggest that industrial sponsorship probably stressed corporate welfare and industrial identity.[8] Mason theorizes that the factory could only do so much in terms of promoting a team. Those workers who played for the industrial team could not afford time off or travel to distant towns for cup matches. Because of this, talented players either became professionals to earn their living or remained amateurs and worked at regular jobs. Furthermore, because industrialists quickly recognized that English soccer was taking on a life of its own, many owners sought to regulate match attendance when it caused worker absenteeism by levying fines or enacting legislation.

As industry increasingly weighed the muscular benefits of soccer against lost productivity, English industry tightened its purse strings. This meant that much of early English soccer financing came from middle-class enthusiasts. Thus, by the turn of the century, English soccer primarily drew supporters and players from the lower and middle classes. The crowds followed the games from the local pubs, or kept abreast of the results via the telegraph; a few enthusiasts even tramped after the teams.

Mason argues that the amateur/professional split grew wider with passing years. The amateur game continued in the spirit of the English sporting tradition as a pastime for educated alumni and youth. By contrast, some clubs sought out the best players and paid them to play. Supported by pub patrons or paying spectators, professional circuits developed alongside their amateur counterparts.[9]

Sociologist Stephen Wagg argues that in the Midlands and the North of England, soccer clubs increasingly embraced professionalism, while those in Southern England did not. Likewise, some Scottish soccer organizations continued to play for sport's sake, while other clubs recruited professionals.[10] Many observers regarded Scotland as the premier football nation at the end of the century, and several of that country's best players signed professional contracts to play in England.[11] Wales, in contrast, embraced the Rugby game, while the Irish played games that did not reflect English cultural importation at all, such as Gaelic football.[12] Still, English soccer grew so popular that 1863 witnessed the formation of the English Football Association (FA), and by 1882 an international football board had formed to regulate the game in Scotland, Wales, and even Ireland. From this point on, one set of rules governed the game.[13]

Late-nineteenth-century British immigrants to North America brought their soccer traditions with them. Many played in school or at their workplace, for their local parish or neighborhood pub. All of these venues were important, as British immigrants constructed new lives and built their communities, but our clearest pictures of early Chicago soccer emanate from the athletic clubs.

Legend suggests that the first organized Chicago soccer game occurred in 1883, when the Wanderers Cricket and Athletic Club played Pullman at the latter's inaugural athletic festival.[14] Unfortunately, no documentation of the match survives. This lacuna is typical for Chicago and indeed much of early U.S. soccer history. Our first newspaper evidence dates to 1886, when a Chicago eleven laced up against a rival team from St. Louis.[15] According to the story, this was a return match, for the Chicago Football Club had played the St. Louis Thistles in 1883.[16] Despite cold weather, the rematch attracted over one thousand fans, who cheered Chicago to a 5–1 victory. Success convinced organizers of the sport's viability, and the Chicago *Inter Ocean* newspaper gushed that the "Chicago Kickers . . . [were] more successful at their game of ball than was Anson's Colts [later known as the Chicago Cubs] against the Browns."[17] For much of the next decade, the two cities put together select teams to contest for the "Championship of the West."

In 1890, the Chicago Football Association (CFA) organized five clubs under its umbrella: the Chicago Cricket Club, the Chicago Swifts, the Colehours, the Thistles, and the Wanderers Cricket and Athletic Club.[18] These were gentlemen's athletic clubs, organizations that restricted membership based on professional or athletic interests and acquired members from the middle and upper classes.[19] While prestigious, they were not at the very top of the social scale. As historian Gerald Gems observes, organizations like the Union League Club drew members only from old, distinguished families, and from the most prominent businessmen in the city. Historian Tom Melville agrees that a club like the Chicago Cricket Club (CCC), "though hardly exclusive, was . . . based upon a uniformity of social outlook and values." The CCC "adopted a statutory requirement that all objectionable persons making an application be screened out." It was a highly respectable organization, but not at the pinnacle of the social pyramid.[20]

Further investigation confirms Gems's and Melville's findings. The *Chicago Blue Book* series listed all of the elite organizations and citizens of Chicago (at least those whom the editors considered worthy). From 1890 to 1892, only two Chicago soccer clubs, the Chicago Cricket Club and the Wanderers Cricket and Athletic Club, were included. Moreover, while all of the members of the CCC were listed, a comparison of the member list and the soccer team roster reveals that only two players, Trevor Webb and F. R. F. Kelly, were on both lists.[21] In other words, the rest of the team simply played soccer for the CCC but were not members of the club.

Moreover, Webb and Kelly were not included in the *Blue Book*'s "Prominent House Holders," and their respective white-collar office jobs of clerk and manager placed them squarely in the middle class, not the elite. Another significant player and later soccer referee, Tom Gibson, also played for the CCC. In 1892, he accepted employment as a clerk with the Pullman Company, and he simultaneously abandoned the CCC in favor of the Pullman team.[22] Wilma Pesavento and Lisa Raymond's study of Pullman athletics further confirms that the Chicago Cricket Club and Wanderers Cricket Club were upper-middle-class clubs, while the Pullman AC was primarily a blue-collar team.[23] This makes Gibson an interesting case. Presumably he left the CCC for a job at Pullman to better his life. However, from a soccer standpoint he left the top team in the city to play for a club unaffiliated with the CFA. This suggests that some of the athletic club soccer players, such as Gibson, saw themselves as workers who played soccer on the side. Secure employment was naturally most important to them.

Records and artifacts from these clubs are scarce at best. Nonetheless, a careful reading of the local newspapers provides a clearer picture of how these groups survived and occasionally prospered. The soccer clubs procured operating funds from private donations, membership dues, dances, and monthly "smokers."[24] When they weren't playing soccer or raising funds, they gathered to debate the direction of the league, to discuss the rules of the game, and to evaluate potential players. The fact that the organizations held these gatherings on both the club and inter-league level suggests that the soccer club captains, presidents, and prominent players knew their way around the inner workings of these establishments and likely subscribed to the clubs' social etiquette.

Other insights about these organizations are found by looking at their leadership. Consider the Swifts' president, S. Archibald Savage, who emigrated from Scotland and was the secretary for A. D. Hannah and David Hogg's whisky distillery.[25] Like Savage, the owners came to Chicago from Scotland. The distillers even trademarked the Scottish Thistle to commemorate their heritage.[26] Savage's salary and connection to the company allowed him to pay travel and league fee bills for the Swift team.[27] In 1891, Savage proudly opened the club's new soccer pitch with a ceremonial kickoff before the Swift/Pullman match.[28] One newspaper account noted of Savage that "several of his lady friends were present, and they applauded [his kickoff]."[29]

In addition to Savage, Chicago Cricket Club member and local socialite Charles W. Jackson presented the CFA a "handsome silver cup" as an annual trophy.[30] Jackson managed a local company and resided in the fashionable Englewood neighborhood. He was a directing member of the Chicago Cricket Club and later joined the Phoenix Club.[31] His trophy gift was very much indicative of his social standing, and for the next two decades the Jackson Cup remained emblematic of the top Chicago soccer team. Even after the rise of the more famous Peel Cup, the Jackson Cup competition continued until the late 1920s. Hence, while club members paid dues to support the club, the CFA's early leaders covered the more costly items.

Gentility, however, did not always prevail. In 1891, the Chicago Thistles visited St. Louis for a five-game series for the Western Championship. The Thistles won the first match 6–2 in a marathon three-hour game, but the second game resulted in a 2–0 victory for the St. Louis side.[32] In addition to a number of officiating protests, the Thistles decried their "shabby" treatment by the St. Louis Foot-Ball Association. Excepting the St. Louis Blue Bells, no other amateur athletic organization recognized the Thistles' visit. Thistle captain Joe McMillan told local newspapers, "You can bet it will be a long time before I or my men will come down here again."[33] Although the Thistles won a third match and the Western Championship in Chicago by 11–1, the Thistles did not again play in St. Louis until 1896.

An additional affront occurred in summer 1891, when the Chicago Cricket Club ventured to Canada for a combined soccer/cricket tournament. The Chicago side lost 2–1 to the famous Canadian Seaforth Hurons.[34] The Chicago captain, Trevor Webb, blamed "rank unfairness" for Chicago's loss. Webb believed the Seaforth officials intentionally made biased calls against the CCC in favor of the local team.[35]

The Chicagoans stopped in Detroit on the way home, where Webb refused to accept a local referee for the games. Surprisingly, he found a sympathetic audience in his Detroit counterpart. The Detroit captain agreed that the Seaforth side employed marginal officials and added that the Seaforth referee had "roasted" the Detroit club the previous Saturday.[36] Clearly, the Chicago and Detroit athletic clubs subscribed to the ethos of gentlemanly conduct in sport. While winning was naturally important, the victory should not happen at the expense of sportsmanship. In this sense too, American soccer reflected its British origins.

Two examples illustrate the treatment that visiting clubs expected and the repercussions that could follow if expectations were not met. In 1892, the Chicago Thistles played the city's first international soccer visitors, the University of Toronto team. The *Tribune* proclaimed the Toronto side the best in Canada for the past seven seasons. The paper lauded its arrival with brief player biographies and a team itinerary. In addition to local soccer players, prominent socialites such as Charles Jackson, Archie Savage, Charles Shaw, R. G. Clarke, and others wined and dined the Canadians at Kinsley's Restaurant. After Toronto's 4–2 victory, the following night's entertainment took place at the Commercial Hotel, where local dignitaries hosted the visitors to a hearty meal, "followed by songs, football reminiscences, etc."[37] The visitors publicly complimented the Chicagoans on their quality football and enthusiastic reception before departing for Detroit the next day.

The next year the prestigious and newly founded Chicago Athletic Association (Chicago AA) hosted the Detroit Athletic Club. The *Tribune*'s front page blasted the Chicago AA for not meeting the Detroit team when they arrived, locking them out of the clubhouse, and failing to provide transportation and tickets to the Columbian Exposition as promised. When the Detroit players returned to the club, they discovered the Chicago members already eating and ignoring them. Furthermore, one of the Detroit players complained that the Chicago athletes "got all that was good to eat" and left only "trifles" of roast beef and bread. The Detroit team had to secure its own transportation—in cattle cars—to the Stock Pavilion for the game. Loose play and "dirty work" characterized the football match, after which the Detroit team returned to the club in the drafty cattle cars, dirty and wet with perspiration. The Chicago AA did not provide soap, towels, or transportation to the Delaware Hotel, where the Detroit team was to sleep. Given the assumptions of gentlemanly sport, the *Tribune*'s outrage was clearly justified.[38]

From these two examples, it is clear that when athletes traveled to other cities, they expected proper hospitality while they mingled among the local elite. But sport was changing. Chicago soccer increasingly became the pastime of the working class more than those higher on the social scale. The ethos of gentlemanly amateurs who scorned professionalism and winning at all cost fell by the wayside. In late 1892, the Chicago Cricket Club sold its Parkside grounds and discontinued support for the soccer team.[39] While many teams continued to play matches near Parkside, the loss of sponsorship meant that the players and fans picked up the costs. By 1894, the Swifts and Wanderers joined the Chicago Cricket Club as defunct teams when both "amalgamated" with the Phoenix club and discontinued soccer support in favor of cricket.[40] Thus, players either formed or joined nonathletic club-funded soccer teams or dropped out of the game. In a case of the former, several of the CCC players briefly became the Chicagos. Likewise, members of the Wanderers became the Wentworths.

One exception to the athletic club teams' decline was the Thistles, who continued to thrive specifically as a soccer club rather than as a more broadly inclusive athletic club. This organization embraced professionalism but still insisted on gentlemanly conduct and exclusive membership. Club sponsors, supporters, and members paid club dues and travel costs for the team. Additionally, because the Thistles were unencumbered with other athletic obligations, the team was able to establish itself as the premier Chicago soccer club. Furthermore, the Thistles actively sought out all competitors. Beyond the Chicago area, their quest for matches brought them into contact with the teams of Braidwood, Joliet, Aurora, Streator, and Spring Valley, into other states, and even outside the country. Where other gentlemen's clubs scorned socially unworthy opponents, the Thistles took on all comers.

In contrast to the members-only clubs, there were also industry-sponsored soccer teams. While not as well documented as the athletic clubs, several generalizations about worker teams can be made. Companies provided facilities for matches, sponsored teams, and advertised the elevens who played under their banner. Teams were sponsored by the Braidwood Mines, Marshall Field Stores, Illinois Steel Company, and the Horlick Food Company of Racine, Wisconsin.[41]

Like their European counterparts, Chicago company teams seemed to reflect the ideology that healthy and sober workers would be more industrious, less susceptible to labor unrest, and appreciative of the benefits of hard work. Such thinking contributed to company towns like Saltaire in England, Guise in France, and Essen in Germany, which all valued the importance of healthy, athletic workers and provided facilities to promote well being.[42] On a modest scale, then, several Chicago companies mirrored European industries by providing playing facilities.

Excepting Braidwood and Illinois Steel, the industrial clubs mostly organized for friendlies—nonleague challenge matches—or for recreation. Still, respectably sized crowds turned out to see the games. For example, in 1891, two hundred spectators cheered the Aurora Hercules Iron Works team against the Chicago Thistles. Even though the Aurora side lost 3–2 on their cramped Herds Island pitch, the *Chicago Tribune* complimented the iron workers' team play.[43] In 1896, the Illinois Steel Company traveled to Racine, Wisconsin, to play the Horlick Food Company team. Over one thousand spectators watched the locals outclass the Chicago side 4–0.[44] Unsurprisingly, James and William Horlick, the company's founders, had emigrated from England. Both were well educated and athletically minded, factors that likely contributed to the company's many sporting endeavors.

Beginning in 1894, Illinois Steel commenced weekly friendlies against Chicago-area clubs. While seldom a formidable side, the team showed enough determination that in the following year, the CFA created a second division in which the Steel Company eleven could compete.[45] Also, by 1895, Illinois Steel laid out a soccer pitch for the team at their Cheltenham facility.[46] This was a part of the company's worker/recreational efforts, which included sponsorship of softball, bowling, and golf.[47] As the decade concluded, the Cheltenham side and the facility at Illinois Steel became synonymous with the Cheltenham neighborhood. Newspapers recognized that all community soccer action reported as "Cheltenham" was in fact sponsored by the Illinois Steel Company, an important intersection of work, community, and recreational identity, and an early example in America of business paternalism.

Another soccer club dependent on workers was the 1890 Colehours, later re-formed as the 1897 Calumet team. The South-Side Colehours first appeared in the Chicago newspapers in 1890.[48] The team's location conveniently corresponded with Charles Colehour's iron works industry near the Calumet River.[49] After the initial CFA season, they did not appear again until seven years later, when members of the team showed up on the Calumet side. The *Chicago Tribune* noted that the Calumets were "mostly Scotchmen employed in the shipyards of South Chicago."

Another example of industrial soccer comes from the Braidwood area. Located about fifty miles south of Chicago, Braidwood fiercely embraced the association game, celebrated their mining occupations, and used soccer as a point of civic pride. As early as 1890, Braidwood fielded a team to compete against the Chicago clubs.[50] This is significant, as the majority of the Chicago clubs at that time were gentlemen's athletic clubs.

For Chicago soccer, Braidwood can claim to be the first team created by unskilled laborers, as all but one player were Scotsmen who worked in the mines.[51] The Braidwood team competed through 1894 and briefly reemerged in 1898.

Braidwood posed distance problems for Chicago soccer teams. In early 1890, the CFA decided that membership eligibility required a team to reside within a twenty-five mile radius of City Hall.[52] While this excluded Braidwood from league competition, it did not mean isolation. An all-Chicago team played the Miners in a charity game for the *Daily News* Fresh Air Fund.[53] Additionally, Chicago teams usually traveled to Braidwood a couple of times per season for friendlies and often came out on the short end of the score.[54] By the close of 1892, a *Tribune* article declared that the "rustics [Braidwood citizens] would sooner play football than eat."[55] Braidwood also sponsored two teams in the 1893 Columbian Exposition World's Fair Championship Football Contest, in which they finished a respectable second and third place.[56] In 1893, a Canadian all-star team once again visited Chicago for a two-game series. On the day off between matches, the Canadians traveled down to Braidwood, where,

8. *Braidwood Miners.* An early photograph of the Braidwood Miners, one of the five founding teams of the 1890 Chicago Football Association. (Photo from *Modesto Joseph Donna, Donna's Story of Braidwood Illinois: Historical Data, Reported Facts, Personal Recollections* [Braidwood, Ill.: Braidwood History Bureau, 1957, p. 243.])

as one account claimed, the "Braidwood boys had worked in the mines all morning before the game." The miners nonetheless won 5–1.[57] The Braidwood team also competed against teams from Joliet, Spring Valley, and Streator. In fact, some of the Spring Valley players were former Braidwood kickers who relocated to more profitable mines. It seems the players transported soccer along with their mining skills.

These examples of the Cheltenham, Calumet, and Braidwood teams indicate that soccer was far from the exclusive property of the middle and upper classes. As in Great Britain, Chicago soccer expanded out of the athletic clubs into the domain of the workers and industries. But in addition to industrial and athletic club teams, mid- and late-1890s Chicago soccer also formed around neighborhoods. These teams included the Rangers and Edgewoods, who played on the West Side, and the Brighton Park Rovers, the Saint Lawrences, and the Parksides, who maintained facilities in the city's South Side. Even in the suburbs, Melrose Park developed and promoted a team.

The two West Side clubs fielded teams during the middle of the decade. The Rangers competed in the 1894–95 seasons, and the Edgewoods played in 1895–96. Despite the Thistles' reputation for signing the top players, the Rangers were able to acquire strong talent, such as A. Goldie, formerly with the Vale of Clyde, a premiere Scottish football club, and Sam Scobie, who later joined the Thistle and Pullman teams, but only after the Rangers folded. The Edgewoods initially debuted in 1895, and played their games at Edgewood Avenue and Humboldt Park.[58] While not a particularly strong team, the Edgewoods maintained the most ethnically diverse lineup. Players' names indicate German, Norwegian, Irish, English, and Scottish ethnicity.[59] The Rangers played on a pitch located at California and Milwaukee Avenues in Logan Square. When the team folded in 1895, the Edgewoods moved to the Rangers' field and added several Rangers to their lineup.

The Brighton Park Rovers competed in the CFA from 1894 to 1897. The Rovers played their games in the community park located at Thirty-fifth and Archer. By 1895, the neighborhood began taking notice of the club; one newspaper reported that "a good crowd of football enthusiasts was on hand" to cheer the team. For the 1896 season, the Rovers' management recruited several players from the defunct Braidwood, Joliet, and Streator teams, which boosted attendance still further. Upwards of eight hundred spectators came out to watch a 2–2 tie between the Brighton team and the Thistles.[60] An even larger crowd turned out for the rematch the next month.[61] Success, however, had its price, and the Rovers are a good example of community control versus professionalism, of local values competing against producing the best possible team. Many of the Brighton players who had been shunted aside to make way for more skilled athletes from other communities made their feelings known, and the following season the Rovers returned to field only Brighton Park boys. Without the star out-of-town players, the team lacked the skills to compete with the top clubs. One reporter declared that their "games . . . were as devoid of life as a drowned kitten."[62] Fans drifted away, and after only three matches, the Rovers no longer secured enough players to continue on a regular basis.[63]

Two additional teams that seldom finished at the top but nonetheless competed for several seasons were the Saint Lawrences (1894–97) and the Parksides (1895–98). Both hailed from the South Side. The Saints played their matches at Forty-sixth Street and Cottage Grove, in the Kenwood neighborhood; the Parksides competed at Sixty-seventh and Stony Island Avenue, on the border of Jackson Park. Although these teams seldom challenged the leaders, their longevity and enthusiastic fans reveal growing neighborhood support for the game.

Many community teams in both the city and the suburbs came and went without much notice. Their transient existence suggests that they depended on local neighborhood residents to provide players and spectators, and that such support could be fickle. These teams played their matches in parks and public spaces. This naturally caused admission and revenue problems and probably contributed to their only marginal success in the CFA. Nonetheless, the community teams' public matches undoubtedly nurtured awareness of soccer and very likely promoted the game to future generations that watched and played in the parks.

One early Chicago organization worth a closer look was the Pullman Car Builders, a team that melded elements of athletic club, workplace, and community-based soccer. The team was a by-product of industrialist George Pullman's social theories. Similar to the already noted company towns in Europe, his "Pullman system" sought to resolve animosity between capital and labor by integrating the workplace and the neighborhood. Pullman reasoned that such a merger would regulate alcoholism, worker absenteeism, and shoddy workmanship. Furthermore, a company town would engender worker pride in the things they built and inhibit the growth of slums and labor agitation.[64]

The Pullman experiment is well documented, and the role of athleticism in the community has received scholarly attention.[65] Theoretically, the promotion of physical fitness created a superior worker. Consequently, athletic competition involved several sports, especially cricket, track and field, rowing, cycling, and football. Unfortunately, and again like much of U.S. soccer research, the account of the association game at Pullman is incomplete. Wilma Pesavento and Lisa Raymond's study of Pullman athletics does include some important pieces of information. They show that Pullman soccer players primarily worked blue-collar jobs, that the team commenced play in 1891, was defunct from 1894–97, and that Pullman was the only organization to field a "B," or second-tier team against the other teams.[66] Pesavento and Raymond relied primarily on the *Chicago Times,* so consulting other dailies augments their findings

As previously noted, the elusive Pullman/Wanderers match is often cited as Chicago's first soccer game, in 1883, but firm evidence indicates that the Pullman Company first showed an interest in the association game at the inaugural 1890 meeting of the Chicago Foot-Ball Association. One V. C. Rhodes represented the Pullman Club, and he voted with the majority to restrict club membership to a twenty-five mile radius of City Hall (the streets of Randolph, Clark, and Washington bordered City Hall). Although the town was well within range, Pullman chose to remain independent of the CFA until 1897.[67] But independence did not mean isolation; as early as 1891, the Pullman Club competed for the Jackson Cup and scheduled games against the Swifts, Thistles, Scottish Athletes, and Chicago Cricket Club.[68] While the final standings are not known, it seems that the inaugural running of the Jackson Cup spilled into the 1892 season. In the final match, the Chicago Cricket Club defeated Pullman 8–0.[69] Although Pullman opted not to compete for the trophy the following year,[70] the Car Builders played friendlies against the Chicagos (formally the Chicago Cricket Club) and Braidwood; they even traveled to Detroit for a match.[71]

By 1893, most of the Pullman players abandoned their old team and instead laced up their boots for the Thistle organization. In fact, no team played against CFA clubs in 1893 under the Pullman banner. Moreover, during the 1894 season (the year of the famous Pullman Strike), the Car Builders continued to remain aloof from the CFA. Nonetheless, the Pullman team played Saturday friendlies against the Chicagos and the Wanderers before and after the labor unrest.[72] Hence, despite the strike, organizers presumably recognized the significance of the soccer team to fans and players. The 1897 season marked the first time that Pullman competed as a member of the CFA and played on Sundays, which suggests a split with the Thistle organization. The last two years of the decade saw the Pullman club dethrone the Thistles, become the top team in Chicago, and develop into one of the premiere soccer organizations in the United States.

The Pullman team shared much with other community, industrial, and athletic club teams. The Car Builders relied on the Pullman neighborhood and labor force to provide players for the team and spectators to cheer them on, much like the West Side Rangers, or Brighton Park.

But the Car Builders also incorporated the workplace by playing at the Pullman complex, competing under the Pullman banner, and recruiting players from the factory. Lastly, the Pullman Athletic Club provided a bridge between blue- and white-collar workers that allowed the sport enthusiasts to compete equally, regardless of employment position.[73] Given these elements—community, workplace, club—it is little wonder Pullman emerged as one of the most powerful teams in the Midwest.

Clearly, 1890s Chicago soccer was alive and well, as the city increasingly made time to play. Athletic clubs and industries sponsored teams, while community groups played in the parks. Nonetheless, the few scholars who examine U.S. soccer today note the disparity of the sport's tepid following in the United States compared to the majority of the world's nations. Some argue that the rise of U.S. football and baseball "crowded U.S. soccer out of a 'sport space.'"[74] Others suggest that the "rugged character" and "newness" of the United States, rather than finite "sport space," encouraged a more physical football game that overshadowed the association game.[75] In terms of popularity, the collegiate game undoubtedly surpassed the association game in the United States during the 1890s. Yet, early in that decade, soccer still had a significant following, so much so that the *Chicago Tribune* contended in 1890 that the "college football craze had yet to catch on in the West as the region still prefers the association game."[76] Soccer was not so much crowded out as overshadowed. From this viewpoint, the United States in the twenty-first century is merely catching up with the rest of the soccer world, while continuing to promote football, baseball, and basketball. That is, soccer is alive and well in the United States, and has been since it was first organized here. But because it had to compete with several other very popular sports, it received less attention than elsewhere

If there is a single benchmark when collegiate football came to overshadow soccer as the city's primary fall sport, it occurred on Thanksgiving Day in 1892. Prior to the formation of the CFA, Chicago soccer teams played annual Thanksgiving Day games. Throughout the 1890s, city soccer clubs used the holiday to showcase their teams, challenge non-CFA teams, and promote awareness of ethnic heritage. For example, the Thistles often played the Gaelic Athletic Association (GAA) in both Gaelic and association football at Thanksgiving Day athletic carnivals that featured food, music, and sports.[77] In 1890, the *Tribune* commented on this developing tradition: "[Soccer] is rapidly growing in favor with the public, being devoid of the roughness of the game under inter-collegiate rules and yet affording great opportunity for scientific play."[78]

All of this changed in 1892, when the Chicago AA hosted the Boston AC in a collegiate football game. Local papers hyped the match for days, providing diagrams and explaining the finer points of collegiate football. In addition to an analysis of the game itself, the next day's *Tribune* reported the attendance, fashion, men and women's attitudes toward the game, even the weather. The turnout of almost five thousand spectators quadrupled the Thistle/Gaelic Association crowds. Furthermore, the *Tribune* devoted three pages to the Chicago/Boston collegiate-style game, compared to one column each for the Thistles/GAA, Braidwood/ Chicagos, and Pullman/Detroit games.[79] Throughout the rest of the decade, Chicago's football coverage increasingly supported the collegiate style over the association game. So long as immigrant-based athletic clubs prospered, so did soccer, but after the early 1890s, not on the level of American football.

Although soccer continued to gain new adherents, British immigrants still dominated the sport through the end of the century. Newspapers often referred to entire teams as the "Sturdy sons of Scotland"; matches, it was said, "resembled the war of the roses." Notable players, such as Dick Jarrett, Ben Govier, and Edward Butcher, hailed from Wales, Scotland, and England, respectively. Others came to Chicago from Britain via Canada. Scots remained the leading lights.[80] In addition to the Colehours and Braidwood, there were also the Scottish Shields, St. Andrews, and the Scottish Athletes.[81] Besides these explicitly Scottish sides, many community teams and worker teams relied almost entirely on Scottish booters. The Thistles, however, emerged as the flagship of Scottish talent. Once a Scottish player established himself in the Chicago area, he usually sought to play for the Thistles.

Benjamin Govier provides a case in point of a turn-of-the century immigrant Chicago soccer player who began with Pullman but was quickly signed by the Thistles. He was born in Coatbridge, Scotland, to English parents, in 1876, learned soccer in primary school, and played for several British school teams. Govier arrived in Chicago at the tender age of fifteen. He secured work with the Pullman Company in 1891, and the following year he debuted with Pullman, alongside veteran players twice his age.[82] From 1895 to 1897, he joined Dick Jarrett in St. Louis, where they formed one of "the greatest left wings the west has ever seen."[83] He returned to Chicago, where he captained championship teams. At the end of Govier's playing career, twenty-four years after he first played for Pullman, Dr. Peter Peel commissioned the sculptor, Charles Mulligan of the Chicago Art Institute, to design a silver trophy of Govier's likeness, which Peel presented to Ben.

Following his retirement, Govier continued to represent Chicago soccer. He was often on hand when teams competed for the Peel Cup and when Chicago teams played in other cities. For example, in 1918 Govier accompanied the Joliet team to a contest in Pennsylvania against the great Bethlehem Steel Club in the semifinal National Open Cup Championship. The *Bethlehem Globe* referred to Govier as the "Honus Wagner of soccer," and fondly recalled his skill and admiration in the Bethlehem soccer community.[84] Obviously, Govier's talent garnered him fame above that of other Chicago players.

As we have seen, soccer helped reestablish ethnic solidarity among immigrants who had played the game back home. But it could also become a touchstone for ethnic groups who did not bring a strong tradition of the game to America. As early as 1891, the Gaelic Athletic Association began holding annual games. Throughout the summer and fall months, the first GAA athletic competitions featured several sport contests, including "football," among nine Irish teams.[85] While the papers did not define "football," the scores indicate either the association game or a hybrid of the association game and the Gaelic football style, which sometimes featured twenty-one men per side.[86]

The GAA not only sponsored sports, it also focused attention on Chicago's Irish community. The organization brought over Irish National League Chairman O'Neal Ryan and Secretary J. C. Sutton as guests of honor for the GAA championship games. Ryan spoke to a small but enthusiastic crowd. He lauded the role of Irish sports and gymnastics, and claimed athletics allowed "the Germans to be where they are today" in U.S. society.[87] Sports, he argued, would serve as a tool for Irish upward mobility. Certainly the Gaelic Athletic Association was upwardly mobile; the very year that Ryan gave his talk in Chicago, the organization showed a $1,000 profit.[88] The following year, the GAA moved from its grounds at Lincoln and Polk to Thirty-seventh and Indiana, which accommodated larger crowds with easier access to the enormous Irish community centered in Bridgeport.[89] The league not only expanded to ten teams, but games now drew crowds of fifteen hundred spectators.[90] Even more significant, the new grounds allowed the Irish to play on Sundays.[91] Sabbath games were generally forbidden among Protestants, but not Catholics, and owning their own private grounds allowed the GAA to circumvent the old blue laws.

In 1893, the GAA proposed competing in the Chicago Football Association.[92] But almost as quickly, the Irish pulled away from soccer and reaffirmed their commitment to Gaelic football. It is unclear why this happened. The desire for opponents who would play on Sundays might have had something to do with it.[93] The World's Columbian Exposition of 1893 also pushed the Gaelic Association back toward the old game. The GAA announced an "Irish Day" at the fair, which would feature a Gaelic football match between the Chicago and New York Gaelic clubs.[94] Even though the game ended in a tie, and despite the absence of a proper ball—the clubs substituted an inflated animal bladder—the game proved so popular among Chicago's Irish that the GAA elected to play the Gaelic game exclusively.

The Gaelic Athletic Association in Ireland might also have contributed to the dominance of the Gaelic style in Chicago. Some historians argue that the cultural nationalism of the Irish GAA culminated in banning members who participated in "association football matches, or any other non-Gaelic games," a striking example of politics shaping sports.[95] Simultaneously, the Chicago GAA abandoned the association game for the rest of the decade. This occurred despite the Irish teams having enough talent to give the Thistles spirited competition in friendlies.

While British immigrants were the most important group bringing soccer to Chicago, their teams were mostly staffed with players who played for the love of the game. A few immigrants were ex-professional players, and some of them were able to use their skills to increase their income by playing for certain organizations or by wrangling time from the company clock to go practice for the company team. But unlike the developing professional game in Northern England and Scotland, 1890s Chicago soccer was mostly an amateur or semiprofessional affair. No player made a living exclusively with his feet, though several secured better-paying jobs, or supplementary income, or time away from their work to hone their football skills.

The Pullman Company clearly recruited players to kick for the team in exchange for employment in the industry.[96] Other players augmented their income by signing with some of the better teams in the city, and these clubs charged a small admission fee to their games, which the players split.[97] There was also some intercity raiding between St. Louis and Chicago (though we can't be sure what individual clubs used to entice players), and this competition is certainly testimony to the health of the game. Several Chicago players took advantage of what can only be described as a St. Louis soccer boom toward the end of the century. In 1895, Edward Butcher and John Aston received and accepted offers from the St. Louis Cycling Club (again, we have no details).[98] In 1897, Ben Govier (whom some called the greatest player in the United States) and Dick Jarrett signed with Saint Theresa's organization and later played for the Cycling Club.[99] Conversely, in 1895, the Thistles convinced J. Middleton to return to Chicago. If we cannot know all that we would like to about how far the professionalization of the game proceeded, it is clear that soccer was following the pattern of baseball, boxing, and other sports at the turn of the century—tough competition and the fans' desire for victories were pressing teams to do whatever they could to secure the best possible players.[100]

Chicago teams apparently followed their Scottish counterparts in stressing the passing game over the dribbling game.[101] With the dribbling game, teams often employed a 7–1–2 formation as opposed to a 5–3–2 lineup when the passing game took precedence. In both of these formations, teams placed emphasis on offense. For dribbling, seven frontmen were backed by a central linkman and then two defenders. The 5–3–2 formation dropped two offensive attackers into the midfield to better facilitate a passing game. Chicago teams of the late nineteenth century favored the passing game's 5–3–2 line-up, which makes sense, since the formation emanated from the Scottish clubs and Scots predominated in organizing the Chicago game.

Of course the stand-out Scottish American club was the Thistles, and statistically, they dominated the Chicago league from 1890 to 1898, a remarkable eight-year run. This is even more astonishing given that their lineup changed frequently as talented players shuffled in and out of it. For example, Harry Boyd was called a "tower of strength" in his 1891 Thistle debut.[102] He soon left the club, but his absence did not keep the Thistles from winning. To give another example, Thistle goalkeeper John Gibbs was a stalwart of the team, and he was selected to travel with the Thistles to Fall River, Massachusetts. Unfortunately, Gibbs died of typhoid fever the day before the team left.[103] Of course he was missed, yet the Thistles replaced him and continued their dominance of the Chicago soccer scene.

The Thistles and other Chicago clubs increasingly went on the road—to Detroit, Fall River, St. Louis, Omaha, Milwaukee, as well as Canadian towns—and these cities sent their teams to Chicago.[104] But the most ambitious plan for competition beyond the city came when the Chicago Football Association proposed to lure the famous Corinthian Football Club from London, as well as teams from Canada, Europe, South America, and the United States to a grand tournament that would be part of the 1893 World's Fair in Chicago, commemorating the four hundredth anniversary of Columbus's voyages. Newspaper accounts reveal the organizers' vision.[105] The Chicago World's Fair Sport Assembly, working in conjunction with the Amateur Athletic Union, designated September 14, 15, and 16 for athletic competition, with the 15th featuring association football.[106] This complemented the Caledonian and Scottish Assembly plans to hold an earlier sports festival in the city from July 28 to August 2, with the final date, "Canadian Day," to feature soccer.[107] When former Toronto resident and Chicago soccer enthusiast William Baird announced that the Corinthians planned to come to Chicago, the *Tribune* ran a full story on the English club that featured player biographies and a history of the organization.[108] By February, Ontario and Philadelphia committed to the tournament.[109] Two months later, the World's Fair Athletic Carnival extended invitations to football clubs in Europe and South America.[110]

Unfortunately, the tournament collapsed in early July, when the Corinthians canceled due to high costs.[111] Following this blow, most of the other teams also pulled out. Chicago's soccer community settled for a two-game visit from a Canadian team and a six-team tournament for the Bain Cup, hosted by the Scottish Athletic Club. But the fact that organizers envisioned an international soccer championship long before the modern Olympics or World Cup gives us a sense of the high hopes of the game's backers.

The Chicago Football Association clearly saw itself as part of a larger national and world game. And despite the growing popularity of collegiate football and professional baseball, soccer tenaciously maintained a following through most of the 1890s. But then came a decline. The game did not disappear, but certainly soccer was less prominent and well organized in 1900 than it had been in 1895. For example, as we have seen, the CFA organized five teams in 1890 and expanded to ten teams in two divisions in 1895, with fall and spring seasons. But in 1899, the league dropped back to five teams, which only competed in spring.

It is unclear why the CFA lost popularity in the final year of the century. Perhaps the Spanish American War distracted attention from sports, though baseball and football certainly did well in this era. Economic hard times, too, might well have had an impact. Or perhaps it was a more local matter. The Thistles disbanded in 1898, for example, and the loss of this flagship team could not have helped matters. Certainly attendance declined. By 1897, upwards of one thousand spectators might show up for a match, but the numbers were far fewer just a couple of years later. By century's end, the CFA canceled its season, and declared that all but Pullman were "too weak to put up teams." The *Tribune* failed to cover the matches that took place in 1899—assuming that they did, in fact, take place.[112]

Still, a beginning had been made. British immigrants initiated the first clubs, matches, and organizations; they created early Chicago soccer. The single most important fruit of their labor was the Chicago Football Association. At its height, the league oversaw ten clubs, structured two seasons per year, codified the rules, enforced proper conduct, and stayed abreast of the game's development in Britain. All of this introduced soccer to countless new fans, who watched accomplished athletes compete in parks and near factories.

True, the newspapers gave much more space to football, baseball, and track and field than to soccer. But neighborhood residents in Pullman, Melrose Park, and throughout south and west Chicago could not help but notice the skillful players and enthusiastic spectators enjoying two seasons of soccer per year. When the original immigrants of the 1890s became too old or too injured to continue playing and the CFA disbanded, Chicago soccer still survived. The game reemerged even stronger in the following decade. A professional team sponsored by Chicago White Sox owner, Charles Comiskey, new semipro teams from Pullman, and a surprising return of the athletic club movement, ensured that many Chicago youths of the early 1900s would be introduced to the game. The setbacks of the late nineteenth century were overshadowed by soccer's rebirth in the twentieth.

Notes

1. Benjamin Rader, *American Sports: From the Age of Folk Games to the Age of Televised Sports*, 2d ed. (Lincoln: University of Nebraska Press, 1990), 55.

2. Ibid., 55–57.

3. Ibid., 80–83.

4. Stephen S. Riess, "Ethnic Sports," in *Ethnic Chicago: A Multicultural Portrait*, ed. Melvin G. Holli and Peter d'A. Jones, 4th ed. (Grand Rapids, Mich.: William B. Eerdmans, 1995), 529–56.

5. Tony Mason, *Association Football and English Society: 1863–1915* (Atlantic Highlands, N.J.: Humanities Press, 1980), 9–13.

6. Ibid., 10–16.

7. Ibid., 26–28.

8. Ibid., 11–13, 21–34.

9. Ibid., 69–78.

10. Stephen Wagg, "The Missionary Position: Football in the Societies of Britain and Ireland," in *Giving the Game Away: Football, Politics, and Culture on Five Continents*, ed. Stephen Wagg (London: Leicester University Press, 1995), 2–4.

11. Ibid., 6.

12. Ibid., 6–8.

13. Ibid., 15–17.

14. Sam Foulds and Paul Harris, *American Soccer Heritage: A History of the Game* (Manhattan Beach, Calif.: Soccer for Americans Publishing Company, 1979), 7–13. Illinois Soccer Commission, *Illinois Soccer Commission 25th Anniversary, 1916–1941: September 25, 1941 Hotel Sherman—Chicago* (Chicago: American Foil Printing Company, 1941), 4. National Soccer League, *National Soccer League 25th Anniversary Program, 1920–1945* (Chicago: American Foil Printing Company, 1945), 7. All of these accounts rely on an undocumented introduction. While the match might have occurred, no record of the inaugural Pullman games notes the soccer match.

15. *Chicago Tribune*, November 26, 1886; *Inter Ocean*, November 25, 1886.

16. *Evening Chronicle* (St. Louis), December 3, 1883.

17. *Inter Ocean*, November 26, 1886.

18. *Chicago Tribune* and *Inter Ocean*, 1890, passim.

19. Gerald R. Gems, *Windy City Wars: Labor, Leisure, and Sport in the Making of Chicago* (Lanham, Md.: Scarecrow, 1997), 32–39.

20. Tom Melville, *The Tented Field: A History of Cricket in America* (Bowling Green, Ohio: Bowling Green State University Popular Press, 1998), 80.

21. *The Chicago Blue Book of Selected Names of Chicago and the Suburban Towns* (Chicago: Chicago Directory Company, 1891, 1892), passim. *The Chicago Blue Book of Selected Names of Chicago and the Suburban Towns* (Chicago: Chicago Directory Company, 1891), 346. I compared this list to the Chicago Cricket Club team roster found in the *Inter Ocean*, February 7, 1892.

22. Wilma J. Pesavento and Lisa C. Raymond, "'Men Must Play, Men Will Play': Occupations of Pullman Athletes, 1880 to 1900," *Journal of Sport History*, 12:3 (Winter 1985): 249. *Chicago Tribune*, October 9, 1862.

23. Pesavento and Raymond, "'Men Must Play, Men Will Play,'" 236–43.

24. Examples of fund-raising dances include the Thistle's "Annual Dance" at Berry's Hall (*Chicago Tribune*, December 7, 1890). Several clubs depended on monthly "smokers" to secure funds. These included the Wanderers (*Chicago Tribune*, October 4, 1891); Bankers/North End Athletic Club (*Chicago Tribune*, November 12, 1892); and the Swifts (*Inter Ocean*, February 19, 1893). Also see the *Wanderers Cricket and Athletic Club Scrapbook* (Chicago Historical Society, ca. 1887–1905).

25. Reuben H. Donnelley, compiler, *Annual Directory of the City of Chicago* (Chicago: Chicago Directory Company, 1893), 1435.

26. Barbara Edmonson, *Historic Shot Glasses: The Prohibition Era*, rev. ed. (Chico, Calif.: Heidelberg Graphics, 1992), 81.

27. Hap Meyer Soccer Collection (1898–1963), Scrapbook, Box 4/19, Southern Illinois University, Edwardsville, Louisa H. Bowen University Archives and Special Collections. *Chicago Tribune*, December 26, 1890.

28. *Chicago Tribune*, November 2, 1891.

29. *Inter Ocean*, November 2, 1891.

30. *Inter Ocean*, October 15, November 1, 1891, and *Chicago Tribune*, November 1, 1891.

31. *Chicago Blue Book*, 1892, p. 362. *Wanderers Scrapbook*.

32. *Chicago Tribune*, March 8, 1891.

33. *Inter Ocean*, March 9, 1891; *Chicago Tribune*, March 9, 1891.

34. *Toronto Mail*, May 29, 1891.

35. *Inter Ocean*, May 31, 1891.

36. Ibid.

37. *Chicago Tribune*, May 28, 1892, and May 29, 1892.

38. *Chicago Tribune*, September 11, 1893.

39. *Chicago Tribune*, November 11, 1892, and December 3, 1892.

40. *Wanderers Scrapbook*.

41. *Chicago Tribune*, and *Inter Ocean*, 1890–99, passim.

42. Wilma J. Pesavento, "Sport and Recreation in the Pullman Experiment, 1880–1900," *Journal of Sport History*, 9:2 (Summer 1982): 38–42.

43. *Chicago Tribune*, May 24, 1891.

44. *Inter Ocean*, December 13, 1896.

45. *Chicago Tribune*, March 2, 1895.

46. *Inter Ocean*, October 14, 1895.

47. A Project by Washington High School, *Chicago's Southeast Side: Teaching of History through Architecture*, http://www.neiu.edu/reseller/scussteel.html.

48. *Chicago Tribune*, October 18, 1890, October 19, 1890, October 26, 1890.

49. Washington High School, *Chicago's Southeast Side*.

50. Donna Modesto, *Donna's Story of Braidwood, Illinois: Historical Data, Reported Facts, Personal Recollections* (Braidwood, Ill.: Braidwood History Bureau, 1957), 245. *Chicago Tribune*, May 25, 1890. *Wanderers Scrapbook*.

51. Modesto, *Donna's Story*, 245.

52. *Chicago Tribune*, April 27, 1890.

53. *Chicago Tribune*, May 25, 1890.

54. *Inter Ocean*, October 23, 1891, May 31, 1892, October 23, 1892, November 20, 1892.

55. *Chicago Tribune*, December 12, 1892.

56. *Chicago Tribune*, July 23, 1893. Modesto reported that Braidwood won the championship. However, the *Tribune*'s report notes scores, lineups, and game summaries, all absent in Modesto's *Donna's Story*.

57. Modesto, *Donna's Story*, 245. Modesto incorrectly listed the year as 1894. However, his date and the score match a Chicago paper's report of the game, except the year played (1893), see *Inter Ocean*, June 18, 1893.

58. *Chicago Tribune*, October 14, 1895.

59. Ibid.

60. *Chicago Tribune*, April 12, 1896; *Inter Ocean*, April 12, 1896.

61. *Chicago Tribune*, May 4, 1896; *Inter Ocean*, May 4, 1896.

62. *Chicago Tribune*, April 26, 1897.

63. Chicago Community Inventory, *Local Community Fact Book: Chicago Metropolitan Area*, 1960, ed. Evelyn M. Kitagawa and Karl E. Taeuber (Chicago: University of Chicago Press, 1963), 130–31; *Inter Ocean*, May 10, 1897.

64. Stanley Buder, *Pullman: An Experiment in Industrial Order and Community Planning, 1880–1930* (New York: Oxford University Press, 1967), 44.

65. Pesavento, "Sport and Recreation in the Pullman Experiment," 38–62. Pesavento and Raymond, "'Men Must Play,'" 233–51.

66. Pesavento and Raymond, "'Men Must Play,'" 238.

67. *Chicago Tribune*, April 27, 1890. National Soccer League, *25th Anniversary Program*, 7. Harold M. Mayer and Richard C. Wade, *Chicago: Growth of a Metropolis* (Chicago: University of Chicago Press, 1969), 37, 186.

68. *Chicago Tribune*, November 1, 1891; *Inter Ocean*, November 1, 1893.

69. *Inter Ocean*, February 7, 1892.

70. *Chicago Tribune*, October 1, 1892.

71. *Chicago Tribune*, October 16, 1892, October 23, 1892, November 25, 1892.

72. Almont Lindsey, *The Pullman Strike: The Story of a Unique Experiment and of a Great Labor Upheaval* (Chicago: University of Chicago Press, 1942), 122–46. Buder, *Pullman*, 147–201. *Chicago Tribune*, March 24, 1894, April 15, 1894, April 25, 1894, December 24, 1894.

73. Pesavento and Raymond, "'Men Must Play,'" 249–51. The authors demonstrate that white- and blue-collar workers competed as equals in athletics. Furthermore, "No worker was excluded due to the type of work they performed." Promoting the company and winning took precedence.

74. Andrei S. Markovits and Steven L. Hellerman, *Offside: Soccer and American Exceptionalism* (Princeton: Princeton University Press, 2001), 7–53.

75. Ivan Waddington and Martin Roderick, "American Exceptionalism: Soccer and American Football," *Sport Historian*, 16 (May 1996): 42–63.

76. *Chicago Tribune*, November 16, 1890.

77. *Chicago Tribune*, November 24, 1892, November 25, 1892, November 30, 1893, November 30, 1894; *Inter Ocean*, November 26, 1896.

78. *Chicago Tribune*, December 25, 1890.

79. *Chicago Tribune*, November 25, 1892.

80. Wayne Retherford and June Skinner Sawyers, *The Scots of Chicago: Quiet Immigrants and Their New Society* (Dubuque, Iowa: Kendall/Hunt, 1997), 121.

81. *Chicago Tribune* and *Inter Ocean*, 1890–93, passim.

82. Joe Davis, "Ben Govier, Captain Pullman Football Club," in *Spalding's Athletic Library, Spalding's Official "Soccer" Football Guide, 1915–1916*, ed. Thomas Cahill, number 55r, group 2 (New York: American Sports Publishing Company, 1915), 81. Ancestory.com., *Data Images from National Archives and Records Administration, 1920 Federal Population Census*. T625, 2,076 rolls, Washington, D.C., National Archives and Records Administration, *http://search .ancestory.com/cgi-bin/sse.dll?db=1920usfedcen&gsfn=&gsln=govier&gsco=2*. *Chicago Tribune*, November 13, 1892.

83. Davis, "Ben Govier," 81.

84. *Bethlehem Globe* (Pennsylvania), March 30, 1918.

85. *Chicago Tribune*, May-November 1891, passim.

86. *Chicago Tribune*, June 1, 1891.

87. *Chicago Tribune*, October 5, 1891.

88. *Chicago Tribune*, October 26, 1891.

89. City of Chicago, Department of Development and Planning, *Historic City: The Settlement of Chicago* (Chicago: GPO, 1976), 61–62.

90. *Chicago Tribune*, October 3, 1892.

91. *Chicago Tribune*, November 7, 1892.

92. Ibid.

93. *Chicago Tribune*, April 17, 1893.

94. *Chicago Tribune*, September 22, 1893.

95. Ibid.

96. Buder, *Pullman*, 125.

97. *Chicago Tribune*, December 25, 1890.

98. *Chicago Tribune*, May 17, 1897; *Inter Ocean*, May 17, 1897.

99. Hap Meyer Soccer Collection (1898–1963), Scrapbook, Box 4/19.

100. *Inter Ocean*, October 4, 1897.

101. Ibid.

102. *Chicago Tribune*, September 7, 1891.

103. *Fall River Daily Globe*, September 18, 1891; *Fall River Daily Evening Herald*, September 21, 1891.

104. *Chicago Tribune*, March 8, 1891; *Inter Ocean*, May 24, 1891, May 31, 1891; *Chicago Tribune*, May 29, 1891; *Toronto Mail*, May 26, 1891, May 29, 1891; *Fall River Daily Evening Herald*, September 21, 1891; *Fall River Daily Evening Herald*, September 22, 1891; *Chicago Tribune*, November 27, 1891; *Chicago Tribune*, November 24, 1892, and November 25, 1892; *Chicago Tribune*, December 20, 1892, December 27, 1892; *Toronto Mail*, May 25, 1893; *Toronto Globe*, May 27, 1893; *Chicago Tribune*, May 27, 1893; *Inter Ocean*, November 27, 1896; *Chicago Tribune*, November 28, 1897, and November 29, 1897. Dan Kubick, (History/Social Science Department, Omaha Public Library) letter to the author, November 21, 2002. *Chicago Tribune*, November 18, 1895. Colin Jose, letter to the author, October 26, 2002.

105. Several monographs examine the events of the 1893 World's Columbian Exposition. However, the following excellent compilation of events, including athletics, does not note the soccer contests. Donna J. Bertuca, senior compiler, Donald Hartman and Susan M. Neumeister, co-compilers, *The World's Columbian Exposition: A Centennial Bibliographic Guide*, Bibliographies and Indexes in American History, number 26, (Westport, Conn.: Greenwood Press, 1996).

106. *Chicago Tribune*, February 19, 1893.

107. *Chicago Tribune*, February 2, 1893.

108. *Chicago Tribune*, January 7, 1893.

109. *Chicago Tribune*, February 12, 1893.

110. *Chicago Tribune*, April 14, 1893.

111. *Chicago Tribune*, July 4, 1893.

112. Markovits et al., *Offsides*, 108. James Francis Robinson, "The History of Soccer in the City of Saint Louis" (Ph.D. diss., Saint Louis University, 1966), 60. *Inter Ocean*, October 11, 1897, November 1, 1897, *Chicago Tribune*, October 8, 1898. *Chicago Tribune*, March 19, 1899. *Chicago Tribune*, November 19, 1899, November 20, 1899.

3

Closing Down
the Open City
The Demise of Boxing and
Horse Racing in Chicago

STEVEN A. RIESS

Chicago at the turn of the twentieth century was a major center of American professional sports. It was one of a handful of cities with two major league baseball franchises, a popular locus for prizefighting (a sport still widely barred throughout the country), and the western center of thoroughbred racing. Greater Chicago had more racetracks than any other metropolitan area except New York, and Washington Park was one of the most prestigious tracks anywhere in the world. The annual opening of the track was considered the start of the summer social season, and its feature event, the American Derby, was one of the richest races in the United States.[1]

Chicago was also one of the most liberal American cities, and its citizens, 80 percent of whom were either immigrants or the children of immigrants, led lives largely free of the social control that old-stock Protestant Americans imposed on urbanites, especially in the East and South. Chicago still had Sunday blue laws but unlike, say, Philadelphia, rarely enforced them. Neighborhood taverns often stayed open well beyond legal closing hours, and prostitution flourished in the Levee district. Beginning in 1893, baseball fans attended major league games on the Sabbath, spectators watched boxing matches with impunity (despite the ban on prizefights), and Chicagoans gambled with little interference from the criminal justice system. Urban machine politicians protected—for a price—gambling halls and brothels against police interference. Betting at the track was legal, and for those who couldn't make it out to watch the races, no officials interfered with offtrack betting at saloons, poolrooms, or in the streets.[2]

This is not to say there was no opposition to the wide-open city. In the late nineteenth century, moral reformers, led by Protestant religious leaders, journalists, temperance advocates, settlement house workers, social scientists, and municipal reform organizations, sought to expose the city's vile amusements, to close them down and replace them with moral recreations. These middle-class urban reformers were the core of the new Progressive movement of the early twentieth century, which sought to promote political democracy, economic opportunity, social justice, and efficiency. Their efforts to improve the quality of life for urban Americans included not only securing cleaner and safer streets, better education, and honest government, but also socializing urban folk, particularly immigrants, into law-abiding citizens. The Progressives believed in imposing their values upon the masses, which meant fighting the saloons, the brothels, and all forms of gambling. They supported clean sports that promoted morality, built character, and improved public health; they also advocated building inner-city parks for the same reasons. However, they disapproved of blood sports and all other recreations that relied on gambling for their popularity. In the early 1900s, they launched vigorous assaults against prizefighting and horse racing.[3]

Boxing in Chicago

Compared to baseball or horse racing, boxing in Chicago was a minor sport. The state banned commercialized prizefighting in 1869, though matches were held surreptitiously or at clubs open to "members only" (simply purchasing a ticket made one a member). Illinois forbade promoting a prizefight, training for one, working as a trainer, or even watching a match. The penalty for fighting was one to ten years in jail, and those abetting boxers could be fined five hundred dollars and spend six months incarcerated. Even a ringside doctor was liable to a five-year sentence, as was a boxer who returned to Illinois after fighting elsewhere.[4] Chicago was not as prominent a boxing locale as New York or New Orleans, the first cities to temporarily legalize pugilism in the late nineteenth century. San

Francisco, too, became a major locus of championship fights in the early twentieth century, when prizefighting was again barred in New York.[5]

Still, Chicago was a significant fight venue. Promoters with political clout evaded anti-prizefighting laws, and several big matches were staged in the city. Back in 1885, for example, heavyweight champion John L. Sullivan won a five-round bout in Chicago against Jack Burke, fighting under the Marquis of Queensbury rules. And in 1899, future world heavyweight champion Jack Johnson fought local black fighter "Klondike" Jack Haines. The main clubs were the Watita League, Battery D, and Ninth Ward Guards, each located on a different side of the city, along with the American Athletic Club, the Lyceum, and the Apollo, all of which promoted top-flight matches. There were also many smaller clubs, and all of this competition resulted in slim profit margins for promoters. Worse, many bouts were fixed, including the Joe Gans–Terry McGovern bout on December 13, 1900. "Terrible" Terry McGovern was the featherweight champion of the world, while Joe Gans was an outstanding African American pugilist, who would go on to become the world lightweight champion. However, Gans had a difficult time getting good bouts because of racial prejudice. Gans agreed to throw the fight against the smaller McGovern because he needed the paycheck. The fix was so obvious that disgruntled spectators staged a riot after the bout.[6]

By 1903, reformers were pressing the authorities to do something about illegal prizefights. The mayor at the time was the popular patrician Carter H. Harrison II, serving the third of his five terms. The son of a previous five-term mayor, he originally was elected with the support of Democratic bosses Johnny Powers, "Hinky Dink" Kenna, and "Bathhouse" John Coughlin. Working-class immigrants formed Harrison's political base. He was a strong supporter of personal freedom when it came to social issues, and during his first terms did not fight the Democratic bosses involved in gambling and prostitution. He gained a lot of national attention in 1897, when first elected, for successfully fighting traction magnate Charles T. Yerkes, who was trying to monopolize mass transit in Chicago. Throughout his mayoralty, Harrison was a strong opponent of corrupt public utilities.[7]

Mayor Harrison told the reformers he would not interfere with boxing, and Sheriff Thomas E. Barrett promised to intervene only on direct orders from the governor. An anti-boxing coalition, however, persuaded Governor Richard Yates to stop the upcoming Benny Yanger–Tommy Mowatt bout promoted by the American Athletic Club. State's Attorney Charles Dineen declared the match illegal early in 1903, and Governor Yates sent Barrett a telegram asking him to stop the bout. With the handwriting on the wall, the American Athletic Club canceled the show.[8]

Disgusted by the growing disorderliness of the ring, the *Chicago Tribune* declared,

> "Fake" fights, dishonest principals, and unscrupulous managers, conniving with equally unscrupulous promoters, have brought pugilism into almost universal disrepute throughout the country. . . . The real fight fan never attends a scheduled bout in these days without misgivings.
>
> Men who might conduct boxing shows honestly fear to besmirch their reputations under the present status of the sport, capable referees are being driven into retirement by the rowdy element which seeks to unfairly influence their decisions by boisterous conduct, and the better class of patrons are being alienated. The sport is thus left in the hands of crooks and sure thing gamblers. Results speak for themselves.[9]

As the ring's corruption continued, and the state increasingly enforced the ban on boxing, some Chicagoans responded with efforts to clean up prizefighting and make it legal. The prime mover in Chicago, besides fight promoters themselves, was the Personal Liberty League, a voluntary association identified with publisher William Randolph Hearst, that supported a more open city. Governor Yates claimed not to be opposed to boxing per se, but he insisted on enforcing the law, so promoters now sought the repeal of the old anti-prizefighting statutes. They proposed the establishment of a state regulatory commission to grant permits to cities under modified rules, including a limit of ten rounds per bout, and the banning of anyone with a criminal record from the sport.[10]

The struggle for boxing's soul continued into the next year. Fresh complaints about fixed fights, corrupt referees, and rough crowds led Mayor Harrison in July 1904 to call for closing the boxing arenas. Even a supporter like sportswriter and part-time referee George Siler advocated a temporary ban. Siler was concerned that much of the ring's "rottenness" grew out of promoters trying to destroy each other. "Managers of small fry clubs were fighting for control," Siler wrote, "one going so far as to have warrants served on his partner and a fighter for engaging in what he termed 'prizefighting.'" Siler concluded: "A layoff of several months will have a tendency to make the patrons of the sport more eager to see the boys together again in the fall, when it is hoped the promoters will cut out their 'dog in the manger' method of conducting business. . . . There is room for three first class clubs in Chicago, and with no conflicting dates and no underhand work in securing matches they could more than make both ends meet. The Waverly, American, and Battery D clubs have staged good attractions in the past, and with a new crop of fighters springing up daily and ready for next fall's market, the game, barring friction, should boom with the shedding of the straw hats."[11]

Others agreed that cutthroat competition among promoters was a major problem. Mayor Harrison concurred that "there is too much dissension among the parties who ran these affairs. They are continually hammering each other, fighting among themselves, pestering headquarters regarding permits." Besides, he added, how could Chicago fairly distribute permits to stage bouts in some neighborhoods, but not in those where residents complained? Better to grant no permits than to grant them unfairly.[12]

The November welterweight championship fight between Chicagoan "Buddy" Ryan and titleholder Billy Mellody of Boston at the Harlem Athletic Club in suburban Harlem (located southwest of Chicago), helped bring the boxing situation to a head. Ryan took the crown in a surprising first-round knockout of the champion. Constable John Small tried to enter the hall to serve a warrant on Howard Carr, manager of the Harlem Athletic Club, but was three times forcibly ejected by Harlem police. Warrants also had been issued for boxers Ryan and Mellody, Sig Hart, Mellody's manager, and referee Abe Pollock. In addition to the fight itself, inspectors found that the arena had no protection in case of fire, which put the 2,200 spectators in considerable danger. Moreover, doorkeepers tried to gouge latecomers, blocking these legitimate ticket holders from entering the arena, demanding five dollars in cash to seat them. On top of everything else, the event ended with the most lawlessness at a sporting event in a decade, which the *Tribune* described on page one as a "Thieves' Carnival at Prize Fight." A large number of pickpockets and holdup men worked the crowd as the Harlem police turned a blind eye or laughed at the chaos. When trains scheduled to transport spectators back to the city failed to materialize, the gangs continued to ply their trade, attacking victims who resisted. Even the renowned referee George Siler had to protect his valuables and fight his way out of the arena.[13]

Although the fiasco took place outside the city limits, Mayor Harrison had had enough, and in December 1904, he took steps to enforce the old anti-prizefighting laws in Chicago. On the advice of corporation counsel Major Edgar B. Tolman, Harrison informed the sports clubs that it was a felony for people to participate in a public bout. The threat worked; thereafter there were no regular prizefights in Chicago, although the Harlem and Blue Island clubs located outside Cook County still held occasional matches.[14]

At least one effort was made to test the ban. In late September 1905, boxing snuck back into Chicago under the guise of a "friendly bout"—

not a sordid and illegal prizefight for money, but a scientific test of skill. The match took place at McGurn's handball court on the Near North Side, permitted by Police Inspector George M. Shippy. Joseph Galley, a local sporting man and saloon manager, arranged the show in an effort to restart boxing under the facade of holding a benefit for some worthy cause. Galley was an influential Democratic ward politician, associated with James Aloysius "Hot Stove" Quinn, a North Side alderman and gambler who had recently been tossed aside by the new mayor, Edward Dunne. However, Police Chief James Collins chastised Inspector Shippy, and a few weeks later he laid down the law, announcing that "when they hire professional sluggers, they violate the state law, and even if the affair is given by a club it is just the same as when an admission is paid to a regular prize fight."[15]

Prizefighting would not return to Chicago until the late 1920s, most spectacularly in 1927, with the Jack Dempsey-Gene Tunney heavyweight title fight, witnessed by over one hundred thousand fans in the new Soldier Field.[16] The circumstances that led to the ring's banishment created a similar situation for horse racing.

The Turf in Chicago

Despite Chicago's liberal traditions, there was always considerable opposition to horse racing because of its ties to gambling, organized crime, and machine politics. Particularly appalling were those who frequented the track, often seen as low-lifes, drunks, and social degenerates. In the late 1880s, for instance, the local press, including the *Times,* the *Daily News,* and the *Inter Ocean,* were critical even of the South Side's Washington Park, the most elite track in Chicago. The *Chicago Times* characterized the crowds there as "sportive preachers, speculative ladies, high roll members of the Board of Trade, blacklegs, [and] peculating clerks," not to mention prostitutes, politicians, and youths, "who extract their working capital from the drawers of their employers."[17] The less prestigious proprietary tracks came in for even harsher criticism. These included the Harlem track, in the town of Harlem, and the short-lived Garfield Park Course, an outlaw track on the West Side, adjacent to the beautiful Garfield Park, operated by local gamblers (including Mike McDonald, the first head of organized crime in Chicago).[18]

Much of the opposition came from religious and moral leaders, as well as South Side property owners in the vicinity of Washington Park, who felt that tracks attracted a tough element and lowered property values. In 1894, the newly formed Civic Federation began a crusade against all

9. *The Finish.* Chicagoans flocked to Hawthorne Race Track, Cicero, Illinois, pictured here in 1902. (Courtesy of the Chicago History Museum.)

forms of gaming. It financed daily raids against gambling houses based on evidence gathered by private investigators. The Civic Federation in late 1894 held its first racetrack raid when agents were sent to break up the pools sold at the Hawthorne Racetrack, located just southwest of the city at the border of working-class Stickney and Cicero.[19] The reformers succeeded in closing Washington Park in 1894, as well as Hawthorne and Harlem a year later. Harlem reopened in 1897, and the other two tracks followed a year later. The improved situation in the Chicago area was undoubtedly abetted by the election of Harrison as mayor, who believed that racing at Washington Park was "a wonderful thing for the city," and was worth, he estimated, one million dollars to Chicago. Washington Park closed the following year under pressure from the Civic Federation, and because of the failure of the state legislature to pass legislation legalizing the sport and gambling at the track. However, it reopened in 1900, and the Chicago turf flourished for the next few years, adding the Worth Track in Will County in 1901, thirty miles from downtown.[20]

A lot of the reform energies in the early 1900s were devoted to enforcing the laws against offtrack gambling, which cut into the legal betting at the racetracks. In 1901, representatives of three leading betting syndicates agreed to halt handbooks (the word referred to how bets were recorded; the more modern term is bookmaking) on neighborhood streets and in stores during the winter. They also agreed to limit gambling to one suburban poolroom. These were illegal betting parlors (as in the movie *The Sting*), mainly located in busy streets downtown, where bettors could wager and then hear announcers re-create the races at the track.[21]

In 1902, however, Jim O'Leary broke the agreement by pushing his operations north into the Central Business District and increasing his presence at the racetracks. O'Leary was the "Gambler Boss 'iv th' yards" and son of Mrs. O'Leary, of Chicago Fire fame. His headquarters at 4187 South Halsted was a combination saloon, restaurant, gambling, bowling, and billiard hall. O'Leary was known nationally for his winter book on the American Derby and for his heavy betting on city and national elections.[22]

More than simply breaking the informal agreement to limit offtrack betting, O'Leary effectively declared war on his competitors. On May 30, 1902, arsonists started a fire at the Hawthorne track. The fire was attributed to O'Leary, whose interests included Hawthorne's rival, the Roby track in Indiana. O'Leary's opponents, the Smith-Perry-White gambling combine (which was protected by Chicago's infamous First Ward bosses, Bathhouse John Coughlin and Hinky Dink Kenna), operated handbooks at Hawthorne. One year later, a fire was set underneath the grandstand at Washington Park. The Smith-Perry crowd retaliated against O'Leary by hiring private police to raid O'Leary's shops. These events came to be known as the "Pineapple War" of 1902–3.[23]

The Pineapple War reveals how horse racing suffered from the same problem as prizefighting: too many competitors for too few fans. There was a lot of unfriendly competition between local tracks, exacerbated by the rivalry between the old Western Jockey Club and the new American Turf Association. Horsemen racing for one group found themselves shut out of tracks affiliated with the other, while promoters ended up in bitter feuds over dates and appearances by horses.[24] The *Tribune* foresaw deep troubles ahead: "The pathway of the local racetrack managers is strewn with thorns. Already there have been signs of a weakening on the part of the Washington Park club in the withholding of its entries, and many will not be surprised if the situation continues to grow worse, to see the south side organization come on with the announcement that it will not hold a meeting. Such an announcement probably would be the signal for the closing of all the Chicago tracks, although there are some who see in all the present strife a scheme to drive the Washington Park club out of the racing field in order that its dates may be divided up among those not so sensitive to public criticism of their favorite sport."[25]

All of these public difficulties led to renewed attacks on the track by reformers. Chicago Police Captain Herman Schuettler led major anti-gambling raids. Mayor Harrison asked the phone company to cut off services used for bookmaking on races and threatened company officials with legal action as accomplices to gambling if they failed. Private citizens also took a hand. Property owners in the vicinity of the Washington Park neighborhood sought to close that track. They formed the Washington Improvement Association and sent letters to residents explaining how the track was a public nuisance. More, the organization began condemnation proceedings to cut streets through the racecourse, and the Board of Local Improvements was asked to recommend an ordinance condemning the streets blocked by the track. President William Rainey Harper of the nearby University of Chicago, as well as several professors and students, joined the crusade against Washington Park.[26]

On April 13, 1904, a special grand jury was called to aid in the growing attack against gambling. The state's attorney, marshaling evidence collected by the police, sent more than one hundred complaints against alleged handbook and poolroom keepers before the jury. His charges named several of the city's largest owners and backers of gambling establishments, including James O'Leary, Patsy King, William Skidmore, and Mont Tennes. King was said to rank with Al Adams of New York as a policy magnate and was considered the financial backer of Skidmore's West Side handbook system. Tennes was the North Side's leading gam-

bler, second overall only to O'Leary, and he soon became the city's leading poolroom and handbook operator.[27]

Meanwhile, Captain Schuettler made plans to end gambling at Washington Park Racetrack. "I cannot tell what we may do in a few weeks,"
he declared; "I can only say that where there is gambling in Chicago we
will stop it. There is no reason to believe that we will permit gambling at
Washington Park when we have stopped it elsewhere." The police organized a special gambling detail and deployed at the track.[28] The *Tribune*
supported the crusade, arguing not only for an end to offtrack bookmaking,
but for the closing of the tracks altogether. The paper took pains to deny
that such draconian measures would—as track partisans alleged—result
in a backlash that opened the city more than ever to the rule of vice.[29]

Gambling took another hit in 1904, when Western Union got out of
the profitable race-information business because of the moral pressure
of Helen Gould, a leading stockholder, who spent much of her life trying
to make up for the misdeeds of her father, the famous robber baron Jay
Gould. Still, police pressure was the key to the turf's difficulties. As one
prominent bookie declared, "[Schuettler] had, by vigorous and indiscrimi-
nate raids and by not standing on technicalities, hammered the players
till they were afraid to be seen around a handbook, and he had killed fully
four-fifths of the play before the Western Union made a move."[30]

Despite the setbacks, the poolroom trust thumbed its nose at Schuettler's
claim that its demise was imminent. The noted bookmaker Kid Weller
declared that the barrier placed on all telegraphic reports at Hawthorne
was "one of the best things that ever happened," since it drove smaller
competitors out of business. The ultimate result, he predicted, would be a
boom for the track betting rings, where the trust was well represented.[31]

Now, however, Mayor Harrison threw his weight behind reform. He
had his eye on the Democratic presidential nomination, and so tried to
present himself as a moral crusader by instructing the police chief not to
allow bookmaking within the city limits and to suppress racetrack gambling. Their efforts focused on elite Washington Park, not only because it
was the standard bearer of Chicago racing, but also because Hawthorne
and Harlem were outside the city limits. Harrison sent a sharp note
to Police Chief Francis O'Neill calling attention to future-book ads in
the *Racing Form*. The mayor mainly had in mind the illegal downtown
poolrooms, but his efforts also affected Washington Park's ability to stay
in operation. Of course, Harrison's sudden conversion was somewhat
disingenuous, since he was closely tied to politicians who thrived on
gambling revenues, including First Ward bosses Coughlin and Kenna.[32]

Racetracks like Washington Park were dependent on gambling to stay
in operation. The wagering not only brought in the admission-paying

10. *The Track.* Derby Day at Washington Park, 1903. (Courtesy of the Chicago History Museum.)

crowds, and fees from Western Union of $700–$1,500 a day, but also significant sums from bookmakers. On Derby Day, 1904, one hundred ordinary bookmakers, who each paid a daily fee of $100, serviced Washington Park. Management anticipated that for the other twenty-four days of the 1904 meet, it would charge fifty ordinary books $100 to operate, or $120,000 for the season.[33]

Washington Park officials feared they would be shut down, and they thought that if they could prevent reports of races from leaking outside to poolrooms and handbooks the sport's public image would be enhanced. The Washington Park managers were certain that offtrack betting was responsible for the anti-gambling crusade, and tried to bend toward the reformers without breaking.[34] But the situation was becoming untenable. Simply put, without outside revenue from gambling, Washington Park was paying out five times in purses what it made at the gate, not to mention the daily overhead expenses that added hundreds of dollars more to the cost of staying open.[35]

City Hall kept the pressure high on the Washington Park Jockey Club, the Midwest's most prestigious racing organization. Fearful of police interference and the mayor's threat to revoke its license, club officials agreed to ban gambling on the premises. However, the club made it clear that without fans coming out to watch the races, the enterprise could not continue. To enforce the law, ninety plainclothesmen were assigned to the track, along with uniformed officers and a contingent of private Pinkerton detectives. Under such scrutiny, the major bookies closed up operations.[36]

The results were predictable. Gate receipts for the 1904 Derby ran $60,000 behind the previous year. Then, on the next racing day, which was a Monday, attendance fell to less than one thousand, compared to about twenty thousand in 1903.[37] On June 21, despite the running of the popular Lakeside Stakes, gate receipts were about $500, a tiny fraction of what was needed to keep the track running. While there was some dispute as to whether the police really were totally effective at suppressing gambling, especially off the track, their efforts were clearly strangling the sport. Officials kept the screws tightened until the Washington Park directors finally decided to discontinue all racing after June 22. The track's remaining races were distributed among Hawthorne, Harlem, and Worth Parks.[38]

The *Chicago Record-Herald* concluded that the closing of Washington Park proved that the track did not exist just for the love of horses. Rather, it was "neither more nor less than a huge gambling enterprise, falsely masking itself under the flag of sportsmanship." The newspaper added that "Chicago has taken no steps during the present anti-gambling crusade that can properly be interpreted as directed against any legitimate sport."[39]

In victory, Mayor Harrison reiterated his insistence that gambling be kept off the track. "As long as I am mayor of Chicago there will be no bookmaking out there," he proclaimed. He added that if the citizens felt that gambling inside the track was a legitimate recreation, then they should go to the state legislature and copy states like New York that legalized gambling.[40]

Harrison elaborated his thoughts further in a *Saturday Evening Post* article entitled "The Dope Sheet," which he hoped would gain him publicity for his ambitions at national office. "Race-track gambling," he declared, "destroys one's ideas of political economy. It takes from one the desire to live by honest work." Harrison urged that, "If congress will take the same cognizance of racetrack gambling that it did of the Louisiana Lottery, it will be possible to exterminate the former as the latter was exterminated." He urged the federal government to forbid the use of the mails for transmitting racing information, declaring that this act alone would do much to eradicate the problem.

Harrison went further, arguing that the state needed to intervene to prevent poolroom gambling by barring publication of dope sheets: "Chicago is now preparing to appeal to the state legislature . . . for legislation that will give a new weapon against this form of gambling. . . . The aldermen have ordered the bill drawn and if the state assembly will pass it we shall be aided materially. It is the purpose of this bill to make illegal the publication of racetrack information, which is used primarily and entirely for the making of bets. It is not a part of our intention to suppress any information for those interested in horse racing as horse racing. I figure that such a person does not care to know in advance what the condition of the track may be, how much weight a horse carries, what the odds against it are."[41]

Yet, while the mayor and the police took strong stands against Washington Park, Cook County Sheriff Thomas E. Barrett dragged his feet. He refused to intervene in gambling at the track without explicit orders to do so, arguing that racing had become a "permanent institution."[42] Barrett's position was strongly criticized by the Citizens' Association, a prominent good-government group. Its president, Louis A. Seeberger, declared the situation intolerable, and vowed to force Barrett into line. The association wrote to the sheriff: "The spectacle of an evil-doer fleeing the authorities of the city and finding conspicuous asylum and refuge in that part of the county which [is] not under the jurisdiction of the mayor, carries with it too grave a suspicion of anarchy and too serious an inferential responsibility to be slightingly dismissed or ignored by the law-abiding element of our community. . . . The Citizens' Association hopes that you will take the same official attitude of Mayor Harrison on the subject of racetrack gambling in your jurisdictions, believing that your determinedly expressed official disapproval will be all sufficient in causing the owners of racetracks within your jurisdiction to follow the example set by the Washington park officials."[43]

At the end of June, the grand jury returned forty-two indictments against alleged Hawthorne bookmakers, with the intention of compelling Sheriff Barrett to take the accused into custody or make them give bonds to appear in criminal court. The true bills were voted under a section of the penal code on the question of racetrack gambling that had been previously ignored. Now, for the first time, indictments were voted against track bookmakers for keeping gambling apparatuses rather than simply for being inmates of gambling houses. Next, the grand jury summoned Barrett. He pledged to enforce the new rulings against gambling, but seemed remarkably uninformed on the subject. He claimed not to have been to Hawthorne for two years and did not remember if he had ever placed a bet on a race. The grand jury directed him to stop the betting at the tracks, a course of action the *Tribune* predicted would shut down Harlem and Hawthorne Parks as surely as it had closed Washington Park.[44] The grand jury then turned its attention to the suppression of racing information, the lifeblood of gambling. Dope sheets published entry names, weights, and odds, and gave advice to bettors. The grand jury passed a resolution asking the press to desist from publishing racing news of any kind.[45]

As a result of all these efforts, 1904 turned out to be an "inglorious season" for turf sports in metropolitan Chicago. After having steadily increased for years, turf attendance plummeted to its lowest point in a decade. Furthermore, the quality of horses dropped significantly, as did the honesty of the races. The attacks in the press, the police actions, the closing of Washington Park, all, as the *Tribune* put it, "alienated a large element that recently had become interested in the pastime, and reduced the patrons of the local tracks largely to 'regulars.'"[46]

The cycle that had worked in the track's favor now ran in reverse. With declining attendance and diminishing revenues, the *Tribune* argued, corruption was inevitable: "The attacks on racing disgusted many of the better class of racing men and racing followers, making them lukewarm in their support, and this naturally gave the dishonest element the better opportunity to come to the front. The change in this respect was gradual, with earlier meetings at Harlem and Hawthorne following the closing of Washington Park being comparatively cleanly conducted. Nevertheless, as the number of stables and more especially of jockeys was reduced, the crooked alliances began to form. . . . The temptations to dishonesty surrounding a jockey, even in times of prosperous and well conducted racing are always great, and many a lad who remains honest during his earlier years in the saddle eventually falls into bad ways."[47]

Carter Harrison framed his actions a bit differently. It was less a matter of corruption than of equity. As he prepared to leave office in April 1905, after four terms (eight years) in office, one term shy of his father's record, Harrison discussed his accomplishments as mayor with the *Tribune.* He was particularly proud of his attack on horse race gambling. Harrison mentioned how he put pressure on the phone company to make transmission of bets difficult, and how he supported the police squads that went after bookies. He saw his decision to attack betting at Washington Park in terms of equity for all citizens:

> The statement has been made that this action on the part of the city government was an injury to the city's business interests. This may

be true, but the fact remains that a community may not safely have one law for the rich and another for the poor. If it be unlawful for the saloonkeeper or the cigar dealer to make a handbook, or to permit the making of a handbook in his place of business, it is equally unlawful for the directors of a great social organization like the Washington Park club to farm out gambling privileges within its enclosure. The charge, indeed, has been made that some of the directors of this great club personally operated the so-called "dollar-book." Whether this be true or not, the immediate closing up of the Washington Park club track, as soon as it was definitely understood the police were in earnest in prohibiting the making of bets within the enclosure, shows it was largely to the financial interest of the club to farm out gambling privileges.[48]

The 1905 season was anticipated with less excitement than any in memory, mainly because fans did not expect racing to take place at all. Washington Park's status was unclear, and continued wrangling between the Western Jockey Club and the American Turf Association threatened to stymie racing at the other Chicago tracks as well. The image of horse racing was further tarnished on April 25, when bombs were planted in the stalls at the Worth Track; this was the second bombing in a week at Worth, but the prior event had not been reported. There was some speculation that the Western Club had instigated the violence to discourage American Turf horsemen from competing there, but the *Tribune* dismissed that explanation.[49]

The final nail in racing's coffin came when State's Attorney John J. Healy announced that he intended not only to stamp out pool selling and handbooks, but to close the remaining tracks. His decision was not a surprise, and leaders at the various racecourses had been hedging the season's new schedule until Healy finally made his position clear. He pledged to "exert every legal power conferred upon me by law" to bring to justice anyone who "commits, aids, abets, or connives in any way" with gamblers. Gambling anywhere and in any form was a criminal offence, he argued; the law granted him full power to prosecute such crimes; as state's attorney, he intended to enforce the law vigorously.[50]

The *Tribune* applauded Healy's decision. At best, racing was a harmless amusement for more-or-less respectable people who wagered small sums they could afford to lose. But in fact, racing in most cases was "an abomination, a scandal, and a disgrace." Chicago would be better off getting rid of it entirely rather than trying to redeem it. The *Tribune* went on to deny the argument of turf proponents that the track brought increased trade to the city. Whatever small amounts flowed into saloons, barbershops, hotels, "and other places of more or less repute" was negated by "the impairment of character among employees of commercial houses, owing to the practice of 'following the races.'" The *Tribune* concluded: "All honor to state's Attorney Healy. He has declared his intention to enforce the law as he knows it, and the community will applaud his efforts, hold up his hands, and say to him, 'Well done, thou good and faithful servant.'"[51]

The racetracks never even opened in 1905. They realized they had no hope of making money without gambling, which the state's attorney was clearly not going to permit. Along with Philadelphia, Chicago was now one of only two of the world's fifteen largest cities to ban thorough-bred racing. This was not the company most Chicagoans would have chosen. Even the *Tribune* noted uneasily Philadelphia's reputation for strict observance of blue laws, and the newspaper attempted to argue that Chicago's problem stemmed from corrupt local practices, rather than anything inherently wrong with racing itself.[52]

Handbook operators were apparently not crestfallen by the news that local tracks were closing. Because they were connected to the Payne Telegraph Service, run by John Payne, a former Western Union employee, they did not have to depend on the Washington and Hawthorne Parks for horses on which to bet; Payne's service kept bookmakers informed of racing results from across the country. According to the *Tribune,* Chicago's handbook syndicate was not fazed by the closings because many racing fans—including high rollers who used to go to the track—now turned to the handbooks. The *Tribune* quoted one sporting man who estimated that $30,000 was bet daily on foreign (out of town) races: "I don't claim to be an expert in such matters, but it seems to me the betting in those downtown places, which are patronized by clerks, and where dollar bets are more common than anything else, does more harm than the betting at the tracks. Of course it is easy to get at the betting at the track and stop it, and it is hard to get at the handbooks."[53]

Opinion makers might have anticipated that the election of Carter Harrison's successor, Democrat Edward Dunne—a political reformer who campaigned on moral issues—would have resulted in an ardent fight against the gambling nexus. Dunne supported a panoply of progressive reforms, yet he got very little accomplished, while managing to alienate both the old-time bosses and the reformers. He appointed as police chief a political ally, John Collins, a veteran of the Haymarket Affair, who appeared at first a fine selection. Collins said upon his appointment, "Gambling in this town is a disgrace. We have handbooks, poker, craps, slot machines, and every gambling device known. Men are waylaid on their way home from work and solicited by barkers and touts. We can drive every damned one of them out of Chicago, and we'll try to do it."[54]

He organized spectacular raids on his first days on the job, including some on Mont Tennes's downtown shops, but these were mainly just for show. The illegal offtrack betting business flourished during Mayor Dunne's tenure, and it continued to flourish for decades.

The successful effort to halt racing and boxing in Chicago was part of the Progressive movement's broader fight against "debased" amusements, especially gambling and prostitution. However, the victories over the track and the ring did not end offtrack gambling, which became bigger than ever. Nor would the city prove any more successful in ending prostitution, even after the closing of the levee district in the early 1910s. Not only did "victimless" crime continue to flourish in Chicago, but in a few years, the city became the heart of the bootleg liquor trade during Prohibition. The raids on Mont Tennes's operations had no long-term ill effects; indeed, he quickly became Chicago's leading offtrack handbook and poolroom operator. In 1911, Tennes gained control over the national racing wire and monopolized the transmission of racing news to illegal betting rooms across the United States.[55]

Ironically, then, amidst a flourishing culture of wagering, the ring and the track died in Chicago. They would not be fully restored for over twenty years. Virtually no races took place in the metropolitan area until Hawthorne reopened in 1921, using evasive oral-betting schemes. The sport was not fully back until 1927, when the state legislature legalized pari-mutuel betting because of political pressure from urban voters, and due to Illinois's need for additional revenues. One year earlier the state had legalized prizefighting, which was then rapidly gaining popular national support following the passage of New York's Walker Act. A generation of abstinence only made Chicagoans more eager for sinful sport.

Notes

1. Steven A. Riess, *City Games: The Evolution of American Urban Society and the Rise of Sports* (Urbana: University of Illinois Press, 1989), 54–55, 184–86, 211.

2. Ibid., 70–71, 93, 185–86.

3. Michael E. McGerr, *A Fierce Discontent: The Rise and Fall of the Progressive Movement in America, 1870–1920* (New York: Free Press, 2003); and Arthur S. Link and Richard L. McCormick, *Progressivism* (Arlington Heights, Ill.: Harlan Davidson, 1983). On progressivism and sports, see Riess, *City Games*, 132–204, 151–53, 158–68, 186–87.

4. Perry R. Duis, *Challenging Chicago: Coping with Everyday Life, 1837–1920* (Urbana: University of Illinois Press, 1998); *Chicago Tribune*, January 25, 1903.

5. Dale A. Somers, *The Rise of Sports in New Orleans, 1850–1900* (Baton Rouge: Louisiana State University Press, 1972), 159–91; Steven A. Riess, "In the Ring and Out: Professional Boxing in New York, 1896–1920," in *Sport in America: New*

Historical Perspectives, ed. Donald Spivey (Westport, Conn.: Greenwood Press, 1985), 95–128.

6. *Chicago Tribune,* December 14, 1900; February 25, 1906; Dan Daniel, "Was McGovern–Gans Fight a Fake?" *Ring,* 39 (June 1960): 8–9, 43; *American National Biography,* s.v. "Gans, Joe."

7. *Dictionary of American Biography,* s.v. "Carter H. Harrison II"; *Chicago Tribune,* March 15, 1897; December 26, 1953.

8. *Chicago Tribune,* January 17, 1903; January 15, 1903.

9. *Chicago Tribune,* January 17, 1903.

10. *Chicago Record-Herald,* September 24, 1905. On the Frawley Act, see Riess, "In the Ring and Out," 105–12.

11. *Chicago Tribune,* July 17, 1904.

12. *Chicago Tribune,* October 7, 1904.

13. *Chicago Tribune,* November 15, 1904.

14. *Chicago Tribune,* December 16, 1904.

15. *Chicago Record-Herald,* September 24, 1905, October 18, 1905.

16. William Nack, "The Long Count," *Sports Illustrated,* September 22, 1997; Bruce J. Evensen, *When Dempsey Fought Tunney: Heroes, Hokum, and Storytelling in the Jazz Age* (Knoxville: University of Tennessee Press, 1996); Elliott J. Gorn, "The Manassa Mauler and the Fighting Marine: An Interpretation of the Dempsey-Tunney Fights," *Journal of American Studies,* 19 (1985): 27–47; Randy Roberts, *Jack Dempsey: The Manassa Mauler* (Baton Rouge: Louisiana State University Press, 1979).

17. *Chicago Times,* June 29, 1887, July 17, 1887, July 20, 1887, July 24, 1887, July 31, 1887, August 7, 1887.

18. Steven A. Riess, "Horse Racing in Chicago, 1883–1894: The Interplay of Class, Politics, and Organized Crime," in Ralph C. Wilcox et al., *Sporting Dystopias: The Making and Meanings of Urban Sport Cultures* (Albany, N.Y.: SUNY Press, 2003), 117–36.

19. *Chicago Daily News,* June 8, 1894, June 10, 1894, September 29, 1894.

20. *Spirit of the Times,* December 15, 1897, August 19, 1899; *Chicago Tribune,* February 7, 1899.

21. Richard Lindberg, *Chicago Ragtime: Another Look at Chicago, 1880–1920* (South Bend, Ind.: Icarus Press, 1979), 177–81.

22. Richard T. Griffin, "Big Jim O'Leary: 'Gambler Boss iv th' Yards,'" *Chicago History,* 5 (1976–77): 213–22.

23. Lindberg, *Chicago Ragtime,* 177–81. See also Lindberg, "The Evolution of an Evil Business," *Chicago History,* 22 (1993): 38–53.

24. *Chicago Tribune,* April 4, 1904.

25. *Chicago Tribune,* April 5, 1904.

26. *Chicago Tribune,* March 30, 1904, April 10, 1904, June 23, 1904.

27. *Chicago Tribune,* April 14, 1904; John Landesco, *Organized Crime in Chicago,* Part 3 of the Illinois Crime Survey (1929; repr., Chicago: University of Chicago Press, 1968), 45–47.

28. *Chicago Tribune,* April 20, 1904.

29. *Chicago Tribune,* April 24, 1904.

30. *Chicago Record-Herald,* May 21, 1904; Riess, *City Games,* 186.

31. *Chicago Tribune,* May 23, 1904.

32. *Chicago Tribune,* June 11, 1904; *Chicago Record-Herald,* June 11, 1904. On

Coughlin and Kenna, see Herman Kogan and Lloyd Wendt, *Lords of the Levee: The Story of Bathhouse John and Hinky Dink* (Indianapolis: Bobbs-Merrill, 1943).

33. *Chicago Tribune,* June 14, 1904.

34. *Chicago Tribune,* June 6, 1904.

35. Ibid.

36. *Chicago Tribune,* June 19, 1904.

37. *Chicago Tribune,* June 20, 1904.

38. *Chicago Tribune,* June 16, 1904, June 20, 1904, June 22, 1904; *New York Times,* June 22, 1904.

39. *Chicago Tribune,* June 23, 1904.

40. Ibid.

41. Carter H. Harrison, "The 'Dope Sheet,'" *Saturday Evening Post,* July 9, 1904, 3, 22; *Chicago Record-Herald,* July 8, 1904.

42. *Chicago Tribune,* May 23, 1904.

43. *Chicago Tribune,* June 26, 1904.

44. *Chicago Tribune,* July 1, 1904, July 22, 1904.

45. *Chicago Tribune,* July 27, 1904, August 5, 1904.

46. *Chicago Tribune,* October 31, 1904.

47. Ibid.

48. *Chicago Tribune,* April 9, 1905. At this time, bookmakers at the track usually took no bets of less than five dollars. Smaller bets were more common with handbook men.

49. *Chicago Tribune,* April 23, 1905.

50. *Chicago Tribune,* April 27, 1905.

51. *Chicago Tribune,* April 28, 1905.

52. *Chicago Tribune,* April 30, 1905.

53. *Chicago Tribune,* April 27, 1905.

54. Landesco, *Organized Crime in Chicago,* 46; Richard Lindberg, *Chicago by Gaslight: A History of Chicago's Netherworld, 1880–1920* (Chicago: Academy Chicago Publishers, 1996), 182–83.

55. Landesco, *Organized Crime in Chicago,* 46–84, 50–61.

4

Jewish Women, Sports, and Chicago History

LINDA J. BORISH

In June 1915, the Chicago Hebrew Institute, a leading Jewish Americanization agency, opened a new athletic facility. Writing in celebration of the occasion, a journalist for the Chicago Jewish American paper, *The Sentinel,* declared that the new building symbolized "the blending of the healthiest in American life and the noblest in Jewish life in the Hebrew Institute's gymnasium and natatorium."[1] The CHI was not unique in providing sporting facilities for Jews. It was not even the only organization that served men *and* women. Other organizations of this era, such as the Young Women's Union in Philadelphia, the Irene Kaufmann Settlement in Pittsburgh, and the Jewish Educational and Charitable Association in St. Louis, also expressed concern about women's physical health. The Chicago Hebrew Institute was part of a trend that linked sporting activities to ideals of citizenship for Jewish immigrants, both male and female.

Yet studies in American Jewish sport history focus on Jewish men, giving scant attention to Jewish women. This is symptomatic of a larger problem in the study of ethnicity. As historian Donna Gabaccia explains about gender and immigrant life, "Most histories of immigrants in the

United States begin with the experiences of migratory men disguised as genderless human beings."[2] Analyzing diverse sources about Jewish immigrant aid associations, including annual reports, bulletins, house organs, newspaper articles, and committee reports, this essay examines the ways physical culture and sports became part of Jewish Americanization efforts for women as well as men.

In his essay on "Jewish Americanization Agencies" Charles Bernheimer declared in the early 1920s that in the "process of adjustment generally called Americanization . . . there is no single formula." He went on, "Americanization has been defined as the process by which an alien acquires our language, citizenship, ideals and an appreciation and love for American traits. . . . It may safely be said that the all-important thinking is the adoption of 'the spirit of America,' and not mere outward conformity to certain habits and customs."[3] Sports were part of this "spirit of America," yet most commentators of this era assumed that only men participated in them. Historian Steven Riess has written that, "Sport was regarded as almost inherently a male sphere, inappropriate for Victorian women, and the contemporary press described nearly all sports as manly." Indeed, manliness and sport went hand in hand so that middle-class men developed their physical and spiritual selves, building character as they built their bodies. As a counterpart to this "Muscular Christian" ideal, middle-class women participated in sporting activities to enhance themselves as moral guardians of home and society. The muscular Christian and the robust mother each pursued physical fitness within gender-prescribed roles. Riess argues persuasively that late-nineteenth-century recreation helped redefine middle-class manliness.[4] But it is equally true that how women adapted their bodies to physical culture shaped perceptions of middle-class femininity.[5]

Historians need to examine more closely the sporting practices of women outside the white, bourgeois mainstream. "There is a tendency for generalizations to be made about all women in sports from examples of white women," sport historian Jennifer Hargreaves has written, and these generalizations stereotypically refer to white, Western bourgeois women.[6] Historians examining Jewish immigrants in sport typically concentrate on males in New York City institutions; examples are Cary Goodman's work on the Educational Alliance and Peter Levine's study on sport and the American Jewish experience, both of which imply that Jewish women participated in very limited sporting activities.[7] Yet Jewish women fought for access to their own sporting venues and athletic opportunities, and some bourgeois reformers aided these women by supporting healthy exercise and recreation as a road to Americanization.[8]

Early Efforts to Promote Athleticism

By 1915, when the *American Hebrew* printed an article titled "Jewesses in Athletics," increasing numbers of Jewish women had already found their way to gymnasiums, tennis courts, and swimming pools.[9] For Jewish immigrant women and children in the late nineteenth century, exposure to American life and sporting activities often occurred at settlement houses and immigrant aid associations. As east European immigrants came to America and populated cities such as New York and Philadelphia, earlier nineteenth-century German Jewish immigrants, many of whom by the 1880s had become acculturated and prosperous, often desired to assist the newcomers' adjustment to American culture. These German Jews opted to promote assimilation rather than nurture the distinct ethnic and religious identities of their east European counterparts.[10]

The Jewish Training School of Chicago, founded by Leon Mandel and other wealthy German Jews in 1888, included physical training in its programs for the newcomers. The founders of the school desired "to equip the sons and daughters of our Jewish poor with the power of making a healthy, honest, and honorable livelihood." The school's first superintendent, Professor Gabriel Bamberger, offered Jewish youngsters classes in physical exercise and manual training (carpentry, metal working, and the like). There was enough of a commitment to athletics that Hilda Satt Polacheck, a young Jewish immigrant from Poland, remembered distinctly that back in 1892–93, "gymnastics were taught in a real gymnasium." The emphasis on physical and athletic skills continued at the Jewish Training School, when Miss Antoinette Belitz took over as gymnastics teacher at the end of the century. The sporting interests of the Jewish students deepened when the 1898 graduating class of the Jewish Training School initiated a fund-raising drive to accumulate the money to open a natatorium.[11]

Such efforts came amidst the larger context of progressive middle-class reformers' attempts to solve urban problems of poverty and overcrowding with cultural institutions such as playgrounds and supervised sports for immigrant youth and children. Jane Addams, founder of Hull-House in Chicago, Jewish philanthropist Isidor Strauss, members of New York City's Educational Alliance, and benefactors and supervisors at the Hebrew Technical School for Girls in New York City, all encouraged young women to engage in physical recreations in a controlled, wholesome environment rather than succumbing to the lure of "immoral" commercial amusements. Similarly, Jewish Americans like Lillian Wald, founder of the Henry Street Settlement in New York City, Lizzie Black Kander, founder of The Settlement in Milwaukee, and Lina F. Hecht, founder of

Boston's Hecht House, were alarmed at the vice and danger they perceived in the chaotic street life of lower-class, east European Jewish immigrants. For these reformers, too, physical culture went hand in hand with immigrant women's welfare and assimilation into American life.[12]

At Hull-House, which served Chicago's Maxwell Street neighborhood with programs designed to promote cultural exchange and urban reform, Jewish girls gained knowledge of sports in their Americanization classes. Hilda Polacheck was a student there after she left the Jewish Training School, and she recalled joining the Hull-House gymnasium with her sisters. The Polacheck girls scraped together the money to buy the regulation gym suit—wide bloomers and a blouse. The girls learned calisthenics and basketball, and social reformers praised such wholesome activities as an alternative to crowded, dirty, and dangerous city streets. Hilda certainly remembered the Hull-House Gymnasium as "an oasis in a desert on Halstead Street."[13]

Even the synagogues helped promote physical culture. The South Side's Temple Sinai Congregation built new social facilities in 1912, and these included a gymnasium and swimming pool. At the annual congregation meeting in 1914, a new director for the center was named, Dr. Joseph Pedott, previously the director of the Chicago Hebrew Institute. He pledged to work closely with the temple's "Ladies Organization." The new center was an instant success, and its director looked back after ten years and saw remarkable progress, especially for the women. He called it a pioneer institution, like no other in the country, with over two thousand members, a range of club sports, and a string of victories against local teams in such events as swimming and basketball. Just to name one athlete, Ethel Bilson—a "Medal-Some Mermaid," as the Chicago *Tribune* called her—represented Sinai in the early 1920s, and had a string of victories in indoor swimming and diving. And the Sinai Social Center, with its excellent coaching, had many years of success in women's sports in the first half of the twentieth century.[14]

The Chicago Hebrew Institute, Americanization, and Women's Athletics

But one social institution stands out from all the rest. The Chicago Hebrew Institute offered men and women a comprehensive range of classes in Citizenship, English, Commerce, Domestic Science, Jewish Culture, Literature, Art, Physical Culture, Drama, and Music. Organized in 1903 by a group of young men on Chicago's lower West Side, the CHI promoted the moral, physical, religious, and civic welfare of Jewish immigrants and residents. Jewish philanthropist and businessman Julius Rosenwald helped secure property for the Institute. President Jacob M. Loeb, elected in 1912, and Dr. Philip L. Seman, director, and superintendent of the Institute from 1913 to 1945, guided the expansion and program development to create a thriving Jewish institution, the forerunner of today's Jewish Community Centers. Superintendent Dr. Philip Seman explained, "The Institute is frankly Jewish and staunchly American." In 1922, the Chicago Hebrew Institute changed its name to the Jewish People's Institute, and in 1927, moved into a new building in Lawndale.[15]

Throughout its history, the CHI underscored the importance of physical well-being for all participants, male and female. In an article titled "'Good, Clean Sport,' Motto of the CHI," the Institute's Director of Physical Culture, Harry Berkman, declared, "The Chicago Hebrew Institute was founded on the idea that athletics are a good thing and dedicated to the idea that mind, body and morals should be developed at one and the same time." Berkman concluded, "We train the boys and girls to be self-reliant, independent, and on the square in everything." But there was an even deeper reason for bringing physical culture to those hundreds of youths who came to the CHI. In a 1914 article in *The Sentinel*, titled "The Temple of the Body: How the Hebrew Institute Is Laboring to Make Jews Physically Fit," journalist Bertha A. Loeb acknowledged the prevailing stereotypes about Jews and physicality in the early twentieth century, but asserted that "the undersized, anaemic 'Jewish weakling' will soon be a recollection of by-gone days." The Chicago Hebrew Institute, therefore, aimed to establish that "one of the first activities to be set into being was a gymnasium for the youth of both sexes."[16]

The Chicago Hebrew Institute paid special attention to the physical welfare of immigrant women and girls by combining gymnasium and athletic work with domestic instruction. In his 1913–14 superintendent's report on the CHI in the *Observer*, Dr. Seman emphasized the link between teaching immigrants English and teaching them physical fitness: "For the past five months, a class now numbering over 200 immigrant women are given instruction, as part of their school work, in calisthenics exercises and drills." He went on, "The girls could not quite see what exercise and calisthenics had to do with the study of English, but it did not take very long before they felt a new life entering their tired, wornout bodies, and the exercise hour was looked forward to with much anticipation." Dr. Seman explained his rationale for exercise: "We recognized that the girls, who work hard in shops or in factories all day long . . . needed physical instructions to invigorate them. The clumsy immigrant girl of the first evening after five months," he observed, "in the majority of instances, has been changed to a graceful and spritely girl, who now moves her arms, her limbs and her body with grace and poise."[17]

The press echoed Seman's enthusiasm. Declared a reporter, "One of the unusual features on Tuesday evening was a calisthenics exhibition by about 100 immigrant young women, members of the English class, who have been in this country only from six months to a year. By such methods of Americanizing the newcomer, the Hebrew Institute does much that counts for civic enlightenment among the immigrants." So successful was the athletic program that the Chicago Hebrew Institute pledged to raise $125,000 to build one of the finest and best-equipped gymnasiums in America.[18]

The new gym revived the old debate over women's physical culture. At first the physical pursuits of girls and women received little attention in the building plans. But President Jacob Moritz Loeb wanted to serve the needs of Jews of both sexes and battled to construct equal athletic facilities for men and women. Loeb and James Davis, the athletic committee chairman during the quest for a new building, believed separate gyms and swimming pools, or "tanks" as they were called, should be included in the new facility. Loeb made his thinking clear in a letter to Mr. and Mrs. Julius Rosenwald (who eventually donated $50,000) in an October 1913 letter: "We can build a gymnasium for $100,000 if we build it for men and boys alone but we cannot build it for $100,000 if we wish to give service to *women, girls and children* (this is for Mrs. J. R. to think about)." Loeb continued, "I impress upon you the great need of the gymnasium, especially of the women's and girls' departments." He added that working-class women in particular needed a neighborhood gymnasium where they could refresh themselves with evening activities and thereby "revive their physical strength for the morrow's hard task."[19]

Over time Loeb raised the necessary funds, and CHI's outstanding athletic facilities served Jewish men and women. In his address to the CHI on March 31, 1914, Loeb praised the sport sites accessible to both genders. "Our demands were different than any Y.M.C.A. or social center building in as much as we wished to accommodate all of our people, namely boys and girls, men and women."[20] Superintendent Seman declared in his 1915–16 report, "With the advent of our new Gymnasium which was dedicated beginning June 6th, a new epoch in our Athletic Work began." The gymnasium offered "equal facilities for men and women, therefore, having a separate Gymnasium, Swimming Tanks, Locker Rooms, Shower Baths and . . . offices for Physical Directors and Swimming Instructors." One journalist remarked, "In a city where the women have as little athletic opportunity as Chicago this is a great step forward. It is only another instance of the aggressiveness that has placed the Hebrew Institute where it is on the athletic map."[21]

CHI officials argued that exercise and sport prepared Jewish boys and girls for "real manhood and real womanhood" in American society. Writing about "Civics and Citizenship," Philip Seman emphasized the importance of immigrants pursuing courses in these subjects. The Institute's literature, addressed to immigrants themselves, stated, "You should become a citizen of the United States because it is the only way you can show your gratitude for the wonderful freedom and opportunity it gives and offers you;—become a part of this government,—a member of it, a citizen." Athletics, of course, were part of this process, and the fact that over three thousand spectators attended CHI swim meets in 1915–16 was evidence of success. With all of its good work, Superintendent Seman concluded, "I feel that we are accomplishing as much, if not more, in making good Jews and Jewesses of the young people who come to us than any other agency, be it the synagogue, temple or institution."[22]

Basketball quickly became a favorite sport of women and girls at the new CHI gym. In 1917, the Institute's ladies' basketball team won thirteen of fifteen games, even though they competed against some of the strongest squads in the Chicago area. The 1921 team enjoyed another impressive season, going 26–0. That year, the Institute won the Central Amateur Athletic Union Girls' Basketball Championship, scoring a total of 447 points to their opponents' 116. Concluded one observer, the JPI (the old CHI was renamed the Jewish People's Institute in 1922) girls' team "has been directly responsible for the popularity of basketball among the girls of Chicago and the towns close by." Always conscious of image, the Institute took pride in the fact that "in all these games, the girls displayed the best sportsmanship."[23]

The CHI natatorium proved equally successful at producing competitive athletes. The 1917–18 girls' swimming team was especially strong, and the pride it engendered was evident: "In our ladies' tank, we have turned out some remarkable young swimmers, every one of whom was trained with us. They have taken first places in swimming competitions held at the Illinois Athletic Club and the Chicago Athletic Club."[24] In 1921, the female swimmers again displayed their prowess when the team won the Open City Swimming Championship of Chicago, hailed as the "biggest of its kind ever held in the city." The next year, JPI girls defeated the YWCA girls' team in a dual meet before three hundred spectators. The team capped its run in 1922 with two prestigious city championships—from the Amateur Athletic Union and the Amateur Athletic Federation—in addition to numerous medals and awards.[25]

Athletic activities for JPI women went beyond the gym and swimming pool. In 1921, the institute's talented track and field team of working-class women demonstrated its skill against the Hawthorne Club, which was made up of women who worked at the Western Electric Company. JPI females also won several events in the Chicago City Track Meet, hosted at the Institute in 1922. The following year, even greater headlines came from the Chicago–Paris Olympic Women's Athletic Meet, sponsored and promoted by the Institute. More than 450 competitors participated, and JPI girls won the meet, taking first place in the 100-yard dash, the 100-yard hurdles, and the 60-yard dash, as well as the shot put and javelin throw. The track and field meet drew much praise from the press. In the Institute's annual report, Dr. Seman declared, "This is the first meet of its kind ever held in this country, and it proved a great success and of much interest." Besides track and field, JPI women and girls competed in tennis, volleyball, and squash, and the Institute founded new teams for girls of various ages.[26]

A few years later, baseball—the most American of sports—became part of the JPI girls' sports program. The 1923 JPI report boasted, "We started out the summer season by winning the Inter-settlement championship in baseball. This is the first time the Institute girls have ever had a baseball team." JPI girls even played in the postseason, earning a tie against the Kewanee Team from Chicago's North Side. Other Jewish organizations also sponsored women's baseball games, introducing women to the national pastime.[27]

In sum, JPI considered physical culture and sport for women an essential component of its Americanization work. A study by the Jewish Welfare Board of Chicago praised JPI's citizenship efforts, and the place of sporting activities in its program: "The large gymnasium building with its many facilities and modern equipment affords opportunities for recreation and physical development to many men and women, young people and children."[28] In serving Jewish girls and seeking civic betterment, JPI's mission integrated sports and athletics with lessons in citizenship.

Leading Jewish Sportswomen

Organizations such as the Chicago Hebrew Institute reveal the desire of countless Jewish women to be part of the growing athleticism of American life. In addition to those who showed up just for refreshment or exercise or the joy of play, a few women became particularly renowned in athletic circles. Elaine Rosenthal, for example, made her mark as a golfer and Jennie Franklin Purvin became known for promoting swimming.

Rosenthal, born in 1896, became one of the most prominent female golfers in the early twentieth century. Mostly she played at the Ravisloe Country Club in Homewood, Illinois, but she came to prominence in 1914, when she competed in the U.S. women's national golf championship in Nassau, New York, reached the finals against Mrs. H. Arnold Jackson, and earned high praise. "Miss Rosenthal made it clear that she will have to be reckoned with in future championships, for she has many shots in her bag, [is] a nervy player, and a heady one, and she is only 18 years old," remarked the *New York Times*. The *American Hebrew* wrote, "In any mention of golfers, the name of Miss Elaine Rosenthal . . . should be included." Referring to "Miss Rosenthal's sensational play on the Nassau links," the magazine anticipated great things from her. In addition, "Miss Schwalbacher, Miss Rosenthal's clubmate, also made a creditable showing. This seems to indicate good days ahead for Jewish women-golfers." Rosenthal's mother, Mrs. Bernard J. Rosenthal, played competitive golf, and her sister, Mrs. Gladys Byfield, was also a championship golfer, at times competing against sister Elaine.[29]

Rosenthal continued her outstanding play in numerous tournaments. In 1917 she won the Western Women's Golf Championship, then repeated this feat in 1918 and 1925, becoming the first woman to wear the "triple crown." She was well enough known by World War I that the Red Cross invited her to participate in charity golf exhibitions that featured the likes of Bobby Jones. Even today, each year's champion at the Illinois Women's Open Golf Tournament is awarded the Elaine Rosenthal Memorial trophy. Though she married in 1921, she remained active on the golf circuit. Yet for all of her accomplishments, it should be remembered that she succeeded in a not fully hospitable social world. After all, the Ravisloe course where she developed her game was part of a Jewish country club; Jews opened their own clubs in part because they had been blackballed from gentile clubs. And during those years at the height of her career, allegations flew that organizers of major tournaments routinely kept the numbers of Jewish golfers low.[30]

For Chicagoans who swam in Lake Michigan, another Jewish American woman, Jennie Franklin Purvin, provided leadership to clean up the beaches. In fact, she became known as the "mother of bathing beaches" because of her long years of work in promoting waterfront recreation. For over twenty-five years, she campaigned for public beaches and comfort stations. Purvin also worked with Dr. Philip Seman, president of the Chicago Hebrew Institute, on the Chicago Recreation Committee in the 1930s.[31]

As a young woman, Jennie Franklin was an avid swimmer. In her diary she recorded some of her swimming excursions. On July 12, 1890, going to a different pool than usual, Franklin wrote, "Swimming; very nice pool; arrangements better than ours"; then on July 15, she added, "Swimming in morning; am considered very good out this way, probably because so few young ladies swim." Another time Franklin tersely noted, "Natatorium in A.M."[32] Her interest in water sports continued

11. *Jewish Sports-women.* Jennie Franklin Purvin was just one of many accomplished Jewish women athletes in the early decades of the twentieth century. (Courtesy of the American Jewish Archives.)

when she became a very active club woman in Chicago. As president of the Chicago Woman's Aid Organization and as chair of the Public Recreation Facilities of the Woman's City Club (she began both offices in 1911), she campaigned vigorously to clean up Lake Michigan. She wrote articles and petitioned local politicians to promote her cause, and in the early 1920s, she organized a group of women to attend meetings of the Lincoln Park Commission and make a plea against destroying beaches for the construction of Lake Shore Drive.[33]

When the commissioners decided to meet behind closed doors, Purvin took her case to the public in articles published in Chicago's Jewish American newspaper, *The Sentinel.* She argued that, "Unless interference comes at once there will be no water sports for the citizen of the north side after another year," and she indicated that until only a few years before, there had been several excellent beaches for swimmers. But now, only Clarendon Beach was left, and it too was threatened. In an article titled "When Is a Bathing Beach Not a Bathing Beach," Purvin reflected on how it used to be that swimming was not considered "lady-like" and that when she learned to swim she had "to go to the natatorium at 5 o'clock in the morning so that we could be well out of the way before any of the boys arrived." But, she went on, "possibly because a few of us found out early what wonderful advantages came from the exercise of swimming, we chafed at the slow progress which the City of Chicago made in utilizing her lake front." Purvin remembered the siege "we laid at the doors of the City Hall fourteen years ago in order to get one little bathing beach at the foot of 39th street." In fact, Purvin advised readers of *The Sentinel*, "We are all agreed that no exercise to which the general public has access is as beneficial in hot weather as is swimming." She urged the city to provide "instruction in swimming on the public beaches," and concluded, "Let us hope that the women of our clubs, who already have so much to their credit in the recreational life of our city, will press the point to accomplishment!"[34]

As fashions changed in the 1920s, Purvin found herself responding to criticisms that women swimmers dressed inappropriately for public venues. Without entirely dismissing the charge, she argued that so long as people used the beaches properly—for active recreation and swimming, not "loafing"—then the city laws spelling out decent dress were sufficient. Above all, she was concerned that such issues not get in the way of women's access to athletic activity.[35] In 1922 she wrote, "The major portion of criticism comes from people who are not yet accustomed to the newer ideas of freedom of movement and who are inclined to allow prudishness to influence judgment." For Purvin, above all, the issue for women was one of "freedom of movement" in the largest sense. As a Jewish woman engaged with the issues and institutions of her time, she was an important example of the ties between activism, athleticism, and citizenship.[36]

Conclusion

The opening of the new Chicago Hebrew Institute gymnasium in the summer of 1915 marked expanded access for Jewish women and girls desiring to hone their athletic skills. This gymnasium garnered the praise of *Chicago Daily News* reporter Fred A. Marquartdt, who wrote, "The building itself, insofar as modern construction is concerned, ranks next to the Patten gymnasium in Evanston as one of the best in the central states, if not in the country." In particular, the journalist proclaimed,

"Hundreds of athletically inclined women and girls and men and boys of all ages already have started to take advantage of it." These Jewish women of the Chicago Hebrew Institute, finding the new gym "a joy to all athletes," extended the participation of sports started in Chicago institutions in the late nineteenth century for Jewish immigrant females.[37] In the environs of settlement houses and educational institutions, Jewish women and girls gained physical and moral health, an orientation to American culture, and access to recreation and sporting competition.

Jewish women in Chicago in the early twentieth century began to excel as they engaged in sports at athletic facilities, and learned skills to compete in swimming, basketball, tennis, track, and golf. At the CHI's natatorium, women obtained proper swimming instruction and training from Miss Sara Hanssen, a noted Olympian from Denmark. Over three hundred girls, from the ages of five to thirty, swam at the pool, and with the new ladies' swimming tank, many Jewish women advanced their swimming skills. The Chicago *Herald* in 1916 even asserted, "The Jewish girls make particularly good swimmers," and the paper told readers, "It is a well known fact that women learn to swim quicker than men. There is more flesh and less bone, consequently her body is more buoyant."[38] These Jewish sportswomen of Chicago in the swimming pools, on the basketball courts, playing fields, or golf links, helped shape the city's rich sporting history and women's participation in America's sporting past.

Notes

1. Chester Foust, "Mother, May I Go Out to Swim?" *Chicago Sunday Herald,* January 2, 1916, and "Imported from Europe—A Swimming Instructor," *Chicago Tribune,* July 8, 1915, Philip L. Seman Collection, Scrapbook; Bertha A. Loeb, "A Gala Day at the Institute," *The Sentinel,* June 11, 1915, Jacob M. Loeb Collection, Chicago Hebrew Institute (CHI), American Jewish Archives, Cincinnati, Ohio (hereafter AJA).

2. Donna Gabaccia, *From the Other Side: Women, Gender, and Immigrant Life in the U.S., 1820–1920* (Bloomington: Indiana University Press, 1994), xi.

3. Charles S. Bernheimer, "Jewish Americanization Agencies," *American Jewish Year Book,* 5682, vol. 23, October 3, 1921–September 22, 1922 (Philadelphia: Jewish Publication Society of America, 1922), 84–85, The Jewish Division, New York Public Library; Linda J. Borish, "The Place of Physical Culture and Sport for Women in Jewish Americanization Organizations" (paper presented at international Conference, Jewish Studies Program, Arizona State University, Tempe, Ariz., February 11–12, 2001).

4. Steven A. Riess, "Sport and the Redefinition of American Middle-Class Masculinity, 1840–1900," in *Major Problems in American Sport History: Documents and Essays,* ed. Steven A. Riess (Boston: Houghton Mifflin, 1997), 190–91,

197; Linda J. Borish, "Catharine Beecher and Thomas W. Higginson on the Need for Physical Fitness," in *Major Problems in American Sport History*, ed. Riess, 95–96.

5. Patricia A. Vertinsky, *The Eternally Wounded Woman: Women, Doctors, and Exercise in the Late Nineteenth Century* (Urbana: University of Illinois Press, 1994), 23.

6. Jennifer Hargreaves, *Sporting Females: Critical Issues in the History and Sociology of Women's Sports* (London: Routledge, 1994), 255.

7. Cary Goodman, "(Re) Creating Americans at the Educational Alliance," *Journal of Ethnic Studies*, 6 (Winter 1979): 1–28; Cary Goodman, *Choosing Sides: Playground and Street Life on the Lower East Side* (New York: Schocken, 1979); Peter Levine, *Ellis Island to Ebbets Field: Sport and the American Jewish Experience* (New York: Oxford University Press, 1992); George Eisen, "Sport, Recreation, and Gender: Jewish Immigrant Women in Turn-of-the Century America (1880–1920)," *Journal of Sport History*, 18 (Spring 1991): 103–20; see also Dominick Cavallo, *Muscles and Morals: Organized Playground and Urban Reforms, 1880–1920* (Philadelphia: University of Pennsylvania Press, 1981).

8. Steven A. Riess, *City Games: The Evolution of American Urban Society and the Rise of Sports* (Urbana: University of Illinois Press, 1991), 133–34.

9. "Jewesses in Athletics," *American Hebrew*, 96:11 (January 8, 1915): 279.

10. On Jewish immigration to America in the Progressive Era, see Gerald Sorin, *A Time for Building: The Third Migration, 1880–1920*, vol. 3, of *The Jewish People in America*, ed. Henry L. Feingold (Baltimore: Johns Hopkins University Press, 1995), 62–63, and Naomi W. Cohen, *Encounter with Emancipation: The German Jews in the United States, 1830–1914* (Philadelphia: Jewish Publication Society of America, 1984). For the immigration of Jewish women in America, selected works include Paula E. Hyman, *Gender and Assimilation in Modern Jewish History*; Rudolf Glanz, *The Jewish Woman in America: Two Immigrant Generations, 1820–1929*, vols. 1 and 2 (n.p. 1976); Hasia R. Diner, *A Time for Gathering: The Second Migration, 1820–1880*, vol. 2, of *The Jewish People in America*, ed. Henry L. Feingold (Baltimore: Johns Hopkins University Press, 1995); Barbara A. Schrier, *Becoming American Women: Clothing and the Jewish Immigrant Experience, 1880–1920* (Chicago: Chicago Historical Society, 1994); Andrew R. Heinze, *Adapting to Abundance: Jewish Immigrants, Mass Consumption, and the Search for American Identity* (New York: Columbia University Press, 1990); Elizabeth Ewen, *Immigrant Women in the Land of Dollars: Life and Culture on the Lower East Side, 1890–1925* (New York: Monthly Review Press, 1985).

11. Linda J. Borish, "Jewish American Women, Jewish Organizations, and Sports, 1880–1940," *Sports and the American Jew*, ed. Steven A. Riess (Syracuse: Syracuse University Press, 1998).

12. On social reformers' perceptions of immigrant youth's need for healthful play and sport as an alternative to the temptations and evils of urban, consumer culture, see Jane Addams, *Twenty Years at Hull House* (1910; repr., New York, 1960) and *Spirit of Youth and the City Street* (New York: Macmillan, 1923); Lillian D. Wald, *The House on Henry Street* (1915; repr., New York: Henry Holt and Co., 1971). Selected historical works on reformers, immigrants, and proper leisure and sport include Kathy Peiss, *Cheap Amusements: Working Women and Leisure in Turn-of-the-Century New York* (Philadelphia: Temple University Press, 1986); Gerald R. Gems, *Windy City Wars: Labor, Leisure, and Sport in the Making of Chicago* (Lanham, Md.: Scarecrow Press, 1997); Gems, "Working Class Women and Sport:

An Untold Story," *Women in Sport and Physical Activity Journal*, 2 (Spring 1993): 17–30; Nancy B. Sinkof, "Education for 'Proper Jewish Womanhood': A Case Study in Domesticity and Vocational Training, 1897–1926," *American Jewish History*, 77 (June 1988): 572–99; Ewen, *Immigrant Women in the Land of Dollars*; Steven A. Riess, *City Games: The Evolution of American Urban Society and the Rise of Sports* (Urbana: University of Illinois Press, 1989); David Nasaw, *Children of the City: At Work and at Play* (New York: Oxford University Press, 1985).

13. Hilda Satt Polacheck, *I Came a Stranger: The Story of a Hull-House Girl*, ed. Dena J. Polacheck Epstein (Urbana: University of Illinois Press, 1989), 76–77; Borish, "Jewish American Women," 115.

14. Chicago, Illinois, Sinai Congregation Manuscript Collection, Series B, Minute Books of the Board of Directors, Box 11, Folder 1, December 29, 1913; Chicago, Illinois Sinai Congregation Manuscript Collection, Folder 3, Report of Executive Director of Sinai Social Center, April 22, 1923, by S. D. Schwartz, AJA; Fifty-Third Annual Meeting of Members of Chicago Sinai Congregation, April 15, 1914, AJA; *Chicago Sinai Congregation: A Pictorial History, 125th Anniversary, 1861–1986* (Chicago: Chicago Sinai Congregation, 1986), 8–9; "A 'Medal-Some' Mermaid," *Chicago Daily Tribune*, December 19, 1920.

15. Bernheimer, "Jewish Americanization Agencies," 90–91; Linda J. Borish, "The Chicago Hebrew Institute," in *Encyclopedia of Chicago History*, ed. James Grossman and Ann Durkin Keating (Chicago: University of Chicago Press, 2004); Hyman L. Meites, *History of the Jews of Chicago* (Chicago: Jewish Historical Society of Illinois, 1927); Philip L. Seman, "Democracy in Action," *Chicago Jewish Forum* (1943): 49–54, Philip L. Seman Collection, Scrapbooks, AJA; Irving Cutler, *The Jews of Chicago From Shtetl to Suburb* (Urbana: University of Illinois Press, 1996); Gerald R. Gems, "Sport and the Forging of a Jewish-American Culture: The Chicago Hebrew Institute," *American Jewish History*, 83 (March 1995): 15–26; Jewish Community Center of Chicago Papers, Archives and Manuscripts Department, Chicago Historical Society, Chicago; Samuel L. Levine, "The Jewish Community Center Movement," *The Sentinel's History of Chicago Jewry, 1911–1961* (Chicago: Sentinel Publishing Co., n.d.), 184–86.

16. "'Good, Clean Sport,' Motto of CHI," Philip L. Seman Collection, Scrapbook, vol. 1, 1910–16; Bertha Loeb, "The Temple of the Body: How the Hebrew Institute Is Laboring to Make Jews Physically Fit," *The Sentinel*, May 1, 1914, Jacob M. Loeb Collection, CHI, AJA.

17. Philip L. Seman, "Report of the Superintendent," *CHI Observer*, 1913–14, pp. 10–11, Philip L. Seman Collection, Scrapbook, vol. 1, AJA.

18. "Exhibition at Hebrew Institute Reveals Athletic Prowess," Philip L. Seman Collection, Scrapbook, vol. 1, 1910–16, CHI, AJA.

19. Jacob M. Loeb to Mr. and Mrs. Julius Rosenwald, October 28, 1913, Jacob M. Loeb Collection, CHI, AJA. For information on this case and the petition to Julius Rosenwald to secure more funding for the CHI gymnasium, see Linda J. Borish, "'Athletic Activities of Various Kinds': Physical Health and Sport Programs for Jewish American Women," *Journal of Sport History*, 26 (Summer 1999): 240–70.

20. Jacob M. Loeb, Address, March 31, 1914, Chicago Hebrew Institute; "Break Ground for New Gymnasium at Hebrew Institute," *Chicago Israelite*, August 15, 1914, Jacob M. Loeb Collection, CHI, AJA; see also Borish, "'Athletic Activities of Various Kinds," for the June 1915 dedication of the CHI gymnasium and speeches by CHI officials.

21. Philip L. Seman, *Chicago Hebrew Institute, Superintendent's Report, 1915–1916*, Chicago Jewish Archives/Spertus Institute of Jewish Studies, Chicago; "Hebrew Institute Dedication Is the Result of Hard Work and Optimism," ca. June 1915, Jacob M. Loeb Collection, CHI, AJA.

22. Chicago Hebrew Institute "News Letter No. 11," on Physical Culture Activities, Jacob M. Loeb Collection, CHI, AJA; Seman, *Chicago Hebrew Institute, Superintendent's Report, 1915–1916*; Philip L. Seman, *Chicago Hebrew Institute, Superintendent's Report, 1917–1918*, 34, Jewish Archives/Spertus Institute of Jewish Studies, Chicago.

23. Seman, *Chicago Hebrew Institute, Superintendent's Report, 1917–1918*, 45; *CHI General Director's Report*, 1921, 56–57, *JPI General Director's Report*, 1922, 80; newspaper clippings, "Girl Cagers Look Impressive in Victory; Team is Host to Large Crowd at Dance," *Observer*, December 13, 1934, Philip L. Seman Collection, Scrapbook, AJA. The JPI Senior women also excelled at volleyball; in 1931, 1932, 1933, the women won the Amateur Athletic Federation Volleyball Championship.

24. Seman, *Chicago Hebrew Institute, Superintendent's Report, 1917–1918*, 45.

25. *CHI General Director's Report*, 1921, 58–59; *JPI General Director's Report*, 1922, 90–91, Philip L. Seman Collection, Scrapbook, AJA.

26. *CHI General Director's Report*, 1921, 58–59; *JPI General Director's Report*, 1922, 85; JPI, *The Community and Its Leisure, Report of the General Director, 1923*, 74, 75–76, Philip L. Seman Collection, Scrapbook, AJA; the *Chicago Daily News* purchased the prizes for the Chicago–Paris Olympic Women's Athletic Meet.

27. JPI, *The Community and Its Leisure, Report of the General Director, 1923*, 74, Philip L. Seman Collection, Scrapbook, AJA. Some YWHAs sponsored baseball games; see Linda J. Borish, "'An Interest in Physical Well-Being among the Feminine Membership': Sporting Activities for Women at Young Men's and Young Women's Hebrew Associations," *American Jewish History*, 87 (March 1999): 61–93.

28. Jewish Welfare Board report, ca. 1922–23 quoted in JPI, *The Community and Its Leisure, Report of the General Director, 1923*, 6–7, Philip L. Seman Collection, Scrapbook, AJA. For information on the Jewish Welfare Board and physical activities at Jewish institutions, see Linda J. Borish, "National Jewish Welfare Board Archives, Young Men's and Young Women's Hebrew Associations Records: A Research Guide," Archives and Manuscript Collections, American Jewish Historical Society, Waltham, Mass. (November 1996): 1–16.

29. Borish, "Jewish American Women," 127–28; "Mrs. Jackson Wins Golf Championship," *New York Times*, September 20, 1914; "Chicago Girl Plays Fine Golf and Wins," *New York Times*, September 19, 1914; "Miss Elaine V. Rosenthal," *American Hebrew*, 95:23 (October 2, 1914): 653; "Jews in Sport," *American Hebrew*, 96:14 (January 29, 1915): 347; Linda J. Borish, "Women, Sports, and American Jewish Identity in the Late Nineteenth and Early Twentieth Centuries," in *With God on Their Side: Sport in the Service of Religion*, ed. Tara Magdalinksi and Timothy J. L. Chandler (London: Routledge Press, 2002); Bernard Postal, Jesse Silver, and Roy Silver, *Encyclopedia of Jews in Sports* (New York: Block Publishing Co., 1965), 294–95; *Fifty Years of Ravisloe, 1901–1951* (Homewood, Ill.: Ravisloe Country Club, 1951), courtesy of Ravisloe Country Club. Also see Paul R. Leach, "See Miss Rosenthal Lead Golfing Field," *Chicago Daily News*, August 23, 1915;

Leach, "Favorites Win Out in Women's Tourney," *Chicago Daily News*, August 24, 1915; Leach, "How Golfers Pair in Semifinal Play," *Chicago Daily News*, August 26, 1915.

30. "Thrice Western Women's Golf Champion," *American Hebrew*, 117 (November 6, 1925): 828; "Miss Rosenthal in Form," *New York Times*, February 15, 1917; "Miss Rosenthal Gets Cup, Chicago Golfer Retains Florida Title by Beating Mrs. Bragg," *New York Times*, February 18, 1917; "Miss Rosenthal Is Victor," *New York Times*, March 27, 1917; "Miss Rosenthal Wins Golf Trophy," *New York Times*, March 30, 1917; "Highlights on Links and Polo Fields," *American Hebrew*, 123 (June 1, 1928): 104, 106; Borish, "Women, Sports, and American Jewish Identity," 84; Nevin H. Gibson, *The Encyclopedia of Golf* (New York: A. S. Barnes and Co., 1958), 42, 70, 156.

31. Biography, Jennie Franklin Purvin Collection, Box 2278, AJA; Karla Goldman, "Purvin, Jennie Franklin," *Jewish Women in America*, vol. 2, 1114; "Purvin, Jennie Franklin," *Who's Who in American Jewry*, vol. 3, 1938–39, 828.

32. Diaries, Jennie Franklin Purvin, July 12, 1890, July 15, 1890, August 2, 1890, Jennie Franklin Purvin Collection, AJA.

33. "Reports of Civic Committees," *Woman's City Club Bulletin*, ca. 1917, 3; Letter, December 12, 1912, from Chicago Woman's Aid Society on Public Comfort Stations, Jennie Purvin Franklin Collections, Box 2278, AJA.

34. Jennie Franklin Purvin, "The Troubled Waters of Lake Michigan," *The Sentinel*, ca. 1923, and Purvin, "When Is a Bathing Beach Not a Bathing Beach?" *The Sentinel*, n.d., Jennie Franklin Purvin Collection, Box 2278, AJA.

35. Jennie Franklin Purvin, "Committee on Bathing Beaches," *Woman's City Bulletin*, 1919; Correspondence, Mrs. M. L. Purvin, March 5, 1920; Correspondence, Rev. M. G. Dickinson, January 17, 1920; Correspondence, Mrs. Moses L. Purvin, March 27, 1920, Jennie Franklin Purvin Collection, Box 2278, AJA.

36. Mrs. M. L. Purvin, "Bathing Beach Committee," *Woman's City Club Bulletin*, September 1922, Jennie Franklin Purvin Collection, Box 2278, AJA.

37. Fred A. Marquardt, "New CHI Gym a Joy to All the Athletes," *Chicago Daily News*, July 9, 1915.

38. Foust, "Mother, May I Go Out to Swim?" and "Imported from Europe—A Swimming Instructor."

5

Baseball Palace of the World

Commercial Recreation and the Building of Comiskey Park

ROBIN F. BACHIN

On a blustery March day in 1910, architect Zachary Taylor Davis laid a solitary green brick on the lot at Thirty-fifth and Wentworth Streets as the cornerstone of what became the new Comiskey Park. Named for Chicago American League baseball club owner Charles Comiskey, the ballpark attracted a large crowd because the ceremony took place on Saint Patrick's Day in Bridgeport, one of the largest Irish communities in Chicago. No subtlety was wasted in the symbolism of the day's ceremonies: the green brick reflected Comiskey's crystal-clear desire to reach out to Irish fellow community residents. Lest anyone miss the connection between ethnic culture and the new ballpark, Comiskey had White Sox catcher Billy Sullivan travel to Ireland to bring back a piece of the "auld sod." On this genuine Irish sod Davis laid his cornerstone. Newspaper reporters, local politicians, and area residents celebrated the glory of the day with tributes to Comiskey, the White Sox, and their new neighborhood ballpark, which many, both in and outside Chicago, came to call the "Baseball Palace of the World."[1]

Yet Comiskey Park was more than just a parochial symbol of urban ethnic working-class culture. It was also an icon of the emerging City beautiful movement, which sought to unite the street grid of the modern city with green spaces and monumental architecture to create large-scale efforts of urban planning. Like the grandiose museums, parks, and boulevards gracing the pages of Daniel Burnham's *Plan of Chicago*, the new ballpark was a site that became a source of civic pride and sociability. Charles Comiskey and other mass-culture entrepreneurs infused their facilities with an aura of respectability in order to justify their business enterprises and establish themselves as legitimate civic leaders. The classically designed physical space of the ballpark pronounced it a place where codes of decorum were observed even as different classes and ethnicities, men and women, mixed with one another. By creating a monumental recreational structure in Chicago, Comiskey could transcend the confines of the immediate neighborhood and make his ballpark an emblem of the emerging links between commercial culture, civic pride, respectability, and Americanism.[2]

At the same time, the rise of commercial mass culture encouraged solidarity among working-class immigrants. Rather than obliterating local, ethnic culture, commercial amusements often grew directly out of that culture. The dance halls, vaudeville theaters, and sporting parks often were sponsored by local businesspeople and drew their support from the localized world of the saloon, the athletic club, and the fraternal lodge. Workers carved out alternative spaces beyond the surveillance of employers and urban reformers, with few restrictions on accessibility (except for race), thereby challenging prevailing notions of appropriate public conduct and social order. By using sites of mass culture as spaces of working-class sociability, new immigrants and their children forged alliances with one another that helped overcome ethnic barriers.[3]

African Americans did not experience this commercial culture in the same way whites did. Often, blacks were excluded from the amusement parks, vaudeville shows, and theaters that welcomed working-class ethnic whites and restructured mass culture, much as they were excluded from public parks. When African Americans were not barred outright, they were segregated into the balconies, with the rowdy crowds that gave those spaces their taint of ill repute. In addition, blacks often were the subject of the show. Vaudeville shows and amusement parks mocked black culture, reinforcing negative black stereotypes in the performative space of the minstrel show and the comedy act. As a result, African Americans created their own spaces of commercial amusement, where popular culture could exist comfortably with respectability as the Black Belt grew into one of the most dynamic cultural districts in Chicago.[4]

Mass Culture and the Spatialization of Vice

In many ways, the rise of mass amusements represented a sharp contrast between the commercial values of entrepreneurs like Comiskey, seeking to attract large audiences, and the civic elite (like park proponents Fredrick Law Olmsted and Henry Foreman), who wished to impose urban social order. Dance halls drew city youth eager to escape the watchful eyes of their Old World parents, as well as the instruction of middle-class and elite reformers. Similarly, working-class women often forged what some considered unsavory alliances with men who took them to the new amusement parks, modeled on Luna Park at Coney Island, which allowed men and women to mingle freely on rides that encouraged intimate contact. Yet the emerging importance of mass amusement to the public culture of the city illustrates how commercial considerations and respectability came together, as entrepreneurs integrated their facilities into the larger legitimate culture of the city.

Part of this legitimation involved spatial distinction. Promoters of commercial culture followed the lead of planners like Daniel Burnham by clearly differentiating the amusement park from the surrounding culture of the city. Indeed, White City Amusement Park, at Sixty-third Street and South Parkway, replicated the Beaux-Arts style of Burnham's 1893 exposition buildings, from which the amusement park took its name. The owners of White City copied the grandiose entrances and ornamented, brightly lit interiors of Coney Island parks to usher customers into an ethereal, dreamlike space. While the experience of leisure was relatively unstructured once patrons paid their admission fee, the park nonetheless offered a safe zone of adventure marked off from the teeming city beyond. Amusement parks posted regulations for behavior and offered a level of respectability that the city streets seldom provided.

Despite the efforts of amusement park promoters to link commercialism with the culture of respectability, many urban reformers still disapproved of these carnivalesque spaces. Many reformers equated commercial leisure with corruption and vice and saw mass culture entrepreneurs as confidence men who profited from the promotion of "unwholesome" amusements, often targeted specifically to children.[5] The creation of public parks and playgrounds grew out of efforts both to regulate places of mass amusement and to encourage the municipality to develop alternative leisure spaces. These alternative recreation opportunities, reformers hoped, would counter the lure of vice districts and places of ill repute that tempted the young in Chicago, and urban Americans in general.

Reformers also recognized that working conditions could lead to immorality and vice, particularly for women, as they were exploited in the factory and department store. Retail sales clerks were especially vulnerable, according to one survey, because they were surrounded by the luxuries they craved but were not paid enough to enjoy them. A 1911 Chicago Women's Trade Union League study showed that between 25 and 30 percent of women employed in department stores did not earn enough "to enable them to procure the necessities of life." A Chicago Vice Commission report pointed to the lure of prostitution for women who could not earn sufficient money elsewhere: "A former salesgirl in a department store was seen in a fashionable all-night restaurant. She said that four weeks previous she had been earning $8.00 per week. She enumerated different articles of clothing which she was wearing, and gave the prices of each, including her hat. The total came to over $200.00. Her eyes had been opened to her earning capacity in the 'sporting' life by a man who laughed at her for wasting her good looks and physical charms behind a counter for a boss who was growing rich from her services, and the services of others like her."[6]

Caroline Meeber, Theodore Dreiser's protagonist in *Sister Carrie,* attests to the lure of fashion amid the bustling downtown department store. "Fine clothes to her were a vast persuasion," writes Dreiser. "When she came within earshot of their pleading, desire in her bent a willing ear." Carrie relied on her associations with wealthy men to supply the finery that so enticed her.[7]

In addition, according to many female reformers, the desire to participate in the culture of mass amusement often enticed women into alliances with unsavory men. A Juvenile Protective Association study claimed that amusement parks often posed the most dangerous risks. "In the first place the gates of every park are surrounded by saloons and many of the men are half intoxicated before they enter the park itself. Almost all of the absurd 'amusements' offered require a separate entrance and fee and young girls stand about unconsciously offering their chastity in order to be invited to see 'the fat folks' convention,' the 'Kansas cyclone,' or the 'human roulette wheel,' for the man who treats them too often demands a return later in the evening."[8] The lure of commercial amusement, combined with the inadequate wages paid to female workers, together threatened the safety and purity of women in the city, many reformers maintained.[9]

Reformers like Jane Addams sought to use municipal government and labor legislation to counter the influences of both workplace exploitation and the temptations of prostitution. Addams also stressed the need for alternative sites of leisure for children and for working-class men and women. Reiterating her belief in the ability of certain public spaces to promote civic discourse and social engagement, Addams showed how outdoor recreation areas, including parks and playgrounds and also athletic fields, could offer working people recreation and release from the "grind of life." "Well considered public games, easily carried out in a park or athletic field," she explained, "might both fill the mind with imaginative material constantly supplied by the theater, and also afford the activity which the cramped muscles of the town dweller so sorely need." For Addams, the spectacle of neighborhood boys and men eagerly entering the neighborhood baseball field illustrated how public life could be enhanced through play and recreation. "Does not this contain a suggestion of the undoubted power of public recreation to bring together all classes of the community in the modern city unhappily so full of devices for keeping them apart?"[10] Athletics offered an alternative to saloons, amusement parks, and dance halls, and a valuable setting for shaping democratic culture and American identity.

Baseball and Team Spirit

Organized recreation was part of a growing movement among urban residents at the turn of the century to recognize the benefits of strenuous activity. Civic leaders also demonstrated that recreation was important to promoting citizenship in the modern industrial city. Proponents of play, such as the leaders of the Playground Association, stressed the benefits of athletics not only in providing wholesome leisure to the city's youth, but also in thwarting the increased inactivity of the growing white-collar population. National leaders, including President Theodore Roosevelt, worried about the effect that office culture had on the physical strength of the nation's workers. As a result, athletics came to be seen as a national imperative, to counter the sedentary character of the American corporate workplace.[11] As historian Daniel T. Rodgers points out, "The cult of strenuosity and the recreation movement grew together, minimizing the distinction between usefulness and sport, toil and recreation, the work ethic and the spirit of play."[12]

The future of America, according to many proponents of athletics, was linked to citizens' physical prowess, manliness, and loyalty. Roosevelt articulated the integral relation between capitalist culture, American nationalism, and organized athletics: "In a perfectly peaceful and commercial civilization such as ours there is always a danger of laying too little stress upon the more virile virtues—upon the virtues which go to make up a race of statesmen and soldiers. . . . These are the very qualities which are fostered by vigorous, manly out-of-doors sports."[13] Athletics promoted patriotism most effectively, according to Roosevelt and other supporters, when part of the larger realm of team play. Team play became, in William James's words, "the moral equivalent of war."[14]

Like many advocates of athletics at the University of Chicago, Jane Addams and other play proponents emphasized the connections between the values inculcated by sports and those that increased productivity in the workplace. Addams linked team play to the modern industrial work process: "It takes thirty-nine people to make a coat in a modern tailoring establishment, yet those same thirty-nine people might produce a coat in a spirit of 'team-work' which would make the entire process as much more exhilarating than the work of the old solitary tailor, as playing in a baseball nine gives more pleasure to a boy than that afforded by a solitary game of handball."[15] The collective experience, according to Addams, was the aspect of athletics that could be most usefully translated to the labor process.

While much of the rhetoric of the play movement related play to industrial capitalism and rising bureaucratic social order, proponents were not merely trying to create efficient industrial workers. Rather, they sought a middle ground between what they perceived as the dangers of the working-class ethnic culture of saloons and the greed and corruption of unregulated capitalism. They tried to strike a balance between advocating individual discipline and skill and encouraging group identification and teamwork. Moreover, for reformers like Addams, the team spirit was the basis for workplace organizing and workers' collective action. The spirit of play also reflected beliefs shared by John Dewey and other educational theorists about the best ways to promote learning, shape experiential knowledge, and foster civic engagement.[16]

The most effective game for instilling team spirit, according to play promoters and reformers, was baseball. Many advocates of organized sport objected to the violence often associated with football. Much of this emphasis on baseball resulted from the collegiate football scandals in 1905, in which the increasing brutality of the game led many educators to reassess its place in collegiate sport. University of Chicago professor Shailer Matthews noted, "From the President of the United States to the humblest members of the school and college faculty there arises a general protest against this boy-killing, man-mutilating, education-prostituting, gladiatorial sport."[17] Instead, sports advocates looked to baseball to promote discipline, order, and self-sacrifice as a means of inculcating nationalism and loyalty. According to sports writer High Fullerton, "Baseball, to my way of thinking is the greatest single force working for Americanization. No other game appeals so much to the foreign-born youngsters and nothing, not even the schools, teaches the

American spirit so quickly, or inculcates the idea of sportsmanship or fair play as thoroughly."[18]

Baseball writers and reformers pointed out that individual skill and success were useful only when used to promote the advancement of the team. Henry Curtis of the Playground Association of America articulated this vision in his discussion of the role of each player in a baseball game: "A long hit or daring run may not be what is needed. The judgment of his play is a social judgment. It is estimated not on the basis of its individual excellence, but by its effect on the success of the team. The boy must come out and practice when he wants to go fishing. He must bat out in order that the man on third may run in. Many a time he must sacrifice himself to the team. This type of loyalty is the same thing we call good citizenship as applied to the city, that we call patriotism as applied to the country. The team game is undoubtedly the best training for these civic virtues."[19] Curtis argued that in baseball the peer group became an instrument of Americanization, as ethnic barriers were overcome in organized team play. Civic culture could be fostered and revitalized by instilling in youth the virtues of cooperation and loyalty as traits to be carried into all phases of public life.

The question of whether football or baseball was the most effective vehicle for promoting civic ideals exposed some of the differences in progressive reformers' ideas about civic culture in Chicago. Promoters of football, like University of Chicago president William Rainey Harper, Amos Alonzo Stagg, and Roosevelt, stressed that sport's function in promoting leadership. In many ways the emphasis on football reflected the belief that the best trained, most highly skilled members of the middle class should be leaders in the workplace and in the nation. Indeed, the opportunity to play football was available, for the most part, only to men who had the means to attend college. By contrast, baseball was available to all urban residents through the newly established athletic fields in public parks. Rather than emphasizing leadership and expertise, proponents of baseball stressed team spirit and self-sacrifice as the basis for organized athletics. Equal opportunity to participate, rather than fostering individual prowess, became their motivation for promoting baseball. Similarly, many critics of football agreed with Shailer Matthews's claim that commercialism was corrupting the college game. Amateur baseball, played in the sandlots and ballfields of municipal parks and playgrounds, was free of this money-making taint.

The Political Economy
of Major League Baseball in Chicago

While promoters of baseball stressed that amateur, participatory sports enhanced American culture, they were less clear about the place of professional spectator sports. University of Chicago president William Rainey Harper's praise of athletics linked its moral benefits to its amateur status. Henry Curtis emphasized how team interaction established the values of citizenship that recreation supervisors hoped children would learn. Reformers were more ambivalent about professional sports. Some worried about the potentially illicit connections between owners of professional ball clubs and the world of vice associated with saloons, dance halls, and gambling dens. Others questioned how the links between commerce and recreation would affect players' motivation for engaging in team play. They worried that the values of cooperation and discipline would be corrupted when athletes played for money.

The rise of professional baseball had its roots in the organized clubs of nineteenth-century cities. These clubs sometimes grew out of earlier fraternal organizations and the urban culture of the saloon. Roy Rosenzweig's classic study of the saloon, *Eight Hours for What We Will*, highlighted the increasingly important role spaces of leisure served in promoting community interaction and fostering class solidarity in industrializing cities. With workers exercising less control over the production process, they often looked to leisure sites as the sources of personal and communal identity. By the late nineteenth century, the rituals associated with leisure played a central role in defining and shaping notions of class, community, and masculinity.

Sports as a means for promoting camaraderie grew out of the ethnic athletic clubs many groups started on entering American cities. German turners, Czech sokols, and Scottish Caledonian clubs all offered alternative spaces for gathering and social activities that helped maintain links to ethnic culture. Baseball clubs followed similar patterns, though they most often comprised skilled craftsmen, like carpenters and shipbuilders, clerks, and shopkeepers. In forming organized baseball clubs, they were part of a redefinition of masculinity and male urban culture. Rather than participating in the rough male sports of prizefighting and cockfights, which flouted Victorian prescriptions for gentility, baseball club members created new terms for defining masculinity that reflected the competitive commercial marketplace. These clubs emphasized that baseball helped establish competitiveness, control, and discipline as features of manly virtue.[20] Baseball also allowed men to reclaim part of the world of sports culture as their own at a time when prescriptions for women's participation in certain forms of athletics were blurring the gendered distinction between male and female leisure and recreation.[21]

As spectatorship grew at games between ball clubs organized by neighborhood, workplace, and church, local businesspeople became active financial supporters of the clubs. Factory owners might provide uniforms, tavern owners could pay for equipment, or booster groups would arrange schedules and charge admission. Before long, ball club sponsors began paying players for their services, as the drive to win games led club managers to look beyond the neighborhood, athletic club, or shop floor for the best talent. These practices removed the game from its local social function and placed it in the world of commerce and work culture that many club members initially sought to counter. Baseball thus moved from a world of loosely organized athletic clubs to become a nationally structured professional sport with standardized rules and prescriptions for work discipline. Competitiveness in sports spurred this link to the marketplace. Baseball became a professional enterprise, firmly entrenched in the urban economy. The game established its place in American culture by demonstrating that the character of professional play was congruent with the work ethic of industrial and corporate America.[22]

Yet baseball was not merely an accommodation to industrial work culture and commerce. Just at the time baseball was becoming more clearly linked with the world of the marketplace and urban commercial culture, and as its popularity was rising, some promoters and former amateur players called for a return to the precommercial era, when money was not associated with the game. In issuing this call, they helped create the myth of baseball's pastoral origins. This harking back to a "golden age," when baseball was uncorrupted by commerce, demonstrated their ambivalence toward associating baseball with the marketplace and the city. Indeed, the baseball field, like parks and playgrounds, became a haven within the expanding built-up environment. By juxtaposing rural and urban, preindustrial and modern, professional baseball became a symbol for the complexities of twentieth-century American culture.[23]

This evocation of the rural elements of baseball also contributed to campaigns to recognize it as America's national pastime, directly linking baseball to nationalism. In 1907, Albert G. Spalding, sporting goods magnate and owner of the National League Chicago White Stockings, argued that baseball was undoubtedly a symbol of a distinctive American culture and called for a formal investigation into the national origins of the game: "To enter upon a deliberate argument to prove that Base Ball is our national game; that it has all the attributes of American origin, American character and unbounded public favor in America, seems a work of supererogation. It is to undertake the elucidation of a patent fact;

the sober demonstration of an axiom; it is like a solemn declaration that two plus two equals four."[24]

Spalding appointed a committee headed by National League President Abraham G. Mills to conduct the study. Several baseball players and writers pointed to the British games of cricket and rounders as clear sources for baseball's origins. Yet the commission's findings argued that future Civil War General Abner Doubleday "drew the first known diagram of the diamond, indicating positions for the players . . . in Cooperstown, New York in 1839."[25] Thus Spalding and his committee linked baseball, American identity, and agrarian culture in a way that denied the centrality of urban culture and the marketplace in the origins and growth of the game.

Spalding, however, had done more to promote the commercial and professional character of baseball than almost any other sponsor of the game. Cincinnati organized the first professional baseball team in 1869, but Spalding launched baseball as a major commercial venture. He became pitcher for the Boston Red Stockings the same year the first professional baseball association was formed. In 1871, ten teams met in New York City to form the National Association of Professional Base Ball Players (NAPBBP). During the meeting, players drew up a constitution that set out provisions for players' contracts, admission prices to league games, and ten-dollar fees to establish a franchise. Spalding used this constitution as the basis for his own commercial venture in Chicago just a few years later, establishing baseball as the recreational equivalent of the corporation and the factory. He became a "captain of industry," forging monopolistic control over the game of baseball and promoting skill, efficiency, and productivity.[26] Moreover, he used this promotion of professionalism and expertise to create one of the leading sporting goods businesses in the nation. The ideals of skill, training, and efficiency could be used in the service of advertising and sales, further linking commerce and baseball.[27]

In 1876, Spalding joined with Chicago coal merchant William S. Hulbert to create a new professional league in baseball, the National League of Professional Baseball Clubs (NLPBC). One of the central features of the league's constitution was the codification and regulation of play. Following the model put forth by the NAPBBP, Spalding diagrammed the proper measurements of the professional baseball field, along with the position of each player on the field. The strict control of space was matched by specialization among players. Players were assigned specific positions and had clearly mapped-out roles within the ballfield.[28] This division of labor, along with the regulation of space, mirrored changes in the modern workplace, where employers looked to gain greater control over production. At the same time, though, the lack of control of time within the ballpark offered an antidote to the factory bell, the pervasive symbol of work discipline in the urban capitalist economy.[29]

Professional baseball's similarities to the modern workplace extended to the control of the work process by management. The league constitution tightened management's control of players, and one of the rules involved binding players more tightly to their current teams. The National League instituted the "reserve clause" in 1882, whereby a club reserved the right to its players' services indefinitely. Players could be blacklisted if they tried to break their club contracts; owners could be expelled for signing another team's players. Spalding and other promoters of baseball argued that these restrictions were necessary to demonstrate baseball's allegiance to professionalism and expertise. Player contracts, paid referees, and uniform ticket prices all contributed to legitimizing baseball as a reputable and well-managed enterprise. These changes also enabled Spalding and other owners to codify rules so that leisure activity could be transformed into commerce and labor.[30]

Organized baseball's respectable status also derived from the understanding among all team owners and promoters that the game would be kept white. As early as 1867, when the National Association for Base Ball Players (NABBP) became the first association to codify playing rules and regulations, African Americans were barred from organized baseball. According to a statement from the Nominating Committee of the NABBP: "It is not presumed by your Committee that any club[s] who have applied are composed of persons of color, or any portion of them; and the recommendations of your Committee in this report are based upon this view, and they unanimously report against the admission of any club which may be composed of one or more colored persons."[31]

Once professionalism overtook the game, the NABBP was supplanted by the NAPBBP, but the color bar remained intact. The new professional league had no formal policy statement restricting African American players because it did not need one. Instead, member clubs maintained a "gentlemen's agreement" that no club would sign black players, a ban carried over into the National League.[32]

But the gentlemen's agreement did not prevent African Americans from playing professional baseball. Many black baseball players enjoyed successful careers in semiprofessional baseball, in the various black clubs that barnstormed throughout the nation even before the organization of the Negro National League in 1920. Some also "disguised" themselves as Cubans or Native Americans and played in the major leagues. Numerous contemporary accounts of black baseball teams praised their skill, grace, and respectability. The *Brooklyn Daily Union* commented on the character of two clubs, the Philadelphia Excelsiors and the Brooklyn

Uniques: "These organizations are composed of very respectable colored people, well-to-do in the world . . . and include many first-class players. The visitors will receive all due attention from the colored brethren of Brooklyn; and we trust, for the good of fraternity, that none of the 'white trash' who disgrace white clubs, by following and bawling for them, will be allowed to mar the pleasure of these colored gatherings."[33]

This passage illustrates both the important place of baseball in the black community and the pervasive connections made between baseball and illicit behavior. For members of the African American community, including elite professionals and businesspeople, as well as the more recent southern migrants who would enter northern cities in huge numbers after World War I, baseball served as a bridge. It could unite the "old settlers" and the new when tensions over class and respectability in other arenas were growing. At the same time, though, white promoters' desire to professionalize baseball reflected their conflation of respectability with whiteness. The black and white professional leagues thus grew up side by side, but rarely intersected.[34]

White club owners also linked professionalism with respectability. Professional baseball still had detractors who complained of its connections to gambling, rowdyism, and saloon culture. Promoters believed they had to overcome this image if baseball was to be a lucrative endeavor. Henry Chadwick, a baseball editor, linked skill, training, and expertise to the professional status of the game. He explained the difference between amateur players and professionals: "[A] professional expert not only requires attentive study to the rules of the game, . . . together with perfect familiarity with each and every rule; but also a regular course of training, to fully develope [sic] the physical powers, in order to ensure the highest degree of skill in each and all of the several departments of the game."[35]

The league constitution spelled out rules for behavior among players, both on and off the field. The National League outlawed Sunday games in many cities, barred the sale of alcohol, charged higher admission fees, and fined players for drinking, swearing, arguing with the umpire, and tardiness.[36] Whereas some reformers linked the value of athletics directly to amateurism, promoters of professional baseball argued that only through professionalization could players develop the skills and expertise needed to ensure baseball's respectability.

Spalding went beyond promoting expertise to ensure baseball's respectability. He made his players pledge abstinence from liquor, set eleven o'clock curfews, and even hired Pinkerton detectives to report on them. By controlling players' behavior, Spalding believed he could make the sport acceptable to bourgeois urban residents. The baseball park could function as a source of well-regulated leisure, fostering civic pride and team loyalty by creating a mythic space of carefree pastoral recreation. Spalding claimed: "The aim of the Chicago management is to secure the highest standard of baseball efficiency obtainable. In fighting the encroachment of drink . . . we are simply striving to give our patrons the full measure of entertainment and satisfaction to which they are entitled. . . . We don't intend to again insult ladies and gentlemen of this city or any other by allowing men who are full of beer and whiskey to go upon the diamond in the uniform of the Chicago club."[37]

The professionalism of the players would attract respectable patrons and make baseball a legitimate form of cultural entertainment. As a result of his legislating morality, Spalding claimed, the crowds at Chicago White Stocking games were "composed of the best of people in Chicago, and no theater, church, or place of amusement contains a finer class of people than can be found in our grandstands."[38] Between 1882 and 1889, attendance at National League games rapidly increased, and between 1885 and 1889 the National League teams earned close to $750,000, with Spalding's team claiming approximately 20 percent of the total.[39]

Spalding was not solely responsible for the overwhelming popularity of the game, of course. While his regulations certainly helped attract a white-collar, middle-class audience, other factors contributed to the growth of the baseball crowd. In the last decades of the nineteenth century, the admission charges for National League games were fifty cents for standard admission, sixty cents for a bleacher seat, and seventy-five cents for a grandstand seat. By contrast, seats at popular theaters and vaudeville shows were between ten and twenty cents. Average income for manufacturing workers in 1890 was $427, which translated to about $1.50 a day. Some baseball players and promoters saw workers as an untapped potential audience, and they created another league to challenge Spalding's.[40]

In 1882 businessmen in six cities launched the American Association (AA) as a challenge to the monopoly of the National League. The AA specifically catered to working-class fans by underselling National League teams and shedding some of the moral constraints Spalding imposed. American Association teams charged an admission fee of twenty-five cents, adopted Sunday baseball, and sold alcohol in the ballpark. Indeed, many of the club owners responsible for creating the AA were saloon keepers, brewers, and liquor manufacturers. Their sponsorship of professional baseball teams showed how "legitimate" and "illegitimate" economies and "rough" and "respectable" cultural norms functioned side by side. Tavern owners joined Spalding in becoming local civic leaders. Moreover, they used baseball as an advertising and sales vehicle for their products, just as Spalding did for sporting goods. Yet the financial strength of the National League ultimately fueled the collapse of the American Association in 1891. The National League then took over many former American Association teams, creating in essence a corporate monopoly over baseball.[41]

In 1900 another challenge to the dominance of Spalding and the National League emerged, this time from a local Chicago competitor. Charles Comiskey and his friend Byron Bancroft "Ban" Johnson discussed the idea of creating an alternative league to challenge the National League. Comiskey and Johnson had become friends during their days with the Western League, one of the minor leagues formed in the 1890s. Johnson, a sportswriter for the *Cincinnati Commercial-Gazette,* became president of the Western League, and Charles Comiskey managed the St. Paul team. The success of the Western League included luring winning teams from major cities and strictly enforcing bans on gambling and rowdiness, striking a delicate balance between excitement and respectability. With fan support and league growth, Johnson and Comiskey changed the name to the American League, giving it a national character. The American League began as a minor league in 1900, and by 1901 it became a second and permanent league.[42]

The story of Charles Comiskey's entry into baseball is a highly romanticized one. It helped establish him as a local hero and contributed to the fans' view that baseball club owners were public-spirited citizens, not just entrepreneurs interested only in making money. According to one of many similar accounts, Comiskey got his baseball start by being drawn uncontrollably to a local sandlot game: "One sunny summer's afternoon in 1876 a gangling, seventeen-year-old from Chicago's teeming West Side was making progress, such as it was, with a horse drawn truckload of bricks destined for immediate use in reconstruction of the City Hall, a major project of the time. As his plodding span drew near Jackson and Laflin Streets, the youth became aware of a ball game in progress between the Hatfields and the McCoys of Chicago's sandlot ranks. The youth, who had some pretensions as a pitcher, drew up his weary steeds and got down from the driver's seat for a more critical survey of the situation."[43]

Comiskey persuaded the "Hatfields'" manager to put him in and save the game for his team. Comiskey left his load of bricks on the street and eagerly entered the game. In the meantime, the workers at the construction site were awaiting their delivery, and it was up to Comiskey's father, "Honest John" Comiskey, alderman for the West Side's Seventh Ward, to take action. He found his son and the load of bricks he had abandoned and was forced to make a quick decision. The story continues: "Honest John made his choice. He took the bricks and drove away. He left his son committed to the game of baseball and thereby set in motion a train of the most interesting events the national pastime has ever recorded."[44]

The story highlights the social geography of the city and illustrates how spaces of leisure played significant roles not just in the daily lives of urban youth, but in their potential careers as well. By his driving past the park on that fateful day, Comiskey's own future and his prominent role in the commercial life of the city were set in motion. That he was delivering bricks to build the new City Hall further links him to the civic life of the city. Yet his alderman father, "Honest John," decided that Comiskey's potential contribution to the city was better served by playing baseball that day than by completing his delivery. John freed his son to pursue baseball as the vehicle through which he would shape Chicago's future.

Comiskey enjoyed a successful career as a player. He joined a semipro team in Elgin, Illinois, in 1875, and by 1878 he was first baseman and outfielder for the Northwestern League's Dubuque, Iowa, team. In 1882, Comiskey signed with the St. Louis Browns of the newly formed American Association, making $125 a month. By 1884, he became manager and led the team to four consecutive American Association pennants. In 1889, Comiskey joined several other players and managers seeking to challenge the rigid wage scale and reserve clause in the National League to create the Players' League.[45]

The Players' League grew out of players' efforts to take back some control over the game of professional baseball. Initially, these efforts resulted in the first union in baseball. In 1885 New York Giants captain John Montgomery Ward initiated the Brotherhood of Professional Base Ball Players to help raise the status of ballplayers as well as their salaries. In arguing for the necessity of the Brotherhood, Ward used the rhetoric of anticommercialism to challenge owners' treatment of players: "There was a time when the National League stood for integrity and fair dealing; today it stands for dollars and cents. . . . Players have been bought, sold, or exchanged as though they were sheep, instead of American citizens. . . . By a combination among themselves, stronger than the strongest trusts, owners were able to enforce the most arbitrary measures, and the player had either to submit or get out of the profession in which he had spent years attaining proficiency."[46]

Ward's use of the language of citizenship and professionalism brilliantly captured the hypocrisy in the owners' rhetoric of Americanism. The union sought to improve wages and increase the respect accorded players by linking them to skilled republican artisans of the preindustrial era. In this way, the organization was similar to the Knights of Labor, with its emphasis on artisan culture and skill. Ward attempted to demonstrate that the players, not the owners, embodied the values of expertise and integrity. In doing so, he tried to force Americans to recognize the crucial links between sporting culture and labor relations in America. He also exposed the ambivalence many Americans continued to feel over commercialism as a defining feature of American sport and recreation.

Members of the Brotherhood organized the Players' League in 1890 to mount a more serious challenge to managers' and owners' control of the labor force. This new league sought not only to raise players' wages but also to weaken the work rules set forth by the National League. The Players' League was defeated after less than two seasons, but not before Comiskey had a chance to bring a team to the South Side of Chicago. Its defeat resulted from Albert Spalding's "war committee," designed to undermine it by offering its financial backers lucrative opportunities to buy into the National League, in much the same way the National League had swallowed up the American Association teams. This defeat effectively lowered salaries and forestalled unionism for decades. The formation of the American League in 1900 only consolidated the power of management and owners against player-workers.[47]

Ironically, Comiskey was one of the owners who fully exploited this power relationship. Comiskey was forced to return to St. Louis after the collapse of the Players' League, but he had established enough of a base of support in Chicago with the Brotherhood team to return in 1900 and form the Chicago White Sox in the new American League. Comiskey also used his political ties to promote his baseball team. He offered free season tickets to local politicians, including aldermen, the city clerk, the chief of police, and the mayor. He also secured favorable licensing fees and had Chicago police deployed for free, to prevent ticket scalping outside the park and gambling inside.[48]

This arrangement points up the connections between the financial interests of the club owners, the promotion of order and respectability in the ballpark, and local political ties. Comiskey courted local politicians and police and exploited his ties to local working-class residents at the same time that he marked the ballpark as a safe and secure leisure space for middle-class patrons. This was a formula for success. Between 1901 and 1911, Comiskey earned over $700,000, proving how lucrative this model of commercial amusement could be.[49] Comiskey pointed to this success as evidence that sport was gaining legitimacy as a respectable enterprise. "Formerly sport was not regarded as a proper calling for young men," he explained. "It is beginning to assume its rightful place in society. To me baseball is as honorable as any other business. It is the most honest pastime in the world."[50] Comiskey's role as owner of the White Sox also showed how thoroughly the ideals of republicanism and player control that animated the Players' League gave way to a "robber baron" style of management that placed professional baseball more firmly in the ranks of corporate America than among either the sporting underworld or the organized play movement.

The Social Geography of the Ballpark

The success of Comiskey's American League White Sox, who won the World Series against their cross-town rivals the Cubs (formerly the White Stockings) in 1906, prompted Comiskey to consider building a modern ballpark for his club. Following the notion that endorsing respectability increased ticket sales, Comiskey set about looking for a site for the park. In planning and building a modern steel and concrete baseball field, Comiskey, like the owners of the other early "baseball palaces," linked the physical control of the game and the crowd to propriety and civic responsibility. By integrating classical design into its structure, Comiskey marked his park as an arena of public gathering and civic pride, much like the field houses in the South Parks and the Civic Center in the Burnham Plan.

When Comiskey founded the White Sox in 1900, he secured a site at Thirty-ninth Street and Wentworth Avenue for the team's ballpark. Part of the agreement reached between the new American League and the rival National League was that the Chicago team could not build a park north of Thirty-fifth Street. Spalding had just built his White Stockings a $30,000 park on the West Side, at Polk and Taylor, in a primarily native-born, white, middle-class neighborhood across the street from Cook County Hospital and just seven minutes from the Loop on the elevated line. By restricting Comiskey to a park south of Thirty-fifth, the National League hoped the American League team would not lure fans away from its franchise. Indeed, the creation of an American League team on the South Side only increased the number of fans and earnings from gate receipts in Chicago.[51]

The South Side Park at Thirty-ninth and Wentworth had been the home of the Chicago Cricket Club. The Chicago ball club of the small Union Association first used the field as a baseball park in 1884. The Union Association lasted less than a year, and it was not until 1900, when the White Sox moved there, that the field again was used for baseball. Comiskey and Ban Johnson got a loan, reportedly with "only their good names" as collateral, and hired workers to construct a grandstand in time for opening day in 1900. Comiskey's political connections evidently helped him meet this goal, for the construction workers, members of the

12. *Comiskey Park, 1915.* Opening Day on the South Side, which included a Prosperity Day Parade. (Courtesy of the Chicago History Museum.)

powerful Building Trades Union, waived labor rules, working overtime and on Sundays in order to have the seats in place by April 21.[52]

The new grandstand held fifteen thousand spectators, and Comiskey had no trouble filling the seats. The grandstand was wooden, with box seats placed in the front of the stands. The park had no bleachers. Players sat on the bench in front of the stands, with little separation between players and fans. On days when the ballpark was crowded (particularly on Sundays) and spectators exceeded the capacity of the grandstands, fans stood in a roped-off area of the outfield, thereby reducing outfield distances and the space available for play. This hardly was a problem for the White Sox, since their park had one of the largest outfields of any major league team. In 1906, when the White Sox won the World Series, they held opponents to an average of 2.28 runs per game.[53]

The proximity of the fans to the players and umpires, though, threatened the safety Comiskey desired. In numerous turn-of-the-century wooden parks, fans tried to attack umpires after unpopular calls and to fight with players on opposing teams. The leagues issued fines for players' fighting and ejected unruly fans, but their success was limited by the unregulated space of the ballpark. Tommy Leach, a Red Sox player, described the mayhem of a World Series game against the Pirates in 1903: "The fans were *part* of the game in those days. They'd pour right out into the field and argue with the players and umpires. Was hard to keep the game going sometimes, to say the least."[54]

The ever-present threat of fire added to the club owners' worries. On August 6, 1894, Spalding's West Side park had a fire in the grandstand, which seated six thousand fans. Between 1900 and 1911 there were at least five fires in major league parks across the country. In 1903, in one of the biggest tragedies since the 1871 fire, Chicago's Iroquois Theater burned, killing 602 people. After that, many cities rewrote fire codes to make public and semipublic buildings more fire resistant. In 1911, Chicago revised its municipal fire codes and added a specific section for ballparks, requiring that they limit the number of tickets sold to the park's seating capacity, have annual inspections, maintain clear aisles for exiting, and use fire-resistant materials for construction.[55]

Comiskey, however, did not wait for the revised codes to build a new park. His lease at the South Side Park was up in 1909, and that same year there was a fire in the grandstand. Comiskey rebuilt the grandstand but also started scouting other locations for his ball club. Several factors shaped his decision in locating a new park. Proximity to transportation was crucial, so the park could draw fans from throughout the city. Equally important was room for expansion. Baseball's popularity was soaring, and club owners across the country looked for grounds on which additional seating could be added. Perhaps most important was the neighborhood, for club owners wanted their parks to be perceived as safe. Pittsburgh Pirates owner Barney Dreyfuss gave his reasons for building a new park: "The game was growing up, and patrons were no longer willing to put up with nineteenth century conditions. Besides, the park was located in a poor neighborhood, and many of the better class of citizens, especially when accompanied by their womenfolk, were loath to go there."[56]

For these reasons, most of the teams that built the steel-and-concrete stadiums that would launch the "Golden Age of the Baseball Park" located their magnificent parks in "respectable" neighborhoods. These included Pittsburgh's Forbes Field and Philadelphia's Shibe Park, both of which opened in 1909 and set the standard for modern construction. Comiskey was the exception.[57]

Comiskey chose to build his new park in the working-class neighborhood of Armour Square, just east of the largely Irish Bridgeport. Comiskey initially wanted to secure the field used by his former Brotherhood team at Thirty-fifth and Wentworth Avenue because the park was accessible from downtown by the Wentworth streetcar line. The neighborhood also was known for its support of professional baseball. The land where the Brotherhood park stood was unavailable, though. Instead, Comiskey chose the site of a municipal dump and cabbage patch, one block west at Thirty-fifth and Shields. This site happened to be on the dumps that Mary McDowell worked with University of Chicago Settlement residents to clean up. By buying the property and locating the ballpark there, Comiskey perhaps did as much to clean up the area as McDowell had.

On December 22, 1908, Comiskey purchased the lot from the estate of former Chicago mayor John Wentworth for $100,000. It was being used by Signor Scavado for his truck garden, which supplied fruit and vegetables to South Side residents. Comiskey bought him out for an undisclosed amount and began plans to construct his stadium on the former dump site. He hired local architect Zachary Taylor Davis, who had contributed to the design of neighboring Armour Institute of Technology, as well as South Side two-flats and St. Ambrose Roman Catholic Church at Forty-seventh Street and Ellis Avenue. Comiskey wanted his new park to be a pitcher's park, like South Side Park, with a deep outfield that favored pitching over hitting. He sent pitcher Ed Walsh and Davis's assistant Karl Vizhum, who also worked on Daniel Burnham's staff, to tour parks across the country for ideas.[58]

Davis submitted his first sketch on October 6, 1909. His design was modeled on Forbes Field in Pittsburgh and called for a double-decked grandstand between first and third bases, with detached single-decked pavilions beyond. Separate uncovered wooden bleachers surrounded the outfield. Plans for the outer facade included a Roman-style design similar to that of ornamental Shibe Park in Philadelphia. Comiskey called for revised plans, however, most likely because of the cost of implementing Davis's design. Instead, Davis created an outer facade of red pressed brick with large archways ringing the stadium. The arcaded masonry exterior with rhythmic archways recalled the Coliseum in Rome. The park embodied the symmetry and grandeur of City Beautiful design even without the more elaborate facade. The design also included Arts and Crafts motifs. Davis had worked as a draftsman in Louis Sullivan's studio, and he incorporated Prairie School design elements into the raised geometric detailing running along the middle and sides of the archways. This design was similar to Allen Pond's prairie motifs in his initial plans for the University of Chicago Settlement. This brick ornamentation subtly blended with the larger facade of the stadium and at the same time provided added decorative detailing.[59]

In addition, the new park's classically inspired design recalled the Armour Square field house immediately to its north, designed by Daniel

Burnham, and echoed the design of churches and factories in the surrounding neighborhood. The red brick archways integrated the ballpark
into the visual landscape of the Bridgeport community. Surrounding the
park were numerous warehouses to the south, including the Chicago
Shipping and Storage Company, C. P. Kimball and Company Automobile Factory, and People's Gas. To the west were the tracks of the Illinois
Central Railroad, along with railroad warehouses. To the east was the
Wentworth streetcar line, as well as the red Romanesque Armour Institute and numerous churches. North of the park, just beyond Armour
Square, were several two-flats, workers' cottages, and apartments.[60]

The construction of Comiskey Park also stimulated small businesses
along the periphery of the park's grounds. McCuddy's Bar, which became
a neighborhood institution, was directly across from the main entrance.
The tavern actually opened before the park was built, evidently based
on inside information. Other vacant lots surrounding the park were used
as parking areas, while a Greek-owned ice-cream parlor opened on the
corner of Thirty-fifth Street and Wentworth Avenue. Writer James T.
Farrell remembered passing the ice-cream parlor on his way to the park
as a youth, always tempted to get a soda and popcorn before he reached
Comiskey. The presence of the park sent real estate values in the neighborhood soaring, almost doubling in value between 1900 and 1916. The
corner of Thirty-fifth and Wentworth, east of the entrance, experienced
the greatest increase, tripling in value between 1910 and 1915.[61]

Davis had to make the park fit within the street grid of the Armour
Square neighborhood. Other ballparks built in urban neighborhoods
during this period took on irregular shapes as they accommodated the
surrounding city. Boston's Fenway Park, for example, had a short left
field and much longer right field because of oddly designed street grids.
Comiskey was fortunate that he secured a big lot, for he wanted a large,
symmetrical outfield in favor of pitching. Davis accommodated Comiskey, creating the first symmetrical ballpark in major league baseball. The
dimensions of the field were 362 feet down the left and right foul lines
and 420 feet to dead center field.[62]

The new ballpark seated 35,000 and, to accommodate working-class
fans, had 7,000 twenty-five-cent bleacher seats, the largest number in
the major leagues. By contrast, New York's Polo Grounds had only 200
twenty-five-cent seats. Groundbreaking for the stadium took place on
February 14, 1910, and, despite a steel strike that delayed the first con-
signment of beams for five weeks, the park hosted its first game on April
15, 1910. The official opening day was on July 1. The park cost a total of
$750,000.[63]

A Day at the Park

The official opening of the new White Sox park was greeted with enormous fanfare. The afternoon's events began with an automobile parade, with Mayor Fred Busse leading the way. The parade commenced at City Hall, and by the time it reached the new grounds, over two hundred vehicles had joined. Decorated with banners, buttons, and emblems, the cars carried Chicago aldermen, police officers, county commissioners, and sportswriters. Once the parade reached the main entrance, five bands joined five marching companies and "marched in to the accompaniment of a storm of cheers that threatened to do damage to Mr. Comiskey's new structure." After the 28,000 fans who came to the opening filed into the park, Mayor Busse offered congratulatory remarks and presented Comiskey with a "shimmering, silken pennant." Comiskey wasted no time in linking patriotism and civic boosterism with professional athletic competition. After the military band raised the Stars and Stripes above the new stadium, he declared, "That flag is with us, they've given us a pennant to-day and we are going out after the other one from this moment."[64] The ceremony recalled the patriotism of the dedication of Davis Square five years earlier and illustrated how both public parks and professional ballfields could be infused with the same rhetoric of civic pride.

Accounts of the opening ceremonies marveled at how easily the unwieldy crowd moved from the parade outside the gates into their seats. The *Chicago Tribune* reported: "Despite the strangeness of it all to everyone concerned and the fact not one in 100 of the visitors had any idea of the location of their seats or the byways and hedges which led to them, the big crowd was handled smoothly and expeditiously. The yawning gates, with their swiftly clicking turnstyles, swallowed the people . . . sweeping them [into] the stands and . . . [toward] the seemingly endless rows of seats."[65]

Indeed, one of the factors that contributed to an atmosphere of refinement and order at the new park was the well-regulated control both of space and of people. New parks like Comiskey introduced crowd-control measures like turnstiles, to slow the surge of entering fans. Color-coded tickets directed spectators to specific gates to avoid a rush at the entrance. For greater safety as spectators entered and left the park, Comiskey installed ramps instead of stairs. Like the public parks and playgrounds, then, the designs of professional sports arenas encompassed ideas about properly ordered space and its ability to control behavior.

Comiskey's prescriptions for crowd control contributed to the segregation of crowds within the ballpark. Of the 35,000 seats, 6,400 were in boxes. In these seats sat local dignitaries. For example, on opening day, several boxes were occupied by friends of Comiskey, as well as Chicago politicians. Mayor Busse sat in the "box of honor" above the players' "cage." Accompanying him were the assistant superintendent of police, the commissioner of public works, a Cook County judge, and several aldermen. Comiskey's box included his immediate family, while friends both from Chicago and from other cities such as St. Louis and St. Paul occupied nearby boxes. The box seats let Chicago's commercial and political elite gather away from the boisterous crowd.[66]

Comiskey further promoted an atmosphere of respectability by charging different admission fees for various parts of the ballpark. In addition to the 6,400 box seats that sold for a dollar or more, there were 12,600 grandstand seats for seventy-five cents each, 9,000 pavilion seats for fifty cents, and the 7,000 twenty-five-cent bleacher seats. This pricing policy effectively confined working-class fans to the bleachers, reserving the grandstand and pavilion for white-collar and middle-class spectators.[67]

Despite this class segregation and all the pretenses toward refinement, the ballpark still was a male space. Comiskey sought to overcome the association between the park and male sporting culture in a variety of ways. For example, his new park had an inscription emblazoned on the grandstand: "No Betting Allowed In This Park." Paradoxically, this visible reminder of ballpark regulations recalled the historical connections between professional sports and gambling. Yet it marked the park as a space where this link was broken, as police and private detectives patrolled the grounds to enforce club policy. In addition, Comiskey instituted ladies' days, when women were admitted free. While it is unclear what effect this had on behavior inside the park, the policy was effective in encouraging female attendance, for by World War I women made up over 10 percent of baseball crowds.[68]

From the start, Comiskey claimed that the park belonged to the people, and he made it available free of charge for local gatherings, including church picnics, union rallies, and athletic club games. In 1911, Comiskey donated the park to the black Eighth Regiment Army for Field Day exercise.[69] The park was also the site of various amusements, including boxing matches, football games, and "auto polo" in 1913, a game in which players drove cars around the field and tried to hit a large ball with oversized mallets hung out the car windows. Comiskey hoped to make the park a site of local pride and to make himself a figure of community respect. In 1915, for example, he sponsored a float celebrating American prosperity and linked this prosperity to the success of the White Sox (fig. 12). For Comiskey, civic pride translated into commercial success and popular appeal.

Comiskey also catered to the press, recognizing, as had Spalding, that favorable newspaper coverage boosted fan support and ballpark attendance. Many sportswriters complained that ballparks did not accommodate them in any way, making it difficult for them to do their job adequately, since they were forced to mingle with fans. Comiskey admitted reporters to his private drinking club on park grounds. The club consisted of politicians, civic leaders, show people, and newsmen. Comiskey called the group the Woodland Bards and invited them all on annual hunting and fishing trips in central Wisconsin. Baseball writing did come to play a large part in increasing the popularity of the game, as reporters like Hugh Fullerton and Ring Lardner, both Bards members, created a unique style of writing that incorporated the street slang of local urban sandlots into sports language and literature.[70]

The rise of baseball writing did much to promote the central place of Comiskey Park in the civic culture of the city. Baseball writers captured the excitement of the ballpark at the same time that they celebrated its atmosphere of civility and comradeship. James T. Farrell, who grew up on the South Side not far from Comiskey Park, remembered nostalgically the prominent part the park had in shaping his sense of local identity: "I visualized Comiskey Park, with roaring and cheering fans, the players swinging, running to the bases. I imagined myself as a player and also spectator seeing all the action. My state of mind was almost describable as one of the walking coma. The sounds around me, the traffic on Grand Boulevard, an occasional horse and wagon, electric car or automobile on Fiftieth Street, of the elevated train, passing one block to the west, these all came to me as though muffled. They might have been the roar of the crowd at Comiskey Park."[71]

For Farrell, the sights and sounds of the ballpark mingled with those of the city around him, structuring his relationship with urban culture. He later discussed his experience of going to the ballpark and camping out overnight to buy bleacher seats for the 1917 World Series. After waiting for dawn to arrive and the ticket office to open, Farrell described his feelings about the crowd of people around him: "These strange men standing in line, sitting on boxes, squatting by a fire, playing poker, chatting intermittently about baseball, showing the same concern as I did about the weather, shivering a bit as I did—they and I were bound together by a common passion. And those around me were kind and friendly. I felt secure and unafraid and I was like them."[72]

This celebration of democratic spirit, while a bit romanticized, attests to the way the local ballpark brought together diverse groups in the city in the shared project of rooting for the team. Within the ballpark, businesspeople, professionals, and politicians joined with artisans and factory workers to overcome class difference for those few hours and to see each other simply as fans. As sports editor Edward B. Moss put it, "Businessmen and professional men forget their standing in the community and shoulder to shoulder with the street urchin 'root' frantically for the hit needed to win the game."[73] Thus, the ballpark functioned in much the same way that park promoters hoped public parks and field houses would, to bring together and even unite diverse groups.

The experience in the ballpark also helped fans transcend ethnic difference. Irish and Germans, especially at Comiskey, celebrated not only their pride in the local team but also their appreciation of fellow ethnic players. Baseball also became popular with the Czech and Polish crowds who came to Comiskey from the neighboring Back of the Yards. Since baseball was a popular sport among ethnic athletic club members, supporters felt a sense of belonging as fans in the major league ballpark. Comiskey even recruited Slavic players from the local sokols to attract fans. Ethnic groups, then, could experience the ballpark both as a site of American civic celebration and as a vehicle of ethnic pride.[74]

Baseball was less popular among Jewish immigrants. Many Jews argued that baseball detracted from the values of study they hoped to instill, and that games like chess promoted. Second-generation Jews spoke about having to overcome their parents' hostility to the game. In addition, there were not many Jewish players fans could root for. Historian Steven Riess's calculations of ethnic professional ballplayers from 1901 to 1906 reveal only two Jewish rookies. No more entered the major leagues between 1910 and 1920, in part because of discrimination against Jews among both club owners and fans. This changed for Chicago fans in the 1920s, when the White Sox signed catcher Moe Berg. Jewish residents of the South Side and throughout the city came to Comiskey Park to cheer for him. In 1928, Jewish White Sox fans were so enthusiastic about Berg that they offered to put up $25,000 for a special day at the park to honor him. Although Berg declined, the offer demonstrated the important part ethnic players had in generating fan support and creating an arena of ethnic diversity.[75]

African Americans had a more ambiguous relationship with the supposed democracy of the ballpark. The Black Belt, which swelled during the Great Migration during World War I, was just east of Comiskey Park. Wentworth Avenue, just a few blocks west of State Street, formed a solid barrier separating the Black Belt from the white ethnic neighborhoods to the west. White fans often complained because the Black Belt was so close to the park. In his autobiographical novel, Farrell described a scene with two friends from the Washington Park area taking the elevated train to the park: "They got off with the crowd at Thirty-fifth Street. Crossing State Street, the sight of so many Negroes . . . talking on the corner made Danny afraid, because at home they always said that niggers would do things to him, and you never could trust a nigger because if you gave him an inch he always took a mile."[76]

African Americans attending games at Comiskey certainly experienced this virulent racism to a certain extent, yet what was more notable for many was that they were welcomed in the park itself. Being spectators at Comiskey Park became a source of pride for many blacks, especially those recently arrived from the South. One migrant from Mississippi exclaimed, "I wish you could have been here to those games. I saw them and believe me they was worth the money I pay to see them."[77] William Everett Samuels, a black musician and officer in Local 208 of the American Federation of Musicians, recalled the proximity of his home in the Black Belt to the new Comiskey Park. "I remember when they built White Sox's Park, that was in 1910. Before that they had a place at 49th [actually 39th] and Wentworth. They leased that to the American Giants, which was a colored ball team, and they moved it. Mr. Cominskey [sic], who owned the White Sox's, lived at 3510 Wabash when he built it. I used to see him everyday when they built White Sox's Park."[78] Though Samuels was not a baseball fan, his memory of Comiskey walking by his home during the building of the park suggested that some of the neighborhood barriers separating the races on the South Side of Chicago could be crossed.

In addition, the *Chicago Defender*, the largest-selling black newspaper in the nation by World War I, featured regular stories and notices about the White Sox. As sociologists St. Clair Drake and Horace R. Cayton explained, "At ball-parks . . . and other spots where crowds congregate as spectators, Negroes [could] be found sitting where they please, booing and applauding, cheering and 'razzing,' with as little restraint as their white fellows." For many African Americans in Chicago, going to a baseball game was an experience of liberation and celebration, of taking part in the shared culture of Chicago civic life.[79]

At the same time, the African American experience at major league ball games differed from that of white ethnic groups. While blacks attended major league ball games and rooted alongside whites, they did not see fellow blacks on the ball field. The sense of pride and ethnic identification that many immigrants experienced was absent for African American spectators. The exclusion of black players suggested that as much as blacks might enjoy attending games, they were not a part of the complete civic experience embodied in the stadium. The creation of a shared American identity in the ballpark, then, contributed to the construction of a civic identity defined, at least in part, by whiteness. . . .[80]

Notes

1. *Chicago Tribune,* March 18, 1910, and *Chicago Record-Herald,* March 18, 1910. For further discussion of the building of Comiskey Park, see Michael Benson, *Ballparks of North America: A Comprehensive Historical Reference to Baseball Grounds, Yards, and Stadiums, 1845 to Present* (Jefferson, N.C.: McFarland, 1989), 88–93; Frank Budreck, *Goodbye Old Friend: A Pictorial Essay on the Final Season at Old Comiskey Park* (Lyons, Ill.: Aland, 1992); Douglas Bukowski, *Baseball Palace of the World: The Last Year of Comiskey Park* (Chicago: Lyceum Books, 1992), 24–25; Richard Lindberg, "Through the Years: A Journey through Comiskey Park's Colorful History from 1910 to 1990," in *Through the Years* (Chicago: Sherman Media, 1990), 4–5; Philip Lowry, *Green Cathedrals: The Ultimate Celebration of 271 Major League and Negro League Ballparks Past and Present* (Reading, Mass.: Addison-Wesley, 1992), 128–31; Lowell Reidenbaugh, *Take Me Out to the Ball Park* (St. Louis: Sporting News, 1987); and Lawrence S. Ritter, *Lost Ballparks: A Celebration of Baseball's Legendary Fields* (New York: Penguin Books, 1992), 29–30.

2. For further discussion of the relation between mass amusement and working-class culture, see Paul Boyer, *Urban Masses and Moral Order in America, 1820–1920* (Cambridge: Harvard University Press, 1978); John F. Kasson, *Amusing the Million: Coney Island at the Turn of the Century* (New York: Hill and Wang, 1978); Kasson, *Rudeness and Civility: Manners in Nineteenth Century Urban America* (New York: W. W. Norton, 1990); and Lawrence Levine, *Highbrow/Lowbrow: The Emergence of Cultural Hierarchy in America* (Cambridge: Harvard University Press, 1988).

3. David Nasaw, *Going Out: The Rise and Fall of Public Amusements* (New York: Basic Books, 1993); Kathy Peiss, *Cheap Amusements: Working Women and Leisure in Turn-of-the Century New York* (Philadelphia: Temple University Press, 1986), 6; and Roy Rosenzweig, *Eight Hours for What We Will: Workers and Leisure in an Industrial City, 1870–1920* (Cambridge: Cambridge University Press, 1983). See also Lewis Erenberg, *Steppin' Out: New York Nightlife and the Transformation of American Culture, 1890–1930* (Westport, Conn.: Greenwood, 1981).

4. As several cultural historians have argued, mass culture helped European immigrants overcome ethnic differences and, in the space of the theater, amusement park, and baseball park, created a shared culture of "whiteness." See Shelley Fisher Fishkin, "Interrogating 'Whiteness,' Complicating 'Blackness': Remapping American Culture," *American Quarterly,* 47 (September 1995): 428–66; George Lipsitz, "The Possessive Investment in Whiteness: Racialized Social Democracy and the 'White' Problem in American Studies," *American Quarterly,* 47 (September 1995): 369–87; Eric Lott, *Love and Theft: Blackface Minstrelsy and the American Working Class* (New York: Oxford University Press, 1993); Nasaw, *Going Out,* especially 47–61; and Michael Rogin, *Blackface, White Noise: Jewish Immigrants in the Hollywood Melting Pot* (Berkeley: University of California Press, 1996). David R. Roediger discusses the role of labor in racializing European ethnics as "white" in *The Wages of Whiteness: Race and the Making of the American Working Class* (London: Verso, 1991).

5. See Louise de Koven Bowen, *Safeguards for City Youth at Work and at Play* (New York: Macmillan, 1914), 4.

6. Vice Commission of Chicago, *The Social Evil in Chicago: A Study of Existing Conditions with Recommendations of the Vice Commission of Chicago* (Chicago: Gunthorp-Warren, 1911), 202, 204.

7. Theodore Dreiser, *Sister Carrie* (1900; New York: Dell, 1959). For further discussion of working-class women's culture in the city, see Edith Abbott, *Women in Industry* (New York: D. Appleton, 1910); Susan Porter Benson, *Counter Cultures: Saleswomen, Managers, and Customers in American Department Stores, 1890–1940* (Urbana: University of Illinois Press, 1986); Angel Kwolek-Folland, *Engendering Business: Men and Women in the Corporate Office, 1870–1930* (Baltimore: Johns Hopkins University Press, 1994); William Leach, *Land of Desire: Merchants, Power, and the Rise of a New American Culture* (New York: Vintage Books, 1993); Joanne J. Meyerowitz, *Women Adrift: Independent Wage Earners in Chicago, 1880–1930* (Chicago: University of Chicago Press, 1988); and Peiss, *Cheap Amusements.*

8. Bowen, *Safeguards for City Youth,* 45.

9. Kathy Peiss argues that working women carefully negotiated their public roles and opened up a range of exchanges between themselves and male suitors. In the process, they reshaped ideas about female sexuality and its place in the public life of the city. See Peiss, *Cheap Amusements,* 3–10.

10. Jane Addams, *The Spirit of Youth and the City Streets* (New York: Macmillan, 1909), 95–96.

11. Benjamin McArthur, "Parks, Playgrounds, and Progressivism," in *A Breath of Fresh Air: Chicago's Neighborhood Parks of the Progressive Reform Era, 1900–1925* (Chicago: Chicago Park District, 1989), 13. For more on the play movement, see Boyer, *Urban Masses;* Dominick Cavallo, *Muscles and Morals: Organized Playgrounds and Urban Reform, 1880–1920* (Philadelphia: University of Pennsylvania Press, 1981); Cary Goodman, *Choosing Sides: Playground and Street Life on the Lower East Side* (New York: Schocken Books, 1979); Elizabeth Halsey, *Development of Public Recreation in Metropolitan Chicago* (Chicago: Chicago Recreation Commission, 1940), 8, 115; and Steven A. Riess, *City Games: The Evolution of American Urban Society and the Rise of Sports* (Urbana: University of Illinois Press, 1989), 132–68. See also Benjamin McArthur, "The Chicago Playground Movement: A Neglected Feature of Social Justice," *Social Science Review,* 49 (September 1975): 376–95, esp. 379.

12. Daniel T. Rodgers, *The Work Ethic in Industrial America, 1850–1920* (Chicago: University of Chicago Press, 1978), 102.

13. Theodore Roosevelt, "The Value of an Athletic Training," *Harper's Weekly,* December 23, 1893, 35–68.

14. See Morris Cohen, "Baseball," *Dial,* July 26, 1919, 57, for a discussion of William James's ideas on the "moral equivalent of war" and their relation to sports.

15. Addams, *Spirit of Youth,* 147.

16. See Cavallo's discussion of progressive theories of play in *Muscles and Morals,* 9, 55–70. Allen Guttmann supports Cavallo's contention that supervised play was not merely an example of bourgeois social control and takes issue with Cary Goodman's argument that the playground movement reflected the hegemony of middle-class aspirations. See Allen Guttmann, *A Whole New Ball Game: An Interpretation of American Sports* (Chapel Hill: University of North Carolina Press, 1988), 88–89. See also David A. Karp, Gregory P. Stone, and William C. Yoels, *Being Urban: A Sociology of City Life* (New York: Praeger, 1991), 200, for

a discussion of the play movement as a contest for the urban space and leisure time of immigrant children.

17. Shailer Matthews, quoted in John S. Watterson, "Chicago's City Championship: Northwestern University versus the University of Chicago, 1892–1905," *Chicago History*, 11:3 (Fall-Winter 1982): 101–74, quotation on 172.

18. Quoted in Steven A. Riess, *Touching Base: Professional Baseball and American Culture in the Progressive Era* (Westport, Conn.: Greenwood Press, 1980), 25.

19. Henry Curtis, *The Practical Conduct of Play* (New York: Macmillan, 1915), 212.

20. For further discussion of ethnic athletic clubs and their role in creating a "bachelor subculture," see Melvin L. Adelman, *A Sporting Time: New York City and the Rise of Modern Athletics, 1820–1870* (Urbana: University of Illinois Press, 1990), 224; Gerald R. Gems, *Windy City Wars: Labor, Leisure, and Sport in the Making of Chicago* (Lanham, Md.: Scarecrow, 1997), 25–30; Elliott J. Gorn and Warren Goldstein, *A Brief History of American Sports* (New York: Hill and Wang, 1993), 14, 70–72; Benjamin G. Rader, *American Sports: From the Age of Folk Games to the Age of Spectators* (Englewood Cliffs, N.J.: Prentice-Hall, 1983), 97–98; Benjamin G. Rader, "The Quest for Subcommunities and the Rise of American Sport," in *The Sporting Image: Readings in American Sport History*, ed. Paul J. Zingg (Lanham, Md.: University Press of America, 1988); and Riess, *City Games*, 16, 22–25. My discussion of changing views of "manliness" is largely informed by Gorn and Goldstein, *Brief History*, 80. See also Mary Ann Clawson, *Constructing Brotherhood: Class, Gender, and Fraternalism* (Princeton, N.J.: Princeton University Press, 1989), chap. 4.

21. For further discussion of gender and athletics, see Susan K. Cahn, *Coming on Strong: Gender and Sexuality in Twentieth-Century Women's Sport* (New York: Free Press, 1994), esp. chaps. 1–3; George Eisen, "Sport, Recreation, and Gender: Jewish Immigrant Women in Turn-of-the-Century America (1880–1920)," *Journal of Sport History*, 18 (Spring 1991): 103–20; Allen Guttmann, *Women's Sports: A History* (New York: Columbia University Press, 1991); Helen Lenskyj, *Out of Bounds: Women, Sport, and Sexuality* (Toronto: Women's Press, 1986); Michael Messner and Don Sabo, eds., *Sport, Men, and the Gender Order: Critical Feminist Perspectives* (Champaign, Ill.: Human Kinetics, 1990); Gregory Kent Stanley, *The Rise and Fall of the Sportswoman: Women's Health, Fitness, and Athletics, 1860–1940* (New York: Peter Lang, 1996); Stephanie L. Twin, *Out of the Bleachers: Writing on Women and Sport* (Old Westbury, N.Y.: Feminist Press, 1979); Stephanie L. Twin, "Women and Sport," in *Sports in America: New Historical Perspectives*, ed. Donald Spivey (Westport, Conn.: Greenwood, 1985), 193–217; and Patricia A. Vertinsky, *The Eternally Wounded Woman: Women, Doctors, and Exercise in the Late Nineteenth Century* (Manchester: Manchester University Press, 1990).

22. For general histories of professional baseball, see Adelman, *Sporting Time*; Charles C. Alexander, *Our Game: An American Baseball History* (New York: Henry Holt, 1991); Warren Goldstein, *Playing for Keeps: A History of Early Baseball* (Ithaca, N.Y.: Cornell University Press, 1989); Allen Guttmann, *From Ritual to Record: The Nature of Modern Sports* (New York: Columbia University Press, 1978); Donald Honig, *Baseball America: The Heroes of the Game and the Times of Their Glory* (New York: Macmillan, 1985); Riess, *Touching Base*; Harold Seymour, *Baseball, vol. 1, The Early Years* (New York: Oxford University Press, 1960), and Harold Seymour, *Baseball, vol. 2, The Golden Age* (New York: Oxford

University Press, 1971); David Q. Voigt, *American Baseball, vol. 1, From Gentlemen's Sport to the Commissioner System* (Norman: University of Oklahoma Press, 1966), and David Q. Voigt, *American Baseball, vol. 2, From the Commissioners to the Continental Expansion* (Norman: University of Oklahoma Press, 1970); G. Edward White, *Creating the National Pastime: Baseball Transforms Itself* (Princeton, N.J.: Princeton University Press, 1996); and Joel Zoss and John Bowman, *Diamonds in the Rough: The Untold History of Baseball* (New York: Contemporary Books, 1996).

23. As Allen Guttmann points out, baseball's attraction "lies in its primitive-pastoral elements and simultaneously in its extraordinary modernity, in its closeness to the seasonal rhythms of nature and, at the same time, in the rarefied realm of numbers" (Guttmann, *From Ritual to Record*, 113–14). For further discussion of industrial work culture, see Herbert G. Gutman, *Work, Culture, and Society in Industrializing America* (New York: Vintage Books, 1976); David Montgomery, "The New Unionism and the Transformation of Workers' Consciousness in America: 1909–1922," *Journal of Social History*, 7 (Summer 1974): 511; and E. P. Thompson, "Time, Work–Discipline, and Industrial Capitalism," *Past and Present*, 38 (December 1967): 56–97. Warren Goldstein argues that baseball has followed two paths throughout its history. Baseball's relationship with money shapes what Goldstein refers to as the "linear" history of the game, while its emotional and mythic element lends itself to a cyclical history, defined by attempts to recreate a "golden age." I agree with this assessment, but would go further and argue that these two elements of baseball history are integrally related. During periods when labor and money issues became more prominent, baseball proponents were more likely to construct baseball as a pastoral, preindustrial activity removed from the world of the marketplace. See Goldstein, *Playing for Keeps*, 70.

24. Quoted in Goldstein, *Playing for Keeps*, 11.

25. Ibid. The Doubleday story is myth. In 1839, Doubleday was about twenty years old and was attending West Point, a long way from Cooperstown. Most scholars agree that baseball evolved from other games that were British in origin, including cricket, rounders, and town ball. Until recently, most scholars also agreed that the first organized baseball game took place in 1846 at the Elysian Fields in Hoboken, New Jersey, and was played not by farmers but by small shopkeepers and clerks.

In 2001, a librarian at New York University came across two newspaper references to organized baseball from an even earlier period. Both articles appeared in New York City newspapers in 1823; an article in the *National Advocate* talked about a game being played in what is today Greenwich Village. The writer stated, "Any person fond of witnessing this game may avail himself of seeing it played with consummate skill and wonderful dexterity . . . it is innocent amusement, and healthy exercise, attended with but little expense, and has no demoralizing tendency." The article, along with another like it, suggests that baseball was familiar to many New Yorkers as early as the 1820s. See *New York Times*, July 8, 2001.

26. Peter Levine, *A. G. Spalding and the Rise of Baseball: The Promise of American Sport* (New York: Oxford University Press, 1985), xiv, 14. Levine compares Spalding to John D. Rockefeller and Frederick Winslow Taylor.

27. *Spalding's Handbook of Sporting Rules and Training, Containing Full and Authentic Codes of Rules Governing All Popular Games and Sports* (New York: A. G. Spalding, 1886).

28. *Constitution and Playing Rules of the National League of Professional Base Ball Clubs* (1876; Chicago: A. G. Spalding, 1886), 2–3, 608, 13–18. See also Honig, *Baseball America*, 10–11; Levine, *Spalding*, 21; Riess, *City Games*, 194–96; Seymour, *Baseball: The Early Years*, chap. 7; and Voigt, *American Baseball*, vol. 1, chap. 1.

29. For further discussion of the relation between spatial arrangements, the division of labor, and the workplace, see Harry Braverman, *Labor and Monopoly Capital: The Degradation of Work in the Twentieth Century* (New York: Monthly Review Press, 1974), 304–10; Alfred D. Chandler Jr., *The Visible Hand: The Managerial Revolution in American Business* (Cambridge, Mass.: Belknap Press, 1977), 6–12, 274–81; David M. Gordon et al., *Segmented Work, Divided Workers: The Historical Transformation of Labor in the United States* (Cambridge: Cambridge University Press, 1982), 151–52; Gutman, *Work, Culture, and Society*, esp. chap 1; Angel Kwolek-Folland, *Engendering Business: Men and Women in the Corporate Office, 1870–1930* (Baltimore: Johns Hopkins University Press, 1994), 94–128; David Montgomery, *Workers' Control in America: Studies in the History of Work, Technology, and Labor Struggles* (Cambridge: Cambridge University Press, 1979), 44–46; David F. Noble, *America by Design: Science, Technology, and the Rise of Corporate Capitalism* (New York: Alfred A. Knopf, 1979), 264–320; Sharon Hartman Strom, *Beyond the Typewriter: Gender, Class, and the Origins of Modern American Office Work, 1900–1930* (Urbana: University of Illinois Press 1992), 235; Thompson, "Time, Work-Discipline, and Industrial Capitalism"; and Alan Trachtenberg, *The Incorporation of America: Culture and Society in the Gilded Age* (New York: Hill and Wang, 1982).

30. *Constitution and Playing Rules*, 8–13. See also Burton J. Bledstein, *The Culture of Professionalism: The Middle Class and the Development of Higher Education in America* (New York: W. W. Norton, 1976), 81, 85.

31. Nominating Committee, National Association of Base Ball Players (1867), quoted in Robert Peterson, *Only the Ball Was White: A History of Legendary Black Players and All-Black Professional Teams before Black Men Played in the Major Leagues* (New York: McGraw-Hill, 1984), 16.

32. For further discussion of African Americans in baseball, see Phil Dixon with Patrick J. Hannigan, *The Negro Baseball Leagues, 1867–1955: A Photographic History* (Mattituck, N.Y.: Amereon House, 1992); David Falkner, *Great Time Coming: The Life of Jackie Robinson from Baseball to Birmingham* (New York: Simon and Schuster, 1995); John B. Holway, *Blackball Stars: Negro League Pioneers* (Westport, Conn.: Meckler Books, 1988); John B. Holway, *Black Diamonds: Life in the Negro Leagues from the Men Who Lived It* (Westport, Conn.: Meckler Books, 1989); Peterson, *Only the Ball*; Mark Ribowsky, *A Complete History of the Negro Leagues, 1884–1955* (Secaucus, N.J.: Carol, 1995); Mark Ribowsky, *The Power and the Darkness: The Life of Josh Gibson in the Shadows of the Game* (New York: Simon and Schuster, 1996); Harold Seymour, *Baseball: The People's Game* (New York: Oxford University Press, 1990), 531–94; Sol White, *Sol White's History of Colored Base Ball, with Other Documents of the Early Black Game, 1886–1936* (Lincoln: University of Nebraska Press, 1995); and Jules Tygiel, *Baseball's Great Experiment: Jackie Robinson and His Legacy* (New York: Oxford University Press, 1983).

33. *Brooklyn Daily Union*, October 1867, quoted in Peterson, *Only the Ball*, 17.

34. For further discussion of the role of sport in African American communi-

ties, see James R. Grossman, *Land of Hope: Chicago, Black Southerners, and the Great Migration* (Chicago: University of Chicago Press, 1989), 86–90; Earl Lewis, *In Their Own Interests: Race, Class, and Power in Twentieth-Century Norfolk, Virginia* (Berkeley: University of California Press, 1991), 90–96; and Rob Ruck, *Sandlot Seasons: Sport in Black Pittsburgh* (Urbana: University of Illinois Press, 1987), esp. 37.

35. Henry Chadwick, *The Game of Baseball: How to Learn It, How to Play It, and How to Teach It* (New York: George Munro, 1868), quoted in Levine, *Spalding*, 82.

36. *Constitution and Playing Rules*, 16, sec. 39; Gorn and Goldstein, *Brief History*, 209; Goldstein, *Playing for Keeps*, 35; Riess, *Touching Base*, 122; Seymour, *Baseball: The Early Years*, 35–59; and Voigt, *American Baseball*, 1:3–34.

37. *Sporting News*, January 22, 1887, quoted in Levine, *Spalding*, 43.

38. Spalding, quoted in Levine, *Spalding*, 42.

39. Riess, *City Games*, 196.

40. *Constitution and Playing Rules*, 8–13; Paul Douglas, *Real Wages in the United States, 1890–1926* (Boston: Houghton-Mifflin, 1930), 112–14; Clarence D. Long, *Wages and Earnings in the United States, 1860–1890* (Princeton: Princeton University Press, 1960), 4; and Riess, *Touching Base*, 33.

41. Riess, *City Games*, 70, 196; Riess, *Touching Base*, 31–34; Seymour, *Baseball: The Early Years*, chap. 13; and Voigt, *American Baseball*, 1:121–30.

42. Seymour, *Baseball: The Early Years*, chap. 13.

43. Warren Brown, *The Chicago White Sox* (New York: G. P. Putnam's Sons, 1952), 1. See also G. W. Axelson, *"Commy": The Life Story of Charles A. Comiskey* (Chicago: Reilly and Lee, 1919), 33–35; and Judith Helm, "Comiskey Family Album," in *Through the Years*, 25–30. See also Richard C. Lindberg, *The White Sox Encyclopedia* (Philadelphia: Temple University Press, 1997).

44. Brown, *Chicago White Sox*, 2.

45. Axelson, *"Commy,"* 73; Brown, *Chicago White Sox*, 7–11; Helm, "Comiskey Family Album," 26; and Riess, *Touching Base*, 156–57.

46. John Montgomery Ward, "The Brotherhood of Professional Base Ball Players' Manifesto" (1889), quoted in Anthony J. Connor, *Baseball for the Love of It: Hall of Famers Tell It Like It Was* (New York: Macmillan, 1982), 216.

47. Riess, *Touching Base*, 156–57; Seymour, *Baseball: The Early Years*, 267–70; and Voigt, *American Baseball*, 1:233–34. The difficulty of challenging the myth of baseball was made clear in 1915, when the Federal League sued the National and American Leagues for violating the Sherman Anti-Trust Act. Owners of Federal League teams initiated the lawsuit after they were unable to compete effectively for players against the two big leagues. They argued that the reserve clause barred fair competition in the marketplace. Judge Kenesaw Mountain Landis presided over the hearing but never issued a verdict because he felt it would forever alter the history of baseball. When the case reached the Supreme Court, Justice Oliver Wendell Holmes argued that baseball leagues were not sources of interstate commerce and therefore could not have violated antitrust laws. See Robert F. Burk, *Never Just a Game: Players, Owners, and American Baseball to 1920* (Chapel Hill: University of North Carolina Press, 1994), 207–9; Guttmann, *Whole New Ball Game*, 65–69; Lee Lowenfish, *Imperfect Diamond: The Story of Baseball's Reserve System and the Men Who Fought to Change It* (New York: Stein and Day, 1980), 88–90; Seymour, *Baseball: The Golden Age*, 212, 230–34; and Voigt, *American Baseball*, 2:21, 81.

48. For licensing fees and taxes on ballparks, see *Proceedings of the Chicago City Council,* April 2, 1919, 1947; December 29, 1919, 1689; and January 4, 1920, 1987. Comiskey claimed that he paid all the police officers working in the park. See *Chicago Daily News,* October 4, 1919. See also Riess, *City Games,* 199; and Reiss, *Touching Base,* 59–61, 73–75. Levine points out that Spalding initiated these connections between ball club owners in Chicago and local politicians. Spalding offered free passes to local politicians, negotiated streetcar schedules with the West Division Rail Company, and encouraged White Stockings investor John R. Walsh, owner of the *Chicago Herald,* to use press coverage to attract fans to the game. See Levine, *Spalding,* 44. Of course, the Brooklyn national league team was the most famous for these types of arrangements. The team was owned by a traction magnate who moved his team to Brownsville, an area served by his trolley line. When Charles Ebbets bought the team in 1898, he moved the team back to Brooklyn with the help of other local traction firms. Ebbets Field's location at the crossing of numerous trolley lines earned Brooklyn fans the moniker "trolley dodgers," hence the team name "the Dodgers." See Robert F. Bluthardt, "Fenway Park and the Golden Age of the Baseball Park, 1909–1915," *Journal of Popular Culture,* 21 (Summer 1987): 43–52, esp. 43; Michael Gershman, *Diamonds: The Evolution of the Ballpark* (Boston: Houghton Mifflin, 1993), 110–15; Riess, *City Games,* 208–16; and Riess, *Touching Base,* 70–71, 80. For a discussion of the politics and business of baseball in Philadelphia, see Bruce Kuklick, *To Every Thing a Season: Shibe Park and Urban Philadelphia, 1909–1976* (Princeton: Princeton University Press, 1991), 13–22, 95–111.

49. Riess, *City Games,* 197: Riess, *Touching Base,* 69–70; Seymour, *Baseball: The Middle Years,* 68–72; and Voigt, *American Baseball,* 2:108–9.

50. Quoted in Axelson, *"Commy,"* 315, 318. I thank Dan Nathan for bringing this quotation to my attention.

51. For further discussion of early Chicago ballparks, see Benson, *Ballparks,* 79–88; *Chicago Tribune,* June 25, 1884; "The Chicago Base-Ball Grounds," *Harper's Weekly,* May 12, 1883, 200; Gershman, *Diamonds,* 19–34, 45, 54; Levine, *Spalding,* 37–47; Lowry, *Green Cathedrals,* 126–31; Riess, *City Games,* 217; Riess, *Touching Base,* 86; and *Sporting News,* January 9, 1892.

52. Axelson, *"Commy,"* 149.

53. Everett Julian Allgood, "The Development of Baseball Architecture in Twentieth Century America" (master's thesis, Emory University, 1989), 6–7; Benson, *Ballparks,* 84; and Bill Shannon and George Kalinsky, *The Ballparks* (New York: Hawthorn Books, 1975), 11.

54. Tommy Leach, in Lawrence S. Ritter, *The Glory of Their Times: The Story of the Early Days of Baseball Told by the Men Who Played It* (New York: Macmillan, 1966), 26–27.

55. Edward Brundage, *The Chicago Code of 1911* (Chicago: Callahan, 1911), 7–10; *Chicago Tribune,* December 24, 1910; Riess, *City Games,* 217; and Riess, *Touching Base,* 95–96.

56. Barney Dreyfuss, quoted in Bluthardt, "Fenway Park," 44.

57. Bluthardt, "Fenway Park," 44–45; Gershman, *Diamonds,* 85–104; Kuklick, *To Every Thing a Season,* 19–29.

58. "Ancient Permit File Index," Department of Inspectional Services, Permit B3833, February 9, 1950, book 61, p. 79, City Hall, Chicago; *Chicago Tribune,* July 2, 1910; *Chicago Record-Herald,* July 2, 1910: George W. Hilton, "Comiskey

Park," *Baseball Historical Review*, 1981, 1–8, esp. 1; and Lindberg, "Through the Years," 5–11.

59. In a similar move of fiscal conservatism, Comiskey decided to incorporate support pillars into the grandstand design, producing seats with obstructed views. Vitzhum's plan to produce a cantilevered grandstand free of posts could have added as much as $350,000 to the cost of the park. For further discussion of the design of Comiskey, see Budreck, *Goodbye Old Friend*, 14, 19, 30; Bukowski, *Baseball Palace*, 24–25, 152, 163; Wayne Guskind, "The Stadium as Civic Architecture" (master's thesis, Georgia Institute of Technology, 1984), 20–24; Hilton, "Comiskey Park," 2; Brian James Nielson, "Dialogue with the City: The Evolution of Baseball Parks," *Landscape*, 29 (1986): 39–47, 45; John Pastier, "The Business of Baseball," *Inland Architect* (Jan.–Feb. 1989), 56–62, 59; and Ritter, *Lost Ballparks*, 40.

60. Bukowski, *Baseball Palace*, 158; *Rascher's Atlas of North Half of Hyde Park* (1890), Chicago Historical Society Library; Riess, *Touching Base*, 97; *Sanborn Fire Insurance Atlas* (1895, corrected to 1909), Chicago Historical Society Library.

61. Homer Hoyt, *One Hundred Years of Land Values in Chicago, 1830–1930* (Chicago: University of Chicago Press, 1933), 148–49, 206, 231, 247, 301; *Olcott's Land Values Blue Book of Chicago, 1909–1930* (Chicago: G. C. Olcott, 1909–30), 101; and Riess, *Touching Base*, 98.

62. Benson, *Ballparks*, 88; Bukowski, *Baseball Palace*, 17; Lindberg, "Through the Years," 3; and Ritter, *Lost Ballparks*, 30–31.

63. Benson, *Ballparks*, 88; Bukowski, *Baseball Palace*, 17; Lindberg, "Through the Years," 3; Ritter, *Lost Ballparks*, 30–31.

64. *Chicago Record-Herald*, July 2, 1910.

65. *Chicago Tribune*, July 2, 1910.

66. *Chicago Record-Herald*, July 2, 1910. See also Bluthardt, "Fenway Park," 48, and Riess, *City Games*, 223, for further discussion of crowd control.

67. Hilton, "Comiskey Park," 3.

68. Riess, *City Games*, 223.

69. *Chicago Defender*, June 27, 1911.

70. Brown, *Chicago White Sox*, 102–3; Jerry Klinkowitz, ed., *Writing Baseball* (Urbana: University of Illinois Press, 1991); Ring Lardner, *You Know Me Al* (1914; rpt. New York: Charles Scribner's Sons, 1960); and Lindberg, "Through the Years," 6.

71. James T. Farrell, *My Baseball Diary* (New York: A. S. Barnes, 1957), 8.

72. Ibid., 60.

73. Edward B. Moss, "The Fan and His Ways," *Harper's Weekly*, June 11, 1910, 13. Also quoted in Riess, *Touching Base*, 24. Yet this public space was mediated by owners seeking to promote a particular vision of baseball that reflected their conception of what would sell. As Warren Goldstein points out, "The democracy of the national pastime could be celebrated only by those who did not play the game and therefore *could* experience the ballpark exclusively as an arena of play." Goldstein, *Playing for Keeps*, 149.

74. *Denni Hlasatel*, September 16, 1911; and *Svornost*, April 8, 1890, in *Chicago Foreign Language Press Survey*, Chicago Public Library Omnibus Project (Chicago: The Project, 1942). See also Steven S. Riess, "Ethnic Sports," in *Ethnic Chicago: A Multicultural Reader*, ed. Melvin G. Holli and Peter d'A. Jones (Grand Rapids, Mich.: William B. Eerdmans, 1995), 529–56, 539–43, and Riess, *Touching Base*, 36–37, 189–91.

75. Riess, *Touching Base*, 189–91; and Nicholas Dawidoff, *The Catcher Was a Spy: The Mysterious Life of Moe Berg* (New York: Vintage Books, 1994), 61.

76. Farrell, *Baseball Diary*, 47.

77. From Charles S. Johnson, "Chicago Study, Migration Interviews," quoted in Grossman, *Land of Hope*, 89.

78. Donald Spivey, *Union and the Black Musician: The Narrative of William Everett Samuels and Chicago Local 208* (Boston: University Press of America, 1984), 21–22.

79. St. Clair Drake and Horace R. Cayton, *Black Metropolis: A Study of Negro Life in a Northern City*, vol. 1 (New York: Harcourt, Brace, 1945), 102. See also *Chicago Defender*, July 2, 1910, May 20, 1911, Aug. 5, 1911.

80. For further discussion of baseball and the construction of whiteness, see Nasaw, *Going Out*, 100; Peterson, *Only the Ball*, 14–15; and Riess, *City Games*, 103.

6

Serbs, Sports, and Whiteness

PETER T. ALTER

"Whiteness Studies" scholars examine what it means to be white. At first glance, it seems obvious that whites are white, and they have always been that way. But it is not that simple. An army of historians, sociologists, literary theorists, and others examine what whiteness signifies, how it has been "constructed," and how it changes across time and place. Essentially, they argue that whiteness is a concept that has been defined and redefined through our own actions, thoughts, belief systems, and social structures. Whiteness, then, is not biological but cultural and historical; like all ideas about race, it is neither static nor easily pinned down.

To be sure, many scholars find Whiteness Studies simplistic. Critics claim that whiteness scholars grossly misread their historical sources, make broad generalizations based on skimpy evidence, and treat data ahistorically.[1] Certainly, the question of race in twenty-first century American life is exceedingly complex, as ethnic, national, and religious groups struggle to define themselves. For example, in this post–September 11th world, Arabs and Arab Americans suddenly hear themselves called "sand niggers," a phrase that explicitly marks them as nonwhite. This raises questions: Who is white and who is not? How, why, and under what circumstances do these categories change? How is power apportioned according to racial status? Even beyond these issues, it is important to realize that race is only one topic in social and cultural studies, that other analytical categories include class, gender, and language, and that, above all, these categories are not fixed, but rather, they interact and overlap.

But what does this line of inquiry have to do with Chicago sports? Chicago, like many cities in the Midwest and East, received thousands of immigrants during the late nineteenth and early twentieth centuries, mostly from southern and eastern Europe. Chicago-area Serbs—who were not considered unequivocally white upon their arrival—serve as a case study to examine the methods by which an immigrant group became white. Serbian immigrants, during the early twentieth century, had a vibrant and active sporting culture, and they used athletics among other activities to combat stereotypes, to demonstrate that they belonged in the American mainstream—indeed, to prove that they were white.[2]

During the 1880s to the 1920s, many native-born Americans believed that Serbs, as well as other southern and eastern European immigrants, constituted a problem. The newcomers generally were Catholic, Orthodox, or Jewish. This diversity of faiths presented a major religious challenge to the predominantly Protestant American mainstream. The immigrants also did not speak English, which reformers believed threatened the American *lingua franca.* Furthermore, the newcomers were mostly from rural areas or villages, and were not accustomed to city life. Typically, these people had lived under authoritarian regimes with little exposure to western democratic institutions. Serbs had encountered prejudice before they ever got to America; neighboring peoples often feared them as war-like, nomadic, backward, savage, primitive, even non-Christian.[3] In the American context, discrimination developed more along lines of race, class, and citizenship. Race was crucial because, although many Americans dismissed Serbian immigrants as uncivilized, the law made all white people eligible for citizenship. Were Serbs (and other east Europeans) white? This was a crucial question because, as potential participants in American civic life, the newcomers raised deep fears among the native-born.

By the second decade of the twentieth century, after millions of new immigrants had arrived, Chicago experienced a crisis of race and citizenship. During the turmoil of World War I, fears arose of people from enemy nations living in the United States, of radicals undermining American democracy, and of violent labor strife (as seen in the steel and coal strikes of 1919). This crisis was particularly pronounced on the city's Southeast Side, where Serbian immigrants lived and worked in the area's steel industry. Local journals, such as the *South Works Review,* published by Illinois Steel (later United States Steel), decried the presence of non-

English-speaking hoards in their midst. A late 1918 *South Works Review* article claimed that unnaturalized steelworkers should leave the United States, because they posed a threat to the "growing [American] Republic." A poem published in the *Review* in the summer of 1921 extolled the virtues of the "American way," claiming that, upon becoming Americans, immigrants learned "How to keep . . . [their] home[s] clean and sanitary." Immigrants could leave behind their backward ways only if they accepted "100% Americanism." This acceptance, the *Review* wrote, meant rejecting their homeland culture and adopting "one country—one flag—one people; America for Americans first, last and all the time."[4]

Issues of culture and nationality were often inseparable from issues of race. The popular label for Serbs and other Slavic immigrants—"hunky" (*plural*, "hunkies")—incorporated all three. Hunkies were considered to be slow, stupid, dull, clannish, primitive, clumsy, and naive. This term came from a combination of Bohemian and Hungarian, Bohunk, and first appeared in print in the early 1900s. Idiomatic usage shortened Bohunk to hunky. While hunky's derivation came from a slang expression for either Czechs or Hungarians, native-born Americans used it as a blanket term for all Slavic immigrants. During the early twentieth century, hunky became popular throughout the Chicago area. Ironically, by the late 1960s, the Black Power movement changed hunky into "honky," a pejorative name for all whites.[5]

The novel *Hunky Johnny* (1945), written by Whiting, Indiana, native Edward J. Nichols, used this stereotype to examine Slavic immigrant whiteness. Nichols's protagonist was a twenty-five-year-old second-generation Slovak named Johnny Opalko living in Gary, Indiana, during the early 1930s. Johnny found himself upon a "fence—part white and part Hunky." Sports became a flashpoint for conflict in Johnny's life. Other Slavic members of the football team kicked Johnny off their squad for dating "white girls." A gridiron star at Gary's Froebel High School, Johnny later chose to play football for the University of Chicago rather than Northwestern University. Johnny's friends in Gary criticized him for jilting a premier athletic program for the smaller and academically more intense South Side institution. The children of Gary immigrants clearly saw sports as a path to success. The native-born American world, however, did not necessarily agree. Johnny's "white" girl friend, Jean Howland, roundly criticized sports, commenting, "Don't ever make a career fooling around with athletics, Johnny. Promise?" While Johnny enjoyed excelling on the playing field, he did not want to be known only for his physical abilities. He mocked people of his background in Gary who wanted him to play for Northwestern, saying, "Us Hunkies is great for da atleticks." But before the novel ends, Johnny decides—and note the wording here—that he is "through with trying to be anything white." He ceased dating women like Jean, abandoned his intellectual ambitions, and stopped thinking he was worth more than his physical talents.[6]

Native-born Americans were not the only ones who thought of Slavic immigrants as nonwhite. African Americans also used the term "hunky." For their major work on African American life in Chicago, *Black Metropolis*, Horace R. Cayton and St. Clair Drake interviewed an African American woman who lived in a multiracial neighborhood. She went so far as to equate hunkies and blacks: "We're not segregated here. Who are these 'hunkies' to segregate you? Most of them are as black as I am." According to her formulation, there was no difference between African Americans and Slavs. Both groups were "black," if not in skin color, at least in status.[7]

Like other groups lumped together as "hunkies," Chicago's Serbs were a distinct people. They practiced a form of Orthodox Christianity called Serbian Orthodoxy; they spoke and wrote Serbo-Croatian, a South Slavic language with two alphabets, Cyrillic and Latin; they were unfamiliar with American-style democratic government; and they knew little of cities, having come from rural portions of the Austro-Hungarian Empire (mostly from Kika-Krbava County in Croatia, where their ancestors had settled beginning in the seventeenth century). Chicago's earliest Serbian immigrants settled on the Southeast Side, in West Town, and in Gary, Indiana. Nationally, the Serbs developed an intricate network of mutual benefit societies that united by the 1930s into the Serbian National Federation. Chicago-based Palandech Press, the major Serbian publishing house in the United States, produced Serbian-language books and newspapers, such as *Balkanski Svijet* [Balkan World], for the Serbian immigrant community.[8]

West Town Serbs resided among other southern and eastern Europeans in what locals called "Polish downtown." The Serbian colony centered on Holy Resurrection Serbian Orthodox Church, next to Wicker Park. Holy Resurrection parishioners lived in the immediate area along Milwaukee Avenue, as well as north at the intersection of Clybourn and Fullerton Avenues. This community included Serbian restaurants, meat markets, bookstores, lodge halls, light industries, saloons, and newspaper offices. A second concentration of mostly working-class Serbs centered around St. Archangel Michael Serbian Orthodox Church, which opened in the 1920s on Chicago's Southeast Side. South Works steel mill in South Chicago, Wisconsin Steel in South Deering, and nearby Republic Steel, were the industrial giants of the region.[9]

South Chicago Neighborhood House (SCNH), a Baptist settlement house on the Southeast Side, worked to "save" local Serbs. The SCNH staff believed that the Baptist faith would Christianize the Serbs. In its biggest offensive against Serbs and other Slavic immigrants, the SCNH condemned them as "menaces to American Christian life" in 1935. The immigrants' religion, the SCNH staff believed, inhibited them from truly participating in American democracy and made them "hunkies." The staff concluded that neighborhood immigrants needed the SCNH's help in "turning white," and becoming civilized. One way to civilize them, the SCNH believed, was through sports. The staff organized "ball teams," and reserved nearby Bessemer Park's gymnasium for athletic events (they built their own gym in 1931). American sports, the SCNH staff argued, would bring these immigrants closer to white culture.[10]

The South Chicago Young Men's Christian Association (SCYMCA) implemented its own "Christian Citizenship Program" for Serbs and other immigrants. The SCYMCA's leaders focused their Americanization efforts on teaching English and citizenship, as well as American "ideals" and "standards of living." They hoped to produce immigrants who were "useful in their employment, intelligent in their citizenship and devoted to the common-weal of home and community"—in other words, people who lived and worked according to native-born American standards and participated in American democracy. Sports became a way to expose immigrants to this message. The SCYMCA sponsored lunchtime athletic events at the local steel mills. If the SCYMCA message did not reach the immigrant steelworkers, their children heard it at school. The SCYMCA set up an exercise program at South Chicago's Bowen High in 1920. A promotional pamphlet declared, "'Puny or strong, patriotic or disloyal, educated or illiterate, moral or untrustworthy, are the choices that America can make for her future citizens and all depends upon her treatment of the boy now.'" In other words, strong boys grew into strong men who rejected the anti-democratic and anti-Christian dogmas of their homelands to become real Americans.[11]

Serbs made up roughly 5 percent of Gary's population throughout the inter-war period. Founded by U.S. Steel in 1906 as a company town, the city was home to a colossal complex of steel mills called Gary Works. Two mainly Serbian neighborhoods developed in town, one on Connecticut Avenue between Nineteenth and Twenty-first Streets, and the other on Twenty-fifth Street west of Broadway. A mixed Slavic settlement, which included Serbs, centered on the railroad tracks in Northeast Gary, near Gary Works. Native-born Americans called the neighborhood "Hunkyville," and the quarter was said to consist of the "fifty cheapest houses" in the entire city. U.S. Steel characterized this area as "miserably unsanitary," and in 1908 ordered residents to vacate it.[12]

Over twenty years later, Hunkyville had not changed. According to a local journalist, "There is the living breathing, sweating, drinking, curs-

ing, laughing, singing Gary. This is the old world. Streets are narrow.
. . . Coffee houses, those rendezvous of the Balkans, shelter gossiping,
card playing men who read newspapers with Ls and Ps crazily inverted;
churches even bearing Byzantine domes, hawkers shouting their wares in
all versions of the bewildering jumble of tongues; children skip and run
half-naked in the streets, mothers sing to dark babies strange alien lul-
labies."[13] These seemingly uncivilized immigrants—mostly Serbs, here,
by the sound of it—drank, gambled, and swore while producing "dark"
offspring. Above all, language, religion, culture, and race have become
inseparable from each other in this passage.

Middle-class Serbian immigrants responded to anti-Serbian propa-
ganda by promoting a more positive image of Serbs through churches,
mutual benefit and singing societies, women's groups, and athletic teams
and leagues. Serbian immigrant leaders used Serbian nationality (srpstvo)
and Yugoslavism (which promoted the unification of all South Slavs,
Serbs, Croats, and Slovenes) to prove they were Christian, democratic,
freedom loving, progressive, thrifty, and most important, civilized. In
1926, Mihail M. Čivančević, a Serbian author, defined civilization and
democracy for Serbs in America. Čivančević pointed to ancient Athens as
the paragon of civilization and democracy As a Balkan people whose ancient culture was respected as the font of democracy in the United States,
the Greeks provided hope for the Serbs that Americans would someday
consider them civilized, too. Serbs, Čivančević concluded, needed to practice civil, religious, political, and individual freedoms before native-born
Americans would consider them civilized. Srpstvo, with its roots in Serbian Orthodoxy and the glorious past of the Serbian medieval kingdoms,
seemed logical ammunition in this war to make Serbs white. Supporters
of Yugoslavism sought the end of "tribal divisions" with the unification
of a single democratic South Slavic state. If Serbs belonged to an entity
such as a Yugoslav state, advocates in the United States argued, surely
they were civilized and democratic—not "hunkies."[14]

Sokols, Serbian gymnastics clubs, led the way in portraying Serbs
as full-fledged members of the American mainstream. Miroslav Tyrš,
a Czech nationalist, created the first sokol (falcon) in 1862, using the
German Turnverein (a nationalistic athletic organization) as his model.[15]
Tyrš formed the sokol in a time of Czech cultural revival and in response
to Habsburg suppression of Czech nationalistic expression. A Chicago-
based Slavic publication described the sokol's founding spirit as keeping
a nation's "physical training . . . in harmony with mental development."
A program for a sokol slet (rally) asserted that the movement combined,
"Health, strength, and bodily beauty together with sterling character,
justice, and culture." From its origins in Czech nationalism, the sokol

spread to other Slavic regions, including the Balkans, during the nineteenth and twentieth centuries. In 1908, the Austro-Hungarian Empire officially annexed Bosnia-Herzegovina from the Ottoman Empire, setting off an anti-Serb riot in the Bosnian capital Sarajevo. With Bosnia under the control of a Roman Catholic monarchy, the rioters reasoned, Serbs were an easy target for anti-Orthodox sentiment. Bosnian Serb *sokols* fought against this oppression by holding *sokol* demonstrations and promoting Serbs as civilized Christians.[16]

Serbs' claims to athletic prowess were in part based on the *hajduk* legends, a key element of Serbian identity, or *srpstvo*. *Hajduks*, the Serbian version of Robin Hood, symbolized the pinnacle of Serbian bravery in the face of Muslim Ottoman oppression. The *hajduks* ambushed the Ottoman Turks whenever possible, often robbing or killing them. The Ottomans were depicted as Muslim barbarians; the Serbs merely defended Christian civilization against them. *Hajduks*, whatever their methods, simply wanted to be free and civilized. Therefore, songs and poems celebrating *hajduks* proclaimed to the world that Christian Serbs defeated the infidel hordes. The Serbian immigrant *sokol* movement carried on this *hajduk* tradition by promoting a physically and mentally healthy Serb nation that was Christian, democratic, egalitarian, and civilized.[17]

In 1909, Serb immigrant supporters of the *sokol* gathered in Cincinnati and organized local *sokols* throughout the United States. One year later, using this meeting as a springboard, Gary Serbs organized the first and most prominent Chicago area *sokol* at St. Sava's. The main objectives of the Gary Serbian *sokol* were threefold: "to prepare for the Serbian and civic call," to become physically fit, and to stay morally upright. Only a year after its creation, Gary *sokol* leaders joined with other *sokols* to form a national organization for all Serbian *sokols*.[18]

Gary's *sokol* became the headquarters for the national Serbian *sokol* publication, entitled *Soko*.[19] A priest from St. Sava Church in Gary, Petar O. Stijačić, served as the journal's first editor. In *Soko*'s first year of publication, 1912, a Southeast Side Serbian priest, Paja Radosavljević, clearly proclaimed a basic *sokol* goal: "The Serbian *sokol* aims to promote democracy. They [*sokols*] accept old and young, poor and rich, teachers and merchants, doctors and laborers. Social and economic differences are erased." By stressing inclusion, Radosavljević displayed the *sokol*'s potential unifying power. *Sokols* promoted Serbian civilization by uniting immigrant Serbs around the common goal of staying physically fit in order to defend Serbia. This pride helped Chicago-area Serbs reject the hunky stereotype.[20]

In 1912, during the First Balkan War in which the Kingdom of Serbia fought, the national Serbian *sokol* organization called a meeting for Vidovdan (St. Vitus's Day, June 27) in Chicago.[21] Michael Pupin, a nationally known Serbian immigrant leader from New York's Columbia University, led the parade, along with the *starešina* (chief) of Gary's *sokol*, Mr. Grkovi. The parade thundered through the Serbian West Town Chicago neighborhood surrounding Holy Resurrection Church. The *sokols* marched to Serbian music and carried Serbian and American flags while chanting, "Gladly goes a Serb into the army." *Sokol* members, in their support of the Serbian Kingdom during the First Balkan War, used the language of democracy, claiming a Serbian victory meant a triumph for freedom and justice. Just as the two flags held high in parade symbolized the compatibility of Serbian and American nationalism, anti-radical sentiment united Serb and American patriots. At Holy Resurrection Church in 1913, several speakers discussed the Serbian war effort. V. Bornemissa, the editor of the Chicago-based Serbian socialist newspaper, *Narodni Glas* (People's Voice), called it the fratricidal Balkan War. He also claimed that the Serbian prime minister, Nikola Pašić, merely wanted to fill his pockets through war profiteering. Dušan Popović, a *starešina* of the West Town Serbian *sokol*, pushed Bornemissa from the stage. Another socialist speaker followed Bornemissa, and he too was banished from the auditorium. Once again, Serbs affiliated themselves with mainstream America by rejecting radicalism and embracing the "America First" ethos of the era.[22]

After World War I, however, a generational change became increasingly noticeable in the Serbian community. American-born Serbs had little enthusiasm for *sokol* gymnastics, associating it negatively with the *stari kraj* (the old country). *Sokol* leaders, in response to this lack of interest, applied their goals to American sports, mainly basketball and baseball, deemphasizing gymnastics. Chicago area Serbs formed teams and leagues within an organization called the Eagles for boys and men and the Eaglettes for girls and women. The St. Archangel Michael Church Eaglettes, for example, had thirty-four members from 1931 to 1934. The Eaglettes created a Serbian girls' basketball league for the Chicago region and sponsored occasional church fund-raisers.[23]

The Eagles of St. Archangel Michael formed both basketball and baseball teams. The Eagle men's basketball squad played other church teams, including Protestants from Chicago's Southeast and North Sides, and Roman Catholics from the Southeast Side. The Eagle men's baseball team played a Romanian immigrant squad occasionally and also faced a Slovenian nine. By playing these inter-ethnic and inter-religious contests, Serbs showed their willingness to mix with non-Serb athletes, thereby contradicting the old stereotype that hunkies were "clannish." Serbs also competed within their own group, and in 1931 the Southeast Side Serbian Eagles reigned as the country's Serbian baseball league champs.

13. *Serbian Men . . .* The Serbian Eagles men's baseball team, 1934. (From *Fiftieth Anniversary, 1919–1969, St. Archangel Michael Serbian Orthodox Church, Spomenica—Monument of the History of the Serbian Orthodox Church in South Chicago.*)

14. *. . . And Serbian Women.* The Serbian Eaglettes women's basketball team, 1935. (From *Fiftieth Anniversary 1919–1969, St. Archangel Michael Serbian Orthodox Church, Spomenica—Monument of the History of the Serbian Orthodox Church in South Chicago.*)

Baseball and basketball teams, such as those associated with Holy Resurrection Church, frequently raised money for their parish, reinforcing the ties between athletics and religion.[24] Other Serbian athletes and teams were held up as emblems of community morality. The Serbian National Federation (SNF) at once promoted athletic teams and established a moral code that condemned alcohol and promoted family life. Sports and morality were part of a package, and the SNF applied its moral aims to its sports programs.[25]

While Serbs formed their own sports leagues, teams, and clubs, they also actively participated in the Southeast Side industrial leagues based at Wisconsin Steel. Joe Kralj, a Serb and captain of the Wisconsin Steel football team, led his men in a gridiron battle during the 1938 Fourth of July celebration. Kralj also played on the Wisconsin Steel baseball squad. Another Serb, Michael Drakulich, a Wisconsin Steel employee and a baseball player, was known simply as the "popular catcher of No. 1 merchant Mill." Men like Kralj and Drakulich crossed a threshold when they played in such leagues. Playing the "national pastime," and being accepted on company teams, was an important symbolic step toward becoming American and becoming white. (In the company magazine, incidentally, Drakulich appeared proudly with his native-born American wife, the former Dorothy Price, who lived in South Deering's Trumbull Park housing project.) Other Slavic Americans played football for the "Real American Club." Founded in 1938 by South and Southeast Side men, the Real American Club fought the "foreign 'isms' such as communism, Nazism, and Fascism." The team brought together immigrants and their sons regardless of "nationality or creed" for fellowship and to display their support for American democracy.[26]

Fourteen years after the founding of the inter-war Yugoslav Kingdom of the Serbs, Croats, and Slovenes, the largest and most public proclamation of Yugoslav unity came with the Century of Progress World's Fair along Chicago's lakefront. From 1928 to 1933, leading members of Chicago's South Slavic communities, headed by Serbian publisher John R. Palandech, planned the Yugoslav Day festivities for July 2, 1933. Palandech strove to make Yugoslav Day as inclusive as possible. Benefit and fraternal societies from the three main Yugoslav groups—Serbs, Croats, and Slovenes—nominated delegates to serve on a committee that planned the festivities. The Yugoslav Committee operated within the larger Committee on Nationalities, which included representatives for most European immigrant groups, some Middle Eastern immigrants, and Chinese and Japanese immigrants. In urging wide participation, Palandech claimed, "The Jugoslav people . . . have always shown themselves loyal and patriotic citizens and have stood for everything that is of civic pride and benefit to Chicago."[27]

Yugoslav Day started at the Indian statues in Grant Park in downtown Chicago at 12:30 p.m. The well-known Croatian sculptor Ivan Mestrović had created these statues. Illinois Attorney General Otto Kerner Sr., himself a second-generation Czech, delivered the day's opening speech. After Kerner's remarks, a large procession moved from the Mestrović statues down to Soldier Field to continue the ceremony. A Yugoslav American Legion post consisting of World War I veterans, carried Yugoslav, Serbian, Croatian, Slovenian, and American flags. Following the veterans were *sokol* youth organizations and South Slavic choral, dance, fraternal, educational, musical, and civic organizations from all three main Yugoslav groups. The major local Serbian communities in Gary, southeast Chicago, and West Town and Serbian colonies from other parts of the country, such as Pittsburgh, all sent representatives.[28]

After the procession assembled on the field, a soccer match between Yugoslav and Polish teams took place. Following this contest, local Serbian and American politicians spoke. After these remarks, the *sokol*s conducted a gymnastics exhibition followed by Yugoslav choral, dance, and musical group performances. Miss Jugoslavia, the winner of a nationwide beauty contest, was also crowned. The Yugoslav day finale was the singing of "My Country 'Tis of Thee" by a Yugoslav woman. Roughly 3,000 Yugoslavs took part in the ceremonies, with a crowd estimated between 20,000 and 50,000. To get participants and spectators from southeast Chicago, the Yugoslav Committee chartered a train from South Chicago's Ninety-first Street station to downtown Chicago. About 250 Serbs reassembled at St. Archangel Michael Church for a banquet following the Soldier Field activities.[29]

"We can stage," Palandech wrote in 1928, "a celebration that would be of everlasting credit to our race." While local newspapers and Serbian, Croatian, and Slovenian colonies throughout the country proclaimed the Yugoslav Day celebration's virtues, the symbolism of the Yugoslav procession, organized by Palandech, a Serb, moving from Mestrović's Indian statues to Soldier Field is unmistakable. The Serbs and other Yugoslavs literally moved from the beautiful yet primitive images of the "red man" created by Mestrović, a Croat, to Soldier Field, where the Yugoslavs displayed their highly developed culture, through sport and music. City-owned Soldier Field was the ultimate public space for such an event; only acceptable groups could perform at this venue. Serbs and other Yugoslavs performing *sokol* gymnastics and playing soccer together illustrated that they were not inferior "hunkies"; rather, their people had a long tradition of athletic and cultural achievements that proved they rightfully belonged in the white American mainstream.[30] Centuries of Serbian literature, theater, religion, music, education, and athletic prowess displayed by the Serbs in West Town, Gary, and the Southeast Side affirmed Serbs' right to partake of American life. Even as they provided exciting entertainment, athletic events also invited participants and spectators to think of themselves as part of America's pluralistic culture. Sports were living performances of civilization and Christianity; athletes and spectators proved themselves just as American and just as white as anyone else.

Historically, whiteness is a moving target, constantly changing, never definitively articulated. This very ambiguity has made the need to be perceived as white—as not disfavored racially—all the more urgent for immigrants. Serbs asserted their right to be thought of as full-fledged Americans—and to be seen as white—not by denying their cultural heritage, but by ennobling it through public displays. Sports became an important part of this Americanizing, whitening, "civilizing" process, necessitated by the fact that the immigrant generation, while not seen as black, was not considered fully white either. Sports, then, were part of the immigrants' great cultural transformation.

Notes

1. Peter Kolchin, "Whiteness Studies: The New History of Race in America," *Journal of American History*, 89 (2002): 154–73; Eric Arnesen, "Whiteness and the Historians' Imagination," *International Labor and Working-Class History*, 60 (2001): 3–32.

2. Many whiteness studies critics argue that until the 1940s the word "race" meant only nationality, implying that race thinking was not well developed. However, evidence to the contrary exists. For example, Franz Boas, working in the early twentieth century, sought to prove that immigrants from various parts of Europe were not of different races. The United States Immigration Commission specifically rejected his claims. In this rejection, the commission demonstrated that it did not consider southern and eastern Europeans the same race as their northern and western European counterparts. See Lee Baker, *From Savage to Negro: Anthropology and the Construction of Race, 1896–1954* (Berkeley: University of California Press, 1998).

3. Kiril Petkov, *Infidels, Turks, and Women: The South Slavs in the German Mind, ca. 1400–1600* (Frankfurt am Main: Peter Lang, 1997), 20–21; Peter F. Sugar, "The Nature of the Non-Germanic Peoples under Habsburg Rule," *Slavic Review*, 22 (1963): 19; Wayne S. Vucinich, "The Serbs in Austria Hungary," *Austrian History Yearbook*, 3 (1967): 9–10; Ivo Banac, *The National Question in Yugoslavia: Origins, History, Politics* (Ithaca, N.Y.: Cornell University Press, 1984), 43, 89; Gunther Rothenberg, *The Austrian Military Border in Croatia, 1740–1881* (Chicago: University of Chicago Press, 1966), 59; Jill A. Irvine, *The Croat Question:*

Partisan Politics in the Formation of the Yugoslav State (Boulder, Colo.: Westview Press, 1993), 20; and Kosta Milutinović, *Vojvodina i Dalmacija, 1760–1914* (Novi Sad: Institute za istorije Vojvodine, 1973), 17.

4. *South Works Review,* July 1916, 9–10; December 1918, 11; June–July 1921, 9.

5. *A Dictionary of Americanisms,* s.v. "bohunk"; *Dictionary of American Regional English,* s.v. "honky"; *Random House Dictionary of American Slang,* s.v. "bohunk"; Emily Greene Balch, *Our Slavic Fellow Citizens* (New York: Charities Publication Committee, 1910), 7; Victor Greene, "Sons of Hunkies: Men With a Past," *Slovakia,* 16 (1966): 80–86; Victor Greene, "The Polish American Worker to 1930: The 'Hunky' Image in Transition," *Polish Review,* 21 (1976): 65–67; and Josephine Wtulich, *American Xenophobia and the Slav Immigrant: A Living Legacy of Mind and Spirit* (Boulder, Colo.: Eastern European Monographs, 1994), 39–70, 89.

6. Edward J. Nichols, *Hunky Johnny* (Boston: Houghton Mifflin, 1945), 5, 38, 95, 190–99, 210.

7. Horace R. Cayton and St. Clair Drake, *Black Metropolis* (London: Jonathan Cape, 1946), 180; and Thaddeus Radzialowski, "The Competition for Jobs and Racial Stereotypes: Poles and Blacks in Chicago," *Polish American Studies,* 33 (1976): 117.

8. Peter T. Alter, "The Serbian Great Migration: Serbs in the Chicago Region, 1880s to 1930s" (Ph.D. diss., University of Arizona, 2000).

9. Edith Abbott, *The Tenements of Chicago, 1908–1935* (Chicago: University of Chicago Press, 1936), 353; Irving Cutler, *The Jews of Chicago: From Shtetl to Suburb* (Urbana: University of Illinois Press, 1996), 233; and *Lakeside Directory of Chicago* (1910 and 1917).

10. *Daily Calumet,* December 28, 1935; and E. Slaught, "South Chicago Neighborhood House, 1939," in South Chicago Neighborhood House Papers, Southeast Historical Museum, Chicago, Illinois.

11. *The Official Bulletin, Annual Review Number* (Feb.-Mar. 1921), 19; "A Matter of Community Pride" (1926), in South Chicago Young Men's Christian Association Papers in Southeast Historical Museum. Also see, for example, Thomas Winter, "Contested Spaces: The YMCA and Workingmen on the Railroads, 1877–1917"; and Nina Mjagkij, "True Manhood: The YMCA and Racial Advancement, 1890–1930," in *Men and Women Adrift: The YMCA and the YWCA in the City,* ed. Nina Mjagkij and Margaret Spratt (New York: New York University Press, 1997), 65–85 and 138–59.

12. Raymond A. Mohl and Neil Betten, *Steel City: Gary, Indiana, 1906–1950* (New York: Holmes and Meier, 1986), 10–11; Ronald D. Cohen, *Children of the Mill: Schooling and Society in Gary, Indiana, 1906–1960* (Bloomington: Indiana University Press, 1989), 9–12.

13. Arthur Shumway, *The American Parade* (1929), quoted in Powell A. Moore, *The Calumet Region: Indiana's Last Frontier* (Indianapolis: Indiana Historical Bureau, 1959), 398–99.

14. For this translation of *srpstvo,* see *Novi Englesko-Hrvatski i Hrvatsko-Engleski Rječnik* (Milwaukee: Caspar Krueger Dory, 1926), 403. Although this was a Croatian dictionary, Serbian immigrants also used it widely. See also *Etimologijski rječnik hrvatskoga ili srpskoga jezika* (Zagreb: Jugoslavenska akademija znanosti i umjetnosti, 1973) for a discussion of *srpstvo* and its origins as a "modern abstraction." *Amerikanksi Srbobran* [*Kalendar*], 1926, 66–70; and Joseph

J. Barton, "Eastern and Southern Europeans," in *Ethnic Leadership in America,* ed. John Higham (Baltimore: Johns Hopkins University Press, 1978), 168–69.

15. Falcons, in Slavic mythology, represent speed, endurance, and fortitude.

16. *Slavs with Special Reference to Americans of Slav Ancestry, Souvenir Edition* (Chicago: New Generation, 1933), 38; *American Sokol Slet,* June 29, 1947; *Spomenica Petdesetgodišnjice Srpskog Pravoslavnog Saveza, 1901–1951, Srbobrana* (Pittsburgh: n.p., 1951), 18–19; and *Karađorđe: Srpski Narodni Kalendar* (1928), 27.

17. *First All-Slavic Singing Festival: Given by the United Slavic Choral Societies, Sunday December 9, 1934 . . . at the Chicago Civic Opera House . . . Representing the Following Groups, Czechoslovakia (Czechs and Slovaks), Poland, Russia, Ukraine, Yugoslavia (Croats, Serbians, and Slovenes), 1,500 Singers* (Chicago: National Print and Publishing Company, 1934), 8; and Miodrag Stojanović, *Hajduci i klefti u narodnom pesništvu* (Beograd [Belgrade]: Srpska akedemija nauka i umetnosti, 1984), 32.

18. Pero Slepčević, *Srbi u Americi: beleške o njihovu stanju, radu i nacionalnoj verdnosti* (Geneva: Ujedinjenja, 1917), 71–76; and *St. Sava Serbian Orthodox Church: Our Religious Heritage in America, 1914–1964, Gary, Indiana* (Chicago: Palandech Press, 1964), 83–84.

19. The Serbo-Croatian words *soko* and *sokol* both mean falcon; the difference in spelling merely stems from Serbo-Croatian dialectic variations.

20. *St. Sava Serbian Orthodox Church,* 83–84; and *Soko,* May 1, 1912 (Chicago Foreign Language Press Survey) (CFLPS).

21. On Vidovdan three major events in Serbian history took place: the Battle of Kosovo Polje in 1389, when the Ottomans defeated and subjugated the Serbian kingdom, the assassination of the Archduke Franz Ferdinand in Sarajevo in 1914, and the adoption of the constitution to create inter-war Yugoslavia in 1918.

22. *Soko: List Srpski Sokola u Americi Vidovdanski Broj,* 20–24; *Radnička Straža,* July 30, 1913 (CFLPS); and *St. Sava Serbian Orthodox Church,* 83–84.

23. *Daily Calumet,* May 14, 1936; Steven A. Riess, *City Games: The Evolution of American Urban Society and the Rise of Sports* (Urbana: University of Illinois Press, 1989), 100.

24. *St. Archangel Michael Serbian Orthodox Church: Fiftieth Anniversary, 1919–1969, Spomenica—Monument of the Serbian Orthodox Church in South Chicago* (Chicago: n.p., 1969), 294–95; *Daily Calumet,* December 8, 1931, January 4, 1932, January 19, 1933, and August 21, 1933; Adam Popović, Scrapbook (CFLPS); *Memorial Book Srpsko Jedinstvo, 1936,* 26 (CFLPS); and National Federation Minute Books of the Official Committee (1939), 447, Immigration History Research Center, Minneapolis, Minnesota.

25. Serbian National Federation Combined Minute Books of the Official Committee, 447; Serbian National Federation Membership Records; Serbian National Federation, Combined Minute Books of the Official Committee, March 4, April 2, May 5, September 4, November 5, 1930, January 5, 1931, February 1, May 6, 1932, February 1, April 6, 1935, Immigration History Research Center; and *Daily Calumet,* June 28, 1926.

26. *Wisconsin Steel Sparks,* July 1938, 8; March 1939, 8; August, 1939, 10; *Calumet Index,* September 29, October 5, December 15, 1938.

27. *Daily Calumet,* June 24, 1933; John R. Palandech to Jugoslav Section, June 4, 1928; June 13, 1928, "List of Appointees of Foreign Races," April 3, 1928;

"Committee on Nationalities, Resolution," May 15, 1929, Century of Progress Papers, Special Collections, University of Illinois at Chicago, Chicago, Illinois.

28. "Yugoslav Day, Press Release," June 30, 1933, Century of Progress Papers; *Daily Calumet*, June 24, 1933.

29. *Chicago Daily Times*, June 30, 1933; *Chicago Tribune*, June 30, 1933; *Chicago Herald Examiner*, June 30, 1933; *Chicago Daily News*, June 30, 1933; "Yugoslav, Press Release," June 30, 1933, Century of Progress Papers; and *Daily Calumet*, June 24, June 30, July 5, 1933.

30. John R. Palandech to Jugoslav Section, August 10, 1928, Century of Progress Papers.

7

"A Dirty Rotten Shame"

The Black Sox Scandal and American Culture

DANIEL A. NATHAN

Few sports stories are as enduring as the Black Sox scandal, which, after more than eighty years, has lost almost none of its resonance, its ability to stoke debates and fire imaginations. The scandal resonates with other moments of betrayal and disillusionment and it is often cited as the equivalent of Watergate in American political history. Both events shocked the entire country, though the Black Sox scandal was a distinctly local event, rooted in a specific place, one well known for winking at chicanery and corruption. But for many Chicagoans, particularly South Siders who rooted for the White Sox, it was—and is—hard to believe that several prominent members of the team conspired with gamblers to lose the 1919 World Series to the Cincinnati Reds. It continues to reverberate, even after the White Sox won the World Series in 2005, beating the Houston Astros, four games to none. A few weeks before the team's victory, Melissa Isaacson of the *Chicago Tribune* correctly observed: "Like Al Capone, the Black Sox scandal remains deeply embedded in Chicago lore, a tale that, with age, grows more intriguing." Later, when the final out was recorded and an eighty-eight-year championship drought had come to an end, nonagenarian and Chicago institution Studs Terkel argued that "We cannot say that a chapter of infamy is over. This is because the players of that infamous team of eighty-six years ago remain on the outside." No doubt, infamy dies hard. More important, the Black Sox scandal has remained vibrant because it offered an occasion to ponder important issues—human frailty and moral responsibility, avarice and corruption, punishment and justice, among others. "To this day," writes sports columnist Frank Deford, "the Black Sox remain a melancholy part of American cultural history, and the whole conflicted saga continues to fascinate us—and affect us, too. Never mind Shoeless Joe Jackson. Pete Rose yet suffers as much from the dark shadows cast by 1919 as from his own modern sins."[1] Rather than provide a detailed accounting of the scandal itself, this essay briefly traces some of the most important and enduring ways it has been remembered and represented in the time since it occurred.

From the beginning, the events that would eventually be known as the Black Sox scandal and the Big Fix were clouded in uncertainty, which probably contributed to the subject's allure as a public spectacle. Uncertainty remains as to who played to the best of their ability during the 1919 World Series, who accepted money from gamblers, who knew what and when. "One thing at least is certain about the 1919 Series," writes archivist Steven P. Gietschier, "and that is that the whole truth will never be known. The principals have gone to their graves, and the evidence that survives is confusing and inconclusive."[2] That, and the fact that in October 1919 the White Sox, led by outfielder "Shoeless" Joe Jackson, pitcher Eddie Cicotte, and second baseman Eddie Collins, were favored to beat the Reds in the World Series but lost, five games to three. (For three years—1919 to 1921—the World Series was a best-of-nine games affair.) The Sox lost four of the first five games, rallied to win two in a row in Cincinnati, but lost the Series on October 9, when the Reds scored four runs in the first inning on their way to 10–5 victory at Comiskey Park.[3]

Many Chicagoans, especially White Sox team owner Charles A. Comiskey and manager William "Kid" Gleason, were bitterly disappointed by the Series outcome. Often brilliant during the regular season, Eddie Cicotte and Claude "Lefty" Williams were unusually erratic on the pitching mound. For example, Cicotte won a league best twenty-nine games with a sterling 1.82 ERA in 1919, but during the World Series he was 1–2, gave up seven earned runs in 21 ⅔ innings, and made several dreadful plays in the field. In addition, Eddie Collins (the so-called Clean Sox because he was uninvolved in the scandal), first baseman Arnold "Chick" Gandil (who organized much of the plot), shortstop Charles

"Swede" Risberg, and centerfielder Oscar "Hap" Felsch, generally played poorly. However, Joe Jackson, third baseman George "Buck" Weaver, and rookie pitcher Dickie Kerr were impressive: Jackson had a World Series record twelve hits (including the only home run during the series) and a .375 batting average, Weaver hit and fielded well, and Kerr won both games he pitched.[4]

A little less than a year later—after the publication of some damning newspaper articles in the *New York Evening World* by the journalist Hugh Fullerton, and as rumors of wrongdoing persisted—Cicotte, Williams, and Jackson testified before a Cook County grand jury about the fixed World Series. Cicotte and Williams confessed that they had conspired with gamblers to lose the series. Jackson explained that he knew of the scam and had unwillingly accepted $5,000 in bribe money, but that he had played to win. It is an apocryphal story, but Jackson was supposedly confronted by a disillusioned street urchin on the steps of the courthouse after his testimony. "It ain't true is it, Joe?" the youngster asked, to which Jackson replied, "Yes, kid, I'm afraid it is."[5] Jackson, it must be noted, always denied that anything like this ever occurred.[6] Nonetheless, this exchange aptly encapsulates how millions of people felt distraught after learning about the Sox's duplicity. As the Chicago writer Nelson Algren later put it, they were "Benedict Arnolds! Betrayers of American Boyhood, not to mention American Girlhood and American Womanhood and American Hoodhood."[7]

All told, eight ballplayers—including Buck Weaver, who forever denied being involved in the scheme—were implicated in the mess. It was news that sent shockwaves of disbelief and indignation across the country. From late September 1920, when the story broke, to early August 1921, when the players were banished, reporters wrote millions of words about the event in newspapers all over the country and scores of editorial cartoons illustrated the scandal's importance (at least to those in the media).

Eventually, the Black Sox and a handful of gamblers received their day in court. It was a strange trial, even by Chicago standards. The novelty of major league ballplayers on trial caused a great deal of public excitement and media interest. Indeed, the *Chicago Herald and Examiner* claimed that a riot was narrowly averted "when 500 men and boys besieged the entrance of the courtroom seeking admission."[8] To add to the drama, the prosecution announced that the ballplayers' original confessions and their immunity waivers had mysteriously disappeared from the state's attorney's office. As a result, Cicotte, Jackson, and Williams recanted their confessions, which were nonetheless read into the record by court reporters. From a legal standpoint, it did not seem to matter. The very nature of the indictments, which outlined five separate conspiracies, made it

15. *"Shoeless" Joe Jackson, 1917.* The great White Sox out-fielder batted .356 over thirteen seasons before his banishment from the game. (Courtesy of the Chicago History Museum.)

difficult for the prosecution to convict the defendants. Furthermore, the judge's instructions to the jury—he explained that the state had to prove that it was the intent of the defendants to defraud the alleged victims identified in the indictments and the public, not merely to intentionally lose the World Series—made a guilty verdict unlikely.

On August 2, 1921, the ballplayers and gamblers were acquitted of all charges. It took the jury one ballot and less than three hours to reach its verdict.[9] While it was a somewhat predictable, even anticlimactic decision, the defendants, their attorneys, and many of the baseball fans in the courtroom were jubilant. The next day, however, baseball commissioner

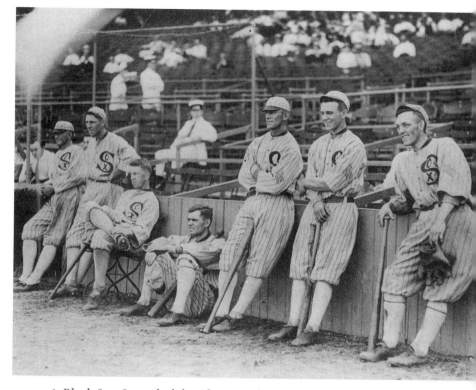

16. *Black Sox.* Several of the Chicago White Sox at the 1919 World Series, including outfielder Joe Jackson on the far left, and third baseman Buck Weaver on the far right. (Courtesy of the Chicago History Museum.)

Judge Kenesaw Mountain Landis, a baseball-loving federal judge who had been hired by nervous team owners in November of 1920 to lend the game the appearance of integrity, declared that all of the ballplayers involved in the incident would be permanently ineligible to play organized baseball.[10] Landis was widely hailed for his decision. One newspaper headline pronounced, "All Agree with Landis."[11] Despite many attempts by some of the ballplayers and their supporters, Landis's ruling has never been reversed. In 1989, baseball commissioner A. Bartlett Giamatti turned down a request to reinstate Joe Jackson, explaining that he did not "wish to play God with history."[12]

In retrospect, the Black Sox scandal happened for a number of complicated reasons. By 1919, there had been a long history of baseball players and gamblers associating with one another; fixed games were nothing new, even if we cannot know precisely how common they were.[13] However, with a few exceptions, the lords of the game chose to ignore or inadequately punish such malfeasance. Moral laxity and a lack of leadership fostered conditions in which game fixing could continue. Moreover, professional baseball had been plagued by exceedingly poor labor-management relations for decades. Many major leaguers felt they were exploited by their employers, partly due to the reserve clause, which was first instituted in 1879 and bound players to their teams indefinitely.[14] This situation engendered a sense of powerlessness and bitterness on the part of some ballplayers. Finally, the 1919 White Sox were beset by tremendous internal dissension and fractiousness: one faction, comprised almost entirely of poorly educated working-class men from rural communities, barely spoke to their teammates and harbored deep enmity toward Comiskey, their penurious employer. (The extent of Comiskey's tightfistedness and the degree of his culpability for the game fixing are often subjects of debate.) All of these conditions helped make the Big Fix possible.

Many have observed that this infamous scandal represented a moment of crisis and transformation. In addition to fostering changes within the organization of the game itself, the Black Sox affair may have affected the way many Americans perceived not only the national pastime, but the nation itself. One critic, George Grella, even suggested that the scandal "may have been more important than World War I in educating the nation in the dubious lessons of disenchantment."[15] In a similar vein, the literary critic Cordelia Candelaria maintains that the Big Fix "marks a crucial milestone in U.S. sociohistory. Before the scandal, baseball's contamination by business and gambling was regarded as minor but necessary evils in a supposedly free-market economy. Afterwards, the painfully disillusioned public could no longer keep up the pretense of the sport's arcadian purity."[16] The historian Donald Honig simply maintains that the Black Sox have become "to baseball history what Benedict Arnold is to American history."[17] Some of these claims may be hyperbolic, but the fact remains that ever since the fixing of the World Series was revealed, many Americans have been mesmerized by the story.

This fascination has been expressed in numerous ways. Most obvious, it can be indexed by the amount of media attention the Black Sox scandal received at the time—and has ever since. From the beginning, the scandal garnered voluminous amounts of newspaper coverage, which usually constructed the event as one of deception, betrayal, and moral disorder. Most journalists and editors tended to see the episode in relatively stark terms: avaricious, depraved ballplayers and gamblers were responsible for the debacle, which made victims of virtually everyone else, including Charles Comiskey, the so-called Clean Sox, like Eddie

Collins and catcher Ray Schalk, the victorious Cincinnati Reds, who had their World Series victory besmirched, and of course baseball fans everywhere. In many ways, it was an ideal news story, combining melodrama, celebrity, and scandal.

Reading the newspaper coverage of the Black Sox scandal today, one can discern many themes, patterns, and tropes. The idea that baseball needed to be "cleansed" was commonly articulated. Occasionally one could detect an undercurrent of anti-Semitism in the media's coverage, as several of the gamblers implicated in the Big Fix were Jewish.[18] But the most frequent and important way in which the media crafted the Black Sox scandal was as a crime story of seemingly epic proportions. Narrating the event in this manner brought the principals and issues into dramatic focus, and effectively simplified the event, which was in reality far from uncomplicated.

First and foremost, the language the press used to tell the "story of the most gigantic sporting swindle in the history of America," as the *New York Tribune* put it, made it clear that the Black Sox affair was *the* crime story of the moment.[19] The *Chicago Tribune* described the tale as "a drama that a scenario writer might well name 'The Great Double Cross.'"[20] Nationally syndicated sportswriter Grantland Rice argued that the individuals "mixed up in this crookedness are worse than thieves and burglars. They are the ultimate scum of the universe, and even the spotted civilization of the present time has no place for them outside of a penitentiary."[21] Clearly beyond the pale of respectable society, the indicted ballplayers and gamblers were quickly vilified and transformed into national objects of disgrace.

With the benefit of hindsight, we can see how the media coverage of the Black Sox scandal was gendered. For those who read about the thrown World Series in the daily press, the scandal offered an extraordinarily dramatic, ongoing narrative written by men, about men, for men. In a sense, it was something akin to a masculine melodrama. By revealing the ugly reality behind baseball's virtuous facade, the scandal made a mockery of the "manly" values the game supposedly upheld. The affair cast its leading actors in various well-known roles. The implicated players were simultaneously depicted as wayward boys (i.e., failed men) and avaricious ingrates. In sharp contrast to his corrupt teammates, Eddie Collins continued to personify baseball's All-American masculine ideal, while White Sox team owner Charles Comiskey embodied the betrayed benefactor, and Judge Kenesaw Mountain Landis became a stern, unforgiving patriarch and baseball's moral savior.

Like many newspapers, the *Chicago Herald and Examiner* was deeply troubled by the verdict in the Black Sox trial. The court's judgment, declared an editorial, "affects every boy in America. Very few of them have any clear conception of the league of nations, or the Penrose bill to make Secretary Mellon the arbiter of our financial destiny, or the problems of the Pacific. But all of them, from Maine to Oregon, will soon learn the verdict in this trial. They will draw their own conclusions. How much preaching and practice by parents, principals and parsons will be required to efface the effect of the conclusions they draw?"[22] This editorial makes clear the anxiety about masculinity that the scandal highlighted. The Big Fix was a meaningful social drama for many Americans because it brought their concerns about middle-class standards of appropriate manly behavior to center stage. The fact that, in the end, the dishonorable players were expelled, that Eddie Collins remained untainted, that Charles Comiskey survived, his reputation for integrity intact, and that Judge Landis had given professional baseball his imprimatur of moral rectitude, made it a satisfying spectacle for the millions of Americans who followed it in the news.

Eventually, all media stories fade and are displaced. Narratives of the Black Sox scandal were no exception. After the implicated White Sox were acquitted in 1921—and Judge Landis immediately dashed any hopes they may have had about being reinstated—the media found new stories to cover. Nevertheless, memories of the Black Sox scandal lived on in the decades immediately following the event. Perhaps most famously, F. Scott Fitzgerald used the Black Sox scandal and the enigmatic Meyer Wolfsheim—Jay Gatsby's nefarious benefactor, commonly believed to have been modeled on Arnold Rothstein, the notorious Jewish "sportsman" and gambler associated with the scandal—in *The Great Gatsby* (1925) to drive home the oft-repeated theme of moral failure.

Sometimes Black Sox memories could be more somber and less judgmental. Whenever someone associated with the Big Fix died, for example, his obituary became an opportunity for Black Sox remembrance. On January 2, 1933, Kid Gleason, the White Sox's manager during the 1919 World Series, died at the age of sixty-seven after a long illness. Gleason's passing did not elicit a great deal of media attention, but eulogizers employed a familiar narrative to describe his post–Black Sox scandal years. The *New York Times* noted: "After the revelations of the 1919 World's Series between the White Sox and the Cincinnati Reds reached the public, the shock of that scandal which involved his players kept Gleason on a sick bed for a long period. His life was despaired of more than once."[23] Gleason, whom the *Times* described as "one of the most picturesque figures in baseball," apparently never fully recovered from the shock of the World Series scandal, despite "his great vitality." At the time of his death, Gleason, like virtually everyone caught in the web of the scandal, was firmly ensconced in Black Sox memories. Thirty years later, Eliot Asinof, a former minor league ballplayer and the author of the widely respected *Eight Men Out: The Black Sox and the 1919 World Series* (1963), maintained that Gleason was "fully aware of how severe a blow he had suffered. He had tried to cover it up with toughness, to forget the old and build up the new. But memories of the betrayal smothered him."[24] Portrayed by eulogizers and historians as a victim of treachery, Gleason remains a depressing example of how the Big Fix made the innocent suffer.

Every so often journalists revived the story, as when John Lardner asked *Saturday Evening Post* readers in 1938, "Remember the Black Sox?"[25] Representative of many Black Sox scandal stories written at the time and for years to come, Lardner's piece vilified the gamblers for the calamity, condemned the ballplayers for their duplicity, disloyalty, and stupidity, and suggested that the whole episode was safely consigned to the past, that baseball's present and future had been purged of such perfidy. But Lardner also suggested that remembering the Black Sox scandal necessarily engaged memories of supposedly heroic men who had failed a generation of American boys and were made to suffer for it. Lardner's article reminded readers that the love of money is the root of all (or at least most) evil, thereby reaffirming the need to keep to the straight and narrow.

Told in such a didactic manner, the scandal was a cautionary tale for boys. As the film critic Richard Schickel puts it: "There was a time when the Black Sox Scandal was central to the moral education of young American males. The fact that it involved baseball players—members of the 1919 Chicago White Sox—who conspired with gamblers to throw the World Series (no less) struck at the very center of boyhood. The fact that the consequence of the act was so dire—permanent banishment from baseball—in comparison with the paltry rewards (a few thousand dollars to each man) imparted ironic force to the story." The scandal, Schickel continues, "was turned by fathers into a parable that helped set several generations of sons on the path of righteousness."[26]

Baseball commissioner Landis ruled the professional game with an iron hand until his death in 1944, so the version of the Black Sox scandal he sought to convey remained alive for almost a quarter of a century. Because he occupied a prominent position, was widely respected, and had a flair for public relations, Landis exerted more influence than any other individual or institution in maintaining a particular remembrance of the affair. In his rendering of it, the Big Fix was an aberrant moral crisis, instigated by avaricious men, and a national tragedy, one that his tireless vigilance would not permit again. Just as Landis brought order to baseball itself, he did much to stabilize individual and collective memories of the event that brought him to power. This is not to suggest that Landis completely controlled how events were remembered. He did not, which is perhaps best illustrated by the different ways some people understood and recalled Joe Jackson and Buck Weaver.

In the decades immediately after the World Series scandal, Joe Jackson represented numerous, sometimes conflicting things. Clearly, he was still widely recognized as a ballplayer endowed with superior natural ability.[27] To at least one constituency, his family and friends, Jackson was shy, unassuming, and considerate. To many others, Jackson was a naive busher, a dupe, a pathetic simpleton. For still others, Jackson represented the worst sort of treachery, deceit, and betrayal; to these people, he was baseball's Judas, its Benedict Arnold. Yet this was (and is) far from the case in Jackson's native South, where a resilient counter-memory of Jackson existed. For more than ten years after his expulsion from the Majors, Jackson played under his own name in the semiprofessional South Georgia League and in numerous promotional contests, where he was advertised in posters and treated warmly by fans.[28] In 1932, Jackson was the subject of a where-are-they-now article by Ward Morehouse, who described Jackson as "clear-eyed, ruddy-faced, big-bellied, slow-moving, soft spoken," and he noted that in Greenville, South Carolina, Jackson's home town, "this ballplaying country boy remains something of a hero. That 1919 business is forgotten. Whatever Joe's cronies may have thought then, they now regard him as a baseball genius who got a tough break."[29] Morehouse's article was corroborated five years later by Richard McCann's "Baseball Remains Joe Jackson's First Love 17 Years After Ban." According to McCann, Jackson "is a respected citizen and a beloved neighbor here [in Greenville]. They just can't believe that Joe did anything wrong. Not their Shoeless Joe."[30] To express their civic pride in Jackson, the people of Brandon Mills, South Carolina twice held "Joe Jackson Night" in the 1940s to celebrate their native son's birthday.[31] Not long after one of those celebrations, *The Sporting News* published a sympathetic article that noted the "gift-bearing delegation of well-wishers at the surprise birthday party was typical of the boys who make almost daily pilgrimages to Joe's home or gang around him in the streets and on sandlots."[32] It is an observation that undercuts the notion that Jackson betrayed and disillusioned the youth of America, or at least the boys in Greenville.

For communities and individuals who saw him as a convenient scapegoat, as a sacrificial lamb, as an icon of victimization—exploited by Charles Comiskey, ensnared by (Jewish) city slickers, punished extralegally by commissioner Landis—Jackson evoked powerful and resilient counter-memories of the Black Sox scandal. These counter-memories resisted the hegemonic version of the Big Fix—which placed blame solely on the players and gamblers—that the baseball establishment and much of the media promulgated. "To the local folk," writes Eliot Asinof, Jackson was always "a hero, well liked and highly respected. He was never without their support, and the dignity of his talent never seemed to dwindle."[33] In fact, it seems likely that Jackson was popular with and respected by some people partly due to his expatriate, outlaw status. The day before he died, Jackson allegedly told an old Greenville friend: "I don't deserve this thing that's happened to me."[34] Those who embraced counter-memories of the Black Sox scandal no doubt agreed.

Buck Weaver likewise engendered counter-memories of the Black Sox scandal, especially on Chicago's south side where he lived until his death in 1956. Weaver—who by all accounts did not take the money offered him to participate in the conspiracy, who played well in the 1919 World Series, and who made several unsuccessful attempts to return to Major League Baseball—was generally treated with respect, warmth, and sympathy by those in his community. During the years immediately after his expulsion, it was not uncommon for Weaver to "go out to the baseball diamonds at Washington Park . . . and hit fly balls to the kids," writes Irving M. Stein in *The Ginger Kid: The Buck Weaver Story* (1992). "They loved Buck and he returned their affection."[35] In 1927, recognizing that Weaver was still a talented ballplayer and a popular local celebrity, representatives of the Mid-West League, a semipro circuit in and around Chicago, voted unanimously to welcome Weaver as a player.[36] During the course of his first Mid-West League season, Weaver was greeted with enthusiasm by thousands of Chicagoans. Twice that summer Weaver was honored with floral tributes and gifts.[37] Stein writes that over the years the local media "sporadically focused on Weaver's situation expressing both sympathy and sorrow. Baseball fans in Chicago, in poll after poll, vouchsafed their confidence in Buck by naming him their choice as the best third baseman in Chicago baseball history. While Buck was still playing semipro ball, south siders set up booths on busy street corners asking passersby to sign petitions asking for his reinstatement."[38] At one point, those petitions numbered thirty thousand signatures.[39] Like Jackson, Weaver was widely seen as a scapegoat. For those who remembered Weaver as a victim of circumstance, as an innocent entangled in a plot he rejected, as a man who refused to be an informer, as someone who was treated unfairly by a baseball commissioner who would not recognize different degrees of culpability, the Black Sox scandal was something other than a simple morality play.[40]

The Black Sox scandal has long intrigued writers—and more recently, a handful of filmmakers and Web page creators—because of its moral complexity, narrative power, and commercial potential.[41] Scores of jour-

17. *Buck Weaver.* The third baseman was one of the most
popular White Sox. Though banned from the game with the
others, Weaver always maintained that he was innocent, and
he pointed to his errorless fielding and .324 batting average
during the 1919 World Series as proof. (Courtesy of the Chicago
History Museum.)

nalists, poets, playwrights, novelists, and historians have reconstructed
the scandal and put it to various uses. One can feel the anguish of the
banished ballplayers in Nelson Algren's prose poem "The Swede Was a
Hard Guy" (1942) and hear clear echoes of the affair in Bernard Malamud's
The Natural (1952). By using magical realism, W. P. Kinsella resurrects Joe
Jackson in *Shoeless Joe* (1982), the novel on which Phil Alden Robinson's

popular film, *Field of Dreams* (1989), is based. For those interested in more critically alert narratives, consider the dueling versions of the event in Harry Stein's book *Hoopla* (1983) and in John Sayles's film *Eight Men Out* (1988), which loosely follows Eliot Asinof's eponymous book.

While less well known than the aforementioned texts, Arnold Hano's novel *The Big Out* (1951), which is dedicated to Joe Jackson, is especially interesting, for it also creatively uses the Black Sox scandal to exemplify how popular culture texts are ultimately political. Hano's book focuses on Brick Palmer, a veteran catcher who is expelled from organized baseball when he is mistakenly caught up in a gambling scandal. (Brick's profligate brother, Johnny, forges Brick's name on a $10,000 betting slip, but Brick refuses to tell the truth because it would ruin his brother.) After much wandering around, Brick signs with an independent Canadian team, the Osage Outlaws. He plays well (despite the fact that his body is failing him), but the fans, his teammates, and the umpires all give him a hard time. It turns out the entire team is comprised of outlaws in a literal sense; all the players have been kicked out of organized baseball for various reasons, mostly acts of violence. Even the team's manager is a former Black Sox player who operates the team as a form of penance. The dramatic climax comes when a gambler makes Brick an offer to throw a game. Brick refuses and is badly beaten by thugs. Johnny reappears and nurses Brick the best he can. Though in tremendous pain, Brick plays the next day and gets the game-winning hit, thus earning the respect of his peers and the fans. For this pariah at least, unlike the actual Black Sox, there is some measure of redemption as readers quickly realize that all is not what it seems.[42]

Fascination with the Black Sox continues. During the 1990s alone, three new books about Joe Jackson were published, as were biographies of Buck Weaver and Kenesaw Mountain Landis.[43] Several baseball histories and encyclopedias devoted significant attention to the scandal.[44] And at least three dramas about the 1919 World Series scandal were staged: Thomas Perry's one-man play *Shoeless Joe*, Brian Cimmet's musical *Black Sox*, and Louis R. Hegeman's *The Trial of Buck Weaver and Shoeless Joe Jackson*.[45] Other works include William A. Cook's *The 1919 World Series: What Really Happened?* (2001), David L. Fleitz's *Shoeless: The Life and Times of Joe Jackson* (2001), and Phil Bildner's *Shoeless Joe and Black Betsy* (2002), a handsome children's book illustrated by C. F. Payne that tells the story of Jackson and his famous bat, Black Betsy—which, by the way, was sold on eBay in 2001 for over $577,000, believed to be the highest price ever paid for a single bat.[46] Even more recently, Gene Carney's *Burying the Black Sox: How Baseball's Cover-Up of the 1919 World Series Fix Almost Succeeded* (2006) and Susan Dellinger's *Red Legs and*

Black Sox: Edd Roush and the Untold Story of the 1919 World Series (2006) have elicited relatively widespread interest, especially among the subscribers to 1919BlackSox@yahoogroups.com, Yahoo.com's Black Sox scandal discussion list. Collectively, these works (not to mention the amnesty movements for Joe Jackson and Buck Weaver) illustrate the Black Sox scandal's remarkable endurance as an American social drama and a profitable cultural commodity, even as it recedes further into the past.

More than any book, however, Pete Rose and his troubles have revived and reinforced Black Sox memories. A former Cincinnati Reds ballplayer and manager and the game's all-time hit leader, Rose was banned for life from the game in 1989 after a six-month investigation into allegations that he had bet on baseball, the game's cardinal sin. The Rose affair ever since has been consistently linked in the media to the Black Sox scandal and to Joe Jackson's exclusion from the Baseball Hall of Fame. Shortly after Rose's exile, for instance, *Newsweek* featured a photograph of him next to an image of Jackson with the caption "Say it ain't so (again)."[47] A few years later, sports columnist Mike Lupica wrote that Rose "spent his whole life trying to be Ty Cobb and ended up as 'Shoeless' Joe Jackson."[48] That the vile Cobb is enshrined in Cooperstown while Jackson and Rose are kept out also draws continuous comment. Rumors in 2002 that baseball commissioner Allan "Bud" Selig might eventually reinstate Rose prompted another round of Rose–Jackson–Black Sox scandal media reports and editorials.[49] To cite but one example, journalist David Kaplan wrote, "Now that Rose is on his way back, it rekindles the Shoeless Joe case. Some baseball insiders say the diplomatic solution is to acknowledge that Jackson has served out his sentence—'banned for life'—and the Hall can take it from there."[50] Regardless of their guilt or innocence, Rose and Jackson have become all but interchangeable tropes for the integrity of American sport (and by implication American culture), and for relations between labor and management, as well as between heroes and their fans.

It may seem obvious, but perhaps it needs to be said: the Black Sox scandal resists closure. There are loose ends, unanswered (and unanswerable) questions, and some unfinished business. "I don't know whether the whole truth of what went on there among the White Sox will ever come out," lamented Edd Roush, a Hall of Fame outfielder and the last surviving member of the 1919 Cincinnati Reds, more than forty years after "winning" the World Series. "Even today nobody really knows exactly what took place. Whatever it was, though, it was a dirty rotten shame."[51] It was that, to be sure. But thankfully, it also provides us with an opportunity to learn some valuable things about the present in addition to the past. "The legend of the Black Sox Scandal," argues critic David

McGimpsey, "has become a centerpiece for discussion about baseball's place in America. This fix has been mythologized to the point where it stands as a historical marker of baseball's so-called 'fall from grace,' where the want of a buck overtook the great national game. Cultural fascination with the scandal is not merely based on a desire to 'get the story straight,' but to map the moral space where baseball is argued."[52] That space is seemingly boundless, far beyond the ability of the best cartographers. Still, something is to be gained by trying to chart the cultural territory the Black Sox scandal occupies, for in so doing we are able to get a sense of the different ways in which people remember the past and make meaning of their cultural politics, prejudices, and particularities. In this way, the Black Sox scandal is what it has always been: an occasion to talk about and reveal ourselves.

Notes

Portions of this essay are drawn from my book *Saying It's So: A Cultural History of the Black Sox Scandal* (Urbana: University of Illinois Press, 2003).

1. Frank Deford, "A Scandal of Such Audacity," *Sports Illustrated*, November 29, 1999, 112; Melissa Isaacson, "Reverse the Curse!" *Chicago Tribune*, October 11, 2005; Studs Terkel, "Nine Men In," *New York Times*, October 28, 2005.

2. Steven P. Gietschier, "They Beat the Black Sox: The 1919 Cincinnati Reds," *Timeline*, 8:5 (Oct.-Nov. 1991): 43.

3. Biart Williams, "The Postseason," in *The White Sox Encyclopedia*, ed. Richard C. Lindberg (Philadelphia: Temple University Press, 1997), 443–44.

4. Daniel E. Ginsburg, *The Fix Is In: A History of Baseball Gambling and Game Fixing Scandals* (Jefferson, N.C.: McFarland, 1995), 128.

5. *Chicago Herald and Examiner*, September 29, 1920.

6. Shoeless Joe Jackson (as told to Furman Bisher), "This is the Truth!" *Sport*, October 1949, 14.

7. Nelson Algren, *Chicago: City on the Make* (New York: McGraw-Hill, 1951; rpt. 1983), 36.

8. *Chicago Herald and Examiner*, July 21, 1921.

9. *Chicago Tribune*, August 3, 1921.

10. *Chicago Herald and Examiner*, August 4, 1921.

11. *Kansas City Star*, August 4, 1921.

12. "Giamatti Turns Down Shoeless Joe Jackson," *New York Post*, August 11, 1989.

13. See Ginsburg, *Fix Is In*, 37–51.

14. For a useful discussion of the reserve clause, see Robert F. Burke, *Never Just a Game: Players, Owners, and American Baseball to 1920* (Chapel Hill: University of North Carolina Press, 1994), 62–63.

15. George Grella, "Baseball and the American Dream," *Massachusetts Review*, 16:3 (Summer 1975): 560.

16. Cordelia Candelaria, *Seeking the Perfect Game: Baseball in American Literature* (Westport, Conn.: Greenwood, 1989), 70.

17. Donald Honig, *The American League: An Illustrated History* (New York: Crown, 1983), 50.

18. See Nathan, *Saying It's So*, 32–36.

19. *New York Tribune*, September 28, 1920.

20. *Chicago Tribune*, September 28, 1920.

21. Grantland Rice, "The Sportlight," *New York Tribune*, September 30, 1920.

22. *Chicago Herald and Examiner*, August 4, 1921.

23. *New York Times*, January 3, 1933. The *Chicago Tribune* reported his death in almost precisely the same manner. See "Heart Attack Fatal; Chicago Boss Five Years," *Chicago Tribune*, January 3, 1933.

24. Eliot Asinof, *Eight Men Out: The Black Sox and the 1919 World Series* (New York: Henry Holt, 1963; rpt. 1987), 283.

25. John Lardner, "Remember the Black Sox?" *Saturday Evening Post*, April 30, 1938, 14–15, 82–85. Lardner's article was later anthologized in Thomas L. Stix's *Say It Ain't So, Joe* (New York: Boni and Gaer, 1947), 2–21.

26. Richard Schickel, "Brave Cuts at a Knuckle Ball," *Time*, September 5, 1988, 63.

27. Arthur Daley, "Finest Natural Hitter of Them All," *Baseball Digest*, February 1949, 8–10.

28. Donald Gropman, *Say It Ain't So, Joe! The True Story of Shoeless Joe Jackson and the 1919 World Series* (New York: Lynx Books, 1979), 203–8.

29. Ward Morehouse, "Joe Jackson at 44 Weighs 220, But He Still Can Slug the Ball," in the "Joe Jackson Folder," National Baseball Library and Archive.

30. Richard McCann, "Baseball Remains Joe Jackson's First Love 17 Years after Ban," in the "Joe Jackson Folder," National Baseball Library and Archive.

31. Harvey Frommer, *Shoeless Joe and Ragtime Baseball* (Dallas: Taylor Publishing Company, 1992), 178.

32. Carter (Scoop) Latimer, "Joe Jackson, Contented Carolinan at 54, Forgets Bitter Dose in His Cup and Glories in His 12 Hits in '19 Series," *Sporting News*, September 24, 1942, 1.

33. Asinof, *Eight Men Out*, 292.

34. Gropman, *Say It Ain't So, Joe!* 229.

35. Irving M. Stein, *The Ginger Kid: The Buck Weaver Story* (Dubuque, Iowa: Elysian Fields, 1992), 300.

36. "Buck Weaver Given Welcome to Diamond," in the "Buck Weaver Folder," National Baseball Library and Archive.

37. *Chicago Tribune*, May 9, 1927.

38. Stein, *Ginger Kid*, 308–9.

39. Edgar Munzel, "Weaver, Former Sox Star, Dies at 64," *Chicago Sun-Times*, February 1, 1956.

40. Bob Broeg, "Buck Weaver's Case Lesson to Remember," in the "Buck Weaver Folder," National Baseball Library and Archive.

41. See http://www.blackbesty.com./joestuff.htm, http://www.gingerkid.com, http://www.chicagohs.org/history/blacksox.html, http://www.law.umkc.edu/faculty/projects/ftrials/blacksox/blacksox.html, and http://www.findagrave.com/reunions/blacksox.html.

42. Arnold Hano, *The Big Out* (New York: A. S. Barnes, 1951).

43. Frommer, *Shoeless Joe and Ragtime Baseball* (1992); Joe Thompson, *Growing Up With "Shoeless Joe": The Greatest Natural Player in Baseball History*

(Laurel Fork, Va.: JTI Publishing, 1997); Donald Gropman, *Say It Ain't So, Joe! The True Story of Shoeless Joe Jackson*, rev. 2d ed. (Secaucus, N.J.: Carol Publishing Group, 1979; rpt. 1999); Irving M. Stein, *The Ginger Kid: The Buck Weaver Story* (Dubuque, Iowa: Elysian Fields, 1992); David Pietrusza, *Judge and Jury: The Life and Times of Judge Kenesaw Mountain Landis* (South Bend, Ind.: Diamond Communications, 1998).

44. Charles C. Alexander, *Our Game: An American Baseball History* (New York: Henry Holt, 1991); Dan Gutman, *Baseball Babylon: From the Black Sox to Pete Rose, the Real Stories Behind the Scandals that Rocked the Game* (New York: Penguin Books, 1992); Benjamin G. Rader, *Baseball: A History of America's Game* (Urbana: University of Illinois Press, 1992); Richard Carl Lindberg, *Stealing First in a Two-Team Town: The White Sox from Comiskey to Reinsdorf* (Champaign, Ill.: Sagamore, 1994); Ginsburg, *Fix Is In*; G. Edward White, *Creating the National Pastime: Baseball Transforms Itself, 1903–1953* (Princeton, N.J.: Princeton University Press, 1996); Lindberg, *White Sox Encyclopedia*; Jonathan Fraser Light, *The Cultural Encyclopedia of Baseball* (Jefferson, N.C.: McFarland, 1997); Leonard Koppett, *Koppett's Concise History of Major League Baseball* (Philadelphia: Temple University Press, 1998).

45. Staci Sturrock, "'Shoeless Joe' Hits a Home Run," *Greenville News*, September 17, 1995; http://www.zuty.com/blacksox.shtml; Louis R. Hegeman, *The Trial of Buck Weaver and Shoeless Joe Jackson*, in the "Joe Jackson Folder," National Baseball Library and Archive.

46. William A. Cook, *The 1919 World Series: What Really Happened?* (Jefferson, N.C.: McFarland, 2001); David L. Fleitz, *Shoeless: The Life and Times of Joe Jackson* (Jefferson, N.C.: McFarland, 2001); Phil Bildner (illustrated by C. F. Payne), *Shoeless Joe and Black Betsy* (New York: Simon and Schuster, 2002); "Shoeless Joe's Black Betsy Bat Nets $577,610," *New York Times*, August 8, 2001; Gene Carney, *Burying the Black Sox: How Baseball's Cover-Up of the 1919 World Series Fix Almost Succeeded* (Dulles, Va.: Potomac Books, 2006); Susan Dellinger, *Red Legs and Black Sox: Edd Roush and the Untold Story of the 1919 World Series* (Cincinnati, Ohio: Emmis Books, 2006).

47. Charles Leerhsen, "The End of the Affair," *Newsweek*, September 4, 1989, 59.

48. Mike Lupica, "Goooood Morning, Cooperstown," *Esquire*, September 1992, 135.

49. Sam Borden, "Might Say It's So for Shoeless Joe," *Daily News*, December 12, 2002; Allen Barra, "Justice Denied? Show the Evidence or Close the Book," *Wall Street Journal*, December 18, 2002; Eric Fettmann, "Bad-Bet Pete," *New York Post*, December 26, 2002.

50. David A. Kaplan, "Baseball: The Other Shoe," *Newsweek*, December 23, 2002, 8.

51. Lawrence S. Ritter, *The Glory of Their Times* (New York: William Marrow, 1966; rpt. 1992), 222.

52. David McGimpsey, *Imagining Baseball: America's Pastime and Popular Culture* (Bloomington: Indiana University Press, 2000), 51.

8

The Plow That
Broke the Midway
Bronko Nagurski

TIMOTHY SPEARS

When Bronko Nagurski joined the Chicago Bears in 1930, he was already a legend throughout the Midwest. At the University of Minnesota, where his raw-boned gift for blocking, tackling, and bulldozing powered a talented football team to an 18–4–2 record over three years, his name evoked the kind of stories found in the Old Testament. The most famous of these, apparently told with some frequency by the Gophers' head coach, Clarence "Doc" Spears, recounts how Spears found Nagurski while driving through the backcountry of northern Minnesota. Stopping at a farm to ask directions of a strapping young man who was plowing the field—without a tractor or horse—the coach asked him the way to Duluth. When the farm boy pointed—with the plow—Spears knew he had discovered something special.

Odds are that anyone familiar with the early history of American football has encountered this story. I must have first heard it as a very young boy because I can't remember a time in my life when I did not know about Bronko Nagurski, his plow, and, most importantly, my grandfather's role in discovering the Bronk. Football in my family was a knotty myth, but like the laces on a football, it was difficult to know which one of the knots kept the air inside the ball.

My grandfather died when I was five years old, so the stories my father told my brother and me about our grandfather were lessons in family history, and freighted with complex emotions. My father, for instance, was part of these stories in ways that are hard for me to decipher even decades after their telling. A talented athlete who played fullback and linebacker for Yale in the early 1950s, captained the team his senior year, and was drafted by the Chicago Bears, he contracted polio in his mid-twenties and never ran again. Still, he swam, played golf (with a brace), and made sports an essential part of our early education, throwing perfect spirals—with a stiff-legged limp—to us on the front yard on autumn afternoons.

Yet if my father showed by example how sports, and football in particular, might order a young man's life, he was also determined to explain why our grandfather was important to us. This was a complicated proposition, since his father was a larger-than-life figure for nearly all the people who knew him, even (I suspect) his family. The proof of this was all around me, on the basement walls of every house I lived in as a child. Team pictures of my grandfather's Dartmouth football team, where he was a two-time Walter Camp All-American, of the Canton (Ohio) Bulldog team, where he played with Jim Thorpe, and of course, snapshots and memorabilia of all the football teams he coached at Dartmouth, University of West Virginia, University of Minnesota, University of Oregon, University of Wisconsin, University of Toledo, and University of Maryland—were all evidence of a remarkable, if tempestuous, College-Hall-of-Fame career. Tempestuous because he rarely got along with administrators and left, or was fired, from several coaching posts. Worthy of respect, however, because my grandfather spoke his mind, did what he wanted, and never lost sight of the broader educational purposes of sports. The "Doc" in his title represented a medical degree, and he managed to hold down a career as a physician throughout his coaching career, even developing training table menus for the Minnesota football team that Bronko Nagurski played on.

A big man with great appetites—one of his nicknames was "Fat," for the 250-plus pounds he sometimes carried on his 5' 10" frame—who grew up poor in western Illinois, my grandfather loved to tell semi-apocryphal stories of the hard-bitten, masculine world of early college football. The point of these stories, I learned through quizzing my father over the years, was to highlight the life lessons inherent in athletic competition, to underscore the fact that football—particularly in the unspecialized, pre-platoon era, when the game was played on both sides of the ball—

could teach young men how to get along, and how to survive. For my father, whose Yale education led away from the gridiron to a career with a steel corporation and a life in the suburbs of Detroit, Cleveland, and Chicago, this conjunction of football and hands-on-learning was an article of faith.

A prime feature of Nagurski's mystique as a football player—to use a phrase often employed by journalists and sports enthusiasts—was his "bone-crushing" power. Late in his life, Red Grange, who starred with Nagurski in the Chicago Bears backfield in the 1920s, claimed he was "the best football player I ever saw," and vouched for his brutal physicality. "Running into him was like getting an electric shock," he said. "If you tried to tackle him anywhere about the ankles, you were liable to get killed."[1] Nagurski's prowess as a running back derived from his speed (he ran the one hundred-yard dash in less than eleven seconds), his low center of gravity (like a plow), and, of course, his size: 6' 2", 230 pounds. As Bears' coach and owner George Halas recalled, "It was all—literally all—muscle, skin, and bone. He didn't have an ounce of fat on him. A lot of men have passed in front of me, but none with a build like that man." Nagurski's physical make-up and athletic skill enabled him to play offense and defense with equal intensity. At the University of Minnesota and with the Bears, he played fullback, linebacker, tackle, and end. On defense, he terrified ball carriers with a weird form of body blocking in which, without using his arms or hands, he threw his body at the runner, steamrolling him with all of his 230 pounds.[2]

Implicit in these assessments of physical prowess and also contributing to his fame was Nagurski's apparent capacity for performing extraordinary athletic feats. Like Red Grange or Babe Ruth and, later, Muhammad Ali, he evoked the uncanny—and occasionally the comic—by narrowing the gap between the imaginary and the real. Reports of Nagurski's feats with the Bears are as well worn as the story about the plow. One of the best known concerns a 1934 game, when Nagurski slammed into the end zone for a touchdown, knocking two linebackers to the ground, running over a safety, and then bouncing off the goalposts before crashing into the wall at Wrigley Field and leaving a crack in the brickwork. Some versions have him complaining as he returned to the huddle that the last guy (the brick wall) hit pretty hard.[3] Nagurski often expressed his fierce will in smaller, less dramatic ways. As *Sports Illustrated* writer Paul Zimmerman discovered while watching old Bears films, Nagurski would become enraged on certain plays and launch himself at a defender, the hunted attacking the hunter.[4] In an irony typical of superlative athletes, Nagurski transcended the terms of play even as he epitomized them.

18. *Bronko.* Bronko Nagurski became the only football player named an All American at two positions when he attended the University of Minnesota in the 1920s. Nagurski led the Chicago Bears to multiple championships in the 1930s. (Courtesy of the Chicago History Museum.)

This is also the point of an anecdote my father once related about a Minnesota football team reunion that he attended with my grandfather at a banquet in Minneapolis in the mid 1950s. Much of the 1929 team was there, getting ready to eat lunch, when someone noticed that the Bronk was missing. An hour later he returned, and when asked where he had been, Nagurski explained that he had been at a local professional wrestling match, filling out a card. Mopping his brow, Nagurski sheepishly explained that he needed the money. But he had finished—and won—the match in time for dessert.

So far as my brother and I were concerned, Bronko Nagurski was the pure embodiment of football might. Not only was he the complete player—the guy who could run and tackle, without a regulation helmet and a groomed playing surface—but his legendary accomplishments were the perfect object for our fantasy that we too might enter the pantheon of football heroes. As eleven- and ten-year-old boys planning careers as

19. *The Legend Beholds Himself.* Nagurski and George MacKinnon (who played center for the University of Minnesota in the 1920s) inspect a portrait of the Bronk at a 1952 team reunion. The inscription "To 'Doc'" was for the author's grandfather.

pro football players, we exercised our fantasies wherever we could, and a front yard, even one scattered with acorns, was a good place for developing a Bronko-style game.

Childhood dreams aside, Bronko Nagurski's importance as a cultural icon extends well beyond his accomplishments on the gridiron and his subsequent installment in both the College and Pro Football Halls of Fame. As Kevin Britz has argued, Nagurski's rise to celebrity status in the 1920s and 1930s had much to do with his northern Minnesota background. Celebrated within the culture as a Paul Bunyan figure with great natural strength and rural values, Nagurski symbolized the residual attractions of the American frontier at a time when actual wilderness conditions had disappeared. Although Nagurski's notoriety placed him in company with sport stars like Babe Ruth, Red Grange, and Jack Dempsey, whose athletic prowess also seemed drawn from some primal source, he appeared more down-to-earth and more modest. While the names of Ruth, Grange, and Dempsey were synonymous with the commercial ballyhoo and high-rolling tenor of the 1920s, Nagurski was most comfortable back on his farm in International Falls, Minnesota. And, in fact, that is where Nagurski went when he retired from the Chicago Bears in 1934, after eight years of playing professional football. Except for a brief return to the NFL in 1943, Nagurski spent the rest of his life at home—raising his family, working his farm, and pumping gas at a station he owned in International Falls. As Britz notes, these qualities established Nagurski as a modern sports hero with a distinctly nostalgic appeal.[5]

Yet if Nagurski was "tailor-made" to exemplify the myth of the American frontier, his evolution as a rough-hewn, professional football star was also a distinctly Chicago phenomenon. When Nagurski joined the Bears in 1930, the team was coming off a 4 and 9 season, its strength debilitated by the conflicting coaching styles of George Halas and Joe Sternaman.[6] During the previous decade, the Chicago Bears had been one of the strongest teams in the nascent National Football League, a shifting confederation of franchises that included the Staten Island Stapletons, the Frankford Yellow Jackets, and the Dayton Triangles. Officially formed in 1920, the NFL still bore the traces of professional football's origins in the factory towns of Ohio and western Pennsylvania, where, during the 1900s and 1910s, jerry-rigged teams like the Canton Bulldogs and the Massillon Tigers, backed by local business interests and fielding an assortment of semipro and college players, competed on fall Sunday afternoons, when businesses were closed and team members who either played or coached for college teams, were free to earn a few dollars. The NFL served to consolidate and rationalize these enterprises during the 1920s. However, playing football was a secondary job for most NFL players; in terms of fan interest and financial outlay, college football was a much bigger game.[7]

To showcase the talents of the University of Illinois star Red Grange, the 1925 Chicago Bears "barnstormed" the country, which helped legitimize the NFL and establish the Bears' identity in Chicago. Close to forty thousand people paid to see Grange play his first game at Wrigley Field, a dramatic rise from the five thousand spectators that usually attended Bears games. The Grange effect, however, could not be sustained, and even as pro football gained in popularity during the 1930s, attendance at games—in Chicago and other NFL cities—seldom exceeded 35,000.[8] By contrast, John Carroll has pointed out, major college teams "could draw thirty to sixty thousand fans to their games on a consistent basis."[9] And in Chicago in 1927, 120,000 people watched Notre Dame play USC at Soldier Field, an attendance record that still stands. Even the city Prep Bowl, which featured the public and Catholic high school champions and drew 50,000 fans when it was first held in 1927, was more popular than a Chicago Bears game.[10]

Characterizing the sport during the first half of the century, Michael Oriard notes that "professional football was not yet every boy's—or even every football player's—dream." What Oriard calls "King Football" pertains to college football, and the campus heroes, like Grange and Nagurski, who translated their skills from one arena to the other, were more the exception than the rule. For most aspiring ballplayers, college football was both the pinnacle and the end of a chiefly amateur game. Hence, when Red Grange signed with the Chicago Bears for an unprecedented $100,000 before graduating from the University of Illinois, he turned the assumptions of the culture upside down. As a business enterprise, source of civic pride, and target for male (and female) fantasies, professional football clearly had a long way to go. And though it gained momentum during the 1930s—in part because of the success of the Chicago Bears—it did not come into its own until after the war, when a surging economy and a tremendous expansion of commercial leisure activities, including television watching, made pro football a very popular form of entertainment.[11]

The relationship between professional and college (or amateur) football had always been close, though vexed. During the early years of professional football, some college players moonlighted for semipro teams, often playing under assumed names. Knute Rockne, for instance, played semipro football while enrolled at Notre Dame; later, as coach, he struggled (sympathetically) to manage talented mavericks like George Gipp, who likewise played on Sundays. During the 1917 season, while coaching at Dartmouth in Hanover, New Hampshire, my grandfather used to ride freight trains to Ohio, where he and a handful of other former All Americans joined Jim Thorpe's Canton Bulldogs; according to my father, he later "worked" his way through Chicago's Rush Medical School by playing for the Bulldogs.[12]

Although educators, administrators, and coaches alike attempted to draw firm boundaries between amateur and professional sports, the smell of money pervaded big-time college football programs in the form of athletic program budgets, alumni largesse, gambling, tramp athletes who moved from one school to another in search of better deals, competing teams that established winner-take-all pots, highly-paid coaches who controlled nearly all aspects of their programs, and universities that built enormous stadiums with the hopes of profiting from lucrative gates. In 1926, as part of an effort to protect the amateur standing of college football players, the six-year-old National Football League passed a rule, recommended by intercollegiate athletic reformers, stipulating that all players must have graduated from college in order to be eligible for league play. The measure clearly separated collegiate from professional competition. But it also acknowledged their shared interests and led to their formal connection, culminating in the draft, instituted in 1934, which gave young players a way of imagining how they might become NFL stars.[13]

College idol that he was, Bronko Nagurski signed with the Chicago Bears in March of 1930, for $5,000 a year—the most lucrative pro contract to date, other than Red Grange's. Yet, when Nagurski joined the Bears, the NFL probably had more in common with the makeshift world of the Canton Bulldogs than the mass-mediated sports culture that it would later come to exemplify. In fact, one of his teammates on the Bears, Hall-of-Fame tackle, Link Lyman, had played for the Bulldogs, while guard Don Murry, quarterback Joey Sternaman, and Hall-of-Fame center George Trafton were also veterans of the very early days of the league.[14]

A sense of tradition lived on in the NFL's very equipment, which, by contemporary standards, was primitive: the leather helmets, resembling aviator headgear, lacked padding and face bars, while the pants included minimal padding; there were no arm pads. The ball, melon-shaped in the 1910s and 1920s, got smaller by 1929, but did not reach a truly passer-friendly size until 1934. The rules, formations, and game strategies heavily favored straight-ahead running and a defensive playing style that sometimes resembled hand-to-hand combat.[15] This was in contrast to the faster, sometimes razzle-dazzle game favored by college coaches like Bob Zuppke at the University of Illinois and Knute Rockne at Notre Dame. Of help in promoting this speedy style of play, Rockne's teams in the 1920s routinely included one hundred fifty players—thirty-five for the varsity traveling squad, thirty-five for the main reserve, and eighty more players for practices and exhibitions. On the other hand, the NFL changed its rules in 1930 to allow teams to carry a maximum of twenty players, which was an increase of four from the previous limit of sixteen.[16] In short, college coaches generally had more resources than professional coaches to develop their teams and their game strategies.

Of course, to underscore the backward-looking nature of professional football at this time is to risk judging the game by contemporary standards. It is important to remember too, as Red Grange emphasized, that professional football players were bigger, stronger, more experienced, and more skilled than their collegiate counterparts.[17] However, the mere fact of Grange's insistence suggests that in 1930 one did not need to be an early-twentieth-first-century time-traveler to recognize professional football's retrograde qualities. One had only to read the sports page or attend one of the many games played each Saturday during the fall to see that college football received far more money and attention.

During the 1930s, this situation began to change as the pro game evolved and gained fans. A prime mover in this evolution was the Chicago Bears, revamped under the direction of head coach Ralph Jones (who came from Lake Forest College, and had assisted Zuppke at the University of Illinois), who installed a T-formation offense. The split T broadened the field of play, took advantage of Grange and Nagurski's contrasting running styles, and provided more options for passing the football.[18] In 1933, as a result of a championship game that the Bears played against the Portsmouth Spartans—held indoors because of the frigid weather—the league passed three rules that further bolstered offensive play. For one, it moved the goal posts forward to the goal lines; second, it established hash marks, which means that following an out-of-bounds play, the ball was placed ten yards in from the sidelines (instead being positioned at the sidelines); and third, it permitted passing from anywhere behind the line of scrimmage (until then, the passer had to be at least five yards behind the line). These new regulations led to higher scores throughout the league and proved critical to the Bears' emergence as the "Monsters of the Midway." By World War II, they became "Chicago's Team" (an obvious snub to the rival Chicago Cardinals).[19]

That Nagurski was a mainstay of Chicago's dynasty during these years is an important aspect of his notoriety: through his ferocious presence on both sides of the ball, he led the Bears to two league championships and five divisional titles. It was not only that Nagurski was physically intimidating, he was also what football analysts call a "skilled player." He could run, catch, and even throw the ball. In fact, it was because of a touchdown pass that Nagurski threw in the Portsmouth game that the NFL loosened its rules on passing behind the line of scrimmage.

Yet the lore about Nagurski registers his significance for pro football in ways that have little to do with athletic talent. Grange referred to the electricity he felt when he hit Nagurski. Ernie Nevers (another Hall-of-Famer), who played for Stanford and the Chicago Cardinals, said tackling him was like running into a downhill train.[20] As the story of Nagurski cracking the brick wall at Wrigley Field suggests, his impact extended beyond the gridiron.

Rooted in the vernacular of modern urban life—electrical currents, locomotive power, and brickwork—these descriptions of Nagurski's wonder-working labor are consistent with Chicago's identity as a rough-and-tumble industrial city. The body imagery recalls Carl Sandburg's poetic evocations of blue-collar work (consider Nagurski's Big Shoulders in this respect) and the violence suggests the disruptive impact of Chicago's gangsters, the most famous of whom, Al Capone, shared a strong tie to the city's immigrants. As Michael Oriard has noted, both Polish and Bohemian Americans claimed Nagurski (who was of Ukrainian descent) as their own, illustrating the extent to which ethnic communities gloried in the success of their fellow countrymen in American sports. Of course, these ethnic and class identifications also worked to underscore Nagurski's difference from the white Protestant middle-class culture that, as Oriard points out, dominated the Ivy League narrative of football success.[21] Depending on the creator and the audiences of such narratives, Nagurski could be anyone's hero. However, given the persisting stories of his football prowess, there was something about Nagurski—that part of him that earned the nickname "monster of the midway"—that was inassimilable and could not be reconciled to a single mythological framework.[22]

The most famous legend about Bronko Nagurski—the one attributed to my grandfather—also reveals the effort to translate his meaning into comprehensible cultural terms. As journalists and commentators have observed, the image of Nagurski pointing with a plow is Bunyanesque. Although they left the connotations unexplained, they presumably had in mind Paul Bunyan's endeavors with Babe, the great Blue Ox, with whom he plowed the Mississippi River Valley and performed various heroic feats in the northern woods of the Midwest. According to one episode, Bunyan was plowing a field with Babe when he reached the end of a row and simply lifted the plow and the ox into the air, turned around, and headed back the way he came.[23] Dating to the early 1900s, the folklore concerning Paul Bunyan had special relevance in northern Minnesota, where in 1937, the town of Bemidji built two large statues of Bunyan and his ox to honor the local folklore and boost the region's sagging timber economy. Citing Bunyan's origins as a "worker-hero" (and the subject of literary portraits by John Dos Passos and Carl Sandburg), Karal Ann Marling has argued that that these gargantuan figures represent the populist spirit of the Midwest. Not incidentally, Nagurski attended high school in Bemidji his senior year before going to the University of Minnesota.[24]

Although many articles over the years have rehashed the account of how Doc Spears discovered his roadside giant, not a single one—at least that I have been able to find—explains the circumstances under which the Minnesota coach first told the story. In place by 1943, when writer Stanley Frank referred to it in an article he published in *Collier's* on Nagurski's return to professional football, the story is curiously absent from earlier written sources. Even in *Collier's* the story is presented indirectly, as a benchmark for measuring other football prospects—and vaguely (and coyly) linked to Nagurski. Frank writes, "Doctor Clarence 'Fat' Spears, raconteur and Nagurski's coach at Minnesota, was asked how he managed to have so many vibrant youths on his teams. 'Every summer I climb into my car and drive down the back roads,' Spears related. 'When I see a boy working in the fields, I stop and talk to him. After a while, I ask him where he lives. If he points with his hand, I can't use him. But if he points with the plow, he's got a chance to play on the same team with Nagurski.'"[25] There is no sign of this anecdote in any of the public relations materials issued by the University of Minnesota during the late 1920s.[26] According to my father, my grandfather denied ever telling the story and instead claimed that he discovered Nagurski when he stopped for gasoline at the Standard Oil station in International Falls and met this strapping young man who looked like a promising football prospect. Yet this explanation also seems suspect, since one of the minor Nagurski myths concerns the stream of fans that visited the retired player's gas station in International Falls in order to meet the legend himself. In this incarnation of the myth, many people left International Falls unable to unscrew the caps on their gas tanks. . . . so strong was Nagurski.[27]

The plow story resembles nothing so much as an rural/urban legend that provided a culturally powerful, if fanciful, explanation for how a Ukrainian football player as uniquely influential as Nagurski found his way from the coldest place in the nation to the University of Minnesota and then Chicago. In this regard, the legend was Bunyanesque in another way; it recalled John Bunyan's seventeenth-century story of urban migration, the didactic *Pilgrim's Progress*. To think of Nagurski in this way—as a prodigiously strong, God-fearing sojourner from the north woods—is to downplay the ethnic aspects of his identity and to underscore his place in the long line of provincial migrants who helped build Chicago. Indeed, the frame of the story hinges on the difference between rural and urban perspectives. Told by an urban outsider who finds himself lost in the countryside, the story concludes with the powerful youth (innocent of his strengths) heading down the road to the big city to develop his talents.

The primary author of this story—if there is one—was likely an enterprising sportswriter, who, in the wake of Nagurski's remarkable career with the Bears, offered a creation account of the hero's rise to success (an account, it is worth emphasizing, that stresses the links between two generations of professional and collegiate football). There was strong precedent for such journalistic myth making in the example of Grantland Rice, who played loose with the facts in his portraits of Notre Dame's Four Horsemen and Grange's "Galloping Ghost."[28] However, given the wide currency and staying power of the Nagurski plow story, there is also good reason to think of it not as one person's construction, but as what Lawrence Levine, in his analysis of African American folklore, calls an "epic," the context of which is "never purely individual."[29]

The scope of Nagurski's epic status may perhaps best be seen closer at hand, through the impact that his 1943 comeback had on the Chicago Bears, professional football, and the city of Chicago. Often deemed a weak spot in NFL history—one football scholar calls it the "nadir"—the 1943 season took place despite the loss of many players to the military draft.[30] Between 1943 and 1945, more than forty roster members, as well as owner George Halas, left the Bears to serve in the military.[31] World War II dramatically affected the league; attendance dropped, some franchises suspended play, others merged—indeed, this last measure led to a Philadelphia-Pittsburgh team known as the "Steagles." Although returning players, including college stars that had never played professionally, fueled the league's resurgence in the postwar years, the conflict itself almost resulted in the dissolution of the NFL.[32]

Faced with a depleted roster, the Bears contacted Nagurski at his farm in International Falls during the summer of 1943 and asked if he would play one more season. Bronk consented, but on the condition that he would play only tackle (he doubted he was in shape to carry the ball) and that he could go back to Minnesota to harvest his crops.[33]

Whether Nagurski's return to action can be called wartime service is a debatable point. However, there is no question that the events and effects of the war permeated most aspects of life in Chicago, and redefined the ways in which professional sports were enjoyed and understood. Like the rest of the nation, Chicago was laboring under a wartime economy that challenged all citizens (including athletes) to make considerable sacrifices. While families had learned during the Depression to adjust their domestic economies to available resources, the war required different sorts of discipline, imposed by federal law. Consumer goods were in short supply, some food products were strictly rationed, and civic groups like the Chicago Nutrition Association provided recipes and advice on how to stretch resources. Fuel, too, was subject to rationing, and families struggled to conserve gasoline and electricity. In 1942, Chicago's industrial economy received a huge boost when billions of dollars in defense contracts were committed to local companies. But though jobs were plentiful, working class families had to adjust to new factory schedules, like the swing shift, which were aimed at increasing productivity.[34] Most importantly, like all Americans, Chicagoans lived with the unrelenting violence of the war, news of which filled the papers every day.

Although the sports page was several sections behind the headlines, it was not removed from the international scene. In its October 10th issue, the *Chicago Tribune* explicitly addressed Nagurski's return to football in an article that appeared next to a photo of him charging ahead under the caption "The Old Hero Returns." To read about Nagurski, however, one had to get past the front page news, which warned of stricter milk rations, described bombing raids in Danzig, Germany, and included a large illustration by the Tribune's long-time cartoonist, John T. Mc-Cutcheon, enjoining citizens to fill the Community Chest with funds to support needy Chicagoans and the federal Lend Lease program. The story of Nagurski's return to the Bears referred to these issues obliquely, noting that the one-time fullback would be "cast as a tackle in the 1943 wartime machine" and that George Halas—among other Bears serving in the military—would not be part of the fall season since he left the year before to serve as a lieutenant commander in the navy.[35]

Football, in other words, was not exempt from the wartime effort: players and fans alike would have to make sacrifices. Nagurski himself had done so, the newspaper implied, by leaving his family and home in Minnesota to help the Bears and the city in this time of need. Although at the beginning of the season he appeared to be in good shape and was still a muscular 230 pounds, the *Tribune* also reported that his "hands show the telltale signs of farm labor."[36] Later that fall, when he missed the Philadelphia-Pittsburgh game to tend to his farm and some family business, the *Tribune* explained in some detail why he was "called home" in a bold-printed sidebar that underscored Nagurski's involvement in several domestic problems. Like other Chicagoans, the football player was striving to balance work and family in a culture stressed by war.[37]

At the same time, Nagurski's return gave sportswriters the opportunity to stress the heroic traditions of professional football, which persisted despite the wartime measures. So, for instance, the *Tribune's* mention that Nagurski had joined "the 1943 wartime machine" cleverly punned on his patriotic contribution by highlighting the Bears' need to turn back the clock and the sport's connection to an earlier era. Similarly (though less humorously), Arch Ward, the sportswriter in charge of the *Tribune's* famous "In the Wake of the News" column, reported that "the return of Bronko Nagurski to the professional football wars has brought a flood of stories about the explosive back."[38] These stories of Nagurski's mythic abilities brought pro football's earlier battles to the attention of younger players and fans. However, they also suggest the war's toll on those who left the NFL for the military or who were leaving college teams to join the armed forces. Football's persistence during a time of war inevitably raised questions about national and local priorities: Why should men play this game while their peers fought overseas?

In September of 1943, just as the football season was beginning for high school, college, and professional teams, the *Chicago Daily News* presented a general answer to this question in an illustrated spread entitled "In Days of War the Games of Peace Still Play Their Role in Nation's Life." More of an editorial gloss than an article, the *News* announced, "Another football season. Again a pageant of youth on fields of friendly strife. In peace we were wont to compare football to war. And in war our generals and captains compare war and its strategies to football. Certainly, no other sport has given more generously of its stars to the nation's defense than football." As the article went on to list specific examples of the sacrifices made by individual football players, it provided concrete evidence that football and war shared a rhetoric and cultural logic—and endorsed that relationship with a sketch of three football players superimposed over three GI's. Framing all six figures was a line drawing of a football.[39] The *Tribune* reported more conventionally on football's new role with the article "Football Gains Approbation as War Time Sport," which noted the public's enthusiastic response to the game. The article went on to compliment administrators and coaches for allowing players and spectators to enjoy the sport's benefits during wartime.[40] Meanwhile, throughout the fall, the *Tribune* tracked the attrition of young men like Alex Agase and Tony Butkovich from the ranks of prominent college players.[41] It did the same for pro football, paying special attention to the war's ongoing impact on the Bears' roster.[42]

In contrast to these departing athletes, Bronko Nagurski figured in the sports pages as a stabilizing presence for the Bears. The notion of the steady, clear-thinking veteran is one of professional sports' great tropes, but in the context of World War II, this old hero's return assumed further gravitas. Hardly a frontiersman, the "Nag," as he was called during his first stint with the Bears, was now reclaimed as a domesticated creature whose connection to midwestern farm life and family values was made manifest by his intention of returning home after the season ended. His thirty-seven-year-old body calloused by farm work and his reputation as a football star already established, he could "come back" to the game—and regenerate it—in a way that no college player ever could. Indeed, Nagurski may well be the first American athlete in a team sport whose return from retirement promised to activate what the *Tribune* called "the magnetism of old time athletic heroes," at a time when Chicago sorely needed a lift.[43] Half a century later, Chicagoans would track the comeback of another sports legend, basketball player Michael Jordan, with considerably more fanfare, though not, ironically, with quite the same attention to the culture's larger needs.

As the season progressed, and Nagurski's contribution to the Bears increased, his significance became more complicated. While in early games, like the Bears' 20–0 victory over the cross-town rival Chicago Cardinals, Nagurski made only a brief appearance at tackle, "his presence seemed to snap the Bears out of their lethargy."[44] Aided by easing the regulations on substitution—introduced because of the wartime shortage of players, free substitution was permanently adopted in 1950—Nagurski's entry seemed mainly symbolic of the team's historical legacy. However, even as writers such as Arch Ward paid tribute to that legacy, they yearned "to see the aged fellow take a turn carrying the ball from his old full back spot."[45] So Nagurski's ascendance, not just as a great player but also as an important figure in Chicago history, went hand in hand with his image as a good family man and cooperative citizen.

During the last game of the regular season Ward and his colleagues got their wish, as Nagurski, filling in for fullback Bill Osmanksi, who was lost to the navy, sparked the Bears' second victory over the Cardinals, clinching the Western Division title. Nagurski's performance—84 yards on 15 carries and a touchdown—allowed the Chicago newspapers to match rhetoric with the legend. The *Tribune* noted the clutch performance of Sid Luckman, who threw four touchdown passes despite having been hospitalized earlier in the week, but paid special tribute to "the man who came out of the past" and "led" the Bears "to the same sort of finish as on Pearl Harbor day two years ago"—in short, a "smashing" offensive effort "of the old and the new." The *Daily News* was more florid, claiming in its headline "Bronko Writes New Chapter in His Grid Career," and likewise pushing the link between Nagurski's age and the Bears' wartime heroism. "This is a story of what men are made of," the article begins. "Fighting-mad, desperate men of football. The right words in the right place might even make it a saga. . . . A saga of one 'old man' of 35, of a couple of kids in their 20s, of raw courage, and—of a little blood." To corroborate this melodramatic lead, writer Harry Sheer included the comments of one "innocent" (read "young") Cardinal who denied Nagurski was thirty-five years old. "That guy's lying. . . . He hits as hard and he's just as tough as that Nagurski of ten years ago."[46]

The story that unfolded in the ensuing weeks as the Bears prepared for, and then defeated, the Washington Redskins on the day after Christmas to win the NFL championship may not have been a saga but it more than lived up to the expectations that Nagurski and his teammates raised in the Cardinals game. The Bears defeated the Redskins 41 to 21 in a game that once again featured sterling performances by Luckman and Nagurski. Although the 34,320 spectators that jammed into Wrigley Field fell short of the season high—more than 42,000 had attended the Green Bay Packers game earlier that season, which was the second largest crowd in the fifty-one game history of that series—the $120,500 set a record for NFL title games.[47] Quite a finish for a season that was almost canceled.

Nagurski's role in the game was also historic, and for reasons that transcended his strong play (including a touchdown) at fullback. Once again, he was the Nag, whose return to football improved the team and thickened its—and Chicago's—connection to the past. On leave from the navy and accentuating the game's sense of tradition, was Lieutenant Commander George Halas, who had personally signed Nagurski to the Bears in 1930 and had been part of the franchise since its original incarnation as the Decatur Staleys. After the game, Halas called the team's fourth NFL championship a return to the "terrible Bears" of old, while coach Hunk Anderson (who played for Knute Rockne and was later a coach at Notre Dame) praised Nagurski's role in the game, explaining that, "The old timer's mere presence, not to mention his powerful play, instilled confidence in the players that a thousand pep talks couldn't have effected."[48] Whatever déjà vu Nagurski experienced during the game (and the season) was also surely reinforced by the presence, on the other side of the field, of the Redskin's coach, Arthur "Dutch" Bergman (also a Rockne player), who was an assistant coach (to my grandfather) at the University of Minnesota when Nagurski had played there.

For Nagurski, this convergence of events generated nostalgia, but not enough to inspire a full-scale comeback. "Well, I am retiring again," he told the *Tribune.* "It's not a game for a 35 year old, and I can't listen to George Halas songs all my life."[49] Still, to mark the occasion, he asked quarterback Sid Luckman if he could keep the game ball. Luckman, who had thrown a record five touchdowns and was facing his own possible retirement, refused. Having played a young man's game one last time, Nagurski went home. The *Minneapolis Morning Tribune* documented his return with a photograph of him, in the Chicago train station, loaded down with suitcases and gifts for his children.[50] Although Nagurski worked the following year as an assistant coach at UCLA, he spent the remainder of his life in International Falls.[51]

"It's always the same," wrote one Chicago reporter in the aftermath of the Bears' victory over the Redskins. "The winners are glad they won; the losers, sad they lost. The coaches will praise the stars, the stars will praise the rest of the players. . . . It's always that way. It always will be."[52] Yet despite the ritualistic uniformity of professional, college, and high school football—a narrative that has persisted with remarkable endurance over the course of the twentieth century and into the twenty-first—all games are not the same. Some unfold in such a way as to bind the game to the cultural needs of the moment and the place. Like the war, the 1943 NFL championship was a good battle fought for a good cause that participants and spectators alike recognized. It would be too much to say that Bronko Nagurski generated or significantly influenced the values that made the game and the season worth playing, but his presence, like the plow, provided direction.

As for the sport's mythic place in my own family history, there came a time when my father stopped throwing footballs in the front yard and I set aside the dreams of sandlot touchdowns. Instead, I struggled to master the specialized skills required of offensive linemen: memorizing plays, recognizing defenses, falling on fumbles, pushing off on the correct foot, and so on. I followed my father to Yale, and was fortunate to play there as a guard. In a tight spot during the last football game I played—the Harvard–Yale game—I ran downfield after a punt and recovered a fumble on Harvard's twenty-yard line. Years later, with the spirit of Nagurski somewhere in the past, I dream of that moment, see the football laces in front of me, and wonder if I should pick up the ball and run.

Notes

1. The stories about Nagurski's strength and football playing are repeated throughout the journalistic and scholarly sources. Red Grange's perspective is covered in John M. Carroll, *Red Grange and the Rise of Modern Football* (Urbana: University of Illinois Press, 1999) 160, and the *Minneapolis Star Tribune*, October 24, 1999 (LexisNexis database).

2. Carroll, *Red Grange*, 160 (Halas quotation). For details on Nagurski's speed and tackling style, see Stanley Frank, "Bronko Bucks Again," *Collier's*, December 11, 1943, 33.

3. *Minneapolis Star Tribune*, October 24, 1999 (LexisNexis).

4. Paul Zimmerman, "The Bronk and the Gazelle: Fifty Years Ago Bronko Nagurski and Don Hutson Dominated Pro Football. But How Would They Do Today?" *Sports Illustrated*, September 11, 1989, 128.

5. Kevin Britz, "Of Football and Frontiers: The Meaning of Bronko Nagurski," *Journal of Sports History*, 20 (Summer 1993): 101–26. For anyone interested in Nagurski's life and career, this well-researched article is the place to start. Although I take a different view of Nagurski's significance, Britz's findings were of great help to me.

6. Britz, "Of Football" 103; Carroll, *Red Grange*, 159.

7. Carroll, *Red Grange*, 164–65.

8. Michael Oriard, *King Football: Sport and Spectacle in the Golden Age of Radio and Newsreels, Movies and Magazines, the Weekly and Daily Press* (Chapel Hill: University of North Carolina Press, 2001), 201–4; Carroll, *Red Grange*, 107–8.

9. Carroll, *Red Grange*, 101.

10. The Chicago college football market was complicated by the tremendous popularity of Notre Dame and the declining fortunes in the late 1920s of the University of Chicago football program. Northwestern was also a popular draw in the late twenties, though not as popular as Notre Dame. Robin Lester, *Stagg's*

University: The Rise, Decline, and Fall of Big-Time Football at Chicago (Urbana: University of Illinois Press, 1995), 131–32; Murray Sperber, *Shake Down the Thunder: The Creation of Notre Dame Football* (Bloomington: Indiana University Press, 2002) 267, photo cap. 314; Gerald R. Gems, "The Prep Bowl: Football and Religious Acculturation in Chicago, 1927–1963," *Journal of Sport History*, 23 (Fall 1996): 288.

11. Oriard, *King Football*, 202 (quotation), 203. Oriard discusses the sporadic acceptance of pro football in the 1930s and its breakthrough in the 1950s on 204–22.

12. Sperber, *Shake Down the Thunder*, 57, 105–10. On early professional football, see Keith McClellan, *The Sunday Game: At the Dawn of Professional Football* (Akron, Ohio: University of Akron Press, 1998).

13. Carroll, *Red Grange*, 104–5.

14. Britz, "Of Football," 111.

15. Carroll, *Red Grange*, 164.

16. On Notre Dame squad sizes and playing style, see Sperber, *Shake Down the Thunder*, 132–33, 247–49; Carroll describes Zuppke's wide-open, innovative game strategy in *Red Grange*, 46–47. On the NFL rule change, see Robert Treat, *The Official National Football League Football Encyclopedia* (New York: A. S. Barnes, 1942), 19.

17. Carroll, *Red Grange*, 164.

18. Carroll, *Red Grange*, 159–60; David S. Neft and Richard M. Cohen, *The Football Encyclopedia: The Complete History of Professional NFL, from 1892 to the Present*, editorial consultants Bob Carroll, John G. Hogrogian, and Rich Korch (New York: St. Martin's, 1991), 112–13.

19. Carl M. Becker, "The 'Tom Thumb' Game: Bears vs. Spartans," *Journal of Sports History*, 22 (Fall 1995): 226; Oriard, *King Football*, 204 ("Chicago's Team").

20. For this anecdote, see the *Washington Post*, January 19, 1990, http://www.washingtonpost.com/wp-srv/sports/longterm/general/povich/launch/bronko.htm.

21. Oriard, *King Football*, 261, 266–67.

22. In the early 1950s, *New York Times* sportswriter Arthur Daley noted, "The Bronk was an original, impossible to duplicate." Arthur Daley, "Sports of the Times," *New York Times*, November 23, 1954. Clippings file, University of Minnesota Archives.

23. The Internet is filled with stories about Paul Bunyan. See, for example, http://www.books-about-california.com/Pages/Paul_Bunyan_and_his_Big_Blue_Ox/Paul_Bunyan_text.html, for an account of his field-plowing exploit.

24. Karal Ann Marling, *The Colossus of Roads: Myth and Symbol along the American Highway* (Minneapolis: University of Minnesota Press, 1984), 1–3; Britz, "Of Football," 104.

25. Frank, "Bronko Bucks Again," 33.

26. This is based on my review of materials in the University of Minnesota Archives in Minneapolis, Minnesota.

27. Britz, "Of Football," 123. As for Nagurski's version of how he was recruited, he claimed that Spears invited him to go fishing with him in nearby Bemidji and convinced him to come to the University of Minnesota. See *Minneapolis Star Tribune*, January 20, 1984 (http://www.startribune.com/stories/507/16792.html).

According to Britz, a physician and Minnesota alum alerted Spears to Nagurski, and the coach followed up on the tip; see "Of Football," 104.

28. Sperber, *Shake Down the Thunder,* 175–82.

29. Lawrence W. Levine, *Black Culture and Black Consciousness: Afro-American Thought from Slavery to Freedom* (New York: Oxford University Press, 1977), 427.

30. Stan Grosshandler, *"1943—The Nadir,"* The Coffin Corner, 15 (1993); http://www.footballresearch.com/articles/frpage.cfm?topic=1943nadir.

31. Howard Roberts, *The Chicago Bears* (New York: G. P. Putnam's Sons, 1947), 216. For a year-by-year listing of the players who left the Bears for military service, see Neft and Cohen, *Football Encyclopedia,* 167.

32. Neft and Cohen, *Football Encyclopedia,* 113.

33. Britz, "Of Football," 120–21.

34. Perry R. Duis, "No Time for Privacy: World War II and Chicago's Families," *The War in American Culture: Society and Consciousness during World War II,* ed. Lewis A. Erenberg and Susan E. Hirsch (Chicago: University of Chicago Press, 1996), 18–33.

35. *Chicago Tribune,* October 10, 1943.

36. *Chicago Tribune,* September 17, 1943.

37. *Chicago Tribune,* October 19, 1943.

38. *Chicago Tribune,* September 20, 1943.

39. *Chicago Daily News,* September 11, 1943.

40. *Chicago Tribune,* December 26, 1943.

41. Agase and Butkovich are discussed under the banner headline "N.U. and Purdue Stars Await Marine Call" in *Chicago Tribune,* October 26, 1943.

42. The war was a steady news item on sports pages, but see the following for a summary of its cumulative impact on the Bears: *Chicago Tribune,* December 25, 1943. One indication of how much interest this subject generated is the false report someone made in November to the Chicago newspapers that quarterback Sid Luckman was leaving immediately for military service. The hoax was attributed to gambling interests. Luckman did depart for the maritime service school, but not until the season was over. See *Chicago Tribune,* November 18, 1943.

43. *Chicago Tribune,* September 18, 1943.

44. The nickname "Nag" is referred to in *Chicago Tribune,* November 29, 1943; "lethargy" quotation, *Chicago Tribune,* October 11, 1943.

45. On the adoption of free substitution, see Treat, *Official National,* 21–22; *Chicago Tribune,* October 11, 1943.

46. *Chicago Tribune,* November 29, 1943; *Chicago Daily News,* November 29, 1943. Ellipses are original to the source.

47. *Chicago Tribune,* December 27, 1943. For statistics on the Green Bay game, see *Chicago Tribune,* November 8, 1943.

48. *Chicago Tribune,* December 27, 1943.

49. Ibid.

50. *Minneapolis Morning Tribune,* December 28, 1943.

51. On Nagurski's life after football and his relative obscurity, see Joel Bierig's piece "The Bronk" in the *Minneapolis Star,* March 1, 1982. The subtitle says it all: "Nagurski lives so quietly many townspeople don't know his legend."

52. *Chicago Daily News,* December 27, 1943.

9

"An Inalienable Right to Play"

African American Participation in the Catholic Youth Organization

TIMOTHY B. NEARY

Full recognition of his inalienable rights to life, liberty
and the pursuit of happiness is the legitimate expectation
of every American child. That is his heritage, and it is his
regardless of the "race," the creed or the position in life
of his parents. . . . Children have therefore an inalienable
right to play.
—Bishop Bernard J. Sheil

Harry Booker, an African American teenager from St. Eliza-
beth's Parish, found himself in the finals of the second annual Catholic
Youth Organization (CYO) boxing tournament by a fluke. He was the
substitute for another CYO boxer and future professional champion,
Leo Rodak, who was out with the flu. Chicago boxing fans had expected
Rodak, representing a German American parish in the shadows of south
Chicago's steel mills, to fight for the 1932 featherweight title against

"Smiling" Jimmy Christy, a "puckish little Irishman" from Our Lady of Mt. Carmel on the North Side.[1] Instead, they witnessed a battle between the black Booker and white Christy. During the semi-finals earlier in the evening, Booker narrowly defeated the reigning national Golden Gloves featherweight champion from Joliet, Illinois. Now, before sixteen thousand fans in the old Chicago Stadium, the African American youth faced Christy, the most popular boxer in the CYO. Bishop Bernard J. Sheil, founder and director of the CYO, adored the redheaded Irish American, as did most of the crowd. Yet, despite his underdog status, Booker soundly defeated Christy in a three-round decision.[2] Like each of the sixteen hundred entrants in the boxing tournament, Booker received a fair chance to compete and win. His racial status, a stigma in almost all other aspects of society, did not preclude him from full participation in this Catholic-sponsored event. Moreover, a month later, he represented not only St. Elizabeth's but also the entire Chicago archdiocese when he defeated a boxer from San Francisco in an exhibition bout at Chicago Stadium.[3]

Booker's victories epitomized African American participation in the CYO, which included black members from its inception in 1930 until its effective termination in 1954. African Americans from St. Elizabeth's, Corpus Christi, St. Anselm's, and—after World War II—other black parishes, took part in CYO activities alongside whites. Although Chicago's Roman Catholic parishes remained almost completely racially segregated during the 1930s, 1940s, and early 1950s, the citywide youth program provided numerous opportunities for black/white interaction. Booker enjoyed full membership in the CYO, because church doctrine recognized the equality of his parish—St. Elizabeth's—to Christy's Our Lady of Mt. Carmel, as well as to the more than 350 parishes in the Archdiocese of Chicago. The neighborhood may have changed from Irish American to African American during the preceding generation, but the parishes remained Catholic.

Bishop Sheil did not establish the CYO to fight racial bigotry. An outgrowth of the Holy Name Big Brothers program and parish athletic leagues, the CYO originally functioned as a means to counter juvenile delinquency, secularism, and anti-democratic ideologies among working-class Catholic boys during the Great Depression. Over the years, however, Sheil became one of the nation's most prominent critics of discriminatory practices against African Americans.

A native of Chicago, Bernard Sheil grew up in a middle-class family on the city's west side at the end of the nineteenth century. Sports and religion profoundly shaped his worldview. Benny, as he was known, excelled at baseball in high school and college. After graduation, he received offers to play professionally but turned them down in order to join the priesthood. The 1891 papal encyclical, *Rerum Novarum*, which called on industrialized societies to protect the rights of workers, shaped his views on social justice. As a young cleric, Sheil thrived under the mentorship of Cardinal George W. Mundelein, who integrated New Deal politics into urban Catholicism. By the late 1930s, Sheil garnered national attention as a champion of organized labor and critic of anti-Semitism. When liberal Catholic thinkers began labeling racism a social sin, Sheil embraced the ideology of Catholic interracialism. During World War II, he spoke out in favor of the "Double V" campaign, victory abroad against fascism and victory at home against racism. After the war, he advocated the elimination of racially restrictive housing covenants.[4]

Black-white relations, however, did not top Mundelein's list of priorities when he granted Sheil permission to inaugurate the CYO. Despite a 137 percent increase in Chicago's black population during the 1920s, African Americans made up only seven percent of the city's residents in 1930, and African American Catholics accounted for less than ten percent of the black populace. Instead, Mundelein and Sheil focused on "Americanization," the process whereby ethnic Catholics set aside na-

20. *Muscular Christians.* Bishop Sheil (left) and Cardinal Mundelein examine the trophy before the first annual CYO boxing tournament. (Courtesy of the Chicago Archdiocese's Joseph Cardinal Bernardin Archives and Records Center.)

tionalistic differences for common participation in the American church and assimilation into American society.

Within the Americanization model, African Americans like Harry Booker became, in many ways, another "ethnic"—like Irish, Poles, Germans, and Italians. In that sense, Booker did not occupy a special place in the CYO paradigm. He simply acted as another young man from one of the city's national parishes participating in the tournament. With some luck (Rodak's illness), he earned his chance to win the championship. Sheil, a proud second-generation Irish American who chose green and white for the CYO colors and held annual corned beef and cabbage fund-raising dinners, may have favored Christy, but he supported fair play above ethnic partisanship.[5] For Sheil, religion trumped race. All Catholic parishes in the archdiocese, whatever their racial compositions, fell under his authority as bishop. Their members, therefore, stood as equals in the eyes of the church. This holistic approach allowed black and white young people to participate on an even playing field—if only between bells of a boxing match or whistles of a basketball game—in a city strictly divided by race.

Sports in Bronzeville

Race and sports shared a long history in Chicago, as well as throughout the nation. Many of the alleged culprits of the 1919 race riot were Irish Catholic members of sporting organizations like the Hamburg Athletic Club, including seventeen-year-old Richard J. Daley, future mayor of Chicago.[6] In his 1927 study of urban gangs, sociologist Frederic Thrasher found that "the dominant social pattern for the conventionalized gang in Chicago is the athletic club." The civic commission charged with investigating the 1919 race riots blamed most of the violence and vandalism on such "athletic" and "social" clubs, which it recommended be closed. Nevertheless, tensions continued to grow after 1919 between blacks and whites, as the South Side's "Black Belt" expanded. African American and white gangs often clashed along the Black Belt's western border, Wentworth Avenue.[7] Progressive-era reformers believed that too much unstructured leisure time led to gang activity, and they advocated recreational programming as a means to avoid criminal behavior among adolescent boys. The Young Men's Christian Association (YMCA) and Boys Clubs, nondenominational Protestant movements, offered two such alternatives to gangs.

Like most American institutions prior to World War II, the YMCA operated under Jim Crow policies designed to serve African American youth in racially segregated settings. By the turn of the twentieth century, most major American cities included a black YMCA. In 1910, Chicago mail-order magnate and philanthropist Julius Rosenwald pledged $25,000 to construct a building to house the African American YMCA in any community that could raise $75,000. The Sears, Roebuck and Company president eventually subsidized the construction of twenty-four so-called Rosenwald YMCAs across the country. In Chicago, he convinced International Harvester boss, Cyrus McCormick, and prominent banker, Norman W. Harris, each to match his donation of $25,000. The resulting five-story building opened in 1913 at Thirty-eighth and Wabash Avenue in the heart of Bronzeville. The "Wabash Y," two blocks east and two blocks south of St. Monica's—Chicago's original black Catholic church— assisted recent African American migrants in their acclimation to urban life. In 1915, historian Carter G. Woodson's Association for the Study of Negro Life and History began meeting at the South Side institution.[8] By World War I, the Wabash Avenue YMCA had become a hub of athletic, social, and intellectual activity in Chicago's rapidly growing African American community.[9]

In the end, however, the Wabash Avenue YMCA could not meet the ever-increasing needs of Bronzeville residents. Demand for more recreational facilities increased as the Black Belt expanded further south during the 1920s and 1930s. "Though this district [Forty-third to Sixty-third Streets between Wentworth Avenue and South Parkway] needs a YMCA, sadly there is none," noted one New Deal worker on the eve of World War II. "The Wabash Avenue YMCA at Thirty-eighth Street and Wabash Avenue is overcrowded, and, apparently, would not be injured if in a city so heavily populated by Negroes another YMCA came into existence and especially to serve this district."[10] A second South Side YMCA did not open until 1949, and racial segregation continued until 1950.[11]

Yet, other institutions besides the YMCA served Bronzeville's youth. In 1924, the South Side Boys Club opened its doors on South Michigan Avenue, one and one-half blocks north of St. Elizabeth's at the same time that the parish was undergoing its transformation from Irish American to African American. Thousands of neighborhood boys came to the club during the 1920s and 1930s. Well-known alumni included Nat King Cole and Ralph Metcalfe. Wealthy white benefactors, like Elliott Donnelly, president of the R. R. Donnelly Publishing Company, helped keep the South Side Boys Club solvent during the lean economic years of the Great Depression. In 1930, author Richard Wright got a job at the South Side Boys Club working with African American street gang members. Wright wrote in the introduction to *Native Son* that his work at the club inspired the creation of the novel's protagonist:

The first event was getting my job in the South Side Boys' Club, an institution which tried to reclaim the thousands of Negro Bigger Thomases from the dives and the alleys of the Black Belt. Here, on a vast scale, I had an opportunity to observe Bigger in all his moods, actions, haunts. Here I felt for the first time that the rich folk who were paying my wages did not really give a good goddam about Bigger, that their kindness was prompted at bottom by selfish motive. They were paying me to distract Bigger with ping-pong, checkers, swimming, marbles, and baseball in order that he might not roam the streets and harm the valuable white property which adjoined the Black Belt. I am not condemning boys' clubs and ping-pong as such; but these little stopgaps were utterly inadequate to fill up the centuries-long chasm of emptiness which American civilization had created in these Biggers. I felt that I was doing a kind of dressed-up police work, and I hated it.[12]

Despite the good work accomplished by the Wabash YMCA and South Side Boys Club, Wright's observations pointed to the failure of most white philanthropists to question the city's racist systems.

Not all African American teenagers, however, reacted to racism like Bigger Thomas. Many found purpose and direction in organized athletics. Public school segregation in Chicago meant that, until the mid-1930s, nearly all of the city's African American high school students attended just one overcrowded institution, Wendell Phillips High School. The all-black school produced excellent basketball teams during the 1920s and 1930s. In 1926, the Phillips lightweight (junior) team advanced to the semifinals of the boys' Public League championship and two years later won the title. Racist admission practices precluded most African American athletes from competing at the collegiate level, but several Phillips basketball alumni played for the Savoy Big Five, an all-black semiprofessional team on the South Side. Coach and promoter Abe Saperstein recruited players from the Savoy Big Five to create his famed Harlem Globetrotters in 1926. Despite its name, the professional touring club operated out of Bronzeville. By 1930, Phillips graduates composed the entire Globetrotter team.[13]

Some Phillips athletes attended college thanks to Katharine Drexel and the Sisters of the Blessed Sacrament (SBS). Three years after sending her missionary sisters to Chicago, Drexel used a portion of her fortune to establish a secondary school for African Americans in New Orleans.[14] Two years later, in 1917, she opened a teaching college, and the school received its charter as "Xavier University of New Orleans" in 1925. By the 1930s, black men and women from across the country attended the southern, Catholic institution, which became known for its strength in the medical sciences. Scores of young people from Chicago's South Side attended Xavier. Many graduated from Catholic grade and high schools operated by the SBS or other Catholic religious orders, but others came from public schools, especially Phillips. Between 1935 and 1938, Chicagoans helped the Xavier men's basketball team compile a record of sixty-seven wins and two losses. For a time during the amazing run, all five Gold Rush starters were Phillips alumni.[15] A virtual pipeline developed between Chicago's South Side and the black Catholic college in New Orleans. Indeed, the first African American to sign with a National Basketball Association (NBA) team and the first African American to play basketball at DePaul University (and later in the NBA) both attended Xavier on athletic scholarships after graduating from Bronzeville public high schools.[16]

Universities closer to home did not necessarily extend the same hospitality to African American athletes, as Jim Crow practices persisted in the urban North. In 1930, the University of Chicago's athletic department broke its longstanding practice of inviting the champion of the Chicago Public League to its annual Amos Alonzo Stagg Basketball Tournament. Phillips won the Public League championship that year, but university officials instead invited runner-up Morgan Park, a white high school, to its Hyde Park campus for participation in the national tournament. Because African American athletes did not find widespread opportunities at the collegiate level until after World War II, Xavier remained particularly attractive to blacks during the 1930s and 1940s.[17]

Wendell Phillips High School, the South Side Boys Club, and the Wabash YMCA formed what one Chicago high school coach has called a "golden triangle" of "great black basketball talent" in the 1930s and 1940s.[18] Eugene Saffold, who played on DuSable High School's first basketball team (1935–36), recalled the importance of these institutions. "We used to meet down at the South Side Boys Club. . . . That's where we all learned to play the game. . . . There were only two or three places where we could go and play inside—Wabash Y and South Side Boys Club."[19] St. Elizabeth's parish plant stood only one and one-half blocks to the south of the golden triangle. Bishop Sheil took advantage of the proximity by inviting black basketball players and other African American athletes to participate in CYO activities.[20] As hundreds of young people from the neighborhood, Catholics and non-Catholics, congregated at a former men's club on the grounds of St. Elizabeth's, the parish-owned building became the center of Catholic-sponsored athletics in Bronzeville.

Sheil House

After its conversion from a high school in 1944, Sheil House became a "magnet for athletes," similar to the three institutions making up the golden triangle. "Bishop Sheil more or less put the Sheil House on Forty-first Street for blacks to have some place to go," according to George Phillips, a standout basketball player on St. Elizabeth's teams of the late 1940s. "St. Elizabeth athletes, the public school athletes, and just about everyone in the neighborhood gravitated to this place to compete." During the day, St. Elizabeth's grammar and high schools used the building's facilities for physical education and other activities. Outside of school hours, however, Sheil House operated as a community center for young people from the surrounding neighborhood. "It was just like a YMCA," recalled Phillips.[21]

Originally known as the Sheridan Club, the four-story building on the southwest corner of Forty-first and Michigan Avenue served several purposes after its completion around the time of the World's Columbian Exposition in 1893.[22] Wealthy, South Side whites built the structure as a private club. Later, Swift and Company used the building as a gymnasium and social club for its executives. Between 1922 and 1926, the Sisters of Mercy operated an academy out of the old Swift Club for the remaining white children of St. Elizabeth's parish. In 1926, the Society of the Divine Word and Sisters of the Blessed Sacrament opened a high school for African American boys and girls in the building. During the late 1930s, the men of St. Elizabeth's Holy Name Society renovated a billiards room and bowling alley in the basement for their use.[23] Conditions became crowded as enrollment in St. Elizabeth High School grew, and in 1944 the high school moved into a more spacious building across the street.[24] This move freed space in the one-time corporate club, which then took the name of the CYO founder and became an after-school destination for St. Elizabeth's students and children living in the surrounding neighborhood.

Sheil House's dark granite exterior "was like a fortress" in the eyes of one South Side boy.[25] Within the walls of the nineteenth-century clubhouse, however, neighborhood children—Catholic and non-Catholic alike—took part in an assortment of athletic, educational, and social activities. Students from St. Elizabeth's grammar and high schools, as well as area public schools, played basketball in the second-floor gymnasium. In the basement, a game room, weight-lifting area, ping-pong tables, and bowling alley provided more recreational opportunities. Baseball, volleyball, shuffleboard, hopscotch, and jumping rope took place on the small patch of grass outside the building, as well as in an adjoining empty lot.

Boy and Girl Scouts created arts and crafts projects in the third-floor workshop, and the Sheil House Players staged dramatic theater productions. Finally, the gymnasium functioned as a ballroom where high school dances regularly took place under the watchful eyes of SBS sisters and lay teachers.[26]

During the summer months, the CYO operated a day camp out of Sheil House. Scores of African American children arrived each weekday morning at the community center, wearing white t-shirts emblazoned with the green CYO logo. A staff composed of laypeople, young priests, and seminarians supervised the youngsters, ages six to thirteen. The program emphasized socialization and recreation; religious instruction was generally absent. In the morning, campers might learn to minuet, polka, or square dance (decidedly non–African American styles), while afternoon field trips exposed them to the city's cultural resources. Edwin Leaner, who lived at Fiftieth and Forrestville Avenue in Corpus Christi's parish, attended camp at Sheil House in the early 1950s with his sister. He recalled taking public transit for outings to the zoo, museums, and the beach: "They would pile all us kids, two by two. We'd get on the el[evated train], because the el stopped right there at Indiana [Avenue] and Thirty-ninth [Street]." Campers generally brought their own lunch, and parents may have paid a small weekly fee. In addition, the children learned about personal hygiene and manners. "We were pretty much a well-mannered bunch," said Leaner.[27]

The Sheil House became a place where African American boys and girls, even those attending public schools, came into contact with the CYO. Bishop Sheil understood the importance of the nation's growing African American population in the urban North, particularly Chicago, during World War II and the postwar years. As the war came to a close, he hired an African American G.I. with an undergraduate degree in sociology from Columbia University to be his liaison to the black community. In 1945, Joseph J. Robichaux became athletic director for St. Elizabeth High School and director of the Sheil House. Robichaux, "a huge tan Buddha of a man," was born in New Orleans in 1916 to a Franco-American father and Creole mother. His family migrated to Chicago, where his father worked for the railroads. Robichaux attended Catholic schools and participated in the CYO during its early years; and after graduating from high school he volunteered as a CYO coach. During World War II, he worked for the USO to organize stateside entertainment for U.S. troops.[28]

Robichaux, who for twenty-five years was known as the South Side "Commissioner" of youth athletics until his death in 1971, oversaw an extensive sports program at St. Elizabeth's and Sheil House. With backing from Bishop Sheil, he recruited talented athletes from Bronzeville's golden triangle. The densely populated, highly segregated Black Belt provided Robichaux and his CYO associates with a rich supply of athletic talent. Several of his protégés went on to successful careers in college athletics, business, and public life. Black participation in Catholic-sponsored athletics, however, predated the postwar era. An entire generation of black athletes took part in the CYO prior to the formation of Sheil House. Boys and girls from St. Elizabeth's, Corpus Christi, and St. Anselm's participated in CYO activities from the program's beginning.

African American Participation in CYO Athletics

The CYO used the popularity of black boxing champion Joe Louis to reach out to African American boys. During the 1930s, the "Brown Bomber" became a symbol of pride and solidarity in the African American community, and his triumphs in the ring presented compelling refutation to ideologies of racial superiority propagated in the United States and overseas. The Detroiter got his start in competitive boxing through the Golden Gloves, winning the 1934 national amateur title at Chicago Stadium. In 1937, Louis won his first world championship by knocking out Jim Braddock at Comiskey Park on Chicago's South Side. He returned to the city a year later to referee a CYO bout at Soldier Field. The endorsement from Louis enhanced the Catholic Youth Organization's standing within Chicago's black community.[29]

The speed, power, and grace of Louis symbolized black strength for millions of African Americans. Richard Wright believed that everyday black men were able to fight racism vicariously through the victories of Louis over white boxers, and Malcolm X later quipped, "The ring was the only place a Negro could whip a white man and not be lynched."[30] In a title fight in New York City during the summer of 1935, for example, Louis soundly defeated Italian boxer, Primo Carnera, who was seen as a representative of Benito Mussolini's racist, fascist regime. Young black athletes found similar (if less publicized) success a few weeks earlier in Chicago. In four championship bouts, African Americans defeated Italians in the International Golden Gloves tournament at Chicago Stadium. One of the black boxers, Lorenzo Lovings, was a Chicago CYO member from the West Side parish of St. Malachy's. Lovings graduated from a Nashville high school in the early 1930s, as economic depression gripped the nation. Unable to find employment in Tennessee, he migrated to Chicago, worked in a grocery store, and began taking boxing instruction from legendary retired fighter Paddy Kane at the CYO downtown gymnasium. After just three years in Chicago, the archdiocesan newspaper dubbed Lovings "the most popular of colored [CYO] boxers." After his success in the Golden Gloves tournament, Lovings entered the CYO Professional Boxing School.[31]

Ralph Leo, an Italian American immigrant, anti-fascist, and CYO public relations director from 1934 to 1942, celebrated the victories of Lovings and the other black Golden Glovers in his tongue-in-cheek weekly sports column: "It should be quite conclusive, after the international pugilistic developments at the [Chicago] Stadium last week, that although Italy can put a rip-roaring argument against the world, Italy cannot lick Ethiopia. . . . And, of course, it may be that the Golden Gloves results did not influence the Italian war department, but it does seem odd that forty-eight hours after Lovings, Clark, Bridges, and Pack had disposed of their Italian adversaries, Mussolini should resolve his dispute with Abyssinia. . . . These international ring thrillers are indeed conducive to international amity!"[32] Italian-Ethiopian peace ended five months later, when Mussolini's troops invaded the east African nation. The multiracial, multiethnic CYO, however, continued to fight racist thinking. In the summer of 1936, three boxers from the CYO's "League of Nations" represented the United States at the Olympic Games in Nazi Germany. Also at the Berlin games, African American stars, Jesse Owens and Ralph Metcalfe, silenced any talk of Aryan superiority on the runner's track.

The CYO sought African American inclusion from its inception. A few months before the first CYO boxing tournament, an article in the archdiocesan newspaper, the *New World,* invited African American boys to enroll in free boxing lessons offered six nights a week at the "first-class" gymnasium on the grounds of St. Elizabeth's. "This is an opportunity for our colored Catholics to get a splendid training in boxing, to enter the tournament and to associate themselves with some of our finest boxers. . . . Anyone passing up this opportunity is missing something really worth while [*sic*]," advised the weekly. A prospective boxer needed to be at least sixteen years of age, an amateur, and a Catholic (the CYO later dropped the religious requirement). Race, color, ethnicity, or class did not matter. St. Elizabeth's pastor, Fr. Joseph Eckert, sat on the first planning committee, and the parish soon became the center of CYO boxing in the Black Belt. In addition, St. Elizabeth's hosted three white teams during one of four sectionals within the South District of the citywide tournament.[33] Winners went on to compete in district competition at De La Salle Institute, a Catholic high school known as "the poor boy's college" for working-class and middle-class Irish Catholics, and alma mater to Chicago's three mayors between 1933 and 1976.[34]

In addition to annual boxing tournaments in December and large intercity and international exhibitions during the summer, the CYO sponsored numerous smaller boxing shows around the city. These matches included interracial lineups in both black and white neighborhoods. In honor of "National Negro Youth Week," for example, Corpus Christi hosted a pageant and boxing show in the parish gymnasium. The *Chicago Defender* reported that CYO champions would display "clean sportsmanship and suberb [*sic*] boxing" in the ring, while close to one hundred boys and girls participated in a spectacle of racial pride outside of the ring.[35] Corpus Christi also sponsored Friday night fights at the famous Savoy Ballroom just two blocks north of the church.[36] Held in a popular, secular setting offering high-caliber boxing, the entertaining exhibitions familiarized Bronzeville's non-Catholic population with the CYO. The stars of the show were more than competitive boxers, however. They served as role models in the community, and some even became parish leaders. In 1937, for example, two of the six officers elected to the parish board of the Corpus Christi's Young Men's Holy Name Society were CYO boxers.[37]

A range of venues provided the Catholic Youth Organization with opportunities to promote its brand of multiracial, multiethnic sportsmanship. African American and white boxers represented the CYO at athletic clubs, banquets, parish gymnasiums, even prisons.[38] During the 1933 World's Fair (Chicago's "A Century of Progress"), CYO boxers put on

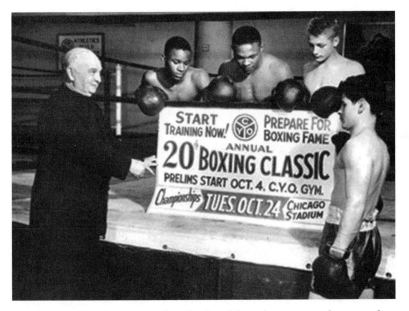

21. *Fisticuffs.* Bishop Bernard J. Sheil and friends promote the annual CYO tournament, 1950. (Courtesy of the Chicago Archdiocese's Joseph Cardinal Bernardin Archives and Records Center.)

exhibition matches in the "Irish Village" on the lakefront fairgrounds.[39] The CYO Open Air Stadium, located at the Mercy Home for Boys on West Jackson Boulevard, became one of the city's most popular settings for amateur boxing during the 1930s. In the summer of 1934, for instance, over thirty-five thousand people attended Thursday night bouts at the outdoor site on the near west side.[40] And as seasons changed, the Thursday night fights moved inside to the second-floor gymnasium at the CYO headquarters in the downtown Loop.[41]

African American boxers found much success in CYO competition. Corpus Christi dominated CYO boxing in the 1930s, winning four team championships in the first ten years of competition. Harold Dade, a flyweight fighter from Corpus Christi, won two CYO titles and two Golden Glove titles in the early 1940s. After serving in the Marines during World War II, Dade entered the professional ranks, winning the world's bantamweight title in 1947.[42] When he started boxing with the CYO at age fourteen, Dade did not show immediate promise, losing his first six fights. But hard work and discipline eventually paid off. The CYO took great pride in Dade's success. "He is one of the finest boys ever to represent the Catholic Youth Organization," declared CYO boxing director Lou Radzienda. "He is a clean-cut, hardworking young man."[43]

African Americans also played a prominent role in the CYO's second most popular sport—basketball. As in boxing, blacks participated from the beginning. St. Elizabeth's fielded two teams in the first CYO season, 1931–32.[44] The lightweight team began the season strong, and both the lights and heavies led the South Division standings by mid-February. Although St. Elizabeth's did not win either the lightweight or heavyweight titles in the inaugural season, the parish's prowess foreshadowed numerous CYO basketball championships won by Black Belt teams in the 1930s and 1940s.[45] Corpus Christi joined St. Elizabeth's in CYO competition during the 1932–33 season. The two African American teams played most of their games at De La Salle's gymnasium and St. Elizabeth's parish clubhouse (the future Sheil House). Corpus Christi also played games at St. Augustine's in the white Back of the Yards neighborhood.[46] Except when they met each other, St. Elizabeth's and Corpus Christi played against white teams.

Interracial competition meant crossing parish—and racial—boundaries. Black teams traveled to white neighborhoods, and white teams traveled to black neighborhoods. For example, during the 1932–33 season, teams representing white parishes played games in St. Elizabeth's gymnasium against black teams from Corpus Christi and St. Elizabeth's, as well as against the other white teams.[47] One of the white parishes, Visitation, was the site of anti-black rioting a generation later.[48] In the

1930s, however, Irish American basketball players from Visitation regularly traveled to the heart of Bronzeville for Sunday afternoon games. Conversely, black teams from St. Anselm's, Corpus Christi, and St. Elizabeth's journeyed to white neighborhoods. Between 1933 and 1940, for example, St. Anselm's played games at the Lady of Good Counsel gymnasium in the white McKinley Park neighborhood, the Grand Crossing Park gymnasium in the white neighborhood of Grand Crossing, Mt. Carmel, an all-boys Catholic high school in the white neighborhood of Woodlawn, and St. Rita's, a Catholic high school in the white neighborhood of Englewood. St. Rita's became infamous in the 1960s for white racist resistance to African Americans, yet the school hosted black teams uneventfully throughout the 1930s.[49] In addition, Corpus Christi traveled to De La Salle, Mt. Carmel, St. Agnes, and Visitation for regular-season games, while St. Elizabeth's competed at De La Salle, Mt. Carmel, and St. Sabina's.[50]

By the late 1930s, St. Sabina's, an Irish American parish in the Englewood neighborhood, became one of the city's primary hubs of Catholic-sponsored basketball. On November 5, 1937, Bishop Sheil dedicated the newly completed St. Sabina Community Center.[51] The state-of-the-art auditorium offered first-class facilities with enough room to accommodate large crowds. In 1938, St. Sabina's began hosting an annual Amateur Athletics Union (AAU) tournament at the parish center.[52] By 1940, the tournament comprised thirty-two teams, including the Hamburg Athletic Association sponsored by Illinois State Senator Richard J. Daley, as well as teams from St. Anselm's, St. Elizabeth's, and St. Sabina's.[53] The event's success prompted St. Sabina's to begin a grammar school tournament in 1939, in which black Catholic schools regularly competed.[54] Although sixty years later St. Sabina's became the center of controversy surrounding interracial competition in a Catholic grammar school sports league, during the Depression and World War II, Catholic-sponsored interracial sports flourished in the Irish American parish.[55]

African American parishes won four team championships in the first decade of CYO basketball competition. Corpus Christi's 1934 lightweight championship team included two stars—forward Charlie Gant and guard William McQuitter—who later played on the phenomenal Phillips and Xavier teams of the 1930s.[56] Such young men became minor celebrities in Bronzeville, often mentoring the next generation of athletes. Gant and Andy Summerlin, Corpus Christi's center, returned to the parish after World War II and coached.[57] Under the leadership of a young Joe Robichaux, the St. Elizabeth's Collegians won CYO heavyweight titles in 1937 and 1938, suffering only a pair of losses in two seasons.[58] St. Elizabeth's stars—Agis Bray, Hillary Brown, and William "Iron Man"

McKinnis—were some of the best basketball players in the country.[59] St. Elizabeth's was the "pride of Chicago's south side and recognized as one of the greatest basketball programs in the country."[60] The collegians even defeated the 1936 U.S. Olympic team.[61]

St. Anselm's followed along the successful path of Corpus Christi and St. Elizabeth's. During the 1939–40 season, the African American lightweights amassed a 56–3 record, winning the 1940 CYO title by upsetting reigning champion, St. Sylvester's, a white parish in the Logan Square neighborhood on the city's northwest side.[62] Postseason competition included an intercity CYO all-star game against Detroit at the St. Sabina Community Center and an interfaith contest with the Albany Park B'nai B'rith Organization (BBYO). A week later, St. Anselm's traveled with CYO athletic director Jack Elder and the St. Columbanus heavies to Cleveland for a second intercity all-star game.[63] St. Columbanus, an Irish American church ten blocks south and four blocks east of St. Anselm's in the white Park Manor neighborhood, drew attention in late 1940s for stiff resistance to African Americans. White parishioners viciously attacked the home of a black Catholic married couple, who moved into the parish in 1949.[64] Nine years earlier, however, St. Columbanus teenage boys made an out-of-town, interracial trip without incident under the auspices of the CYO. Bishop Sheil's organization used sports to transcend Catholic parochialism, so evident in postwar housing conflicts.

In addition, the CYO challenged gendered parochialism in modest ways. Unlike boxing, basketball offered an opportunity for girls to take part in CYO competition. More than ninety girls' teams competed in the first CYO basketball season, 1931–32.[65] A girls' team from St. Elizabeth's entered the second season, playing most of their games at the Lady of Good Counsel gymnasium, Thirty-fifth and South Hermitage Avenue, in the white McKinley Park neighborhood, three and one-half miles west of St. Elizabeth's. The St. Elizabeth's girls competed against white teams from Our Lady of Good Counsel, Sacred Heart (a Jesuit parish in the Czech neighborhood of Pilsen), St. Augustine's (in the white Back of the Yards neighborhood), St. Anthony's (a German parish in the white Bridgeport neighborhood), and St. George's (a German American parish).[66] Corpus Christi entered the girls' league during the 1933–34 season, competing at St. Agnes's, an Irish American parish in the white Brighton Park neighborhood.[67]

The CYO may have included girls, but it did not give them equal attention. Boys' sports dominated CYO athletics coverage in the archdiocesan and city newspapers. In his biography of Cardinal Mundelein, Edward Kantowicz described the CYO as a Roman Catholic form of "muscular Christianity."[68] In the early 1930s, an African American mother expressed concern to Sheil about her son boxing in the CYO, because he suffered nosebleeds easily. The bishop curtly replied, "That's good. . . . He'll learn how to protect himself."[69] Despite his macho persona, Sheil always included girls in CYO programming. When he negotiated with the Boy Scouts of America to take over responsibility for sponsoring Catholic Boy Scouts, for example, he also began sponsoring Catholic Girl Scouts. Girls participated, but with less fanfare than boys. That changed, though, when girls' track became the premier CYO sport of the 1950s.

African American boys dominated CYO track starting in the mid-1930s. St. Elizabeth's juniors (eighteen and younger) won seven consecutive CYO titles between 1935 and 1941, for example, while St. Anselm's seniors (nineteen-years-old and older) won four consecutive titles between 1938 and 1941. Championship meets took place at Loyola University's campus in the Rogers Park neighborhood on the far north side of the city and at Ogden Park in the white Englewood neighborhood on the southwest side.[70] Talented CYO athletes, like Agis Bray and "Iron Man" McKinnis, competed in multiple sports, running track in the spring after participating in boxing and basketball in the fall and winter.

As much success as Bronzeville's young men enjoyed in track and field, the CYO women surpassed them. During the CYO's first ten years, female athletes struggled to gain much notice. They could not even use the facilities at the CYO Center until 1943, when large numbers of men went away to serve in World War II. By the late 1940s, however, women commanded their fair share of the CYO spotlight. After taking charge of Sheil House and St. Elizabeth's athletics, Joe Robichaux began assembling an extremely talented group of female athletes. The CYO women's track team soon became a national powerhouse. Instead of individual parish teams, Robichaux coached a citywide squad—blacks and whites together—that competed in AAU meets across the country. The interracial approach did not play well everywhere, especially in the South. The sight of black and white CYO girls draping their arms over each other's shoulders after a 1950 race scandalized spectators at a national AAU tournament in Freeport, Texas. Two men standing next to Robichaux recoiled in disgust, one saying to the other, "Now I've seen everything. Let's get out of here." Natural camaraderie and easy give-and-take between black and white girls remained a radical notion to most Americans.[71]

The CYO women's track team produced two great individual talents in the 1950s. Sheil House's Mabel Landry was a four-time national AAU champion in the long jump and two-time champion in the 50-meter sprint, while Barbara Jones was a two-time winner in the 100 meters.[72] Their victories brought widespread attention to Robichaux's program and garnered unique opportunities for the young women. In 1952, Landry traveled to Helsinki, Finland, where she represented the United States in the long jump competition at the Olympic Games. Jones also competed at the Helsinki games and became the youngest woman ever (at age fifteen) to win an Olympic gold medal in track and field, capturing a second gold medal as a member of the U.S. 4 x 100–meter relay team at the 1960 games. She later credited the CYO with providing her the opportunity to become a world-class competitor regardless of race. "CYO was mixed, so, you know, I didn't know anything about segregation," recalled Jones, who grew up in Chicago's Ida B. Wells public housing project and received a full athletic scholarship to track and field powerhouse, Tennessee State University.[73]

Boxing, basketball, and track and field made up the big three CYO sports, but African Americans competed in other activities as well. For example, St. Elizabeth's girls played volleyball against white parishes across the city, and boys from Corpus Christi competed in CYO horseshoes tournaments in Lincoln Park.[74] Bronzeville youth were exposed to a greater variety of games after the CYO expanded its mission in 1938 to include social services.[75] While defending the Catholic Church's sponsorship of boxing, Sheil once quipped, "Show me how you can lead boys from saloons with a checkers tournament, and I'll put on the biggest checkers tournament you ever saw."[76] Apparently, someone convinced him. In 1939, the CYO held its first annual checkers tournament at the CYO Center in the downtown Loop, with youth from Bronzeville among the more than five hundred entrants.[77] Finally, boys and girls from the Black Belt found success in CYO table tennis tournaments.[78] Richard Wright may have questioned ping-pong's ability to affect social change, but St. Anselm's took great pride in its 1939 table tennis team championship at the CYO Center.[79] By playing everyday games with white children—table tennis, checkers, marbles, horseshoes, or volleyball—African Americans crossed social boundaries. It was one thing to punch a black opponent in a boxing ring; it was quite another to rub shoulders with him while lining up a marbles shot.

The CYO crossed its most formidable boundary, however, in the swimming pool. Society held a longstanding taboo against interracial swimming. The 1919 Chicago Race Riot erupted from an incident along the shores of Lake Michigan, and some of the ugliest confrontations in the modern civil rights movement took place around pools.[80] It was as if whites thought that African Americans "polluted" water with their "blackness." Yet, African Americans swam in CYO meets beginning as early as the mid-1930s. When the CYO held its sixth annual swim meet on the seventeenth floor of the Illinois Club for Catholic Women's North Michigan Avenue building, a boy from St. Elizabeth's came in third in the 40-yard breaststroke.[81]

22. *Water Sports.* 1950 CYO swim team poses in the second floor gymnasium at the CYO Center on East Congress Street. (Courtesy of the Chicago Archdiocese's Joseph Cardinal Bernardin Archives and Records Center.)

District playoffs took place at Mt. Carmel High School's pool, with finals often held at Loyola University's Rogers Park campus.[82]

In 1950, the CYO established its own citywide team to compete against area swim clubs. The CYO held its first open meet in the Washington Park swimming pool at Fifty-sixth and South Park Way (Dr. Martin Luther King Jr. Drive after 1968).[83] Whites and blacks swam and dove in the same pool, including a white girl from the Gage Park neighborhood, which later earned a reputation for white Catholic racism.[84] The Lake Shore Club from the tony Gold Coast neighborhood captured first place, while Portage Park, a white neighborhood on the northwest side and the Lawson YMCA on the near north side took second and third, respectively. Teams from the Back of the Yards and Washington Park neighborhoods also competed.[85] At a time when de jure racial segregation ruled the South and de facto segregation existed almost everywhere else, the CYO defied conventions by bringing blacks and whites together—even in water.

Playing to the Crowd

Although Sheil's inclusive policies guaranteed African American participation in the CYO, black athletes did not always receive full support from majority white crowds. The CYO boxing team, undefeated for seven consecutive years in intercity and international competition, got a scare during an international tournament at Soldier Field in the summer of 1938. Entering the second-to-last bout of the night, the CYO and Ireland were tied, four wins apiece. The CYO light heavyweight champion from St. Cecilia's, a white parish east of the stockyards in the Fuller Park neighborhood, won in a decision. The win guaranteed the CYO would not lose the tournament, but the final bout offered a chance to win it outright. Clarence Brown, an African American heavyweight champion from St. Nicholas's parish in Evanston, represented the CYO. His Irish opponent was Matt Lacey, described by a sportswriter as a "dock worker and able seaman." Brown knocked Lacey to the canvas in the first round, where he stayed a full eight counts. In the final round, though, the Irishman recovered and pummeled Brown with punches that "had the big colored boy staggering almost helpless around the ring."[86] The Chicago crowd booed when officials announced Brown the winner, even though his triumph ensured a tournament victory for the CYO, which retained its undefeated record.[87]

Crowds usually cheer for the hometown competitor. In this case, however, loyalty toward the black heavyweight appeared absent. It is difficult to determine whether the booing resulted from racist thinking or a sincere difference of opinion with the judges. Yet another possibility might explain the crowd's reaction: ethnic allegiance. During the 1930s, fight promoters often appealed to ethnic loyalties by highlighting the nationality of boxers. Some fighters even changed their names to appeal to certain ethnic groups. The CYO, playing up its "League of Nations" theme, publicized boxers based on their national origins.[88] Perhaps the undoubtedly large number of Irish American spectators at Soldier Field that night simply chose ethnic allegiance over loyalty to their city and the CYO. Whatever the case, the incident underscored a harsh reality for black athletes—success did not necessarily translate into acceptance.

However much individual whites may have harbored racist feelings toward black CYO participants, Bishop Sheil's organization still provided African American athletes with opportunities to compete on a level playing field—at least within the confines of organized athletics, where the long-cherished principles of sport included fair play and equal opportunity. Yet, every so often, racist behavior poisoned supervised competition. St. Elizabeth's alumnus George Phillips recalled his eighth-grade basketball team encountering racial bigotry during a 1947 tournament at St. Sabina's, an Irish American parish on the southwest side of the city. St. Elizabeth's was routing its opponent (not St. Sabina's), when the opposing coach, a white priest, ordered St Elizabeth's to "take the good niggers out." With the game out of reach for the opposing team, the St. Elizabeth's coach, Melvin Cash, sat Phillips and the other St. Elizabeth's starters on the bench. After the game, the racist priest then offered to buy ice cream as payoff to the "good niggers." In response, an enraged Phillips began "cussing out" the priest and threatened to throw a basketball at him. Cash quickly restrained Phillips and explained to the angry boy, "You're going to encounter this. You can't fight everybody." Phillips found it particularly painful to accept that a priest could be racist, since, in his experience, the German American missionaries at St. Elizabeth's were "authoritative" but "not racist." The incident taught Phillips that all priests were not necessarily as enlightened on race as the members of the Society of the Divine Word. "Just because you wear a Roman collar," he decided, "doesn't mean you're what you're supposed to be." In the end, St. Elizabeth's won the tournament. Phillips said the experience taught him to ignore race-baiting tactics and concentrate on his own successes.[89]

Phillips's painful experience underscores the prevalence of racism among Chicago's white Catholics. Sheil could use his authority as bishop to include African Americans in CYO competition, but he could not necessarily change the hearts and minds of racists living in white parishes. Black CYO teams, therefore, regularly faced hostilities while traveling in white neighborhoods for competitions. Since the archdiocese included the entire city, black athletes traveled into white neighborhoods everywhere. African Americans competed in downtown Chicago, in the stockyards district, in the suburbs, and in white neighborhoods on the south, west, and north sides of the city.[90] Basketball teams or boxing squads from St. Elizabeth's, Corpus Christi, or St. Anselm's often met near their local streetcar or elevated train stop and traveled together into white neighborhoods for protection.[91] Racism had not disappeared, but the CYO provided regular opportunities for blacks and whites to play together. As the second great migration of blacks arrived in Chicago during World War II and the immediate postwar years, however, mutual distrust grew between blacks and whites.

"League of Nations" to "Colored Youth Organization"

After the first large wave of migration in the 1910s and 1920s of African Americans from the South, the 1930 census revealed that blacks made up just 7 percent of Chicago's population. By 1940, that number barely increased, to 8 percent, due mostly to a decade of economic depression.[92] As a result, black CYO participants, in many respects, acted as another ethnic group, like German Americans, Italian Americans, or Polish Americans. More precisely, an amorphous concept of race extended to various groups.[93] Irish American Catholics and Italian American Catholics, for example, were considered members of two different races. Sheil and the CYO, however, attempted to downplay "interracial" differences as part of Mundelein's Americanization of Chicago Catholicism—the plan to create a church "100 percent American and 100 percent Catholic."

The second great migration of African Americans that began during World War II dramatically affected this situation. By 1950, African Americans composed 14 percent of the city's residents and that number would jump to 25 percent by 1960. As Chicago's black population expanded, the participation levels of African Americans in the CYO grew correspondingly. In 1932, Harry Booker was the only African American to make it to the finals of the CYO boxing tournament, but by 1940 nine of the thirty-two finalists were African Americans. And when the CYO held its final boxing tournament in 1953, more than 40 percent of the finalists were black. In addition to individual black competitors, African American teams also found success in the CYO. Between 1931 and 1949, 46 percent of the team champions in CYO basketball, boxing, and track and field were African American teams.[94] In 1937, for instance, Corpus Christi won the team boxing championship; St. Elizabeth's took the boys' heavies basketball championship; St. Elizabeth's won the junior track title; and a St. Elizabeth's athlete won the men's singles title in tennis.[95] Bronzeville parishes dominated the CYO again in 1938, when Corpus Christi won the team boxing championship; St. Elizabeth's took the boys' heavies basketball championship; and St. Anselm's won the senior track title, while St. Elizabeth's took the junior track title.[96] The trend accelerated through World War II and the postwar period.[97]

As African Americans played an increasingly prominent role in CYO athletics, many white Catholics began to believe the CYO had reached a "tipping point." They no longer saw blacks as just one ethnic group among many; rather, they felt that African Americans had overrun the organization. Some even referred to the CYO derisively as the "Colored Youth Organization."[98] For these white Catholics, the competition from black athletes seemed overwhelming. They no longer felt a sense of ownership in the CYO. Losses on the basketball floor and in the boxing ring represented more profound "losses," like the racial transformation of neighborhoods from white to black.

The CYO responded to white fears by showing that African Americans, if given proper opportunities, did not pose a threat. The organization consistently depicted its members as "clean, honest and upright."[99] Such characterizations were particularly crucial for black participants, stereotyped in American society as lazy, untrustworthy, and immoral.

Bishop Sheil and his staff portrayed African American members, like all CYO participants, as virtuous citizens committed to Christian principles. In 1940, for example, Hiner Thomas, a black boxer from Corpus Christi, won the CYO Club of Champions prize. The award recognized Thomas for "upholding the C.Y.O. principles of fair play and sportsmanship."[100] CYO public relations director Ralph Leo often used his weekly column in the archdiocesan newspaper to promulgate accounts of honorable young men living out CYO ideals.

In one Depression-era account, Leo chose Westerfield Millen, an African American boxer who lived in Corpus Christi's parish, to serve as the model CYO youngster of the week. One night, Millen found himself outside of the Black Belt (near Wrigley Field on the North Side) without fare for the elevated train ride home. "Westerfield solved his dilemma by doing what any other intelligent young man would have done—walked into the Town Hall Police Station, smiled at the sergeant and proceeded to explain his predicament," Leo recounted in an idealized narrative. "By way of adducing further evidence as to his bona-fide status in the community, Westerfield mentioned the fact that he was member of the C.Y.O. boxing club and knew Boxing Director T. F. O'Connell personally." According to Leo, this piece of information carried great weight with the desk sergeant, who gave the African American teenager a dime for carfare. Millen promptly returned the ten cents to O'Connell, who kept it on his desk in the CYO headquarters, promising to give it to the policeman the next time they met. The sergeant, however, forgot about the loan and never asked for the money. When the exceptionally conscientious Millen insisted that the loan be repaid, O'Connell went so far as to send a note to the police station with the dime enclosed.[101]

The tale, however contrived, captured several dynamics at work in the CYO. First, the organization had established citywide prominence by the mid-1930s. Therefore, Millen garnered immediate respect from the police officer when he revealed his connection to the sports league. Second, the desk sergeant's friendship with boxing coach O'Connell suggested Chicago's influential network of Irish Catholics. Irish Americans dominated police and fire departments, politics, and leadership positions in the Catholic Church. As a black teenager alone in a white neighborhood at night, Millen himself did not command much respect, but his association with the CYO mitigated his precarious status. Finally, Millen's behavior and the police response exemplified the organization's approach to fighting racism: Millen showed respect for authority and worked within the system, demonstrating his personal integrity by conducting himself in a manner beyond reproach, and for that he was treated with respect. The story encapsulated an optimistic view of race relations, for despite the prevalence of bigotry and discrimination, African Americans could find protection within the city's Euro-American Catholic fold through association with the CYO. A number of African Americans took advantage of their connection to Catholic-sponsored athletics to access Chicago's influential network of Irish American contacts in business and politics. Their link to Catholicism and the Democratic Party often mitigated the effects of racism and gave them an inside track to power and influence.

"The Club"

As a "minority within a minority," black Catholics comprised a relatively small part of Chicago's African American population.[102] Yet, by the mid twentieth century, they were leaders in business, politics, and the professions in significant numbers. Sociological studies have found that African American Catholics attained higher levels of education, income, and influence than their black Protestant counterparts.[103] But in Chicago, black Catholics had a particular advantage. In a city dominated by Irish Catholic leadership and power, connections to the Roman Catholic Church and the Democratic Party helped African Americans gain access to areas otherwise off limits to them. For many black men, Catholic-sponsored sports provided a particularly useful entry into the world of Irish Catholic power and influence.

Two-time Olympian Ralph Metcalfe epitomized this process. Born in Atlanta in 1910, Metcalfe's family relocated to Chicago during the first great migration of African Americans to the urban North. A track star at Tilden Technical High School, Metcalfe received an athletic scholarship to Marquette University in Milwaukee, where he won the national collegiate championship in the 100- and 220-yard dashes for three consecutive years. The phenomenal sprinter earned international fame as a member of the U.S. track team, winning silver medals in the 100-meter dash at both the 1932 and 1936 Olympic Games. At the Berlin games, Metcalfe joined Jesse Owens on the historic 4 x 100–meter U.S. relay team that dramatically refuted Aryan theories of physical superiority.[104]

While at Marquette, Metcalfe converted to Catholicism. Chicago's Catholic *New World* proudly reported on "one of their own," using Metcalfe's story to evangelize African Americans. A gentleman, scholar, and athlete, he became a kind of Catholic Paul Robeson.[105] Metcalfe helped Bishop Sheil by running exhibition races during CYO track meets in Chicago.[106] CYO members must have felt great pride when it was reported that Metcalfe received communion on the morning of his gold medal victory in Berlin, making the sign of the cross just prior to the race.[107] After coaching track and field at Xavier University in New Orleans and serving in the army during World War II, Metcalfe returned to Chicago. He became the first black appointed to the Illinois State Athletic Commission and served as an assistant to the Chicago Board of Examiners under Mayor Martin Kennelly. In 1952, African American U.S. congressman William Dawson helped the former track star secure the job of committeeman for the city's Third Ward. Loyal to Chicago's Democratic machine, Metcalfe eventually won Dawson's vacated congressional seat in 1970.

Metcalfe became the most prominent member of a group of black Catholics that political scientist William Grimshaw has called Mayor Richard J. Daley's "loyalist black elites."[108] They included John Stroger, president of the Cook County Board of Commissioners. A native of Helena, Arkansas, Stroger converted to Catholicism in grammar school. After graduating from Xavier University in New Orleans, he moved to Chicago in 1955. He plugged into the black Catholic network and began attending mass at Corpus Christi. Then someone suggested he meet Ralph Metcalfe. "Metcalfe had once taught at Xavier before I came. He had been the track coach. And then his wife was from Arkansas. So when I came up, people suggested that I should go and talk with Ralph, and I went up and talked with him. We developed a relationship." That relationship led to a fifty-year career in Chicago politics. A staunch machine loyalist, Stroger became the Eighth Ward committeeman and later Cook County commissioner. In 2001, Mayor Richard M. Daley appointed Stroger's son, Todd, a Xavier graduate, to fill the vacated aldermanic seat representing the Eighth Ward.[109]

In addition to acting as the "Commissioner" of South Side athletics, Joe Robichaux was also one of the loyal black elite in Richard J. Daley's machine. In 1963, Daley named Robichaux committeeman of the Twenty-first Ward. He was also the president of an ice cream company, integrating politics, sports, and business into his South Side leadership. Through programs at St. Elizabeth's and Sheil House, Robichaux groomed numerous future leaders in the African American community. His most famous protégé was Joseph Bertrand, a standout athlete at St. Elizabeth High School. Bertrand starred on St. Elizabeth's Iron Man team, which won the 1950 National Negro Basketball Championship, and received an athletic scholarship to the University of Notre Dame.[110] In 1971, Mayor Richard J. Daley chose Bertrand as the Democratic Party's nominee for city treasurer. A Catholic, he became the first African American elected to citywide office in Chicago's history. Bertrand's son, Jason, described the network of black men involved in Democratic Party politics, sports, and Catholicism as "the club."[111]

Members of "the club" received advantages through their network and, in turn, served the black community. However, when the interests of their constituents diverged with those of the machine, black loyalists paid a price for dissent. Mayor Daley dropped his support of Metcalfe, for example, when the congressman raised charges of police brutality during the 1970s.[112] Nevertheless, relationships formed through sports and religion provided unique opportunities for a cadre of black men in postwar Chicago. They became role models for the next generation and used their gifts to serve the community, whether they became a famous television personality, esteemed judge, or just an everyday member of their community.[113]

Conclusion

Between 1930 and 1954, the CYO reached hundreds of thousands of Chicagoans with its message of equality and universalism. Chicago's experiment in Catholic interracialism ended in the same year that the U.S. Supreme Court found racial segregation "inherently unequal" and unconstitutional. Just as the modern civil rights movement was beginning, the CYO and Sheil's progressive Catholic politics faded from national consciousness. The CYO name continued as a way to describe Catholic intramural sports, but neither Chicago nor any other American city would again have the same kind of commitment to Catholic-sponsored interracialism as seen in Chicago during the 1930s and 1940s. Liberal Catholic activists, like Chicago's Monsignor John Egan, and Catholic organizations like the Catholic Interracial Council, fought for racial justice, but they did not possess the authority of a bishop or the comprehensive scope of a diocesan program that reached every parish.

The CYO offers a counter-narrative to the story of white Catholic racism in twentieth-century urban America. A number of recent studies illustrate a pattern of working-class, Euro-American Catholics resisting the movement of African American residents into previously all-white, urban areas during the mid twentieth century.[114] High rates of home ownership as well as deep psychological and financial investments in parishes created strong neighborhood ties for white Catholics. While Protestants and Jews commonly moved away—"white flight" in the parlance of the day—many Catholics remained in the old neighborhoods, fighting to "protect" their parishes from African American "invasion." In several cases, white Catholics in the urban North used violence to intimidate African Americans who were moving into their parishes. Typically, historians have accepted such racist behavior as representative of urban Catholics. The regular interracialism of the CYO, however, complicates this interpretation by presenting evidence of cooperation between blacks and whites.

In 1942, Bishop Sheil proclaimed, "Jim Crowism in the Mystical Body of Christ is a disgraceful anomaly."[115] He viewed racism simply as an inconsistency (albeit a formidable one) in the American Catholic experience. In speeches across the country, Sheil spoke out against racial restrictive covenants and employment discrimination. But perhaps more important than his rhetoric were twenty-five years' worth of opportunities for interracial sporting contact among everyday Chicagoans.

Notes

The epigraph to this chapter is drawn from Bernard J. Sheil, "Speech to Negro Press Association," October 14, 1943, Folder 38, Box 1, Bernard J. Sheil Papers, Archdiocese of Chicago's Joseph Cardinal Bernadin Archives and Records Center (hereafter AAC).

1. Roger L. Treat, *Bishop Sheil and the CYO: The Story of the Catholic Youth Organization and the Man Who Influenced a Generation* (New York: Messner, 1951), 81–82, 191–94.

2. *New World*, December 2, 1932; Wilfrid Smith, "C.Y.O. Boxing Champions Crowned Before 16,000," *Chicago Tribune*, December 3, 1932. Jack Elder, "The Tournament Finals Reviewed for the Record," *New World*, December 9, 1932.

3. "Inter-City Bouts Draw Interest: Civic Reception for Pacific Coast Teams Who Will Meet C.Y.O. Champs," *New World*, December 30, 1932; Jack Elder, "Capacity Attendance Expected at C.Y.O. Inter-City Tournament," January 6, 1933; and Elder, "Coast Teams Say Good-Bye," January 13, 1933.

4. On Sheil, see Treat, *Bishop Sheil*; Edward R. Kantowicz, *Corporation Sole: Cardinal Mundelein and Chicago Catholicism* (Notre Dame, Ind.: University of Notre Dame Press, 1983), chap. 12; Mark B. Sorvillo, "Bishop Bernard J. Sheil: Hero of the Catholic Left" (Ph.D. diss., University of Chicago, 1990); Steven M. Avella, *This Confident Church: Catholic Leadership and Life in Chicago, 1940–1965* (Notre Dame, Ind.: University of Notre Dame Press, 1992), chap. 4; and Timothy B. Neary, "Crossing Parochial Boundaries: African Americans and Interracial Catholic Social Action in Chicago, 1914–1954" (Ph.D. diss., Loyola University Chicago, 2004), chap. 3.

5. Timuel Black, an African American historian who grew up in Bronzeville during the 1930s and played basketball at St. Elizabeth's gymnasium, recalled that Sheil was simply "fair." Timuel Black, interview by author, Chicago, Illinois, February 27, 2003.

6. There is no evidence to either confirm or deny that Daley took part in the rioting. The best works on Chicago's 1919 race riot are William M. Tuttle Jr., *Race Riot: Chicago in the Red Summer of 1919* (New York: Atheneum, 1970), and Dominic A. Pacyga, "Chicago's 1919 Race Riot: Ethnicity, Class, and Urban Violence," in Raymond A. Mohl, ed., *The Making of Urban America* (Wilmington, Del.: Scholarly Resources, 1997), 187–207.

7. Chicago Commission on Race Relations, *The Negro in Chicago: A Study of Race Relations and a Race Riot* (Chicago: University of Chicago Press, 1922), 16. Frederic M. Thrasher, *The Gang: A Study of 1,313 Gangs in Chicago* (Chicago: University of Chicago Press, 1968), 43, 52, 139–40.

8. This group organized Negro History week, which eventually became Black History Month.

9. For more on the Rosenwald YMCAs, see Nina Mjagkij, *Light in the Darkness: African Americans and the YMCA, 1852–1946* (Lexington: University Press of Kentucky, 1994), 74–83. For more on the Wabash YMCA, see James R. Grossman, *Land of Hope: Chicago, Black Southerners, and the Great Migration* (Chicago: University of Chicago Press, 1989), 81, 116, 128–29, 134, 140–43, 150, 200–202, 228–29, 235, and 240.

10. Margaret Brennan, "Recreation Facilities in Chicago's Negro District," Federal Writers' Project: Negro Studies Project, Box A875, Library of Congress, quoted in Maren Stange, ed., *Bronzeville: Black Chicago in Pictures, 1941–1943* (New York: New Press, 2003), 189.

11. "Y Integrated—After Five Years," *Chicago Defender*, June 10, 1950.

12. Richard Wright, "How 'Bigger' Was Born," *Native Son* (New York: Perennial, 2001), xxvi–xxvii.

13. Robert Pruter, "Early Phillips High School Basketball Teams," Illinois High School Association's "Illinois H.S.toric" web page: http://ihsa.org/feature/hstoric/phillips.htm.

14. For more on SBS work in Chicago, see Suellen Hoy, "Ministering Hope to Chicago," *Chicago History* (Fall 2002): 4–23, and Neary, "Crossing Parochial Boundaries," chaps. 1, 2.

15. Pruter, "Early Phillips High School Basketball Teams." Four of the five participated in CYO athletics and represented Bronzeville parishes: Cleveland Bray and Leroy Rhodes came from St. Elizabeth's, while Charles Gant and William McQuitter came from Corpus Christi.

16. Sam Smith, "'Sweetwater' Keeps Rollin': First Black to Sign in NBA Now on Taxi Squad," *Chicago Tribune*, June 9, 1985; John W. Fountain, "'Sweetwater' Clifton, Former Globetrotter," September 2, 1990; and Fred Mitchell, "Robinzine Remembered at DePaul," July 25, 2000.

17. Pruter, "Early Phillips High School Basketball Teams." On racial discrimination against African Americans in college athletics, see Ocania Chalk, *Black College Sport* (New York: Dodd, Mead, 1976), and David Kenneth Wiggins, *Black Athletes in White America* (Syracuse, N.Y.: Syracuse University Press, 1997), chap. 7.

18. Larry Hawkins, former Public League coach and director of Special Programs at the University of Chicago, dubbed the three institutions only blocks apart a "golden triangle." Pruter, "Early Phillips High School Basketball Teams."

19. Eugene Saffold, interview by author, tape recording, Hazel Crest, Illinois, November 8, 2001.

20. John Woodford, interview by author, tape recording, Chicago, Illinois, April 26, 2002.

21. George Phillips, interview by author, tape recording, Chicago, Illinois, August 8, 2001.

22. The building opened on Thanksgiving Day, 1892. "Minor Locals," *Chicago Daily Sun*, October 31, 1892.

23. "St. Elizabeth's Club House Remodeled," *New World*, September 16, 1938, and Duncan E. Roudette, "St. Elizabeth Branch," *New World*, September 1, 1939.

24. The building at 4062 South Michigan Avenue was the former LaSalle University Extension.

25. Edwin W. Leaner, III, interview by author, tape recording, Chicago, Illinois, June 27, 2001.

26. Marie C. Davis, interview by author, tape recording, Chicago, Illinois, July 6, 2001; Leaner interview; Phillips interview; Saffold interview; and Warner Saunders, interview by author, tape recording, Chicago, Illinois, August 24, 2001.

27. Leaner interview.

28. Treat, *Bishop Sheil*, 130–34; "Joseph J. Robichaux Dies at 54; Political Figure, Molder of Athlete," *Chicago Sun-Times*, April 27, 1971; "Athletic-Political Activist Succumbs," *Jet*, May 13, 1971; and A. S. "Doc" Young, *Negro Firsts in Sports* (Chicago: Johnson, 1963), 197.

29. Wilfred Smith, "C.Y.O. Boxers Defeat Irish, Six Bouts to Four: Retain Perfect 7 Year Record Before 30,000," *Chicago Tribune*, July 15, 1938.

30. Richard Wright, "High Tide in Harlem: Joe Louis as Symbol of Freedom," *New Masses*, July 5, 1938, reprinted in David K. Wiggins and Patrick B. Miller, eds., *The Unlevel Playing Field: A Documentary History of the African American Experience in Sport* (Urbana: University of Illinois Press, 2003), 169–74. Alex Haley and Malcolm X, *The Autobiography of Malcolm X* (New York: Ballantine, 1999), 25.

31. "Lorenzo Lovings," *New World*, April 21, 1935; "C.Y.O. Boxing Notes," September 7, 1934; and "C.Y.O. Boxing Notes," August 23, 1935.

32. Ralph C. Leo, "Looking 'Em Over," *New World*, May 31, 1935.

33. "Colored Boys to Take Part in C.Y.O. Glove Tournament: Catholic Boys of Colored Race Invited to Enter Great Boxing Tournament," *New World*, October 23, 1931. "Youth Organization to Back a Giant Program of Athletic Bouts," October 9, 1931. M. Price Jones, "Many Applications for C.Y.O. Athletic Event Are Received," October 2, 1931.

34. Pacyga, "Chicago's 1919 Race Riot," 194.

35. "Corpus Christi to Hold Pageant Jan. Thirteenth," *Chicago Defender*, January 9, 1937; "Corpus Christi C.Y.O. Makes Plan for Pageant Jan. 13," *New World*, January 8, 1937.

36. "C.Y.O. Sports Summary: Week of March 8 to 15," *New World*, March 8, 1935.

37. Boxers Hiner Thomas and Jimmy Martin served as vice president and marshal, respectively. "Corpus Christi Young Men's Branch Selects New Officers for Year," *New World*, January 8, 1937.

38. "C.Y.O. Boxers Win in I.A.C. Tournament," *New World*, February 2, 1934; "All-Star Entertainment for Bishop Sheil Dinner," January 17, 1936; "Capacity Crowd at St. Andrew's C.Y.O. Bouts," August 23, 1935; and "C.Y.O. Boxers in Benefit at Statesville, Ill., April 16," April 15, 1932.

39. "C.Y.O. Boxers Give Exhibition at the Fair This Week," *New World*, July 13, 1934; "The Irish Village at A Century of Progress" [advertisement], July 20, 1934; and "Make Irish Village Irish," August 3, 1934.

40. "C.Y.O. Boxing Notes," *New World*, September 7, 1934; "C.Y.O. Boxing Notes," June 14, 1935; and Leo, "Looking 'Em Over," June 28, 1935.

41. "C.Y.O. Boxing Notes," *New World*, December 21, 1934.

42. "Young, Canadeo and Dade, of C.Y.O., Win Golden Glove Titles," *New World*, March 15, 1940; Treat, *Bishop Sheil*, 88.

43. "Former CYO Boxer Wins World Title," *C.Y.O Voice*, February 1947, 1, 8, Box 11, Folder 11, Edward Victor Cardinal Papers, University of Notre Dame Archives.

44. *New World*, January 1, 1932.

45. *New World*, January 15, 1932; January 22, 1932; January 29, 1932; February 5, 1932; February 12, 1932; February 19, 1932; February 26, 1932; and March 4, 1932.

46. *New World*, January 6, 1933; "St. Elizabeth's Gym Center of C.Y.O. Games," *New World*, December 2, 1932, and December 9, 1932.

47. St. Agnes (an Irish American parish in the white neighborhood of Brighton Park), St. Carthage (an Irish American parish in the white neighborhood of Park Manor), St. Mary of Perpetual Help (a Polish American parish in the white neighborhood of Bridgeport), St. Rose of Lima (an Irish American parish in the white Back of the Yards neighborhood), and Visitation (an Irish American parish in the white Englewood and Back of the Yards neighborhoods), played at St. Elizabeth's gymnasium. "Boys' Division Scores," *New World*, January 27, 1933; "Boys' Division Scores," *New World*, January 20, 1933. The 1933–34 season witnessed similar dynamics. White teams—St. John the Baptist (an Irish American parish in the Back of the Yards neighborhood), St. Gabriel's (an Irish American parish in the Canaryville neighborhood), and Sacred Heart (a Jesuit parish in the Czech neighborhood of Pilsen)—competed at St. Elizabeth's gymnasium with black teams from St. Anselm's, Corpus Christi, and St. Elizabeth's, as well as against the other white teams. "C.Y.O. Men's Basketball Divisions, 1933–34," *New World*, December 8, 1933.

48. For an account of the 1949 rioting, see John T. McGreevy, *Parish Boundaries: The Catholic Encounter with Race in the Twentieth-Century Urban North* (Chicago: University of Chicago Press, 1996), 94–97.

49. In the late 1960s, Francis X. Lawlor, an Augustinian priest at St. Rita's High School (Seventy-seventh and Western Avenue), spearheaded white resistance by spewing racist rhetoric about "holding the line" against black encroachment. McGreevy, *Parish Boundaries*, 232.

50. "C.Y.O. Boys' Standings," *New World*, February 20, 1933; "Field of Undefeated Teams in C.Y.O. Race Cut to Twelve," February 9, 1934; December 13, 1935; *New World* sports schedules, 1937 and 1938, January 6, 1939, January 20, 1939, January 27, 1939, February 3, 1939, February 10, 1939, February 17, 1939; "Final Week of Sectional Play Remains in Cage Tourney," February 24, 1939; and *New World* sports schedules, 1939–40.

51. Harry C. Koenig, *A History of the Archdiocese of Chicago* (Chicago: Archdiocese of Chicago, 1980), 860.

52. St. Elizabeth's played in St. Sabina's first AAU tournament. "St. Sabina Cage Tourney Finals Sunday Afternoon: Capacity Crowd Expected to See Climax of Colorful Cage Tournament," *New World*, March 18, 1938.

53. "Third Annual A.A.U. Cage Tourney Opens at St. Sabina's Gym," *New World*, March 15, 1940.

54. "St. Sabina Cage Tourney Slated for Dec. 4–13," *New World*, December 2, 1949.

55. On the controversy surrounding St. Sabina's in 2001, see Neary, "Crossing Parochial Boundaries," prologue; and "'An Inalienable Right to Play,'" *Chicago Tribune*, June 17, 2001.

56. "C.Y.O. Crowns Three New Champs in Basketball: Cicero Five Wins Title in Heavyweight Class," *New World*, March 12, 1934. Ralph C. Leo, "1933–34 Is Most Successful Season in C.Y.O. Basketball," *New World*, March 23, 1934.

57. Phillips, Saffold, and Saunders interviews.

58. "400 Quintets Entered for 1937–38 Play," *New World*, December 19, 1937; "C.Y.O. Quints in Torrid Race for Cage Supremacy," *New World*, January 13, 1939.

59. Brown was named AAU outstanding player of the Midwest in 1937. "Chicago Centennial Basketball Classic," *New World*, March 26, 1937.

60. "6,500 Fans See Final of C.Y.O. Cage Tourney: St. Elizabeth, St. Dorothy and Sacred Heart Take 1938 Crowns," *New World*, March 11, 1938.

61. "Loyola University Beats DePaul, 46–43," *New World*, April 2, 1937. USA Basketball, Inc., http://www.usabasketball.com/history/moly_1936.html.

62. Mike Murphy, "St. Columbanus, St. Anselm Win C.Y.O. Basketball Titles," *New World*, March 22, 1940.

63. Murphy, "C.Y.O. Cage Champs Meet Detroit at St. Sabina Gym," *New World*, April 5, 1940. "Chicago C.Y.O. Basket Teams Defeat Detroit," April 8, 1940. Murphy, "C.Y.O. Champs Meet Cleveland Sunday: St. Columbanus, St. Anselm Journey to Ohio City for Title," April 12, 1940.

64. McGreevy, *Parish Boundaries*, 93; Vernon Jarrett, "Church Myths vs. New Sabina," *Chicago Defender*, June 20, 2001.

65. "Try for Division Championship in C.Y.O. Girls' League," *New World*, February 26, 1932.

66. *New World*, December 9, 1933, February 24, 1934.

67. *New World*, February 16, 1934.

68. Kantowicz, *Corporation Sole*, 173–88.

69. Woodford interview.

70. Jack Elder, "C.Y.O. Track Meet Begins Tomorrow," *New World*, August 12, 1932; "Leonas and Bodeau Win C.Y.O. Titles: New Records Set in the Fifth Annual Meet at Loyola Field," July 3, 1936; "C.Y.O. Track, Field Meet at Loyola Field: Marquardt, Gill, Bray, Brunton to Run," July 30, 1937; "St. Elizabeth, St. Thomas Win in C.Y.O. Track: Marquardt, Brunton, Bowles, Star," August 6, 1937; and "Shatter 5 Records in C.Y.O. Track and Field Title," June 24, 1938.

71. Treat, *Bishop Sheil*, 139.

72. Landry won the long jump in 1949, 1950, 1952, and 1953. She won the 50 meters in 1953 and 1954. Jones won the 100 meters in 1953 and 1954. USA Track and Field, the sport's national governing body: http://www.usatf.org/statistics/champions/outdoor/women.shtml.

73. J. S. Fuerst and D. Bradford Hunt, eds., *When Public Housing Was Paradise: Building Community in Chicago* (Westport, Conn.: Praeger, 2003), 170.

74. "Girls' Volleyball Playoffs Open Next Sunday Afternoon," *New World*, April 21, 1939. "Playoffs in the C.Y.O. Horseshoe Meet Tomorrow: Lincoln Park Is Scene of Event as Finalists Vie for Coveted Divisional Crowns," *New World*, September 16, 1938.

75. For a discussion of the 1938 transformation, see Neary, "Crossing Parochial Boundaries," chap. 3.

76. "'People's Bishop' Has a Silver Jubilee: Chicago Gives Its Beloved 'Benny' Sheil a Well-Earned Celebration," *Life*, May 18, 1953, 63.

77. "Keen Competition Features Checker Finals at the C.Y.O.," *New World*, February 3, 1939.

78. Jack Elder, "Swimming, Volleyball and Table Tennis to the Fore in C.Y.O. Program," *New World*, March 15, 1935.

79. "Bartolini, Gant Snare Individual Honors of Table Tennis Meet," *New World*, March 17, 1939.

80. See James H. Madison, *A Lynching in the Heartland: Race and Memory in America* (New York: Palgrave, 2001), 130–38.

81. "St. Viator Takes C.Y.O. Swimming Championship," *New World*, May 1, 1936.

82. "C.Y.O. Swimming Meet Entries Being Accepted," *New World*, April 8, 1938. The CYO did not confine interracial swimming to competitive meets. Marie Davis, an African American woman who grew up in Corpus Christi parish, swam in 1942 with white girls at a CYO camp in Libertyville, Illinois. Davis interview.

83. "CYO Open Swim Meet Slated for Aug. 12–13: Mermaids Set to Splash," *New World*, August 11, 1950.

84. On anti-black rioting in Gage Park, see McGreevy, *Parish Boundaries*, 187–88.

85. "12-Year-Old Marilyn Stars in Swim Meet: Lake Shore Wins Title," *New World*, August 18, 1950.

86. Smith, "C.Y.O. Boxers Defeat Irish, Six Bouts to Four: Retain Perfect Seven Year Record Before 30,000," *Chicago Tribune*, July 15, 1938.

87. *New World*, July 22, 1938.

88. For a discussion of the CYO "League of Nations" imagery, see Neary, "Crossing Parochial Boundaries," chap. 3.

89. Phillips interview.

90. There are numerous examples of interracial competition in both black and white neighborhoods. For example, in the 1932 district championships, Harry Booker faced a boxer from St. Anthony's (Twenty-fourth and Canal Street in the South Loop) at the CYO gymnasium in the downtown Loop (*New World*, November 4, 1932). In November 1935, two St. Anselm's athletes boxed in the gymnasium at St. Bernard's, Sixty-fifth and Harvard Avenue in the white Hamilton Park neighborhood (*New World*, November 15, 1935). In June 1937, three Corpus Christi boxers fought in the auditorium of Sacred Heart, a Jesuit parish in the Southwest Side Czech neighborhood of Pilsen ("Review of C.Y.O. Boxing in Recent Weeks," *New World*, June 4, 1937). In one week during January of 1937, boxing shows were held on Monday at St. George's Catholic High School in north suburban Evanston, on Tuesday at St. Pius parish in Pilsen, and on Wednesday at Corpus Christi in Bronzeville. "C.Y.O. Boxers Face Busy Month," *New World*, January 8, 1937.

91. Phillips interview.

92. U.S. Census Bureau, Working Paper no. 76, "Historical Census Statistics on Population Totals by Race, 1790–1990," table 14, Illinois, Race and Hispanic Origin for Selected Large Cities.

93. On definitions of race in the United States prior to 1940, see McGreevy, *Parish Boundaries*, 9–13.

94. *Chicago Tribune* and *New World*, 1931–53.

95. "CYO History and Information" Folder, Box 4263, CYO Papers, AAC.

96. "'Hail the Victors!' C.Y.O. Presents 1938 Crop of Champs," *New World*, January 6, 1939.

97. In addition to African Americans, Latinos participated in the CYO in large numbers during the postwar period. In 1948, for example, nine boxers from St. Francis Mexican Youth Center qualified for the CYO finals—the largest number ever from one parish. Frank Mastro, "South Boxers Beat North in C.Y.O. Finals," *Chicago Tribune*, December 10, 1948.

98. "Roman Catholics: Winning the Kingdom of God," *Time,* September 26, 1969, 63.

99. This phrase is taken from the CYO pledge. Treat, *Bishop Sheil,* 70–71.

100. "Club of Champions Award Given to 6 by Bishop Sheil," *New World,* May 31, 1940.

101. Ralph C. Leo, "Looking 'Em Over," *New World,* May 1, 1936.

102. The phrase is borrowed from Albert J. Raboteau, "Minority within a Minority: History of Black Catholicism in America," in *A Fire in the Bones: Reflections on African-American Religious History* (Boston: Beacon, 1995), 117–37.

103. See J. L. Alston and E. Warrick, "Black Catholics: Social and Cultural Characteristics," *Journal of Black Studies,* 3:2 (December 1971): 245–55; William Feigelman et al., "The Social Characteristics of Black Catholics," *Society and Social Research,* 75:3 (April 1991): 133–43; and Larry L. Hunt, "Religious Affiliation among Blacks in the United States: Black Catholic Status Advantages Revisited," *Social Science Quarterly,* 79:1 (March 1998): 170–92.

104. "This Week in Black History: Ralph Metcalfe: October 10, 1978," *Jet,* October 10, 1994, 29.

105. "Metcalfe, Sprint Star, Olympic Hope, Baptized Catholic," *New World,* June 24, 1932; "Metcalfe at Marquette," September 9, 1932; "Colored College Man Elected," May 12, 1933; "Ralph Metcalfe: Hopes for National Championship Here," June 16, 1933; "Metcalfe Out for Law," September 22, 1933; "Metcalfe Honored for Oratory," February 2, 1934; "Metcalfe to Defend Title," April 20, 1934; "Metcalfe Returns," February 1, 1935; and "Metcalfe Starts Summer Training," May 10, 1935.

106. "C.Y.O. Track and Field Meet: Metcalfe to Run in Invitational Hundred," *New World,* July 29, 1932; Jack Elder, "St. Brenda's Boys Declared Winners in Sunday's Track Meet," August 26, 1932.

107. "Sign of Cross Made by Athlete, Winner of Olympic Race: Metcalfe, American Star, Received Communion before Victory," *New World,* August 28, 1936.

108. William J. Grimshaw, *Bitter Fruit: Black Politics and the Chicago Machine, 1931–1991* (Chicago: University of Chicago Press, 1992), 118.

109. Honorable John H. Stroger Jr., interview by author, tape recording, Chicago, Illinois, April 8, 2002.

110. "National Negro Title Goes to St. Elizabeth," *New World,* March 31, 1950.

111. Jason Bertrand, interview with author, Chicago, Illinois, November 4, 2000.

112. Grimshaw, *Bitter Fruit,* 134–38.

113. For example, Warner Saunders, a newscaster for Chicago's NBC affiliate, graduated from Corpus Christi in 1953 and attended Xavier University in New Orleans on a basketball scholarship. Mitchell Ware, founder of the largest minority-owned law firm in the United States and a Cook County judge, was a standout athlete at St. Elizabeth High School and attended St. Ambrose College in Davenport, Iowa, and DePaul University's school of law.

114. See Gerald Gamm, *Urban Exodus: Why the Jews Left Boston and the Catholics Stayed* (Cambridge, Mass.: Harvard University Press, 1999); Arnold Hirsch, *Making the Second Ghetto: Race and Housing in Chicago, 1940–1960* (Chicago: University of Chicago Press, 1998); John T. McGreevy, *Parish Boundaries*; Eileen McMahon, *What Parish Are You From? A Chicago Irish Community and Race Relations* (Lexington: University of Kentucky Press, 1993); and Thomas

J. Sugrue, *The Origins of the New Urban Crisis: Race and Inequality in Postwar Detroit* (Princeton, N.J.: Princeton University Press, 1996).

115. "Paper to be read by the Most Reverend Bernard J. Sheil, D.D., Auxiliary Bishop of Chicago and Founder-Director of the CYO before the Annual Conference of Catholic Charities, September 27–30, 1942, in Kansas City, MO," Box 1, Folder 25, Sheil Papers, AAC.

10

An Athlete Dying Young

Kenny Hubbs, Memory, and the Chicago Cubs

RICHARD KIMBALL

The time you won your town the race
We chaired you through the market-place;
Man and boy stood cheering by,
And home we brought you shoulder-high.

To-day, the road all runners come,
Shoulder-high we bring you home,
And set you at your threshold down,
Townsman of a stiller town.
　　—A. E. Housman, "To an Athlete Dying Young"

Death, youth, and beauty form a potent combination in American society. One need only remember the nonstop coverage of the tragic ends of Princess Diana and John F. Kennedy Jr. to appreciate the American obsession with celebrity death. When an individual is killed during the prime of life the tragedy is multiplied. If the victim is beautiful and enjoys wide recognition, Americans who never knew the deceased personally mourn the loss as though a close family member had died.

Celebrity deaths remind us of our own mortality, but the deaths of famous athletes often appear even more poignant because, unlike other celebrities, their physical gifts seem to defy the possibility of the grave. Perhaps the most indelible memory of an athlete cut down in the prime of life was Lou Gehrig. After playing in 2,130 straight games for the New York Yankees in the 1920s and 1930s, the Iron Horse's skills deteriorated almost in front of the fan's eyes. Within a matter of months, Gehrig's body betrayed him, and in 1941, at the age of thirty-seven, he died from amyotrophic lateral sclerosis (ALS). Immortalized by Gary Cooper in *Pride of the Yankees,* Gehrig's declaration that he was the luckiest man on the face of the earth always brings tears because his strength, skill, and determination were impotent against the scourge that came to be known as Lou Gehrig's disease.

The premature deaths of other athletes—Roberto Clemente, Thurman Munson, Dale Earnhardt—have been seared into the American consciousness. In Chicago, the death of Bears running back Brian Piccolo in 1970 did for embryonal cell carcinoma what Lou Gehrig had done for ALS. More recently, on Saturday, June 22, 2002, Wrigley Field fell silent when Cubs catcher Joe Girardi announced to forty thousand people that St. Louis Cardinal's pitcher Darryl Kile had been found dead in his Chicago hotel room earlier that day. The game canceled, fans filed out quietly, their thoughts focused on the tragedy that befell the thirty-three-year-old Kile, his family, and the Cardinal organization. The typical tension between Cub and Cardinal fans evaporated as all shouldered some burden of grief.

Later that week, on June 26, Cubs fans returned to Wrigley Field to remember one of their own who had been cut down in his prime, Kenny Hubbs, the Cub second baseman who won the Rookie of the Year award in 1962 and then was killed in a plane crash in Utah a year later. More than thirty thousand fans attended Ken Hubbs Memorial Night and received a facsimile of Hubbs's baseball card from his rookie season forty years before. Most fans would not have remembered the fresh-faced visage on the front of the commemorative card but many choked up when they read on the back of the card that Hubbs "looks like he can't miss."

Kenny Hubbs, the All-American Boy

Kenneth Douglas Hubbs had not always been a "can't miss" athletic prospect. When he was just six months old, in the spring of 1942, Kenny ruptured a hernia. Too young for a restorative operation, he wore a truss until he was five or six years old. In fact, the doctor who initially fitted Kenny for the truss told his parents, "You will need to watch him his whole life." Kenny eventually grew out of the hernia, discarded the truss, and almost immediately began to make his mark on the athletic fields of his hometown, Colton, California, a working-class community sixty miles east of Los Angeles.[1]

Athletic success in Colton had long been a Hubbs family tradition. Kenny's mother ran track during high school and Kenny's father had been an all-star football player in the California Interscholastic Federation, as well as a high school record holder in the 440-yard dash. Kenny's older brother, Keith, likewise excelled in sports, captaining the basketball team and winning All-American honors as a running back at Colton Union High School. Later, Keith played football at Brigham Young University in Provo, Utah.

Nonetheless, Kenny's athletic gifts set him apart. At age nine he enrolled in the local YMCA boxing tournament, where he quickly worked through the ranks of boxers his age. After all of the nine-year-olds fell prey to Kenny's lightning blows, he took on the ten-year-olds, then the eleven-year-olds. By the end of the tournament, Kenny stood toe-to-toe with twelve-year-olds, whose bodies towered over him but whose hands had trouble keeping up. Yet it was on Colton's baseball diamonds that Kenny really came to the town's attention.

In 1954, twelve-year-old Kenny led the Colton All-Stars to the final game of the Little League World Series in Williamsport, Pennsylvania. In a tournament that featured five future major leaguers (Jim Barbieri, Boog Powell, Bill Connors, Carl Taylor, and Hubbs), Kenny stole the show. His exploits at the Series have become legendary. Suffering from a broken toe, Kenny nonetheless rose to the occasion when Colton faced Schenectady, New York, in the final game. Early in the game, he smashed a home run that cleared the bleachers and struck a bus parked outside the stadium, then he hobbled around the bases in pain. Later, playing shortstop, Kenny made the fielding play of the Series when he ran, lunged, and barehanded a pop-up that was headed over second base. Yankees broadcaster Mel Allen, who called the game for a national television audience, gushed in admiration: "You don't see that in the big leagues. That's one of the greatest plays I've ever seen."[2] Broadcast into homes throughout the country, baseball fans beyond Colton began to have great expectations for young Kenny.

On the trip east to Williamsport, Kenny became acquainted with his future home and the friendly confines of Wrigley Field. During a stopover in Chicago, the Colton All-Stars toured the city and attended a Cubs game. The 1954 Cubs, led by Hank Sauer and Ralph Kiner, finished in seventh place, with a record of sixty-four wins and ninety losses. Team standings were of secondary importance to the young fans from Colton, however. More exciting was the opportunity to watch major league baseball (the Dodgers had not yet moved to Los Angeles), especially the gifted new Cub shortstop Ernie Banks, who was playing in his first full season. Banks later became one of Kenny's closest friends when Hubbs joined the team just seven years later. Kenny also took particular interest in the Cubs first baseman, Dee Fondy, who had grown up in neighboring San Bernardino, California.

After returning from the Little League World Series, where Colton lost in the final game to the Schenectady team led by future Baltimore Orioles star Boog Powell, Kenny Hubbs settled into the life of a teen athlete. He lettered in four sports at Colton Union High School. Before graduating, he was named as the quarterback on the All-American football team; leading Colton's hoop squad in scoring, rebounds, and assists, he was elected to basketball's All-American team, making him the nation's first athlete to achieve that honor in two sports in the same year. Kenny also starred in track and field, and in baseball. In addition, he was an excellent scholar and was student body president at Colton. A fictional Jack Armstrong might have been the All-American boy on the radio during the 1930s and 1940s, but Kenny Hubbs was the real-life version in 1950s southern California.[3]

23. *Little League Hero.* Kenny Hubbs crossing first base in the 1954 Little League World Series.

Hubbs and the Cubs

As high school graduation approached, Hubbs weighed his options. College scholarships in football, basketball, and baseball promised education and sports, while major league scouts dangled offers that included sizable signing bonuses. On the morning following graduation in June 1959, Hubbs chose to defer college and signed a $50,000 contract with the Chicago Cubs. For the next three summers, the shortstop worked his way through the Cubs minor league teams, starting in the Appalachian League in Morristown, Tennessee, and moving on to Fort Worth, Texas (Texas League); Lancaster, Pennsylvania (Eastern League); and Wenatchee, Washington (Northern League). Though Hubbs succeeded at each level of the minor leagues, he realized that it would be difficult to make the major league club as a shortstop. Ernie Banks, the Cubs' regular shortstop, was already a two-time National League MVP (1958 and 1959), and winner of the Gold Glove award in 1960.

With help from Hall of Fame shortstop (and Cubs broadcaster) Lou Boudreau, Hubbs made the transition to second base. By the spring of 1962, Kenny Hubbs made the Cubs roster as the team's starting second baseman. He played a sparkling defense, breaking major league records for errorless games and consecutive chances without an error. For seventy-eight straight games in the middle of the season, Hubbs handled 418 chances without an error, breaking Bobby Doerr's record of 414. The slick-fielding second baseman hit .260 with 172 base hits, 49 runs batted in, and was awarded the 1962 Gold Glove and the National League Rookie of the Year award, joining teammate Billy Williams, who had been named Rookie of the Year the previous season.

Kenny Hubbs was one of the most promising young players in the major leagues. Boudreau compared his skills to Hall of Fame second baseman Bobby Doerr and Yankee great Joe Gordon. Though Hubbs struggled at the plate during his sophomore season (hitting only .235), the Cubs believed that they had solved their second base problem for the next decade. Sportscaster Tom Harmon, speaking in 1964, called Hubbs "the greatest defensive second baseman in the history of baseball." Though such extreme praise may not yet have been warranted, Hubbs clearly had the potential to prove Harmon right.[4]

Hubbs's off-field image grew during his time with the Cubs. In fact, former teammates recall his character traits more often than they recite his baseball skill. By all accounts, Hubbs never refused to sign an autograph, often standing outside of the stadium for hours. The day before he broke the major league fielding record, Hubbs visited Chicago's Rehabilitation Institute and spent his day off cheering up the patients.

He explained, "If I make an error tomorrow it won't be because I was nice to somebody." In fact, Hubbs seemed to be nice to everybody. Ernie Banks called Hubbs "a perfect hero for kids to have. He's a Mormon. He doesn't drink or smoke. None of that. It's a pleasure to be on the same team with Kenny." Endless speaking assignments kept Hubbs busy, but he still managed to find time to coach a Midget football team in Colton. Teammate Ron Santo captured Hubbs's character perfectly, in terms that we have come to expect: "You know those movies where they show the All-American boy? Well, that's Kenny."

On many of the Cubs' flights, Hubbs could be found in the cockpit talking to the pilots and observing their technique. The flying bug had bit Kenny. He took pilot lessons, earned his license in January 1964, and purchased a red Cessna 172. Kenny's parents were concerned about his new hobby and his brother Keith asked Kenny to give up flying. Instead, as Keith recalls, Kenny "had a certain way about him—he could convince you that you should try anything. The next thing I knew, he's introducing me to his flight instructor and then *I'm* taking flying lessons."[5] Kenny, just a month removed from earning his license, and days after agreeing to a new contract with the Cubs, flew with friend Denny Doyle from Colton to Provo, Utah. The two wanted to surprise Denny's wife and newborn baby girl, who were visiting relatives in Utah. The trip was to be a quick one, as Kenny was scheduled to play in a church basketball tournament in San Diego the next weekend. Spring training was just two weeks away.

On Thursday, February 13, 1964, Kenny Hubbs and Denny Doyle left the Provo airport for their return trip to Colton. A storm was dumping snow in the mountains surrounding Provo but Hubbs received clearance for takeoff. Hoping to be out of Provo before the storm hit, Hubbs and Doyle took off heading south. Within a few minutes, Hubbs turned the plane around and headed back toward the airport, but too late. They crashed into the ice of Utah Lake. Hubbs was twenty-two years old; Denny Doyle was twenty-three.

An outpouring of respect, admiration, and sadness flooded toward Colton and the Hubbs family. Newspapers in Chicago, Los Angeles, and Salt Lake City (where the Mormon Hubbs had become a favorite son) followed the details of the crash investigation and the impact that Hubbs's death had on his hometown and his adopted hometowns. Colton shut down for Hubbs's funeral. More than two thousand mourners attended the services held in the auditorium at Colton Union High because the Latter-day Saints chapel could not accommodate the crowd. LDS Bishop Lyman Madsen officiated, and he read a telegram from Chicago Mayor Richard J. Daley that captured the feeling of the gathering: "Ken Hubbs had the affection and respect of all of Chicago. There isn't a man in Chicago who wouldn't have been proud to have him as a son. His great humility and fine sportsmanship won him a place in the hearts of the nation." Kenny's teammates served as his pallbearers and a procession of more than five hundred cars followed the casket to Montecito Memorial Park.[6]

To Perpetuate His Memory

The recounting of Kenny Hubbs's life and athletic accomplishments tells only part of the story. As anthropologist Katherine Verdery writes, dead bodies have political lives; they continue to influence society and morality not just through their legacies but through the reinterpretation of those legacies by the living. Athletes have posthumous lives as well. By recalling the lives of sporting heroes past, the living cannot unbury the dead, but they do use them to help create meaning for a new generation of athletes and fans. Verdery concludes, "No matter which conceptions of cosmic order, ancestors, space, and time we human beings employ, it seems our dead . . . are always with us. The important thing is what we do with them."[7]

Almost from the moment of Kenny Hubbs's death, the living began to "do" things with his memory and construct a living legacy that has continued for four decades. More than sports necrophilia, the uses that dead athletes are put to help to shape contemporary athletic culture and transmit ideals and values from one generation to the next. Following Hubbs's tragic plane crash, memorials appeared almost immediately. As we might expect, Topps Baseball Card Company was one of the first institutions to memorialize and capitalize on Hubbs's death. In 1964, Topps card number 550 showed a close-up picture of Hubbs in his batting helmet with a black band "In Memoriam" across the top and his name on a black band across the bottom.[8]

Other organizations, perhaps with less of a pecuniary interest in Hubbs's legacy, were created shortly after Kenny's death. The Ken Hubbs Foundation, the most prominent Hubbs-related association, was organized in Colton by the local chapter of the Kiwanis Club. The Foundation's letterhead announced its mission clearly. Complete with picture of a kneeling Kenny Hubbs in the background, the foundation's motto is emblazoned in red across the bottom of the page: "Dedicated to preserving the superb example Ken Hubbs set for the youth of America." The foundation, run by civic and church leaders in Colton, uses Hubbs's local fame to support and strengthen youth athletics in Colton. To preserve Hubbs's "superb example," the foundation honors a local high school athlete (currently drawn from eighteen high schools around the

San Bernardino valley) who has succeeded not only on the field of play, but in the classroom and community as well. The list of winners contains names that, like Kenny Hubbs, first gained fame in southern California and then went on to garner national recognition. Initiated in 1973, Ken Hubbs Athlete of the Year winners include future NFL star Ronnie Lott (and his son Ryan Nece of the Tampa Bay Buccaneers), Mark Collins (New York Giants), Charles Johnson (major league baseball), and Greg Colbrunn (major league baseball).[9]

The Ken Hubbs Foundation attracted support from throughout the nation, and from fans of all ages. As evidenced by two letters the foundation received in 1964, the organization *was* helping young people to remember Kenny's example. A letter arrived in June 1964 from twelve-year-old Holly Schindler: "I am enclosing fifty cents for the Ken Hubbs' Foundation. . . . I am a loyal Cub fan and Ken Hubbs was my hero. I knew all statistics of him, height, weight, etc., and even the color of his eyes. I have even converted a Sox fan to a Cub fan. I was grieved to hear of the young athlete's death and I feel terribly sorry for the Hubbs family." Connecting the living to the dead, the letter concludes: "This is a part of my allowance and I feel better by contributing."[10] Kathy Kort, from Aurora, Illinois, included the following with her donation: "I only wish I could give more but my babysitting job isn't very regular. . . . I was quite an admirer of Ken and I hope that this money will help guide other boys to be as great as he was."[11] The foundation, and even Kenny Hubbs himself, could have hoped for nothing more.

In addition to recognizing the outstanding accomplishments of individual athletes, the Ken Hubbs Foundation has perpetuated Kenny's memory by associating his name with sports leagues and athletic venues in Colton. Kids there still learn the game of baseball by playing in the Ken Hubbs Little League. When they get a little older, the Ken Hubbs Gymnasium at Colton High School is home to the school's basketball teams and houses several of Kenny's awards, including the Gold Glove he won during his rookie year. Although adolescent athletes in Colton no longer play in Kenny Hubbs's shadow, his legacy continues to influence local athletics in his hometown.

The Cubs organization maintained Hubbs's memory by creating the Ken Hubbs Memorial Award, which honored a player "for excellence and exemplary conduct on and off the playing field." Described by the Cubs as "an attempt to perpetuate [Hubbs's] memory," the first award was given to Ernie Banks in 1965.[12]

Hubbs's legendary accomplishments as a schoolboy athlete in southern California prompted Los Angeles television station KTLA to produce *A Glimpse of Greatness: The Story of Kenny Hubbs*, a documentary about

the Cubs star. Produced and written by Bob Speck, the KTLA sports director who later married Kenny's ex-fiancé, the ninety-minute documentary
first aired in Los Angeles during the summer following Hubbs's death and
was later broadcast in Chicago, New York, and Salt Lake City. Proceeds
from each showing were donated to the Ken Hubbs Foundation. Complete
with footage from Kenny's Little League days (including film of the hobbled
Hubbs rounding the bases after his monumental home run in the Little
League World Series) and high school games, the film contains interviews
with Hubbs's coaches and family members. The documentary clearly illustrates Hubbs's athletic gifts, while lavishing praise on his accomplishments. Kenny's legend grew as viewers were told that his name would
"stand forever" with the immortals Babe Ruth, Ty Cobb, and Stan Musial.
Understandably sentimental in the wake of Hubbs's death, *A Glimpse of
Greatness* not only perpetuated Kenny's memory, it promoted the legend
of Ken Hubbs throughout southern California and the nation.[13]

Less prominent memorials to Kenny Hubbs continue to proliferate
forty years after his death. The Internet has provided a new medium
for Hubbs's fans. For example, Tom Meling manages the Slippery Rock
Cubs in the fantasy "Trans American Baseball League." The Slippery
Rock Cubs "play" their fantasy games in the fictional Ken Hubbs Memorial Park. When asked about the name of the park, Meling replied,
"I chose Kenny Hubbs as a name for my fictional stadium because as
an eight year old he was my favorite Cub player and also because of his
tragic death."[14] Other Internet memorials are not as kind to Hubbs. The
Internet site baseballprimer.com, which presents itself as "baseball for
the thinking fan," offered fans a venue to revisit Hubbs's career in the
summer of 2002. In a fairly typical posting, one fan questioned Hubbs's
potential: "Hubbs, had he lived, probably would have been compared to
Julian Javier, Bobby Knoop, maybe Frank White as the absolute upside.
If Ken Hubbs was Ryne Sandberg," the writer noted with skepticism,
"then Daryl [*sic*] Kile was Roger Clemens."[15] More macabre memorials find Hubbs included on the "Premature Death All-Star Team," with
teammates Roberto Clemente, Lou Gehrig, and Josh Gibson—all of whom
died before the age of forty.[16]

Perhaps the most persistent theme that follows the death of a young
athlete focuses on unfulfilled potential. In Hubbs's case, the "what ifs"
began immediately, reaching their fantastic crescendo in "What Might
Have Been," a 1993 *Sports Illustrated* article that rewrote the history of
the Cubs as though Kenny Hubbs had lived. Author Steve Rushin had
the North Side nine, led by Hubbs, hold off the Mets in 1969 and go on to
defeat the Baltimore Orioles in the World Series. The "Big Blue Machine"
then won four consecutive World Series from 1972 to 1975. Wearing five

championship rings, Hubbs retired at age thirty-three. Awash in the glow of unfulfilled potential, Rushin recorded Hubbs's revisionist legacy: "Though the Hubbs Cubs joined the Yankees, Montreal Canadiens and Boston Celtics as teams synonymous with the word *champions,* Hubbs cast a long shadow over future Cub second basemen: Since '76, eighty-one men have filled the position. As journeyman Ryne Sandberg, now of the St. Petersburg White Sox, says, 'No matter what I did, it was never enough.'"[17]

When the Cubs sponsored Ken Hubbs Night at Wrigley Field in June 2002, the free baseball cards that were passed out showed the unlined

24. *Ken Hubbs.* A commemorative baseball card, issued in 2002, reveals how long the memory of Hubbs's tragic death lingered among Cubs fans.

face of a rookie peering forward into a future that promised glory and fame. The mixture of physical beauty and timelessness give the portrait a haunting quality because the stories of Kenny Hubbs's athletic achievements cannot describe what Hubbs might have accomplished had he lived more than his twenty-two years.

Memories of dead athletes—like Kenny Hubbs, Darryl Kile, Lou Gehrig, and Brian Piccolo—adhere to the American psyche with unusual poignancy. Perhaps it is because as athletes they belong to entire communities. In Hubbs's case, people from Colton to Chicago felt the loss of one of their own. By playing in the public eye, athletes become integrated into the daily lives of countless others. Perhaps it is because athletes who die young remain forever in their prime; the grainy footage of their physical exploits is never juxtaposed with pictures from their declining years. But in the end, early mortality alone is not enough to turn athletes into immortals. That task is left to the aging fans to revisit their hero's accomplishments and perpetuate their memories.

More particular to Chicago, Kenny Hubbs's death symbolizes the plight of Cubs fans everywhere—the hope of a bright future consistently denied. Fate, this time manifested by a snowstorm in central Utah, struck the Cubs down again. The questions surrounding Hubbs's future fit easily into the litany of "what-ifs" that connects Cubs fans to the past and to the future. Hubbs's potential seems so high in retrospect partly because Cubs fans have been hungry for a winner for nearly a century. By remembering the life and death of Kenny Hubbs, the annual cries of "wait 'til next year" seem more poignant, and more plaintive. Unlike the legend of Babe Ruth's ghost and the curse of the Bambino, which reaches back into the past to define the identity of the Boston Red Sox, the memories of Kenny Hubbs—full of youth, beauty, and promise—focus on the past and the future at the same time. Kenny, then, acts as the patron saint of the eternally hopeful; Cubs fans' veneration of his memory connects their dashed dreams of the past with their hopes of a brighter future.

Notes

The author wishes to thank Keith and Roxy Hubbs of Rialto, California, for their willingness to share their extensive collection of artifacts and memories of Kenny Hubbs.

1. For more on the life and career of Kenny Hubbs, see James L. Ison, *Mormons in the Major Leagues* (Cincinnati: Action Sports, 1991), 66–69; and *Great Infielders of the Major Leagues* (New York: Random House, 1972), 57; see also Early Gustkey, "Memories of Ken Hubbs Live On," *Los Angeles Times*, July 5, 1993.

2. *A Glimpse of Greatness: The Story of Kenny Hubbs*, produced by KTLA television, 1964; video copy in possession of the author.

3. Like Kenny Hubbs, the fictional Jack Armstrong had a connection to Chicago as well. The program, which aired from 1933 to 1950, originated from WBBM in Chicago.

4. *Glimpse of Greatness.*

5. Gustkey, "Memories of Ken Hubbs."

6. "Nation, Colton Honor Hubbs in Funeral Rites," February 21, 1964; clipping in Ken Hubbs folder, Mormon Athletics Collection, Salt Lake City, 1970–2000.

7. Katherine Verdery, *The Political Lives of Dead Bodies: Reburial and Postsocialist Change* (New York: Columbia University Press, 1999), 127. Peter Brown discusses the roles that dead bodies played in Latin Christianity in *The Cult of the Saints* (Chicago: University of Chicago Press, 1981).

8. Interestingly, the Topps Company issued an unwitting memorial to Hubbs two years later. The 1966 Dick Ellsworth card inadvertently contained Hubbs's picture. Ellsworth, a left-hander who went 22–10 for the Cubs in 1963, pitched for the Cubs from 1958 to 1966. See Dan Albaugh, "'Hey! That's Not Me!': Dan Albaugh Takes a Look at Baseball Cards That Don't Match the Name with the Face," *Sports Cards* (March 1997).

9. "Ken Hubbs, Athlete of the Year, Presented by the Ken Hubbs Foundation"; copy of a brochure in possession of the author.

10. Holly Schindler to Ken Hubbs Foundation, June 6, 1964; copy of letter in possession of the author. Other kids donated to the foundation as well. On June 24, 1964, the Youth Symphony of San Bernardino County held a memorial concert to benefit the Ken Hubbs Foundation; photocopy of program in possession of the author.

11. Kathy Kort to Keith Hubbs, May 28, 1964; copy of letter in possession of the author.

12. "Ken Hubbs Memorial Award," photocopy in possession of the author.

13. *Glimpse of Greatness.* Information on the marketing of the film comes from an oral interview with Keith Hubbs, December 14, 2002; notes in possession of author.

14. Tom Meling to author, December 17, 2002; copy of letter in possession of the author.

15. See http://www.baseballprimer.com/clutch/archives/00003695.shtml. Darryl Kile had died just three days before this posting appeared on the Internet.

16. See http://baseballspot.warpkeen.com/article.php?sid=102.

17. Steve Rushin, "What Might Have Been . . . ," *Sports Illustrated*, July 19, 1993, 97–98 (quote on 98).

11

The Social Logic of Boxing in Black Chicago

Toward a Sociology of Pugilism

LOÏC J. D. WACQUANT

Any group of persons—prisoners, primitives, pilots or
patients—develop a life of their own that becomes meaningful, reasonable and normal once you get close to it.
—Erving Goffman, *Asylums*

Boxing presents the paradox of being perhaps the most widely
recognized and popular sport worldwide and yet the most profoundly
misknown. Top pugilists are the highest paid athletes or single-event per-
formers of all time and their bouts command immense public attention—
even though their social impact is considerably less today than earlier in
this [the twentieth] century when a heavyweight title fight seemingly
brought society in toto, including its political and economic elites, to
a complete standstill (Roberts 1978; Edmond 1973). The "Manly Art"
has long held a fascination for artists and intellectuals. Few today are
unfamiliar with the stereotypical images conveyed by the mass media

(Barbara Walters interviewing Mike Tyson and his then-wife Robin Givens set record ratings for primetime TV), the more aestheticized depictions of novelists (Jack London, Ernest Hemingway, Nelson Algren, and Joyce Carol Oates, to mention but a few), and the realist or caricatural characters of movies, from John Huston's intimist *Fat City* to Scorsese's studied *Raging Bull* to Stallone's self-parodic celluloid saga of *Rocky.* The life of champions has been exposed in countless biographies and autobiographies and "fights of the century" have been lionized in print and immortalized in video (e.g., Mead 1985; Mailer 1971; NBC 1990). And former world heavyweight titlist Muhammad Ali may rightfully lay claim to being the most famous person on earth (Hauser 1991).

In keeping with its popularity, boxing has also been the subject of stubborn attack and sometimes vitriolic criticism. The litany of complaints is familiar (Donnelly 1988). The sport is exploitative, dangerous if not murderous, dehumanizing, and uncivilized. Calls are periodically sounded for federal regulation of the game. In 1984, the American Medical Association launched a campaign to ban the "sweet science of bruising." The most comprehensive and best historical study of the sport available to this day concludes by calling it "one of the supreme anomalies of our time" (Sammons 1988, 235). Boxing elicits near-schizophrenic reactions (Early 1988): it fascinates and revulses; it is adored or abhorred, celebrated or castigated, but leaves few indifferent.

Yet it is hard to think of a sporting practice that has also been so thoroughly mythologized and so little researched by social scientists. While sociological studies of pugilism could be listed on a single half-page, one would need a whole book to inventory all the misconceptions that float about concerning the sport, its practitioners, and its social roots and meaning. A stylized synthesis, of which the media construction of the meteoritic rise of former champion Mike Tyson provides a good approximation,[1] would look something like this: Boxers are rugged, near-illiterate young men who, raised in broken homes and deprivation, manage single-handedly to elevate themselves from the gutter to fame and fortune, parlaying their anger at the world and sadomasochistic craving for violence into million-dollar purses, save for those who, ruthlessly exploited by callous managers and promoters alike, end up on the dole with broken bones and hearts. With a precious few exceptions (Weinberg and Around 1952; Hare 1971; Sugden 1987), existing studies of boxers, dominated as they are by the writings of "natives" and quasi-insiders such as journalists (Hauser 1986, is the best of them), concentrate on the *public* side of the sport at the *top* echelons of the game. Boxing is seen as an *individual and competitive* quest for glamour and riches in *isolation* from the concrete social context that endows it with meaning and value.

A contrario, the necessary first step of a rigorous sociology of boxing must be to deny itself the easy recourse to the prefabricated exoticism of the publicized side of the institution—the fights, great or small, the heroism of the social climb of the excluded ("Marvelous Marvin Hagler: From Ghetto to Glory," proudly proclaims a feature article in a 1986 issue of *KO Magazine* that can be found taped on the walls of many a gym), the exceptional life and career of the champions. It must instead approach boxing through its least known and least spectacular side; the drab and obsessing routine of the daily workout, of the endless and thankless preparation, inseparably physical and moral, leading to the all-too-brief appearances in the limelight, the minute and mundane rituals of daily life in the gym that produce and reproduce the belief underlying this very peculiar symbolic and material economy that constitutes the pugilistic world. To do so, it must not simply "defocus" (Douglas 1976) but more decisively *break with the spectator's point of view* that informs the preconstructed object of collective mythology, that is, the theoretical gaze—*theorein*, it may be recalled, means to contemplate—fostered by the status of distant analyst and consumer of this "show business with blood" (to borrow Budd Schulberg's apt expression). In short, to avoid the pitfalls of "spontaneous sociology" that the evocation of fights inevitably leads into, one must not step by proxy into the ring with the extraordinary figure of the "champ," but "hit the bags" alongside anonymous boxers in their habitual environment of the "gym.

This paper, based on the first long-term ethnography and intensive participant observation of boxing carried out in the United States, centers on the collective "counterworld of the boxer's training" (Oates 1988, 244), grasped in its internal makeup and contradictory relation to its proximate social matrix of the ghetto. It draws on materials gathered during three years of fieldwork in a boxing gym located in a segregated inner-city neighborhood of Chicago, conducted as part of a larger investigation of the changing intersection of race, class, and state in the formation of the contemporary black subproletariat (Wacquant 1989b, 1992). Prior to enrolling at the Stoneland Boys Club,[2] I had no contact with the pugilistic world: I had but the vaguest knowledge of the sport and had never so much as contemplated getting close to a ring, let alone getting *in* it. Starting from this situation of perfect novice, I trained regularly at the Stoneland Boys Club, alongside local fighters, both amateur and professional, spending anywhere from three to seven days a week at the gym, participating in all phases of the boxer's strenuous preparation, from the basic shadow-boxing drills to sparring in the ring.

I also "followed the animal in the foliage," as Harold Garfinkel says. I attended official amateur tournaments and professional "cards" (boxing shows) at scores of venues throughout the greater Chicago area, under the various covers of gym photographer, cornerman, fan, and sparring partner, which afforded me complete access to the front- and backstages of the pugilistic scene. I accompanied fighters from my gym on the road when they fought in other midwestern cities, as well as in Atlantic City, where they had a "shot at the big time." I also followed them in their daily rounds, looking for jobs and housing, hunting for bargain buys in thrift stores, and visiting "homeys" in nearby projects. We developed strong bonds of friendship as they took me to picnics, taverns, churches, and pool halls, or simply indulged in "hanging' around" on the South Side. I witnessed marriages, funerals, cheered Public Enemy on stage, and attended a rally with Minister Farrakhan along with some of my "gym buddies."

The analyses presented here are based on the detailed notes from my ethnographic diary, which I filled daily after each training session, and informal conversations recorded on a tape player I carried around after nearly two years in the gym. Writing this diary initially helped me overcome the vivid feeling of physical awkwardness and the overwhelming sense of being out of place among these remarkable and unusually dedicated athletes, a sense of strangeness no doubt reinforced by the fact of being the only white member in an all-black boxing gym at the time of my entrance in the field. In the final four months of data collection, I conducted over one hundred formal in-depth interviews with professional fighters, trainers, managers, referees, cornermen, and other boxing officials in the Chicagoland and Northwest Indiana area. I also trained at three other professional gyms in Chicago and visited gyms in numerous other cities in the United States and in France. Finally, I monitored the boxing press, subscribed to trade newsletters, and watched televised fights on a regular basis with my coach. Although this chapter centers on one boxing gym and relies heavily on the views of the trainers and boxers from that gym, I am confident that the analyses built on them have a validity that extends beyond the monographic. Indeed, comparison across time or space reveals a striking predominance of invariants over variations in the boxing universe (viz., the numerous empirical commonalities between my materials and those gathered by John Sugden [1987] in a Connecticut gym).

The aims of this partial report on an initiation to the world of pugilism[3] are twofold. A first, mainly empirical, purpose of this paper is to provide fresh ethnographic data on a little-known universe on which factual misconceptions are as abundant as rigorously collected data are scant. At a second, theoretical level, this paper had a dual goal: first, to uncover some of the principles that organize boxing as it is practiced in a black ghetto, highlighting the social regulation of violence it effects, visible in the peculiar relation of *simultaneous symbiosis and opposition* that links the boxing gym to the universe of the street and its culture. Second, it seeks to contribute to a rethinking of the "logic of practice" (Bourdieu 1990) by reflecting on the nature of a *practice of which the body is at once the seat, the instrument, and the target.* This is to say that my intent is neither to condemn nor to defend this reputedly most "barbaric" of all sports, so passionately revered and denigrated, but rather to show how boxing makes sense in its context and to suggest what its specific logic, and especially that of its inculcation, might teach us about the logic of all human social action.

To anticipate some of the tentative results of this inquiry, I propose that the inculcation of what may be called the *pugilistic habitus*,[4] that is, the specific set of bodily and mental schemata that define the competent boxer, rests on a twofold antinomy. The first owes to the fact that boxing is a sport situated at the borderline between nature and culture, a sort of empirically realized limiting case of practice, and yet that it simultaneously requires an exceptionally complex, quasi-rational management of the body and of time, whose transmission is effected in a purely practical mode, without the mediation of a theory, on the basis of an implicit and largely uncodified pedagogy. Thence the second antinomy: Boxing is an individual sport, perhaps the prototype of the individual sport insofar as it puts into play—and in danger—the sole body of the fighter, whose proper learning is nevertheless quintessentially collective, in particular because it presupposes a belief in the game which, like all "language games" according to Wittgenstein (1953), is born and lasts only in and through the group that it defines through a circular process. In other words, the dispositions that make up the accomplished pugilist are, as all "techniques of body," "the work of individual and *collective practical reason*" (Mauss 1950, 368, emphasis added).

Finally, to become a boxer is to appropriate through progressive impregnation a set of bodily and mental dispositions that are so intimately interwoven that they erase the distinction between the physical and the spiritual, between what pertains to athletic "talent" and what belongs to moral capacities and will. The boxer is a living gearing of the body and the mind that explodes the opposition between action and representation and transcends *in actu* the dichotomy of the individual and the collective that underlies accepted theories of social action. Here again, I concur with Marcel Mauss when he speaks of "the physio-psycho-sociological assembly of series of acts . . . more or less habitual or more or less ancient in the life of the individual and in the history of the society . . . [that] are assembled by and for social authority" (Mauss 1950, 383).

An Island of Order: The Gym Versus the Street

A fundamental hypothesis guiding this research is that there are deep structural relations between boxing as a (sub-)proletarian bodily craft and certain forms of social life and cultural practices found in the lower regions of social space, and particularly in the black American ghetto; that the "idioculture" (Fine 1979) of the gym develops in ruptural continuity with that of the inner city. True, at one level, boxing "is a unique, closed, self-referential world" (Oates 1987, 13). Yet, at another, it is nurtured and held together by definite social forces and cultural repertoires; it arises and reproduces itself both as reflection of and reaction against (masculine) street culture or, to be more precise, as a functional rearticulation of some of its core elements.

This means that one cannot grasp the inner logic that regulates the apparently autonomous universe of pugilism outside of its social and ecological context and independently of the space of social possibles

25. *Pugilism.* Boxing has long been associated with working-class and ethnic neighborhoods. Here, two lads square off outside the Chicago Hebrew Institute Gymnasium, 1915. (Courtesy of the Chicago History Museum.)

that this context assigns young men. Indeed, much like joining a gang (Sanchez-Jankowski 1991) or becoming involved in street crime (Sullivan 1989), two germane careers to which it offers a potential alternative, going to the gym acquires its full social meaning only in regard of the local structure of opportunities, including those offered—or denied—by the school, the labor market, and street-based networks and activities. In this section, I argue that *the boxing gym defines itself in a relation of symbiotic opposition to the ghetto* in which it is situated, and from which it both draws its sustenance and protects its members. Before we venture into the gym, then, it is necessary to provide a brief sketch of the environment of the Boys and Girls Club of Stoneland.

The Context: From "Miracle Mile" to "Murdertown"

The Boys and Girls Club of Stoneland (or Stoneland Boys Club, as it is commonly referred to) is located on Sixtine Street, one of the most devastated streets of the neighborhood, in the midst of a barren urban landscape emblematic of the tragic demise of the "Black Metropolis" of Chicago (Drake and Cayton 1945). This section of the South Side is by no means unusually destitute by the standards of the city's ghetto. Indeed it ranks only thirteenth on the scale of poverty among the city's seventy-seven "community areas," twenty-five of which have over a fifth of their population under the official federal poverty line (Chicago Fact Book Consortium 1984). Yet, following a pattern common to other inner-city neighborhoods throughout America (Wilson 1987), Stoneland has experienced spectacular decline and a rapid cumulation of social dislocations in recent decades.

At the end of World War II, Stoneland was a stable and prosperous white neighborhood, satellite of Hyde Park, the nearby stronghold of the University of Chicago. The area attracted businesses, consumers, and renters, who flocked in and saturated its real estate market and commercial outlets. The corner of Sixtine Street and Cottage Grove Avenue was reputedly one of the liveliest in the city, as people streamed in to patronize the area's countless restaurants, taverns, movie houses, and jazz clubs. Indeed, Sixtine Street itself was such a booming artery that local merchants nicknamed it "The Miracle Mile." Forty years later, the neighborhood has turned into a virtual Bantustan of segregated poverty, material dilapidation, and social decay. (Limitations of space do not allow me to provide a more nuanced description of the ecological and social structure of Stoneland. I am well aware that the compressed, monochromous portrait drawn here in bold strokes risks reinforcing the stereotypical vision of the ghetto as a "disorganized" social wasteland devoid of sociability and patterning.)[5] Between 1950 and 1980, the number of residents fell from about eighty-one thousand to thirty-six thousand as the racial makeup of the population went from 38 to 96 percent black. The swelling inflow of Afro-American migrants from the South, spilling over the rigid boundaries of the city's historic "Black Belt," set off a massive exodus of whites, whose number plummeted from fifty thousand to a few hundred. The ensuing out-migration of the (small) black middle class and stable working class to more pleasant, if still racially segregated, areas at the periphery of the traditional ghetto left in its wake the most disadvantaged segment of the black community. This change in the composition of the local population, further solidified by the massive "urban renewal" programs of the 1950s (Hirsch 1983) and accelerated by the "gang wars" of the '60s, when the Blackstone Rangers ruled the streets of the neighborhood, determined in turn a crisis of communal institutions. The mutually reinforcing decline in housing, schools, and public and private services combined with rising levels of joblessness to transform Stoneland into a veritable economic and social purgatory.

A few empirical indicators may serve to gauge the exclusion and hardship visited upon the people of Stoneland (Chicago Fact Book Consortium 1984). According to the latest usable census figures, those of 1980, a third of the families live under the official federal poverty line and the average annual family income of $10,500 amounts to barely half of the city's average figure. The percentage of households recorded as female-headed has reached 60 percent (compared to 34 percent ten years earlier), the official unemployment rate is 20 percent (twice the city average after tripling over a decade), and fewer than one in ten households own their home. Only a third of all women and 44 percent of all men hold a job; 61 percent of the households have to rely in part or whole on grossly inadequate welfare programs for their survival. Among the workforce, the single largest occupational category is that of clerical workers (31 percent), with private household and service personnel coming in second at 22 percent. Over half of the adult residents did not finish high school, while the current dropout rate for high school students from the area is believed to fluctuate between one-half and two-thirds. The neighborhood no longer has a secondary school, movie theater, library, or job training facility. Nor does it have a bank, supermarket, or insurance agency. Despite the proximity of one of the world's most advanced centers of medical innovation, the University of Chicago Hospital, infant mortality in Stoneland is estimated at about 3 percent and rising, a figure almost three times the national average and comparable to many Third World countries.

Like other inner-city public establishments in Chicago (*Chicago Tribune* 1986, 149), local schools are "hostage to poverty and crime." Plagued by massive shortages of supplies, inadequate if not crumbling facilities, and demoralized and unstable teaching personnel, they have become akin to custodial institutions that merely process students until their eventual discharge. No wonder so many youth find the expanding illegal economy more attractive when schools lead nowhere—they do not even offer college preparatory classes. Once powerful agents of social integration, churches have also declined significantly; most of the thirty or so religious institutions still operative two decades ago have closed their doors. The most visible active institutions of Stoneland are liquor stores, lotto outlets, and "Currency exchanges" where residents can cash checks, pay bills, and obtain car stickers and other public certificates for a fee. The absence of new construction for decades and the gradual erosion of the existing housing stock—which was cut by nearly one-half between 1950 and 1980, 70 percent of all remaining units predating World War II—in an area situated near the city's lakefront, less than ten miles from the heart of the third largest metropolis of the country, testifies to the abandonment of this community.

Today the "Miracle Mile" resembles a ghost town, complete with burned out stores, vacant lots strewn with debris and broken glass, and boarded-up buildings left to rot in the shadow of the elevated train line. The few commercial establishments that have survived (mostly liquor outlets, clothing and food stores, small catering places, and providers of personal service that each employs a handful of workers at best) are huddled behind iron bars. Here is how a member of the gym describes the street we ride down in his car after a workout:

> You have a lotta street walkers, you have yo' gang-bangers, you have yo' dope dealers and yo' dope users—I mean, that's in every neighborhood, I'm not just saying' around here. An' it's bad for the kids that's comin' up in the neighborhood 'cause that's who they gotta look up to. . . . You see like guys like this [pointing to a group of men standing by the entrance of a liquor store] hangin' out, bummin' for quarters an' dimes and stuff to buy 'em wine. It's bad that these guys, they messed up they lives and stuff. . . . You see that's boarded up. Here it's a store that sell liquor, with another store that's boarded up that useta sell liquor. You see people walkin' down the street that jus' live on a wish and a prayer. You know you can never say what's on these guys' min's you know: they out there to live, they live day by day.

The Stoneland Boys Club is surrounded on one side by the crumbling remnants of the former Maryland Theater, of which only the boarded-up facade, covered with posters advertising the latest rap concert or a Farrakhan meeting ("A New Dawn Is Coming") remain, and on the other side by a vacant lot occupied in part by a children's playground, where jobless men from the neighborhood come share a "taste" on sunny days. Immediately behind the club is a large, abandoned brick building whose doors and windows are condemned by metal bars and locks. On windy days, garbage and flying papers accumulate in the back of the building at the boxers' entrance.

More than physical degradation, however, it is the erosion of public space brought about by rampant crime that is chiefly responsible for the constricted and oppressive tenor of daily life on Chicago's South Side (Wacquant 1992). In today's ghetto, battery, shootings, and homicides are a common occurrence, creating a climate of pervasive insecurity, if not terror, on the streets that borders on a state of "war of all against all" (Bourgois 1989; Kotlowitz 1991). The rise in crime that has accompanied the deepening of poverty caused by the retrenchment of the welfare state and the continual contraction of the wage economy is readily visible in Stoneland. Residents fear going to the nearby public park and many will avoid public transportation if they can (several stations on the local Chicago Transit Authority train line have been closed to entry; CTA buses are trailed by special police cars). Though gang activity has subsided, purse snatching, muggings, rackets, and prostitution are not uncommon in the area. And the growing drug trade and wide availability of guns have made violence endemic. A fourteen-year-old gym member spoke these words to describe his place of residence not far from the club: "This project where I stay here ain't too bad. The one over there is something else. I mean *they all bad,* you know, but *this one's badder: it's 'Murdertown' over there."*

The club shelters itself from this hostile environment in the manner of a fortress: all entries to the building are protected by metal bars and solidly padlocked; the windows of the daycare and Headstart center are latticed with iron; the back-door entrance has two enormous bolts that cannot be opened or shut without a hammer, and an electronic alarm system is set by the last person leaving the building. A baseball bat is at hand near each entrance, one behind the counter of the daycare office, the other behind the coach's desk, in case it proves necessary to repel the intrusion of unwanted visitors *manu militari.*

> The conversation returns to the situation of the city's black neighborhoods, Chuck (trainer) and O'Grady agree on the surrounding devastation and on the insecurity that pervades the community. Of his area, a couple of miles south of the gym, Chuck says, "It's full of drugs everywhere, you can buy dope on the street from just about any guy you see. Young punks who bother you, getting' in your face. Ain't got no schoolin'. No jobs, runnin' the streets—what they gonna do? Me, I don't care but that ain't my neighborhood, it's too much punks and

low-lifes. It ain't my class of neighborhood." The building where he lives is a well-known selling spot for Karachi, cocaine and PCP. (field notes, August 1988)

Today Gaby called the gym from the hospital. Two members of a rival gang shot him on the street not far from here. Luckily he saw them coming and took off running, but a bullet pierced his calf. He hobbled behind an abandoned building, pulled out his own gun from his gym bag and opened fire on them, forcing them into retreat. He says he'd better get out of the hospital real quick because they're probably out to get him now. I ask Richie [the head coach of the gym, a reputable boxing trainer for over fifty years] if they shot him in the leg as a warning: "Shit, Louie! They don't shoot to injure no leg, they shoot to kill you. If Gaby don't have his gun with him and pull it, they'd track him down and kill him, yeah: he be dead now." (field notes, September 1990)

I told Richie that I went to interview Ray at his place last night. He was furious: "I told you not to go there! You might end up in the middle of shootin'. That's a terrible vicinity. Them prostitutes might try to snatch you money or your tape recorder. Yeah, it's a *real* rough neighborhood." (field notes, July 1991)

Violent crime is indeed so commonplace that nearly all members of the gym have personally witnessed killings and have either been shot at or stabbed themselves. Many also grew up having to fight on the street, sometimes on a daily basis, to keep their lunch money, their coats, their reputation, or simply to go about. One of them recalls a typical childhood scene: "Right in that square block area it was definitely rough, it was *dog-eat-dog*. I had to be a mean dog. A lotta concentrated people, young guys wan'ed to take yer money and beat ya up an' you jus' had to fight or move out of the neighbo'hood. I couldn't move, so I had to start fightin'."

Many gym members were thus "pretrained" on the street in the art of self-defense, if not from choice, then by necessity. In fact, a good number of them are former "street fighters" reconverted to boxing. "I used to fight alot when I was younger *anyway so*," recounts Mitch; "my father figure like, you know, 'If you gonna fight, well why don't you take it to a gym where you gonna learn, you know, a little more basics to it, maybe make some money, go further and do somethin' . . . insteada jus' bein' on the streets you know, an' fightin' for nothin'." This is to say that young men raised and living in the contemporary ghetto are, very early on, accustomed to a range of predatory behaviors entailing the most varied and seemingly anarchic (though in fact patterned) forms of physical and economic violence, forms before which the controlled violence of boxing cannot but pale.

"Another World of Its Own"

By contrast to this hostile environment, and despite its severe dearth of resources, the Boys and Girls Club constitutes *an island of stability and order where social relations forbidden on the outside become once again possible.* The gym offers a relatively self-enclosed site for a protected sociability where one can find respite from the pressures of the street and the ghetto, a world in which external events rarely penetrate and upon which they have little impact (the [first] war against Iraq went virtually unremarked; the Clarence Thomas/Anita Hill soap-operatic hearings elicited little reaction or interest). This collective closure, which borders on claustrophilia, is what makes life in the gym possible and goes a long way toward explaining its attractions.

> I can go to the gym an' I can fin' a peace of min'. I can relax in my min'. . . . I don' have ta *worry abou' thin's that's on the street* right here bein' in the gym, because my min' is on one thin' an' my min' is on conditionin' an' my min' is on makin' somethin' outa what it is that I'm doin' that I really like an' hum, susseedin' in it. When I get to the gym, it's like I'm in a *whole new diff'ren' atmosphere,* a whole differen' place. It's jus' like a whole new diff'ren' worl' to me an' that's why in my blood, I don't know what it is, it's jus' in my blood, like I was spoon-fed the gym . . . The gym is jus' like havin' another family. Like I said, the gym is *another world of its own.* (professional, age twenty-six, stockman)

> You can go there and you feel good about yourself. Like I said, you feel *protected, secure.* You in there, aw, you're alright—it's like a second family. You know you can go there for support. . . . If you feelin' down, somebody be there to pump you up. I say, take your frustration out on the bags. Gettin' up in there and sparring, you might have felt down when you got there, then [?] make you feel a whole lot better. (amateur, age nineteen, still in high school)

An older member of the club whose pro career was recently brought to a premature close by a hand injury explains what keeps bringing him to the gym in between his two jobs: "I ju' like watchin' the guys train an' do somethin' positive with theyself, burn energy in a way where it's not gonna git them in trouble and they're lettin' them *gangs* and *drugs* and *jail* go all aroun' them, 'cause they in the gym doin' somethin' with theyselves, so tha's real goo' to see that." (interview, August 1991).

The gym functions in the manner of a buffer against the (often illicit) attractions and dangers of ghetto life. It is not uncommon to hear a boxer say that the more time spent in the gym, the less time given to the street. Many professional athletes willingly confess that, were it not for the discovery of boxing, they would most likely have become criminals and delinquents; numerous well-known boxers (Sonny Liston, Floyd Patterson, and Mike Tyson, among others) learned their trade in prison or correctional facilities. Pinklon Thomas (cited in Hauser 1986, 186), a former heavyweight champion, once confessed, "Boxing brought me out of a hole and made me a worthwhile person. Without it, I'd be selling heroin, dead, or in jail." Several participants in the 1989 edition of the Chicago Golden Gloves tournament do not hesitate to mention this in the biographical capsule that accompanies their picture in the official tournament program ("Vaughn Bean, 16, 5' 11", 178 lbs. Representing the Valentine Boys Club, he has been boxing for 1 year. A freshman at Calumet High School, his brother brought him to boxing to keep him out of trouble"). Members of the Stoneland Boys Club agree:

Q: Where would you be today if you hadn't found boxing?
A: Uh, prob'y in jail, dead or on the streets turnin' up a bottle. [Really?] Yeah. 'Cause it was tha' peer pressure I was goin' through at the age of sixteen and fifteen, hangin' out with the wron' guys an' tryin' ta blend in an' you know, not bein' what they woul' call *a punk, a poot-butt*,[6] you know, not lettin' guys bully you on the street an' stuff. You know, it's peer pressure tha' every teenager go through at tha' age, see what I'm sayin'? You wanna be *a'cepted* by the group o' people tha' you surroun' yourself in comin' through the neighbo'hood an' the community. (professional, age twenty-eight, custodian)

I figure if it weren't for the gym I might be doin' somethin' that I wouldn't wanna do, you know so it's, it's good, the gym help me alot. [Like?] Like you know, prob'ly *killin' somebody*, you know, stick-up, you know drugs—anythin': you can't never tell! You never know what the world holds. [The gym has taken you away from that?] Yeah, alotta outside. [You feel protected in the gym?] Yeah, gym takes me mind off alotta things, you know, especially outside a—when you have problems too, you know, you come to the gym workout, it seem like it jus' *blanks out the mind*, like all you know you're in the gym work out on the bags. (professional, age twenty-four, supported by his manager)

I figure well, the bes' thin' for me to do is to chan' my life style, 'cause I saw a lot of my frien's git hurt an' kill' from the thin's that we were doin' an' thin's like that. I said, before I wan'ed [that] to happen to me, I ha' to change my life an' that idea [that I can't go on] hangin' on the streets an' thin's like that. It was on me. What did I wanna do in life? you know. The gym show me that I coul' do somethin'. The gym show me that I can be my own man. The gym show me that I can do other thin's than the *gang bang, use drugs, steal, rob people, stick people up, or jus' bein' in jail.* (professional, age twenty-six, stockman)

A protective shield against worldly temptations and risks, the gym is not only the site of a rigorous training of the body; it is also the locus and support of what Georg Simmel (1949) calls "sociability," that is, processes of pure sociation that are an end in themselves, social forms of interaction devoid of significant content and purpose. This is possible because of the unspoken code according to which members do not carry into the gym their obligations and problems from outside, be they work, family, or love. The "relevance rules" that define the gym as a "situated activity system" (Goffman 1961, 19, 8), tend to strip the boxer of all his external statuses and to exclude all issues and values not directly related to his athletic pursuit. Everything takes place as if a tacit pact of nonaggression governed interpersonal relations and ruled out any topic of conversation that might threaten this "play form of association," hamper the smooth functioning of daily individual exchanges, and thereby endanger the specific masculine subculture that the gym perpetuates (much like the Irish working-class bar described by Zola [1964] in his study of gambling).

Not surprisingly, favorite topics for chatter are boxing and other sports, with a marked preference for "rough" ones (the games of the Chicago Bears football team are much more talked about than those of the Chicago Bulls basketball team). Politics is rarely touched upon. Issues of "race" are sometimes addressed, but they are unlikely to lead to disagreement, given the homogeneity of the gym on this count. Crime and "hustling" are a common topic of conversation, just as they are a banal component of daily life. The brunt of shoptalk revolves around the problems of "making the weight," the day's sparring sessions, and various technical subtleties of the game. Advice and tips are continually traded; boxing bouts, local and national, are avidly dissected.

In the course of these endless conversations, head coach Richie and the older members of the gym reveal a near-encyclopedic knowledge of the names, places, and events that make up the pugilistic folklore. The outstanding fights of history, especially regional, are frequently evoked, as are the successes and setbacks of boxers on the rise or on the decline. Through a deliberate upturning of the official hierarchy of values, the great televised clashes (e.g., Leonard vs. Hagler or Holyfield vs. Foreman) are less prized than are local confrontations, and the strings of names mentioned in gym gossip include many more obscure fighters than famous boxers known by the media or general public. Conversations insensibly shift back and forth between boxing and stories of street fights, shady traffics, "hustles," and street tricks and crime, of which everyone seems to possess an extended repertory. Under this angle, Richie's office—a small back room adorned with old boxing posters and pictures, and which looks into the gym proper through a large window—functions in the manner of the Parisian salon, as the stage where each can attest his excellence in the manipulation of the specific cultural capital, namely pugilistic knowledge and street smarts, and display his mastery of the informal code of the ghetto and its *demi-monde.*

The significance of these ongoing mundane gym conversations should not be overlooked, for they are an essential ingredient of the "hidden curriculum" of the gym. They insensibly teach its members the lore of the game. In the form of stories, gossip, fight anecdotes, and other street tales, they orally impregnate the boxers with the core values and categories of judgment of the pugilistic universe, many of which are the same that anchor ghetto street culture (Abrahams 1970; Folb 1980; Kochman 1972; Sanchez-Jankowski 1991): a mix of limited peer-group solidarity and defiant individualism, physical toughness and courage ("heart"), an uncompromising sense of masculine honor, and an expressive stress on personal performance and style.

The "Boys Who Beat the Street"[7]

It is generally accepted, though without much supporting data, that the overwhelming majority of boxers come from the popular classes (Weinberg and Arond 1952; Hare 1971; Sugden 1987). Thus, Chicago, the predominance first of the Irish, then of the Central European Jews, Italians, and blacks, and, lately, the rise of Latinos, closely mirrors the succession of these groups at the bottom of the class ladder. The upsurge of Chicano fighters (and the strong presence of Puerto Ricans) this past decade, which even a casual survey of the program of the annual Chicago Golden Gloves tournament makes immediately apparent, results directly from the massive influx of Mexican immigrants into the lowest regions of the social space of the Midwest. A similar process of ethnic succession can be observed in the other major boxing markets of the country, the New York–New Jersey area, Florida, and Southern California.

However, it is necessary to stress that, contrary to a widespread opinion, backed by the native myth of the "hungry fighter" (Jenkins 1955) and periodically revalidated by selective media attention to the more exotic figures of the fight game, such as "thugs" and former inmates, boxers do not generally come from the most disenfranchised fractions of the ghetto subproletariat, but rather from those fractions of the minority working class that struggle at the threshold of stable socioeconomic integration. This self-selection, which tends to exclude the most excluded, does not operate via the constraint of a lack of financial resources but through the mediation of the moral and bodily dispositions that are within reach of these two segments of the black population. There is no direct economic barrier to boxing to speak of. Yearly dues to enroll at Stoneland Boys Club amount to ten dollars; the mandatory license from the Amateur Boxing Federation costs an additional twelve dollars a year, and all the necessary equipment is graciously loaned by the club (save for the handwraps and mouthpiece, which can be purchased for less than ten dollars in the few sport stores that carry them).[8] Youngsters from the most disadvantaged families are eliminated because they lack the habits and inclinations objectively demanded by pugilism—for to become a boxer requires a regularity of life, a sense of discipline (especially temporal), and a physical and mental asceticism that cannot take root in social and economic conditions marred by extreme instability and temporal disorganization. Below a certain threshold of personal and family constancy, one is very unlikely to acquire the minimal physical and mental dispositions necessary successfully to endure the learning of this sport.[9]

Preliminary analysis of the profiles of the twenty-seven fighters (all but two of them black, with ages ranging from twenty to thirty-seven) active in the summer and fall of 1991 in the three main gyms of Chicago confirms that professional boxers do, on the whole, stand above the lower tier of the inner-city male population. Only one-third of them grew up receiving public aid and 22 percent are currently jobless, the remainder being either employed or drawing a "weekly salary" from their manager. Nearly half of them have attended a community college, if only for a short while, and with little or no educational and economic gain to show for it. One had earned an associate degree and another a bachelor's. Only three have not graduated from high school, and a full 48 percent have a current checking account. For comparison, of the men ages eighteen to forty-five living in Chicago's South Side and West Side ghettos, 36 percent have grown up on welfare, 44 percent do not hold a job, half have not completed their high school education, and only 18 percent have a current checking account (Wacquant and Wilson 1989, 17, 19, 22). So the educational, employment, and economic status of professional pugilists is somewhat higher than that of the average ghetto resident. Most distinctive about their background is that none of their fathers received more than a high school education and nearly all held typical blue-collar working-class jobs (with the exception of the son of a wealthy white entrepreneur from the suburbs). And sketchy evidence suggests that the social recruitment of fighters rises slightly, rather than descends, as one climbs up the pugilistic ladder, possibly for the reasons adduced above: "Most of my boys," says veteran trainer and founder of the world-renowned Kronk Gym in Detroit, Emanuel Steward, "contrary to what people think, are not that poor. They come from good areas around the country" (cited in Halpern 1988, 279).

Far, then, from belonging to this disorganized and desocialized "dangerous class" designated by the recent flood of discourses on the consolidation of a black "underclass" supposedly cut off from "mainstream society" (e.g., Auletta 1982; Jencks and Peterson 1991), everything indicates that most professional boxers come from traditional working-class backgrounds and are attempting to maintain or recapture this precarious status by entering what they see as a skilled trade, highly regarded by their immediate entourage, and with potential for big earnings. The majority of adults at the Boys Club are employed, if only part time, as janitors, steel mill workers, gas station attendants, messengers, bricklayers, sports instructors, stockmen, firemen, counselors at youth detention centers, or baggers at a supermarket. To be sure, these working-class attachments are in most cases tenuous, for these jobs are, as a rule, insecure, low-paying, and do not obviate the chronic need for "hustling" to make ends meet at the end of the month (Valentine 1978). And a contingent of professional fighters does not come from the lower echelons of society, that is, from larger female-headed families raised on public aid in stigmatized public housing projects for most of their youth, and plagued with quasi-permanent joblessness. But they are not the majority, nor are they the more successful competitors in the pugilistic field. Furthermore, if their mediocre income and educational disaffection do not differentiate them noticeably from the mass of ghetto residents of their age category, boxers tend to live with their wife or girlfriend and children more often than the latter do, and have the important distinction of belonging to at least one formal organization—the boxing gym—whereas the overwhelming majority of the inhabitants of the inner-city belong to none (with the partial exception of the few remaining middle-class residents, cf. Wacquant and Wilson 1989, 24).

The enrollment of the Boys Club of Stoneland fluctuates markedly over the months. Somewhere between 100 and 150 men, young and not so young (the oldest is in his mid-fifties, the youngest is twelve) sign up for a twelve-month period, but most of them will stay no more than a few weeks, as they find the workout of the boxer too demanding. An attrition rate in excess of 90 percent is common for a boxing gym. Attendance is maximum in the winter just before the Golden Gloves tournament, whose preliminary rounds take place in early February every year, and in the late spring. A nucleus composed of a score of "regulars," including an inner circle of eight older members, most of them professionals who came into the game together, forms the backbone of this shifting membership. Most of the regulars train assiduously to compete officially in the amateur or professional divisions. Others come to the gym primarily to get and keep in physical shape, to stay in contact with boxing friends, or to learn techniques of self-defense. In addition to the fighters and trainers, many former pugilists in their old age come to chat with Richie, spending countless hours in the windowless back room reminiscing about the old days when "fighters were fighters."

The single most important divide among members is that between amateurs and professionals. Amateur and professional boxing are two structurally interdependent and tightly linked, yet experientially very remote, universes. Boxers may spend years in the amateurs and yet know fairly little about the factors and mores that shape the career of their pro counterparts, especially in its economic aspects. In addition, differences in rules and regulations are so vast as to make the amateur and professional divisions almost two different sports. To simplify, in amateur boxing the goal is to pile up points by touching one's opponent in rapid flurries, and the referee has ample latitude to stop the contest before one of the boxers gets visibly hurt; in the latter, the goal is to hurt one's opponent by landing heavy blows. As an experienced trainer from another gym remarked, "Professional fighting is, you know, it'll knock you *outta your mind*, you know. Rough game, you turn professional, it's a rough game—it's *not* a game. Amateur, you have fun. Professional, they're tryin' to kill you." The overwhelming majority of amateur boxers do not cross over into the pros, so the latter group is a highly (self-) selected group; again, a minimally stable background is more conducive to a successful transition into the professionals. Numerous additional distractions have currency within each of these classes, which refer to style and tactics: boxer (or stylist), brawler or slugger, counterpuncher, banger, "animal," and so forth.

Beyond these distinctions, the gym culture is self-consciously egalitarian in that all participants are treated basically alike: Irrespective of their status and goal, they all have the same rights and the same duties, particularly that of "working" hard at their trade and displaying a modicum of ring bravery when called for. True, those who have their personal trainer command more attention, and the professionals go through a more structured and demanding workout. But Richie is as keen on teaching a sixteen-year-old novice, who might not show up after a week of trial, how to throw a left jab as he is on polishing the defensive moves of a ring veteran. Whatever level of pugilistic proficiency he reaches, he who "pays his dues" is accepted as a good-faith member of the club.

Needless to say, all members are men: The gym is a *quintessentially masculine space* into which the trespassing of females is tolerated only as long as it remains incidental. Though no formal barrier blocks their participation—some trainers even deny having any reticence at women boxing[10]—women are not welcome in the gym because their physical presence symbolically, if not actually, disrupts the whole pugilistic universe (Wacquant 1991b). Only under special circumstances (such as before a "big-time fight" or right after a decisive victory) will the girlfriends or wives of fighters attend the workout of their men. When they do, they always remain quietly seated, motionless, on the few chairs that line each side of the ring; and they generally walk carefully along the walls, so as to avoid penetrating the "floor," even if it is not being occupied. Of course they are not to interfere in any way with the training regimen, except to assist at home by taking care of daily tasks, cooking special foods, and by providing emotional and even financial support. At Stoneland, if a woman is present, the boxers are not even allowed to come out of the dressing room bare-chested to use the scale in the back room—as if the semi-nude bodies of men could be seen at work in the ring but not at rest in the backstage of the shop floor. At another gym, the head coach resorts to the following methods to keep women away: He first warns his boxers to not bring their "girl" to the gym; if they do, he has them spar with a much stronger fighter so that they get beat up in the ring and lose face. In yet another gym, a separate area enclosed by a hip-high wall is reserved for visitors to sit in; in practice it is used solely by women. At the famed Top Rank Gym in Las Vegas, women are explicitly disallowed from entering.

As they progress in the game, some boxers find that they are more comfortable remaining at the "gym" level, where they train and spar more or less frequently, occasionally entering a tournament. Others decide to venture further in competition, going on the regular amateur circuit before eventually "turning pro." The differentiation between the noncompetitive boxer and the full-fledged pugilist is rendered visible by the expenses each makes to acquire his equipment, and by the use of a permanent locker. Only competitive fighters train with their own gloves, of which they generally possess several worn-out pairs accumulated over the years, their own headguard, and their own rope, which they keep under lock in their individual locker. The purchasing of boxing boots (about $35 to $60) and, even more so, of a sparring helmet ($60 minimum) rarely fails to signal a long-term commitment to competition. The dress of athletes is also a good indicator of their degree of involvement in the sport, although it is easier to manipulate and thus less reliable: The firm Ringside, which supplies boxing equipment by mail order, sells custom-made shirts, shorts, and training sweaters at moderate prices. In sum, investment in training gear provides a generally trustworthy measure of moral and physical investment in the pugilistic field.

We have seen how the environment of the inner city and specific features of its street culture predispose youngsters to construe boxing as a meaningful and valuable activity that offers a stage on which to enact core values of its masculine ethos. Under that angle, the gym and the ghetto stand in continuity. However, once *in* the gym, this relation is ruptured and reversed by the Spartan discipline that boxers have to obey, which harnesses street qualities to the pursuit of different goals, more stringently structured and distant.

The first thing trainers always stress is what you are *not* supposed to do in the gym. Stoneland's coach-in-second offers the following compressed enumeration of the gym's don'ts: "Cursin'. Smokin'. Loud talkin'. Disrespect for the women, disrespect for the coaches, disrespect for each other. No animosity, no bragging." To which could be added a host of smaller, often implicit rules forming a tightly woven web of restrictions that converge to *pacify* behavior in the gym: It is forbidden to bring food or drink in the club, to talk during training, to rest leaning on the sides of tables, to alter the sequence of drills (for instance, to start a session by skipping jump rope instead of loosening up and shadow-boxing). It is mandatory to wear a jockstrap under one's towel when coming out of the shower and dry clothes when coming out of the gym. There is no using the equipment in an unconventional fashion, throwing punches against objects, sparring if one is not fully equipped for it, or worse, starting or even simply faking a fight outside the ring. Indeed, such floor incidents are so rare that they are remembered by all, quite in contrast with the routine occurrences of street violence.

Most of the implicit "internal regulations" of the club are visible only in the conduct and demeanor of the regulars who have progressively internalized them, and they are brought to explicit attention only when violated.[11] Those who do not manage to assimilate this unwritten code of conduct are promptly dismissed or advised by Richie to transfer to another gym. All in all, as I shall demonstrate below, the gym functions in the manner of a quasi-total institution that purports to regiment the whole existence of the fighter—his use of time and space, the management of his body, even his state of mind—so much so that boxers frequently compare it to being in the military:

> In the gym, you learn discipline, self control. You learn tha' you s'pose to go to bed early, git up early, do road work, take care of yerself, eat the right foods. Uh, yer body is a *machine*; it's s'pose to be well-tuned. You learn to have some control so far as rippin' an' runnin' the streets, social life. It jus' gives you kin' of like an' *army, solider mentality* an' that's real good for folks. (professional, age thirty-one, firefighter)

> The average guy th' trains in this gym, kid or man, he *matures*, see, 85 perzent, 85 perzent more than if he was out on the street. 'Cause it discipline him to try to be a young man, to try to have sportsmanship, ring generalship, you know, uh, I don't know. . . . It's more like,

26. *Golden Gloves.* The amateur "Golden Gloves" boxing tournaments began in Chicago in the 1920s and were fed by neighborhood ethnic athletic clubs. Chicago stadium housed the 1930 New York-Chicago inter-city championship. (Courtesy of the Chicago History Museum.)

I coul' sit up here an' give you a line of tin's, you know, but [you can] break it down to: it works *like bein' in the military,* it show you how to be a *gentleman* and all, and learn *respect.* (professional, age twenty-nine, custodian)

Thus, the boxing gym defines itself in a relation of symbiotic opposition to the surrounding ghetto: at the same time that it recruits its residents and draws on its masculine culture of toughness, physical prowess, and bodily performance, it stands opposed to the street as the individual and collective regulation of passions is to their private and public anarchy, as the constructive—from the standpoint of the social life and identity of the fighter—and controlled violence of a strictly policed and circumscribed exchange is to the violence seemingly devoid of rhyme or reason, of the unpredictable and unbounded confrontations symbolized by the rampant crime and drug trafficking that infest the neighborhood.

Boxing as a "Social Art"

If the hallmark of practice is, as Bourdieu (1990) contends, that it follows "a logic that unfolds directly in bodily gymnastics" without the intervention of discursive consciousness and reflexive explication, that is, by excluding the contemplative and detemporalizing posture of the theoretical gaze, then few practices may be said to be more "practical" than boxing. For most rules of the pugilistic art boil down to bodily moves that can only be intellectually grasped and made sense of. Moreover, boxing consists of a series of strategic exchanges in which hermeneutical mistakes are paid for at once, the force and frequency of the blows taken (or the "punishment" received, in pugilistic parlance) standing as the inescapable and instantaneous assessment of the performance: action and its evaluation are confounded, and reflexive return is by definition excluded from the activity. This amounts to saying that one cannot construct a science of the "social art" of boxing, that is, "pure practice without theory," as Durkheim (1956, 78) defines it, without undergoing a practical initiation into it. To understand the universe of boxing requires one to immerse oneself in it firsthand, to learn it and to experience it from the inside, *intus et in cute*. Native understanding of the object is here a necessary condition of an adequate knowledge of the object.

The culture of the boxer is not made up of a finite and discrete sum of information and normative models that exist independently of their application and can be transmitted in some logical, self-reinforcing sequence. Rather, it is formed of a diffuse complex of postures and (physical and mental) moves that, being continually reproduced in and through the functioning of the gym, exist only *in action*, as well as in the traces that this action leaves within and upon the body. Pugilistic knowledge consists of a practical knowledge composed of schemata that are thoroughly immanent to practice. It follows that the inculcation of the dispositions that make the boxer resolves itself in a process of *Bildung* of the body, in a particular (re)socialization of physiology in which "the function of pedagogical work is to substitute to the savage body . . . a body 'habituated,' that is, temporally structured" (Bourdieu 1972, 196) and physically remodeled according to the specific demands of the field.

An Endless Ascesis

The training of the boxer is an intensive and exacting discipline—the more so, in this case, given that the Stoneland Boys Club is among the best in the city and the coach a staunch disciplinarian behind his nonchalant attitude—that aims at transmitting, in a practical manner, by way of *direct embodiment*, a practical mastery of the fundamental corporeal, visual, and mental schemata of boxing. It is not for nothing that the most striking character of the workout is its repetitive, denuded, ascetic quality: Its different phases are repeated ad nauseam, day after day, week after week, with only barely perceptible variations.

Among the most frequent misrepresentations of the "sweet science" is the idea that the training of professional boxers consists essentially of punching each other silly on end. In fact, pugilists spend only a small fraction of their total preparation time facing an opponent—or partner: the importance of the distinction will become clearer below—in the ring. Much of the workout does not consist of "ring work" but of "floor work" and "table work." The members of the Boys Club train in the gym an average of four to five times a week, sometimes more (professional fighters nearing a bout train every day). The typical menu of a workout, which can last from forty-five to ninety minutes or more, is made up of the same five basic ingredients that each boxer doses to his taste and needs of the moment: *in seriatim*, shadow-boxing, hitting the bags, speed bag, jumping rope, and stomach exercises. A typical workout might include five rounds of shadow boxing in front of the mirror and three more working on moves and combinations in the ring in front of an imaginary opponent; three rounds on the heavy bag and one each on the double-end bag and uppercut bag; three rounds improving one's hand speed and hand-eye coordination on the speed bag, and three more skipping rope before closing the session with sit-ups, push-ups, neck tractions with a loaded helmet, and various other calisthenics. Absent sparring, one can "work on the pads" (by firing punches at padded mitts held by a trainer who moves about in the ring in mock simulation of an opponent, varying the angles and height of the pads and asking for specific combinations) or build up stomach muscles by having a fellow boxer hit you repeatedly on the belly with a medicine ball or with special mitts. Add to this a demanding daily regimen of "roadwork": professional boxers from the Boys Club run an average three to five miles a day, six days a week (three days on, one day off, and so on).

Professional pugilists have often been compared to artists. A more apposite analogy would look toward the world of the factory or artisanal workshop (Wacquant 1991a, 16–17). For learning the "Manly Art" is very much like a repetitive, yet skilled, manual craft.[12] Boxers themselves consider training as work—"it's a job I gotta do," "I gotta do my homework," "it's like having a second job"—and their body as their tool. Knowing that condition is critical to performance, they toil in the gym so they can step into the ring in the best possible shape, their skills sharpened and their anxiety partially allayed by knowledge that they did their utmost before getting in the ring: "You win your fight in the gym" says a well-known boxing proverb. The grueling preparation can be so consuming that it makes the bout seem easy by comparison; and some indeed find it is the training that is the hardest facet of their trade. McIlvanney's (1988, 173) description of champion Joe Frazier's training could be borrowed to depict many an anonymous club fighter: "He is a joyful masochist in the gym, flogging himself without respite in pursuit of the toughness that will make him oblivious of his opponent's aggression. . . . 'I work so hard in camp, punish myself, and then when I get to the real thing it's that much more easy for me. When the bell rings, I'm ready. I'm turned on.'"

But the sacrifice does not end in the gym. The monastic devotion demanded by preparation for a bout extends deep into the boxer's private life and cuts into his social life. To reach his optimal fight weight, he must abide by a strict diet (avoid all sugar and fried foods, stick to white meats and steamed vegetables, drink tea or water). He must maintain regular hours and impose on himself an early curfew to adequately rest his body. And he is taught early on that he must forsake sexual contact with women for weeks before the fight for fear of losing bodily fluids and sapping both his physical strength or his mental resolve (Wacquant 1991b). This, more so than the training, can make the life of the professional fighter a truly harsh existence, as complains a twenty-four-year-old contender in the welterweight division, for whom the biggest sacrifice is not the training itself, but,

> Layin' off the junk-food—the-hamburger-the-French-fries, *no sex* you know. I like drinkin' beer: no beer, you know no light beer, you know *dedication* when you gotta really dig deep down inside of you and go for what you want—you gotta say like "well no women this month," you know, an' no hamburgers. (Then, quickly, his voice rising to a feverish pitch as if revolted at the mere thought) You know what it's like to eat no junk food for a whole month, no Cokes or ice cream or chocolate cookies? *It be hell* wouldn't it!?

Yet the extreme repetitiousness and monotony of training does not preclude taking pleasure in it. Among the sources of enjoyment on the gym floor are the virile friendship of the club, expressed through glances and smiles, chunks of conversation, jokes and encouragements uttered during "time-outs," or affectionate taps on the hand (boxers ritually salute one another by hitting each other's gloved fists alternately from above and from below). The pleasure of feeling one's body blossom, get "tuned," and progressively adapt to the specific discipline of boxing is another important payoff. Besides the sometimes acute sentiment of wholeness and "flow" it provides,[13] training becomes its own reward when it leads one to master a difficult move or to win a victory over one's limitations (as when one surmounts the anguish of sparring with a tough opponent). Finally, boxers relish the fact that they "share membership in the same small guild," renowned for its physical toughness and bravery. They enjoy the sentiment that "they are different from other people. They are

fighters" (Bennett and Hamill 1978), a satisfaction that the regulars of
the gym express by proudly wearing boxing patches, shirts, and jackets
bearing the insignia of the trade.

> Yeah, uh, it's almost like a uh, *brother thing*, you know everybody's
> like a brother. They see you doin' somethin' wrong they try to help
> you, they try to *encourage* you, you know. They, uh, jokin' every now
> an' then, talk about themselves, but all in all, it's just like a friend,
> you know: ev'rybody in the gym, we become *friends*, with ev'rybody.
> (professional, age twenty-four, formerly telemarketing agent, now
> full-time boxer in Atlantic City)

> I like the sound of hitting the bag four-five times real fast, and then
> sliding out of the way, just watching my body git *tuned up*, feelin'
> the good conditionin' comin', an' jus' havin' people look at me and
> see that I got *talent* and I'm doin' somethin' and fixin' to git loose
> and tear somebody's head off. Tha's what I like. (professional, age
> thirty-one, firefighter)

A former world-ranked middleweight who recently retired had this to
say:

> The best memory of my career was . . . (pensive) *tie a pair of gloves
> on,* lacin' a pair of gloves on. [Really?] Right, right, anyday, in the gym.
> The day-to-day. [What feeling does it give you?] Like, like, comin' to
> orgasm, just lacin' the gloves on, yeah. Because I know I'm gonna step
> in the ring and I know it's time to rumble. For a fight, for trainin', *as
> long as they gloves.* (interview, August 1991)

Boxing resembles sociology in that it is an eminently esoteric practice
that has every appearance of being exoteric. The surface simplicity of the
boxer's moves could not be more deceiving. Far from being natural and
self-evident, the basic punches (left jab and hook, right cross, straight right
hand and uppercuts) are difficult to execute properly and presuppose a
thorough physical "rehabilitation," a genuine reshaping of one's kinetic
coordination and even a psychic conversion. It is one thing to visualize
and to understand them in thought, but quite another to realize them
and, even more, to combine them in the heat of the action. Virtually a
thousand conditions must be fulfilled for a punch to be thrown perfectly.
For instance, an effective jab requires, among other conditions, the correct
placement of feet, hips, shoulders, and arms; one must "pump" one's left
arm out at the right time, turn the wrist clockwise a half-turn at the moment of impact but no sooner, and transfer one's body weight alternately
to the front and to the back leg, all the time holding one's right hand close
by the cheekbone, ready to block or parry the opponent's counter.

Theoretical mastery is of little help as long as the move is not inscribed within one's bodily schema; and it is only after it has been assimilated by the body in and through endless physical drills that constitute so many "incorporating practices" (Connerton 1989) that a punch becomes in turn fully intelligible intellectually. There is in fact an *intelligence and a comprehension of the body* that goes beyond, and comes before, visual and mental mastery. The regulated bodily experimentation of training permits a "practical comprehension" of the rules of pugilism that satisfies the condition of dispensing with the need to constitute their meaning in consciousness.

To provide an adequate account of this imperceptible process that leads one to become involved and to invest in the game—in the twofold sense of economics and psychoanalysis—the long climb that takes the novice from the initial horror or indifference to curiosity and thence to pugilistic interest, and even to the carnal pleasure to box and desire to "go at it" in the ring (*libido pugilistic*), I would need to quote at length the field notes taken daily after each workout over the months. Their very mundanity and redundancy would help the reader grasp concretely the maddeningly slow progression that occurs, from week to week, in the mastery of the moves, in the comprehension—most often retrospective and purely gestural—of pugilistic technique, and in the modification that takes place in one's relation to the body. They would also convey, if imperfectly, the holistic and collective nature of the pugilistic education, in which each collaborates in teaching all others, every boxer functioning at every moment as a real or potential model for his peers to emulate or avoid. Even the material setting itself—from the life-size painting of Joe Louis high on the back-room wall to the colorful posters announcing past and upcoming bouts, and the worn gloves, ropes, and headguards lined up on the coach's table—exerts a real if subtle educative influence.

Yet, what is most likely to elude the outside observer[14] is the *extreme sensuousness of the initiation to pugilism.* One would need to call up all the tools of visual sociology (Becker 1981; Harper 1988), or even those of a sensual sociology that has yet to be invented (the possibility of which is suggested by Katz 1988), to convey the process whereby the boxer becomes orgasmically "invested" by the game as he progressively makes it his—boxers often use metaphors of blood and drugs to explain this particular relation akin to *mutual possession*. For it is with all of one's senses that one becomes converted to the world of boxing and its stakes. To give this proposition its full force, one would need to capture and communicate at once: the odors (the heady smell of sweat and embrocation, the leathery scent of the bags and gloves); the cadenced thump of punches against the bags and the clanking of the chains on which they hang; the machine-gun-like rattle of the speed-bag and the lighter tap-tap of feet galloping on the wooden floor while skipping rope, or the muffled squeak they let out as they move gingerly on the canvas of the ring; also the rhythmic snuffle of the fighters, each blowing, groaning, and sighing in a characteristic manner; and especially the synchronized disposition of the bodies in the space of the gym, whose mere view suffices to produce lasting pedagogical effects (Wacquant 1989b, 38–39, 58–61); not to forget the temperature, whose variation and intensity are not the least relevant properties of the gym. Their combination produces a sort of sensuous elation that is a key dimension of the education of the apprentice-boxer:

> I come because I love to come there to work out. I hate it when I don't come. You know like a doctor who love to perform surgery: gotta be there, it's like a *natural high*. I can't explain it, it's just a natural high. It's somethin' I guess like a dope fiend who's shooting up dope. Gotta have it, I just gotta have it! It's just part of my life. (amateur, age thirty-one, delivery driver by day and security guard by night).

Sluggin' It Out: The Social Logic of Sparring

If the professional boxer typically spends the bulk of his time outside the ring, endlessly rehearsing his moves in front of a mirror or building his stamina and honing his coordination by hitting an assortment of bags, and even outside the gym eating away miles and miles of daily roadwork, the climax and yardstick of training remains the sparring. Without regular practice in the ring against an opponent, the rest of the preparation would make precious little sense, for the peculiar mix of skills and qualities required by fighting cannot be assembled other than between the ropes. Many a boxer who "looks a million dollars on the floor" turns out to be inept and helpless once faced with an adversary. As Richie explains,

> Hittin' bags is one damn thing—runnin', hittin' bags, shadow box-in's one thin' and' sparrin' is a hun'red percent diff'rent. 'Cause it's diff'rent use of muscles, so *you have to spar to git in shape to spar.* Yeah, I don't give a damn who you are, 'less you're a helluva damn good fighter tha's *relax.* . . . You gotta be relax, cool, the breathin's diff'ren' an' everythin'. Tha's what it's all abou'. Tha's from experience. [So you can't instruct a boxer on how to relax or breathe on the floor?] Hell no! No, uh-huh, you can't tell. You can talk abou' it, but it don't work.

Sparring, which has its own temporality (unless he is about to fight, a boxer should spar lightly or at distant intervals so as to minimize the "wear and tear" on his body),[15] is both a reward and a challenge. It first represents the tangible payoff of a long week of hard labor and seemingly boundless "sacrificing." Trainers at Stoneland pay close attention to the condition of their charges and do not hesitate to bar from sparring those who have too blatantly neglected their preparation. "Little Anthony ain't puttin' no gloves on, Richie. He don't do no runnin', he got no gas, no stamina, it's a waste of time to get him up there. It's a disgrace."

But sparring is also a redoubtable test of strength, cunning, and courage, if only because the possibility of serious injury can never be completely eliminated, in spite of all precaution. Three boxers suffered a broken nose in sparring during my sojourn in the gym, a fourth had his tongue lacerated by an uppercut that required sixteen stitches; cuts are rare because of the protective headgear, but bloody noses and black eyes are plentiful. Not to mention that every time a boxer steps into the ring, even to "shake out" with a novice, he puts a fraction of his symbolic capital at stake. The slightest failing or slip-up, such as a knockdown or a sloppy performance, brings immediate embarrassment to the fighter, no less than to his gym mates, who dutifully assist his "corrective face-work" (Goffman 1966) so as to restabilize the fuzzy and labile status order of the gym. A variety of socially validated excuses are available for this purpose, ranging from minor sickness ("I been battling the flu, man, it's killing me") to imaginary injuries (a bad hand, a sore shoulder) to that most readily called upon, especially by trainers, a breach of the sacred code of sexual abstinence while in training (Wacquant 1991b).

Although it occupies only a small fraction of the pugilist's time in quantitative terms, sparring warrants close analysis because it demonstrates the highly *codified and collectively managed nature of pugilistic violence.* Also, being situated midway between shadow-boxing and the actual fighting of a competitive bout, sparring allows us to discern more clearly, as if through a magnifying glass, the subtle and apparently contradictory mix of instinct and rationality, emotion and calculation, individual abandon and group control that gives the work of fabrication of the pugilist its distinctive touch and stamps the totality of the training process.

1. *Choosing a Partner.* Everything in sparring hinges on the choice of partners, and for this reason it must imperatively be approved by the head coach.[16] Richie will not let a pairing slip by that he has not endorsed. Even regular sparring partners are careful to ask him, before they get in full gear (i.e., put their cup and headguard on, grease their face with Vaseline, and are "gloved up" with special, heavily padded gloves), whether they can step in the ring together. This is because the matching of opponents must always be adjusted in such a way that both boxers benefit from the exercise, and risks of physical injury are kept below an acceptable level.

As suggested above, considerations of honor also enter into the picture. Ideally, one does not spar with an opponent who is too superior, for fear of "getting a good ass-whuppin'," or one who is so weak that he cannot defend himself. However, vagaries in attendance and divergences in the training and fighting schedules of members of the club can make it difficult to find a steady partner who fits under the threefold rubric of weight, skill, and style. Therefore, it is good policy to maintain amicable relations in the gym with the one(s) you have, to not hurt his feelings by ensuring a degree of balance in the confrontation, and to always be ready and willing to give back a few rounds of sparring (at least three) to someone who bailed you out on another occasion. This is why asking a boxer if he wants to spar is a delicate matter. It means interfering in the network of reciprocal obligations that ties him to his current and past partners. It is better not to ask if you surmise that the answer will be negative.

In the absence of an adequate sparring partner, one can have recourse to boxers of lesser caliber or even beginners, as a last resort (I have once helped a cruiserweight get ready for a fight in England, despite the 50 lb. weight gap between us). Club members will travel to another gym to spar there but infrequently, as this will likely get them embroiled in the tangle of characteristically invidious and distrustful relationships that the coaches, trainers, and managers from different gyms entertain with one another. In all cases, there *must always be a measure of equilibrium between partners*, even if that requires purposefully handicapping one of them. In the case of an excessively uneven matching, the most experienced fighter tacitly, sometimes explicitly, commits himself to "holding back his punches," and will concentrate on his speed, "footwork," and defense while the weaker boxer puts the stress on punching and offense. When one of them is a novice, it is critical to select an initiator who perfectly masters his punches and temperament. If Richie waited almost ten weeks before letting me enter "the lion's den," it is not only because I needed to improve my conditioning and gain a handle on the basics of the trade, but also because he had to find me an adequate partner. And several regulars remained off limits for me even after I had progressed enough to "mix it up" with seasoned pros.

> During my training for the Golden Gloves, Shante suggested that I spar with Mark H., a thin but tough white amateur from Hammond who drives sixty miles every day to come prepare for the tournament here. I mentioned this to Richie, who replied, "Shante don't know nothin' and you don't know nothin'. Mark whip your butt, he's strong as hell, strongest guy in the gym! Look at his upper-body: he's only 135 but *he can crack*. I don't need you to get your nose busted again." (field notes, January 1990)

Some fighters have a style and mindset that make them difficult to work with because of their lack of adaptability to their partner:

> See, Alphonzo, he'll bang you. He get in there to bang you hard, he don't lay offa you. I wouldn't put John in there till he got his legs back: you gotta be able to move and get away from him 'cause he hit so damn hard. (former gym member advising the manager of John S., an older fighter attempting a comeback, on whom to approach as the latter's sparring mate, April 1991)

2. *A Controlled Violence.* Just as one does not spar with anyone, one does not spar anyhow either. The brutality of the exchange is a function of the balance of forces between partners on the one hand (it is more limited the more uneven this balance) and of the goals of the particular sparring session on the other, that is, of its coordinates in the twofold temporal axis of training and competition. As the date of the fight draws nearer, sparring sessions become more frequent and last longer—up to eight or ten rounds daily during the final week, with a letup in the final two or three days to make sure you "don't leave your fight in the gym"—the confrontation becomes more intense, and inexperienced boxers are temporarily held away from the ring. On the eve of an important bout, sparring can become almost as brutal as the fight itself. While gearing up for his much-awaited confrontation with Gerry Cooney, the latest "Great White Hope," heavyweight world champion Larry Holmes offered a bounty of $10,000 to the sparring partner who would send him to the canvas (Hauser 1986, 199). Yet, as with every well-run training camp, these sparring partners themselves were carefully selected to give Holmes an edge so as to preserve his strength and bolster his confidence for the fight.

During a session, the level of violence fluctuates in cycles according to a dialectic of challenge and response, within moving limits set by the sense of equity that founds the original agreement between sparring partners, which is neither a norm nor a contract but what Erving Goffman (1969, 21) calls a "working consensus." If one of the fighters picks up his pace and "gets off," the other immediately and "instinctively" reacts by hardening his response. There follows a sudden burst of violence that can escalate to the point where the two partners are hitting each other full force, before they step back and tacitly agree to resume their pugilistic dialogue a notch or two below. The task of the coach is to monitor this "fistic conversation" to see that the weaker fighter is not being overwhelmed, in which case he will instruct his opponent accordingly ("Circle and jab, Shante, I told you not to load up! And you keep that damn left hand up Lou!"), or that the two partners do not let the intensity of the sparring sag too far below that of a fight, thereby defeating the very purpose of the exercise ("What you be doin' up there, makin' love? Start workin' off that jab, I wanna see some nice right hands and counters off the block").

Competent pugilists relish the hands-on, one-on-one contest of sparring, but understand that this competitive clash is bounded by "noncontractual" clauses and, though close to an actual bout, is quite distinct from it because it involves an element of "antagonistic cooperation" that is expressly banned from the latter. Says one veteran gym member,

> I don't dislike anything [about sparring]. I like it all, 'cause ya learn at the same time. In a gym you not tryin' to win a fight, you in here *learnin'*. It's all about *learnin'*. Practicin' on doin' what you wanna do when [the] upcomin' fight come, ya know. . . . I can't hurt my opponent—I mean my sparrin' *partners*. They helpin' *me* out, just like I helpin' *them* out. They not gonna get in there and try and hurt me. . . . Here and again, now and then, ya know, ya have your little flashy stuff, where he might hit you hard, you might get caught with a nice punch and you gonna try and retaliate and come back with somethin'.

Many boxers take long to adjust to these tacit norms of cooperation that stand in apparent contradiction with the public dictate and ethos of unlimited competition. As in the case of bicycle racing (Albert 1991), this "cooperative informal order" is particularly problematic for novices who, taking the game at face value, are incapable of controlling their aggression and believe they must go all out to prove themselves, as the following field note indicates: "This new kid, he think he can beat everybody up: 'I can whup this guy, I can kick his ass! I'm better than 'im, lemme get in the ring!' and he just wanna fight with everybody. We gonna have problems with him. I don't know what to do 'cause I can't let him spar with this kinda attitude" (Richie, November 1989). They will have to be taught *in actu* how to read cues as to when to back off to give their partner respite and when to keep pressing to make him work harder.

3. Sparring as Perceptual, Emotional, and Physical Work. A hybrid between training and fighting, sparring effects a thorough reeducation of the body and mind, during which is forged what Foucault (1963, 168) calls a "multisensorial structure" quite specific to boxing that can be articulated or discerned only in action. Ring experience expands the boxer's capacity for perception and concentration; it forces him to curb his emotions and it refashions and hardens his body in preparation for the clashes of competition. First, sparring is an education of the senses, and notably of visual faculties; the state of emergency it creates effects a progressive

reorganization of perceptual abilities and habits. A transformation occurs in the structure and scope of one's visual field as one climbs up the
hierarchy of sparring. Instead of seeming cluttered and entropic, this field
progressively achieves pattern and regularity; one becomes better able to
sort stimuli, to shut out unneeded sensory information, and to interpret
and even anticipate relevant ones as one acquires the "eye of the boxer"
(Wacquant 1989a, 52–53).

Sparring is also the means and support of a particularly intense form
of "emotion work" (Hochschild 1983, 7). Early on, boxers must learn
to control and hide their emotions in the ring. For they must not only
exercise constant surveillance of their internal feelings, but also exert
continual "expressive control" (Goffman 1969) over their external signaling so as never to let their opponent know if and when they are hurt by
punches. Legendary trainer-manager Cus D'Amato (cited in Brunt 1987,
55), who discovered Mike Tyson, sums up the matter thus: "The fighter
has mastered his emotions to the extent that he can conceal and control
them. Fear is an asset to a fighter. It makes him move faster, be quicker
and more alert. Heroes and cowards feel exactly the same fear. Heroes
react to it differently." This difference is not innate, but is an acquired
ability collectively produced by prolonged habituation of the body to
the specific discipline of sparring. A middleweight with a record of five
consecutive professional wins explains:

> You have to stay in control, because yer emotions will burn up all
> yer oxygen, so you have to stay calm and relaxed. So you have to deal
> with the situation.
>
> Q: Was it hard learning to control emotions, like to not get mad
> or frustrated if a guy is slippery and you can't hit him with clean
> shots?
> A: It was hard for me. It took me years-and-years-and-years to git that
> and *juuus'* when I was gittin' it under control real goo', then thin's,
> um, started movin' for me. It works, well, I guess when it was time,
> it worked itself into place.
>
> Q: Is that something that Richie taught you?
> A: He kept tellin' me to stay calm, relax. Jus' breathe, take it easy—
> but I foun' it har' to stay calm and relax when this guy's trin' to kill
> ya over in the next corner, but eventually it sunk in and I understood
> what he was sayin'.

Indeed, the deep imbrication between gesture, conscious experience,
and physiological processes—to recall Gerth and Mills' (1964) distinction between the three constituent elements of emotion—is such that a
change in each brings instantaneous modification of the other. Failure to

monitor the sensory experience of punches coming at you disrupts your ability to act and thus alters your bodily states. Conversely, to be physically fit allows one to be mentally ready and therefore to better muster the feelings triggered by the actual flow of blows.

Because the slightest lapse of self-control is instantly punished once between the ropes, the boxer must be capable of managing his emotions and know, according to the circumstances, how to contain or repress them or, on the contrary, how to trigger and fuel them. He must know how to muzzle certain feelings, such as frustration or anxiety, so as to resist the blows, provocations, and eventual verbal abuse and rough tactics dished out by his opponent—hitting low or with the elbows, head-butting, rubbing one's gloves into the other fighter's eyes or over a cut in order to open it further, and so forth. He must be able to call forth and amplify feelings of anger or "controlled fury" at will without ever letting them get out of hand. Most boxers strive to be "businesslike" in the ring, to channel all their emotional and mental energies toward "getting the job done" in the most effective and painless fashion. Sparring teaches them the "feeling rules" specific to their occupation.

Finally, the strictly physical aspect of sparring should not go unnoticed on account of being self-evident; it must not be forgotten that professional prizefighting is first and foremost an *economy of pain (and money)*. The aim of a fight is to outmaneuver or subdue one's opponent by hitting him, which necessarily involves getting hit. The boxing vernacular is replete with terms referring to the ability to "take a punch" and glorifies the capacity to endure pain. Now, beyond one's natural endowment, such as an "iron chin" and the mysterious and revered quality called "heart" (also central to the masculine street culture of the ghetto), there is only one way to harden oneself to pain, to get one's organism used to taking blows: to get hit regularly and progressively adjust to it. For, contrary to another popular stereotype, boxers have no particular liking for pain and do not enjoy getting hit, or even, for many of them, hurting their opponent. Says a young welterweight who recently turned professional, "*Nah, we're human man! We're human,* you know, we're ju' like anybody else, our feelings are jus' as much as your feelins', we—you can't put us outside, you know, *we're not no different than you:* we're in the same world, we're the same flesh, same blood, same everything, you know."

What they have done is to elevate their threshold of tolerance of pain via its controlled routinization (Weber's *Veralltaglichung*). This brings us right back to emotional regimentation, inasmuch as this learning of indifference to physical dolor goes hand in hand with the acquisition of the form of *sang froid* specific to pugilism. The adequate socialization of the boxer presupposes an endurance to punches whose basis is the ability to master the first reflex of self-protection that undoes the coordination of movements and gives a decisive advantage to the opponent. More than the actual force of the punches borne, it is this progressive acquisition of "resistance to excitement" [*resistance a l' emoi*] as Mauss (1950, 385) aptly labels it, that is impossible to neatly apportion undivided either to the realm of will or to the physiological order, which exhausts the novice during the first sparring sessions as well as inexperienced fighters during their bouts.

Thus, from an alien space where one feels awkward, out of place, or plain endangered, the ring progressively becomes a "place of work," a stage for self-expression, where pugilists are "at home"—this is the expression they use most often when asked how it feels to step into the ring. This is because their habitus has been so thoroughly reorganized that its structure now corresponds to the basic structure of the game, thereby producing the peculiar *sense of felicity* that comes from the prereflective agreement of the body with the microcosm in which it evolves.

Pugilistic Rationality: The Boxer as Embodied Practical Reason

To learn how to box is imperceptibly to modify one's bodily schema, one's relation to the body and to its uses so as to internalize a set of dispositions that are inseparably physical and mental and, in the long run, that turn the body into a virtual punching machine—but *an intelligent and creative machine capable of self-regulation while innovating* within a fixed and relatively limited panoply of moves as an instantaneous function of the actions of the opponent in time. The mutual interpenetration of corporal and mental dispositions reaches such a degree that even willpower, morale, determination, concentration, and the control of one's emotions become so many reflexes inscribed within the organism. In the accomplished boxer, the mental becomes part of the physical and vice versa; body and mind function in total symbiosis.

This is what is expressed in this scornful comment that Richie opposes to fighters who argue that they are not "mentally ready" for a fight. After Jason's loss in his first nationally televised fight in Atlantic City, the old trainer is fuming: "He don't lose 'cause he's not 'mentally ready.' That don't mean nothin', 'mentally ready,' that's bullshit! If you're a fighter, you get up in the ring and you *fight*, there's no bein' mentally ready or not ready. It's not mental, ain't nothin' mental about it; if you're not a fighter, you don't get up there, you don't fight. If you're a fighter, you're ready and you fight—that's all. All the rest is just *bullshit for the birds.*" (field notes, April 1989)

It is this mutual overlapping of the physical and the mental that allows experienced boxers to continue to defend themselves and eventually rebound after having been nearly knocked out. In such moments of quasi-unconsciousness, their body continues to box, as it were, on its own, until they recover their senses, sometimes after a lapse of several minutes. Former world heavyweight champion Gene Tunney recounts this experience in training:

> I went into a clinch with my head down and my partner's head came up and butted me over the left eye, cutting and dazing me badly. Then he stepped back and swung his right against my jaw with every bit of his power. It landed flush and stiffened me where I stood. Without going down or staggering, *I lost all consciousness, but instinctively proceeded* to knock him out. Another sparring partner entered the ring. We boxed three rounds, I have no recollection of this. (cited in Sammons 1988, 246, emphasis added)

In the famous "Thrilla in Manila," one of the most brutal fights in heavyweight history, Joe Frazier and Muhammad Ali fought much of the bout in a state of near unconsciousness. "Smokin' Joe" recalled, several years after the event, that by the sixth round, "I couldn't think anymore. All I know is the fight is there. The heat [over 110°], the humidity. . . . That particular fight, like, I just couldn't think; I was there, I had a job to do. I just wanted to get the job done" (NBC Sports, 190).

Interviews with boxers and trainers on the question of the mental aspect of the game turn up a seeming contradiction. On the one hand, they assert that boxing is a "thinking man's game," which they frequently liken to chess; on the other hand, they also insist that, once in the ring, you have far too little time to ratiocinate: "Ain't no place for thinkin' in the ring; it's reflex! When it's time to think, it's time to quit," lectures Richie. Yet, at the same time, the Stoneland trainer fully agrees with Ray Arcel, the doyen of trainers, still active at age ninety-two after having groomed eighteen world champions, that "boxing is brain over brawn. I don't care how much ability you've got as a fighter. If you can't think, you're just another bum in the park" (cited in Anderson 1991, 121). The riddle is resolved as soon as one realizes that the ability of the boxer to cogitate and reason in the ring has become a faculty of his organism *in globo*, or of an indivisible "body-mind" complex (Dewey 1929, 277). This blurring of the divide between the corporeal and the mental is highlighted in the following comment by a local contender in the cruiserweight division:

> It's a mental aspect, because the computer, the *brain* is what controls the body. If the computer isn't strong, then it can't sen' a strong message to the body, so yes, you have to be strong mentally to carry out

the task. You have to think what position this man is in, where you wanna hit him, maybe you wanna open up, give him a face, make him swing so you can slide and duck and hit him. It's a *constant thinkin' thing*—if you wanna git there and git out without gittin' hit, but if you jus' wanna go in there bombs away, well then it doesn't take any thinkin' to do that.

Q: But you don't have that much time to think, do you?

A: [snapping his fingers nervously to give cadence] But it's all like a split second: yer mind is like a spark plug [click-click with his fingers, voice picking up the same tempo], *jus' constantly thinking, jus' constantly thinkin'. Everythin' you do, move, is thinkin' for a reason*, to make somethin' happen, that's how you have to think in the ring. Tha's how you have to think [stops finger snapping]. There's a sayin' that once you train so much an' get so good, you don't even have to think anymore. It's jus' *natural*, but your body naturally does what it's suppose' to do, but it's still, *the thinkin' is so much faster than you*, you don't have a chance to *think about it.* You got the answers before you even did it, so you have to be well tuned to get like that.

Once in the ring, it is the trained body that learns and understands, sorts and stores information, finds the correct answer in its repertory of preprogrammed actions and reactions. Pugilistic excellence can thus be defined by the fact that the body of the fighter computes and decides for him, instantaneously, without the mediation and the costly delay that it would cause, of abstract thinking, prior representation, the strategic computation. *The body is the immediate, spontaneous strategist of the game:* It knows, understands, judges, and reacts all at the same time. To be a competent boxer, then, is not much different from being a competent jazz pianist. For both, to achieve flowing utterance—of punches in one case, of notes in the others—takes a specific form of habitual knowledge, "an embodied way of accomplishing distances" that can be acquired only through "a long course of incorporation" (Sudnow 1978, 12, 13) upon which the "disciplined body assumes the essential postures of the mind" (Levao 1988, 13).

The strategy of the boxer is thus the product, not of the technology of individual rational choice or of mechanical submission to the normative dictates of the coach or gym "subculture," but of the encounter of a pugilistic habitus with the very field that has produced it. The social art of pugilism effaces a whole series of scholastic distinctions, between the intentional and the habitual, the rational and the emotional, the corporeal and the mental, that are so deeply entrenched in the dualistic ontology of modern social science that we do not even notice how much they truncate the fundamental reality of human social action. For boxing thrives on the juxtaposition, indeed the *fusion,* of these opposites. It expresses an embodied practical reason that escapes the logic of individual consciousness and computation. Confrontation in the ring calls for synoptic judgments, informed by pugilistic sensitivity and responsiveness, made in and for the moment, which are the very antithesis of the systematically planned and measured decisions of the kind of "calculating reason" that underlies rational-choice and game-theoretical models of social action. Indeed, one could characterize the strategy of the boxer in the ring by what Brody (1982, 37, emphasis added) says of the Athabascan Eskimo hunters of the Canadian Northwest: "To make a good, wise, sensitive hunting choice is to accept the interconnection of all possible factors, and [to avoid] the mistake of seeking rationally to focus on any one consideration that I held as primary. What is more, *the decision is taken in the doing;* there is no step or pause between theory and practice. As a consequence, the decision—like the action from which it is inseparable—is always alterable (and therefore may not properly even be termed a decision)."

The successful learning of boxing thus requires the combination of quasi-antinomic dispositions: impulses and drives rooted deep within the "biologic individual" dear to George Herbert Mead (1934), in a body that may be said to be "savage," at the borderline of the cultural, and the ability to master them at every moment, to regulate, transform, and tap them according to a plan that is objectively rational even though it remains beyond the reach of rational consciousness. This contradiction, inherent in the pugilistic habitus, explains that the belief in the innate character of the boxer's ability can peacefully coexist with an unrelenting and rigid ethic of work and striving. As with religion according to Durkheim (1965), the myth of the gift of the boxer is "an illusion founded in reality" (*cum fundamento in rei*). What fighters take for a natural ability ("you gotta have it in you," "you're a born boxer") is in effect this peculiar nature that results from the long process of inculcation of the pugilistic habitus, a process that is facilitated to the extent that recruits are predisposed to it by the congruent conditionings of this antechamber to the gym that is the ghetto street. The native concept of the "natural," frequently invoked to explain why certain boxers learn quickly or succeed with apparent ease, denotes this *cultivated nature,* whose social genesis has become literally invisible to those who perceive it through the mental categories that are its product.

Thus we reach, through a different, quasi-experimental route as it were, the same conclusion as Merleau-Ponty (1962) in his *Phenomenology of Perception:* that the "lived body" is not in the first instance an *object* of consciousness but the pre-objective medium of consciousness, indeed the veritable *subject* of human social practice if there is ever to be one.

By demonstrating the egregious inadequacy of the two theoretical models of action that have recently polarized thinking on the question (Elster, 1989), rational choice and normative constraint, boxing suggests the need to place the *socialized lived body*, and the incorporating practices that shape its structures, at the center of the analysis of social action.[17]

References

Abrahams, R. D. 1970. *Positively Black*. Englewood Cliffs, N.J.: Prentice Hall.
Albert, E. 1991. "Riding a Line: Competition and Cooperation in the Sport of Bicycle Racing," *Sociology of Sport Journal*, 8: 341–61.
Anderson, D. 1991. *In the Corner: Great Boxing Trainers Talk about Their Art*. New York: Morrow.
Auletta, K. 1982. *The Underclass*. New York: Pantheon.
Baldwin, J. B. 1988. "Habit, Emotion, and Self-conscious Action," *Sociological Perspectives*, 31: 35–58.
Becker, H., ed. 1981. *Exploring Society Photographically*. Chicago: University of Chicago Press.
Bennet, G., and P. Hamill. 1978. *Boxers*. New York: Dolphin Books.
Blacking, J. 1973. *How Musical Is Man?* Seattle: University of Washington Press.
Bourdieu, P. 1972. *Esquisse d'une theorie de la pratique. Precede de trios études d'ethnologie kabyle*. Geneva: Droz.
———. 1977. *Outline of a Theory of Practice*. Cambridge: Cambridge University Press.
———. 1990. *The Logic of Practice*. Cambridge: Polity Press (original work published 1980).
Bourgois, P. 1989. "Just Another Night on Crack Street." *New York Times Magazine*, November 12.
Brody, H. 1982. *Maps and Dreams*. New York: Pantheon.
Brunt, S. 1987. *Mean Business: The Rise and Fall of Shawn O'Sullivan*. Harmondsworth, U.K.: Penguin.
Chicago Fact Book Consortium. 1984. *Local Community Fact Book: Chicago Metropolitan Area*. Chicago: Chicago Review Press.
Chicago Tribune. 1986. *An American Millstone: An Examination of the Nation's Permanent Underclass*. Chicago: Contemporary Press.
Connerton, P. 1989. *How Societies Remember*. Cambridge: Cambridge University Press.
Csikszentmihalyi, M. 1975. *Beyond Boredom and Anxiety*. San Francisco: Jossey-Bass.
Dewey, J. 1929. *Experience and Nature*. Chicago: Open Court.
Donnelly, P. 1988. "On Boxing: Notes on the Past, Present, and Future of a Sport in Transition," *Current Psychology*, 7: 331–46.
Douglas, J. D. 1976. *Investigative Social Research*. Beverly Hills, Calif.: Sage.
Durkheim, E. 1956. *Education and Sociology*. New York: Free Press (original work published in 1922).
———. 1965. *The Elementary Forms of the Religious Life*. New York: Free Press (original work published in 1912).

Drake, St. C., and Cayton, H. R. 1945. *Black Metropolis: A Study of Negro Life in a Northern City*. New York: Harcourt Brace Jovanovich.

Early, G. 1988. "Three Notes toward a Cultural Definition of Boxing." In J. C. Oates and D. Halpern, eds., *Reading the Fights*. New York: Prentice Hall. 20–38.

Edmond, A. O. 1973. "The Second Louis–Schmeling Fight: Sport, Symbol, and Culture," *Journal of Popular Culture*, 7: 42–50.

Elster, J. 1989. *The Cement of Society: A Study in Social Order*. Cambridge: Cambridge University Press.

Fine, G. A. 1979. "Small Groups and Culture Creation: The Idioculture of Little League Baseball," *American Sociological Review*, 44: 733–45.

Folb, J. 1980. *Runnin' Down Some Lines: The Language and Culture of Black Teenagers*. Cambridge: Harvard University Press.

Foucault, M. 1963. *Naissance de la clinique. Une archeologie du regard medical* [Birth of the Clinic. An Archeology of Medical Perception]. Paris: Presses Universitaires de France.

Gerth, H., and Mills, C. W. 1964. *Character and Social Structure*. New York: Harcourt Brace Jovanovich.

Goffman, E. 1961. *Encounters: Two Studies in the Sociology of Interaction*. Indianapolis: Bobbs-Merrill.

———. 1966. *Interaction Rituals*. New York: Vintage.

———. 1969. *The Presentation of Self in Everyday Life*. Harmondsworth: Penguin (original work published 1959).

Halpern, D. 1988. "Distance and Embrace," in J. C. Oates and D. Halpern, eds., *Reading the Fights*. New York: Prentice Hall. 275–85.

Hare, N. 1971. "A Study of the Black Fighter," *Black Scholar* 3: 2–9.

Harper, D. 1988. "Visual Sociology: Expanding Sociological Vision," *The American Sociologist* (Spring): 54–70.

Hauser, T. 1986. *The Black Lights: Inside the World of Professional Boxing*. New York: McGraw-Hill.

———. 1991. *Muhammad Ali: His Life and Times*. New York: Simon & Schuster.

Heller, P. 1989. *Bad Intentions: The Mike Tyson Story*. New York: New American Library.

Hirsch, A. R. 1983. *The Managed Heart: Commercialization of Human Feeling*. Berkeley: University of California Press.

Jackson, M 1989. *Paths toward a Clearing*. Bloomington: Indiana University Press.

Jencks, C., and Peterson, P., eds. 1991. *The Urban Underclass*. Washington, D.C.: Brookings Institution.

Jenkins, T. J. 1955. *Changes in Ethnic and Racial Representation among Professional Boxers: A Study in Ethnic Succession*. Master's thesis, University of Chicago.

Katz, J. 1988. *Seductions of Crime*. New York: Basic Books.

Kochman, T., ed. 1972. *Rappin' and Stylin' Out: Communication in Urban Black America*. Urbana: University of Illinois Press.

Kotlowitz, A. 1991. *There Are No Children Here*. New York: Morrow.

Levao, R. 1988. "Reading the Fights: Making Sense of Professional Boxing," in J. C. Oates and D. Halpern, eds., *Reading the Fights*. New York: Prentice Hall. 1–19.

Mailer, N. 1971. "*King of the Hill*": *On the Fight of the Century.* New York: New American Library.

Mauss, M. 1950. "Les techniques du corps." [Techniques of the Body]. In *Sociologie et anthropologie,* 365–86. Paris: Presses Universitaires de France (English translation published in *Economy and Society* 2: 70–88).

McIlvanney, H. 1988. "Superman at Bay. Joe Frazier v. Muhammad Ali, New York, March 8, 1971," in J. C. Oates and D. Halpern, eds., *Reading the Fights.* New York: Prentice Hall (original work published 1982). 170–84.

Mead, C. 1985. *Champion: Joe Louis, Black Hero in White America.* New York: Charles Scribner's Sons.

Mead, G. H. 1934. "The Biologic Individual," in *Mind, Self, and Society from the Standpoint of a Social Behaviorist.* Chicago: University of Chicago Press. 347–53.

Merleau-Ponty, M. 1962. *The Phenomenology of Perception.* Atlantic Highlands, N.J.: Humanities Press (original work published 1945).

Mitchell, R. G., Jr. 1983. *Mountain Experience: The Psychology and Sociology of Adventure.* Chicago: University of Chicago Press.

Mosca, D. 1991. *A Boxing Enclave: Preserving the Great White Hope* (fieldwork project at Newman's Gym, San Francisco). Manuscript, San Francisco State University, Department of Anthropology.

Muel-Dreyfus, F. 1983. *Le métier d'educateur* [The Educator's Craft]. Paris: Editions de Minuit.

NBC Sports (Producer). 1990. *The Thrilla in Manila* (VHS video of the 1975 Ali-Frazier heavyweight title fight). NBC Sports Venture.

Oates, J. C. 1987. *On Boxing.* Garden City, N.Y.: Doubleday.

———. 1988. "Mike Tyson," in *(Woman) Writer: Occasions and Opportunities.* New York: E. P. Dutton. 225–53.

Ostrow, J. M. 1990. *Social Sensitivity: An Analysis of Experience and Habit.* Stony Brook: State University of New York Press.

Roberts, R. 1978. *Jack Dempsey: The Manassa Mauler.* Baton Rouge: Louisiana University Press.

Sammons, J. T. 1988. *Beyond the Ring: The Role of Boxing in American Society.* Urbana: University of Illinois Press.

Sanchez-Jankowski, M. 1991. *Islands in the Street: Gangs in Urban American Society.* Berkeley: University of California Press.

Simmel, G. 1949. "The Sociology of Sociability," *American Journal of Sociology,* 55: 254–68.

Suaud, C. 1978. *La vocation. Conversion et reconversion des pretres ruraux* [The Calling. Conversion and Reconversion of Rural Priests]. Paris: Editions de Minuit.

Sudnow, D. 1978. *Ways of the Hand: The Organization of Improvised Conduct.* Cambridge: Harvard University Press.

Sugden, J. 1987. "The Exploration of Disadvantage: The Occupational Sub-culture of the Boxer," in J. Horne, D. Jary, and A. Tomlinson, eds., *Sports, Leisure, and Social Relations.* London: Routledge and Kegan Paul. 187–209.

Sullivan, M. 1989. *"Getting Paid": Youth, Crime, and Work in the Inner City.* Ithaca, N.Y.: Cornell University Press.

Torres, J. 1989. *Fire and Fear: The Inside Story of Mike Tyson.* New York: Popular Library.

Valentine, B. L. 1978. *Hustling and Other Hard Work: Life Styles in the Ghetto.* New York: Free Press.

Wacquant, L. J. D. 1989a. "Corps et âme: Notes ethnographiques d'un apprenti-boxeur" [Body and soul: Ethnographic notes of an apprentice-boxer]. *Actes de la recherché en sciences socials,* 80, 33–67.

——. 1989b. "The Ghetto, the State, and the New Capitalist Economy," *Dissent* (Fall): 508–20.

——. 1991a. "'Busy Louie' aux Golden Gloves," *Gulliver,* 6: 12–33.

——. 1991b. "The Meaning of the Manly Art: Boxers, Sex and Women." Lecture delivered to Program on Gender and Meaning, Sociology Department, Smith College, November.

——. 1992. "Redrawing the Urban Color Line: The State of the Ghetto in the 1980s," in C. J. Calhoun and G. Ritzer, eds., *Social Problems.* New York: McGraw-Hill.

——. 1995. "The Comparative Social Structure and Experience of Urban Exclusion: 'Race,' Class, and Space in Chicago and Paris," in R. Lawson, C. McFate and W. J. Wilson, eds., *Poverty, Inequality, and the Future of Social Policy: Western States in the New World Order.* Newbury Park, Calif.: Sage.

Wacquant, L. J. D., and Wilson, W. J. 1989. "The Cost of Racial and Class Exclusions in the Inner City," *Annals of the American Academy of Political and Social Science,* 501: 8–25.

Weinberg, S. K., and Around, H. 1952. "The Occupational Culture of the Boxer," *American Journal of Sociology,* 62: 460–69.

Willener, A. 1988. "Le concerto pour trompette de Haydn [Haydn's trumpet concerto]," *Actes de la recherché en science socials,* 75: 54–63.

Wilson, W. J. 1987. *The Truly Disadvantaged: The Inner City, the Underclass, and Public Policy.* Chicago: University of Chicago Press.

Wittgenstein, L. 1953. *Philosophical Investigations.* Oxford: Blackwell.

Zola, I. K. 1964. "Observations on Gambling in a Lower-class Setting," in H. S. Becker, ed., *The Other Side: Perspectives on Deviance.* New York: Free Press. 247–60.

Notes

This chapter originally appeared in *Sociology of Sport Journal,* 9 (1992): 221–54. Reprinted with permission.

1. Tyson grew up in a single-headed family living on public aid in the tenements of Brownsville, a ghetto of Brooklyn, and was introduced to boxing while in a juvenile detention center. The youngest heavyweight world champion in history, he has been typically portrayed as a "bad nigger" (Heller 1989; Torres 1989).

2. This is a pseudonym. Names of persons and places have been changed to preserve the anonymity of my informants.

3. For a more detailed account of the process of fabrication of the boxer that analyzes the collective logic of the pugilistic pedagogy in the gym and includes large excerpts of the supporting field materials, see Wacquant (1989a); for a first-person, literary narrative of my experiences at the Golden Gloves tournament, see Wacquant (1991a); for a preliminary analysis of boxing as a ritual of consecration of an embattled plebeian masculinity, see Wacquant (1991b).

4. On the notion of habitus as a system of durable, transposable dispositions to perceive, appreciate, and act, see Bourdieu (1977, 1990). For an insightful study of the inculcation of the "sacerdotal habitus" among French rural priests that has many parallels with the case of boxers, see Suaud (1978); compare also with the formation of the habitus of primary school teachers in two historical epochs in Muel-Dreyfus (1983).

5. For a more detailed sociography of social change in Stoneland, see Wacquant (1995); for a comparative analysis of the accelerating degradation of the other ghetto neighborhoods of Chicago's South Side and West Side, see Wacquant and Wilson (1989). Suffice to note here that, beneath its appearance of uniform devastation, the ghetto remains a differentiated and hierarchized universe.

6. A "poot-butt," a subcategory of the "lame," is somebody who is socially inexperienced, too young (literally or emotionally) "to take care of business," though he "may blunder or bully ahead as if he knew what to do or how to act. . . . 'He's tryin' to be so old, don't know shit! Still wet under d'lip. . . . Momma didn't teach 'im enough. Let 'im out on d' streets too young'" (Folb 1980, 39).

7. Title inspired by the motto of the Chicago Boys and Girls Club, which runs the Stoneland unit: "The Club That Beats the Street" (club brochure).

8. Municipal Park District gyms are even less costly since they levy no dues; one other professional gym in Chicago requires monthly payments of $5 for amateurs and $20 for professionals, but allows many waivers. Higher gym dues are not unheard of (e.g., $55 per quarter at the Somerville Boxing Gym in Boston's suburbs, $50 a month at the Tenderloin gym in San Francisco).

9. Or lack of internal government must be compensated by truly exceptional aggressivity, physical prowess, and ring "toughness." However, such fighters tend to "burn out" early or leave their potential unfulfilled. A boxing prodigy such as former three-time world champion Wilfredo Benitez, the son of a Puerto Rican sugar cane cutter, is a good case in point: pro at age fourteen and world champion by age seventeen, his lack of training and eating discipline cut his career short of its potential.

10. There are exceptions to the rule: a female kick-boxer trained at Stoneland for part of my stay in the gym but she had a special relation to its star fighter. A well-known female professional boxer trains at another Chicago gym but at separate hours. The gender closure of the pugilistic universe is highlighted by the reaction to the entry of a female ethnographer in a San Francisco boxing gym (Mosca 1991).

11. At most other gyms I have visited, regulations are more clearly spelled out, taking the form of a standard list of rules posted on the entrance door or on a wall, or hung from the ceiling for all to see. The more unstable and socially dispersed the membership of the club, the more explicit the regulations.

12. As Gerald Early (1988, 20) perceptively puts it, "The one word that comes to mind more than any other watching the fighters work in the gym is 'proletariat.' These men are honestly, and in a most ghastly way, *toiling*, and what is most striking is how much more grotesque this work is than, say, the nightmare of an assembly line. And proletariat is such an appropriate word for fighters whom we also call stiffs and bums."

13. Boxers talk about "a natural high" and compare the feeling of the experience in intensive training (or fighting) to taking drugs or having sex. On the notion of flow, see Csikszentmihalyi (1975) and Mitchell (1983, 153–69) for an interesting

parallel analysis of the management of risk and uncertainty in the experience of flow among mountain climbers.

14. And a fortiori the reader: One wonders whether the mere passage to a written medium of communication does not irretrievably transform the experience to be conveyed. Willener's (1988, 61) remark on music is very apposite to boxing: "One of the obstacles to any sociology of music remains that one does not know how to talk about it. One must translate a musical sense in a non-musical language."

15. Some boxers become "punchy" (i.e., suffer from the "punch drunk" syndrome) not so much from getting hit during fights as from excessive pounding absorbed in the gym. This is of particular concern to boxers who enter the game at an early age or stay too long in the amateur division, running upwards of three hundred amateur bouts before turning pro, by which time they may be "washed up" or "shot." For a more detailed discussion of the management of the boxer's "bodily capital" in and out of the gym, see Wacquant (1989a, 63–67).

16. The personality and coaching philosophy of the head trainer is decisive because it determines the main parameters for the social management of ring violence. In more impersonal, even anomic, gyms devoid of a clear authority structure and formal membership (such as many municipal "park district" facilities), the rules that govern sparring are much looser and the results can be disastrous.

17. See the work of Bourdieu (1990, especially book 1, chap. 4), Jackson (1989), Blacking (1973), and various recent reinterpretations of the notion of habit (e.g., Baldwin 1988; Connerton 1989; Ostrow 1990) for substantial efforts in this direction.

Acknowledgments

This paper is dedicated to the memory of Aaron, Spanish man-child and gym buddy, whom the ring could not save from the street.

This paper benefited from the reactions, critical comments, and encouragement of a number of colleagues, among them Pierre Bourdieu, Rogers Brubaker, Lynn S. Chancer, Rick Fantasia, Harvey Molotch, Bill Wilson, Viviana Zelizzer, and members of the Center for European Sociology in Paris. My gratitude also goes to my colleagues in the "sweet science" who taught me much more than how to throw a left jab, and to the friends and family who supported me morally during this strenuous project (with special mention to Elizabeth Bonamour du Tarte for a major on-site assist). This research was made possible in part by the financial support of the Maison des sciences de l'homme, a Lavoisier Fellowship from the French government, and the Milton Fund of Harvard University.

12

Recent Stadium Development Projects in Chicago

A Tale of Three Neighborhoods

COSTAS SPIROU
and LARRY BENNETT

On February 25, 1988, the Chicago City Council approved an agreement between the city government and the Chicago Cubs permitting the baseball franchise to erect stadium lights at Wrigley Field. The council's action ended the Cubs' longstanding status as the eccentric among major league sports franchises in America, the only major league team whose home contests were performed exclusively during daytime hours. The prelude to the momentous city council vote on lights at Wrigley Field had been seven years of often rancorous maneuvering involving the Chicago Cubs baseball franchise, the City of Chicago, and residents of the Lake View neighborhood on the city's North Side. Yet within a few years, three of Chicago's four remaining major league franchises moved from pre–Great Depression facilities into newly built sports palaces:

the American League's Chicago White Sox welcomed the Detroit Tigers to their home opener in 1991 at the new Comiskey Park, the Chicago Blackhawks of the National Hockey League and the National Basketball Association's Chicago Bulls inaugurated the United Center during their 1994–95 seasons.

The stories of how these three projects—the modernization of Wrigley Field, the construction of the new Comiskey Park, and the United Center—came to fruition offer important insights about the changing economic profile of Chicago, the dynamics of contemporary deal-making in the city, and the ambiguous future of Chicago's fabled neighborhoods. We recount these stories with the intent of highlighting how important professional sports have become in defining Chicago's identity, and also, to note how the effort to accommodate professional sports franchises can produce highly variable consequences for neighboring residents, businesses, and other community institutions.

Wrigley Field, Lake View, and Evening Baseball

Since the 1920s, the Wrigley family, of chewing gum fame, owned the Chicago Cubs, and for much of that period Philip K. Wrigley resisted the seemingly irresistible: major league baseball's move toward night baseball. However, in 1981, Philip Wrigley's son William, facing substantial estate tax obligations, sold the Cubs to the Tribune Corporation, the corporate entity controlling the *Chicago Tribune* and a variety of other media properties, including WGN-TV. Following its purchase of the Cubs, the Tribune Corporation began to explore ways of harnessing the team's drawing power to its other assets. Already, WGN-TV was operating as a national cable TV station. The Cubs' new owners, from the very beginning, considered the baseball franchise to be an excellent source of programming. At the time, WOR-TV in New Jersey was transmitting New York Mets games, while in Atlanta, Ted Turner's "super station," WTBS, offered a heavy dose of Atlanta Braves baseball. WGN was reaching millions of homes across the country, and the motivation behind the corporate purchase of the Cubs quickly became apparent. According to John Madigan, executive president of the Tribune Corporation, obtaining the Cubs "was an opportunity to control live programming, which is the most important thing to a television and radio station" (Gershman 1993, 218).

An unlighted Wrigley Field presented an obstacle to these plans, and by early 1982 a Cubs official, general manager Dallas Green, acknowledged that the franchise intended to install lights at their ballpark. His March 10 announcement marked the beginning of an intense and complicated process of political negotiation. Local opponents of the Cubs' plans for Wrigley Field mobilized in adjoining Lake View. The Cubs, for their part, orchestrated a public relations campaign aimed at furthering their case. Inevitably—given the Cubs' status as one of the city's prized sports franchises, and Wrigley Field's at least informal status as a local landmark—City Hall was drawn into the fray. The Cubs' campaign succeeded, though it took years, and on August 8, 1988, night baseball was played for the first time at the friendly confines of Wrigley Field.

The Cubs engaged in a series of strategies aimed at showcasing the importance of the team to the city's economy, the psychic importance of the team to its fans, and the value of historic Wrigley Field. In effect, the Cubs franchise claimed that if it did not win approval for lights at Wrigley Field, the team's departure to a suburban location, and as a consequence, the demolition of Wrigley Field, would be assured. According to Donald Grenesko, the Cubs Vice President for Operations: "Lights is still our first choice and without them we cannot stay at Wrigley" (McCarron and Burton 1986). The franchise commissioned a series of studies (Market Facts 1985a) showing that the Cubs were Chicago's favorite professional team among baseball fans (77.4 percent), and that the majority of the fans (64.6 percent) were willing to accept either unrestricted use of lights, or lights at eighteen to twenty games during the season. Other research commissioned by the Cubs showed that an overwhelming majority (77.6 percent) of those living within a half mile of Wrigley viewed the ballpark as a neighborhood asset (Market Facts 1985b) and that the annual value of the Cubs to the local economy was $90.7 million (Melaniphy and Associates 1986). That same year, a study by the City of Chicago Department of Economic Development (1986, 2) concluded that "the consulting reports prepared come to remarkably similar conclusions about the total impact of a baseball team on the local economy—about $100 million."

This research did little to sway the opinions of community activists in Lake View, a prosperous area composed of several stable residential neighborhoods and bustling commercial activity along Broadway, Clark, and Halsted streets. Though Lake View had been losing population since the 1950s, by the 1980s homeownership and property values began to climb, a trend that continued into the 1990s. Longstanding community organizations such as the Lake View Citizens Council (LVCC) vigorously opposed the Cubs' plans to illuminate Wrigley Field, as did a newly formed group, the Citizens United for Baseball in Sunshine (CUBS).

The LVCC, CUBS, and supportive local officials argued that the installation of lights would bring increased traffic, noise, public drunkenness, and rowdiness, which in turn, would decrease property values and tarnish

27. *Wrigley Field.* Pictured here at the beginning of the twenty-first century, looking toward the right-field bleachers and centerfield scoreboard. (Courtesy of Larry Bennett.)

Lake View's favorable community reputation. The Lake View activists, through their use of multiple political strategies, proved a formidable opponent for the Cubs. They organized their fellow residents, threatened legal action, advanced a referendum to tap local public opinion regarding the future of Wrigley Field, and persuaded elected officials to support legislation blocking the Cubs' plans. Their community meetings were well attended, often with crowds of several hundred residents, and their press conferences were polished affairs featuring formal news releases, with articulate local activists on hand to provide additional information to reporters.

For a time, it appeared that the LVCC/CUBS trump card was state legislation signed into law by Governor James Thompson in 1982. The new enactment, applied to sporting facilities where night sports had not been played before July 1, 1982, specified that evening events would be in violation of Illinois noise pollution standards. As back-up, Lake View activists also won Chicago City Council approval of an ordinance making night sporting events illegal in facilities with more than fifteen thousand seats that were located within five hundred feet of one hundred or more residential units (Elie 1986).

Fearing the flight of the franchise to the suburbs, the destruction of Wrigley Field, the loss of perceived economic benefits, and possibly worst of all, a political backlash, Chicago's city government sought to mediate the dispute between the Cubs and their Lake View neighbors. Robert Mier, commissioner of economic development under Mayor Harold Washington and an advisor to Washington's successor, Eugene Sawyer, warned in a 1988 city council meeting that without lights the Cubs might be forced to leave Wrigley Field, possibly for a new site beyond Chicago's municipal boundaries: "I have always taken business seriously when they say they have problems and are going to move. I've seen too many say that, and when there is no solution, they move" (Strong 1988a).

Beginning in the fall of 1986, Mayor Harold Washington took direct steps to bring together Lake View community leaders and Cubs representatives to resolve the lights issue, sponsoring several closed-door discussions and two public meetings involving neighborhood, Cubs, and municipal representatives. However, in the face of continued resident opposition to any compromise, Washington took a stronger stance in May 1987, when the Cubs threatened to play their postseason games in upcoming years in St. Louis. Within a few months, Washington adopted a position that he considered middle ground: the addition of field lights at Wrigley Field, but a limited annual schedule of night games. This compromise approach to the issue was likely to have received the city council's support, which in early November of 1987 was considering an ordinance allowing the Cubs to play eight night games during the 1988 season and eighteen night games in subsequent seasons. However, the untimely death of Mayor Washington two weeks later held up the council's vote. Eventually, newly selected Mayor Sawyer won passage of the Wrigley Field lights-enabling legislation on February 25, 1988. Sawyer's public comment overstated the degree of consensus that backed the legislation: "Thanks to the input of the residents of the community and the responsiveness of the Chicago Cubs, I'm confident that we have come up with a compromise proposal which will ensure that one of America's most loved baseball teams stays in Chicago for all of us to enjoy" (Strong 1988b). In fact, many LVCC and CUBS activists continued to oppose the baseball franchise's plans for Wrigley Field. Moreover, city council action on the lights compromise was dictated as much by the *Chicago Tribune*'s aggressive editorial page lobbying on behalf of the deal as members' inherent enthusiasm for the agreement.

Despite ongoing neighborhood misgivings, the Wrigley Field compromise offered Lake View residents a number of benefits. These centered on the development of a "Neighborhood Protection and Improvement Plan." The plan authorized regular discussions between city, community, and Cubs' representatives to address baseball-generated problems and to ensure the viability of the neighborhood. A residential parking permit program and a police hotline were put in place. On game days, bus service to the area was expanded, as were police patrols to assist with area traffic and to address fan-related disorderly conduct. The Cubs organization further agreed to work with the city government to develop more effective litter collection in the vicinity of the ballpark. The Cubs also pledged to restrict the sale of beer during games and to promote public awareness of the plan via their public relations staff. Finally, all parties agreed that, based on community input, the neighborhood protection plan would be regularly updated (City of Chicago 1988).

In many respects, the future did not turn out as either side had planned. Although the Chicago Cubs have made four brief national league playoff appearances since 1988, a resurgent Cubs team playing in the World Series—the presumed result of the Tribune Corporation's infusion of capital to the long-suffering Cubs—has not come to pass. Nor has night baseball brought ruin to Lake View. The commercial streets adjoining Wrigley Field have thrived, and to the surprise of many local residents, property values and new residential construction within earshot of Wrigley Field have skyrocketed. Indeed, several residential property owners along Sheffield and Waveland avenues, across from Wrigley Field's right and left fields respectively, have made small fortunes by converting their roofs and upper floors to private boxes offering bird's eye views of the action. Meanwhile, the Cubs advanced a new plan for upgrading Wrigley Field, and between the 2005 and 2006 baseball seasons, rebuilt and substantially expanded the ballpark's outfield bleachers.

New Comiskey Park: Public Funding of Private Enterprise

In the early months of 1981, nearly coinciding with the Wrigley family's sale of the Cubs, another of Chicago's legendary sports franchise owners, Bill Veeck, turned over the reins of the Chicago White Sox to a consortium headed by Jerry Reinsdorf and Eddie Einhorn. Although Veeck was known as a consummate sports marketer, by the 1970s his bag of crowd-pleasing tricks, such as the notorious Disco Demolition night of July 12, 1979—which produced a near-riot on the playing field and the Sox forfeiture of the second game of the scheduled doubleheader—had clearly taken a turn toward the carnivalesque. Jerry Reinsdorf, for his part, described Comiskey Park, major league baseball's oldest stadium, as "the world's largest outdoor saloon," and clearly the new Sox owners wished to take their franchise in a different direction (Fitzpatrick 1986). During the late 1960s and 1970s, cities around the country had begun to build a new type of sports stadium. Construction of domed stadiums in Houston and Minneapolis, single-purpose stadiums within large sport complexes in Kansas City, and multi-purpose, coliseum-like structures in Cincinnati, Philadelphia, and Pittsburgh all pointed to the fact that a new era in the presentation of sport had emerged. Among the features shared by these facilities were their imposing physical presence, large spectator capacities, and most importantly, revenue-gushing skyboxes, a feature absent from pre–World War II facilities such as Comiskey Park.

Built in 1910, Comiskey not only lacked luxury skyboxes but was also burdened with two thousand support column–obstructed seats in its lower grandstand. The new owners of the White Sox made much of the fact that newer facilities, such as Riverfront Stadium in Cincinnati and Royals Stadium in Kansas City, contained no such seating (Bess 1989). As such, Comiskey Park in its own way posed a challenge to Jerry Reinsdorf and Eddie Einhorn comparable to the liabilities Wrigley Field brought to the doorstep of the Tribune Corporation. Soon after the White Sox ownership transfer, the City of Chicago issued five million dollars in industrial revenue bonds to support the construction of a bank of skyboxes attached to Comiskey Park's upper grandstand, yet even at this point, the new owners of the team had set their sights on a more compelling prize. Dissatisfied with their aging home field, Reinsdorf and Einhorn embarked on a course of action aimed at solidifying exist-

28. *New Comiskey Park.* The new ballpark was built right beside the old one, and several early structures remain. (Courtesy of Larry Bennett.)

ing revenue streams while opening up new markets for their ball club. Central to their plans was the construction of a new home for the White Sox, which would be loaded with the latest in spectator amenities.

The new owners' first step was to document that Comiskey Park's deterioration had reached the point necessitating "significant expenditures on an annual basis to keep the park in safe and usable condition," accomplished by way of an engineer's report completed in 1986 (Krallitch 1986). The next step was to play the field, that is, find communities willing to offer public financing of a new ballpark. During the mid to late 1980s, the White Sox engaged in serious stadium talks with suburban Addison, Illinois, and St. Petersburg, Florida, clearly signaling that the White Sox owners were willing to depart Chicago if a franchise move yielded a new home field.

Suburban Addison could bring the White Sox closer to their principal fan base in DuPage County (Hersh 1986), and the availability of a 140–acre parcel in that community already owned by the White Sox (which had purchased the site in 1984 for $7 million) made it an attractive option. The proposed structure, a $100 million, fifty-five thousand-seat arena, would have a retractable, shell-shaped dome roof and would provide parking space for fifteen thousand cars. The facility would be publicly owned, financed through tax-free state bonds. The facility also promised to yield substantial local economic benefits—$41.4 million for the county and $1.7 million for the city (Presecky and Fuentes 1985). However, the effort to relocate to Addison failed in the face of a close referendum vote in which 50.3 percent of local residents objected to the White Sox project. The upshot of the failed Addison referendum was a series of breakneck meetings among White Sox officials, representatives of the state government, and Washington administration officials, which yielded the initial new Comiskey Park deal in December 1986. This agreement mandated the state and city governments to share the cost of building a new $120 million stadium in the vicinity of the original Comiskey Park (McCarron and Egler 1986).

In fact, by late 1987 Jerry Reinsdorf and Eddie Einhorn took advantage of the slow start-up of the Illinois Stadium Facilities Authority (ISFA) to contact St. Petersburg, Florida, an aspiring Sunbelt city with a stadium under construction but no major league occupants to fill it. St. Petersburg area political and business leaders wanted to attract a professional baseball team, and the White Sox, seemingly unwanted by their hometown of Chicago, qualified as a good match. The city promised to complete the Suncoast Dome by the start of the 1989 baseball season, and Florida's state legislature chipped in with a $30 million appropriation to assist the prompt completion of the new stadium.

Throughout this convoluted series of negotiations there was in fact much concern expressed in Chicago concerning the possibility of a White Sox relocation. A study commissioned by the White Sox had claimed that the baseball team contributed $100.3 million annually to the economy of the city (Laventhol and Horwath 1985). Such calculations were not lost on the municipal government. Ira Edelson, an advisor to Mayor Washington, observed that "losing a major-league baseball team is no different than losing a Wisconsin Steel" (one of the South Side Chicago steel plants) (McCarron 1985). In 1986, a Department of Economic Development study linked new stadium development to additional economic stimulus for the local economy. The study (1986, 8) concluded that: "A team is a substantial source of revenue for the City, County, and State." Stories in the local press offered similar assessments, one for example, claiming that the White Sox would help "retain an estimated $112 million to $162 million in annual local spending, taxes and economic activity" in Chicago (Hornung 1988).

Media support for the public funding of a new White Sox stadium sometimes bordered on the hysterical. A *Chicago Tribune* editorial in early 1988—even as the White Sox negotiated with both St. Petersburg and Illinois officials—asserted that "if the stadium authority persists in refusing to negotiate, it virtually guarantees that Sox will move, and puts much of the blame on itself." *Tribune* sports columnist Bob Verdi (1988) adopted an even harsher tone: "Should Reinsdorf and Einhorn depart for clearly a better situation is St. Petersburg, they will be gone, out of sight, out of mind. But not forgotten will be those striped suits who helped arrange the going-away party. They are the ones who will have to stand up for a change and explain what happened. They are the ones who will have to answer questions from voters who put them in office. They are the ones who will beg for an expansion franchise and be laughed at by major league baseball. . . . Does he [Governor Thompson] want the St. Petersburg White Sox on his resume?" Quickly enough, Governor Thompson in July of 1988 signed an amended new Comiskey Park deal—in one stroke committing the state to a more ambitious stadium project and scotching the franchise's negotiations with St. Petersburg. This agreement provided the team with a new, publicly funded stadium costing in excess of $150 million. The legislation also gave the White Sox exclusive rights to sales within and around the new ballpark. Special auxiliary ticket purchases would be made by the state if minimum annual ticket sales were not met, and taxpayer dollars were committed for annual maintenance (Kass 1988a).

Though these details were not specified in the second stadium agreement, the construction of the new Comiskey Park would require the acquisition of land resulting in the removal of 178 privately owned housing units and 12 community businesses in the South Armour Square neighborhood. Relocation costs were also covered by the agreement. According to a 1989 state audit, Illinois taxpayers would pay a grand total of $657 million in the following twenty years to keep the White Sox in Chicago (Pearson and McCarron 1989).

Opposition to the new Comiskey Park plan emerged on two fronts. A group called Save Our Sox (SOS) sought to keep the team in Chicago and to retain historic Comiskey Park. The second group of opponents consisted of residents of South Armour Square, the small neighborhood across Thirty-fifth Street to the south of the original Comiskey Park. Though both SOS and the South Armour Square residents employed creative tactics to convey their messages, neither was able to reach a large audience or win support from influential political allies.

The SOS group proposed to convert the old stadium into an "urban park," designate it a national monument, and use the resulting revenues to renovate it. They saw a renovated Comiskey as part of a larger district in which tourists to Chicago's South Side could visit additional social/cultural institutions such as the nearby Illinois Institute of Technology and its distinctive collection of campus buildings, historic South Side churches, old ethnic neighborhoods, and legendary blues clubs (Bukowski, O'Connell, and Aranza 1987). However, the SOS plan never captured the public's attention. Nor did SOS and the South Armour Square residents manage to forge an alliance.

South Armour Square was a small, predominantly African American enclave on the south flank of the old ballpark. Covering a modest fifteen city blocks, South Armour Square's residents numbered about fifteen hundred. Though not an economically thriving community, it nonetheless possessed a strong sense of residential identity. As the details of White Sox plans for the new Comiskey Park began to emerge, local residents attempted to organize under the banner of the South Amour Square Neighborhood Coalition (SASNC), staging demonstrations at City Hall and Comiskey Park. Beyond seeking citywide attention, the SASNC also sought the support of various local political figures, including Mayor Washington. However, little came of these demonstrations and overtures to local elected officials. Similarly, when the SASNC leadership met with SOS representatives, the two groups did not find a basis for joint action. Indeed, once the White Sox owners unequivocally demonstrated their willingness to depart Chicago in search of a new home field, SOS switched gears in favor of local public funding of a new ball park (O'Connell 1995).

The politically isolated SASNC came apart in the summer of 1988, as the State of Illinois offered relocation packages to local homeowners and tenants who were willing to acknowledge acceptance of the south-of-Thirty-fifth Street siting of the new Comiskey Park. Compensation was not provided to the residents of the TE Brown Apartments, a senior citizen building, or to those residing in Wentworth Gardens, a low-rise public housing complex, both to the south of the proposed stadium site. All of the residents offered relocation assistance chose to accept the ISFA's terms. For their part, a group of the uncompensated South Armour Square residents filed a civil rights lawsuit against the State of Illinois, the City of Chicago, and the White Sox franchise. In 1996, the federal district judge sided with the defendants, stating that: "There is no evidence that the southern site for the new Comiskey Park was selected for racial reasons" (*Laramore v. ISFA* 1996, 33).

In the fifteen years since the new Comiskey Park opened (it was renamed "U.S. Cellular Field" in 2003), neighborhood revitalization has not come to the areas adjoining the White Sox ball club's new home. During baseball season, the residents of the remnant South Armour Square area experience considerable inconvenience due to the traffic management program used to route motorists to and from the Dan Ryan Expressway.

Nor have the White Sox made a sustained effort to win local friends through community outreach programs or by employing local residents. To the west of the new U.S. Cellular Field, relatively little stadium activity spills over to the Bridgeport neighborhood's commercial district. As such, the deal to build a new Comiskey Park increasingly looks like an expensive case of public subsidy of a well-connected private enterprise.

The United Center in the New Near West Side

During the 1980s, Chicago's Near West Side, a sprawling jumble of public housing developments, aging industrial facilities, and abandoned properties—strategically located within a few minutes of Chicago's downtown core—was a virtual honeycomb for stadium development advocates. Stadium plans for both the White Sox (briefly) and the Chicago Bears of the National Football League were attempted on the Near West Side during that time. Yet only at the beginning of the next decade, when the owners of the Chicago Blackhawks and Bulls won neighborhood support for a new indoor arena, the United Center, to replace Chicago Stadium, was a viable West Side Stadium project achieved.

The Near West Side experienced massive disinvestment and population loss during the 1960s and 1970s, with the neighborhood's low point reached during the destructive riots of April 1968, following the assassination of Martin Luther King Jr. Although the post–World War II period brought a number of major public projects to the Near West Side, including the Chicago Housing Authority's Henry Horner Homes, the new campus of the University of Illinois at Chicago, and Malcolm X College (a two-year institution), the area's acre upon acre of vacant land offered an alluring prize for space-hungry stadium development proponents.

The Chicago Bears' Super Bowl victory in 1986 was the impetus for the team's quest for a new home. Tenants since the 1970s of the Chicago Park District's lakefront Soldier Field, the Bears were unhappy with the terms of their lease as well as the park district's maintenance of their playing field. Although Soldier Field recently had been retrofitted with sixty skyboxes, newly built stadiums around the country featured several times that number, generating substantial revenue streams. In January of 1987, Illinois Governor Thompson expressed support for a West Side site for a new Bears stadium. Additional interest in the project by William Wirtz, owner of the Chicago Stadium and the Blackhawks, as well as by the Rush Presbyterian–St. Luke's Medical Center, morphed into a joint proposal for a massive complex yielding physical spaces for all three partners. The plan included a 72,000–78,000–seat stadium with 15,000 parking spaces and 240 luxury suites, an "Olympic-class" sports medicine and education facility, and a refurbished Chicago Stadium. Initial press coverage was highly favorable. At a time when stadium development proposals seemed to be emerging on a daily basis, one commentary asserted that this plan would "yield far more benefits to the city in terms of jobs and urban redevelopment than would any of the others under consideration" (McCarron 1987). As with the new Comiskey Park, sports development was promoted as a means of neighborhood revitalization. According to a local observer: "It would be hard to find a neighborhood more in need of such help" (Reardon 1987).

Residents of the Near West Side, led by the Interfaith Organizing Project (IOP), a coalition of clergy and lay-persons founded in November of 1985, questioned this form of urban redevelopment. They viewed the stadium proposal as a "land grab" by white developers and wealthy downtown interests. Many residents echoed the concerns of Trimina O'Connor, a member of the IOP, who argued: "We don't want members of the neighborhood's churches and schools displaced so we can become a service heaven for the rich" (Wilson 1987). Moreover, the IOP successfully won the attention of the city's news media via a series of creative public actions including two visits to the Bears' preseason training camp and a touch football game staged in a public park near the home of Bears' president Michael McCaskey (Interfaith Organizing Project 1992). Mayor Harold Washington was also cautious about the community impact of this proposal, which was estimated to displace 328 families and approximately 1,000 to 1,500 low-income and elderly residents. By the summer of 1987, the sports complex proposal had begun to lose steam. Extensive community dissatisfaction and difficulties with securing financing for such a large project redirected the Bears' attention to a new stadium plan.

Paralleling the events surrounding the Wrigley Field lights agreement and the new Comiskey Park proposal, Mayor Harold Washington's death in late 1987 added confusion to the West Side stadium picture. In the succeeding months, not only would a new development team seek to advance an amended version of the Bears stadium proposal, but Governor Thompson would, at one point, weigh in on behalf of a two-stadium proposal (for the Bears and White Sox) on the Near West Side. Although the City of Chicago and the Bears announced an agreement in June 1988, to proceed with a privately funded stadium project—which would be assisted via public infrastructure improvements—this proposal never received the required state legislative approval. Ironically, the lawmakers in Springfield were diverted via the lobbying efforts of William Wirtz, partner to the earlier Near West Side stadium plan but opposed to the eminent domain provisions in the new plan, which would claim some of his property holdings near the Chicago Stadium (McCarron 1988).

With the demise of the Bears stadium initiatives, William Wirtz, joined by the recent purchaser of the Chicago Bulls (as well as lead owner of the Chicago White Sox) Jerry Reinsdorf, made a new entry in the Near West Side stadium sweepstakes. The owners of the Blackhawks and Bulls proposed to replace the Chicago Stadium. Lacking luxury seating, restaurants, and new concession areas, "The Stadium" limited the profit potential for both its owners and sport franchise operators, especially at a time when Michael Jordan and the Bulls were the hottest ticket in town and a growing national sports attraction. Wirtz described the Chicago Stadium as "economically obsolete," and according to an associate: "There comes a point when you realize that you could hurt the health of the franchise by not making a move. The numbers right now don't favor keeping things the way they are" (Kass 1988b).

Given the earlier conflict between Near West Siders and the Bears, Jerry Reinsdorf learned his lesson, declaring himself "determined not to do battle with the community. That is what Mike McCaskey [president of the Bears] did, and he lost. One person can never win these battles—everyone has to get something" (Interfaith Organizing Project 1992, 3). Near West Siders also took a different approach to the proposed basketball and hockey facility. According to a community organizer: "This second time around we wanted to use this opportunity to get something out of it" (Schmich 1992). Finally, Mayor Richard M. Daley's approach to this proposal, in effect, added to the leverage of the community. According to Daley: "What this community needs most is jobs and economic development, but not at the expense of homes and neighborhoods" (Reardon 1991). By refusing to intervene in talks between developers and the IOP from 1989 to 1991, the new mayor in effect enhanced the power of the community groups.

These on-again, off-again negotiations—which broke off for several months in early 1990—resulted in the following "neighborhood package." The agreement mandated the removal of forty homes for the project, but in exchange developers provided replacement housing nearby. The IOP additionally won funding for the reopening of a community health center, a new public library and park, a no-interest loan for the development of seventy-five "for sale" homes, and the use of United Center parking spaces for local churchgoers.

Once the Wirtz/Reinsdorf team and IOP had come to terms, the city stepped in to cement their agreement. The city government collaborated on land acquisition, funded substantial infrastructure improvements, offered a 40 percent break on amusement taxes, and agreed to tax 60 percent of the income derived from the United Center's 216 skyboxes, at a low 4 percent rate (Kass 1991). Although the City of Chicago turned the United Center agreement into a neighborhood development initiative, Mayor Daley's unwillingness to dictate a developer/neighborhood agreement was viewed as crucial by the IOP. According to Earnest Gates (1995) of the IOP: "I knew that if we could keep the government out of the negotiations we would have a chance to get something out of the agreement. You see that was our goal. You can never beat the government. That's why we were successful."

One must accept Gates's comments with a few grains of salt. The attraction-rich United Center has been a major economic success, particularly during the Bulls' second run of NBA championships in the mid-1990s. Moreover, the 1990s brought a new wave of upscale residential investment to the Near West Side. At the same time, the IOP fragmented, and some local residents question whether or not the ongoing gentrification of their neighborhood will provide them much in the way of economic opportunity, or for that matter, even permit them to hold onto to their homes and apartments. Chicago's Near West Side is indeed a new neighborhood, but the most reasonable interpretation of the United Center's role in local transformation suggests that it has been more a marker than cause of the neighborhood turnaround.

29. *United Center.* The United Center—home to the Bulls and the Bears— was built next door to the old Chicago Stadium, Chicago's previous home for professional basketball and hockey. (Courtesy of Larry Bennett.)

Stadiums, Neighborhoods, and the Future of Chicago

The flurry of stadium projects that struck Chicago in the late 1980s like a plains-driven winter storm did not completely dissipate until the early 2000s. In 2001, the Chicago Cubs franchise began negotiating with the City of Chicago and Lake View residents for a proposal to add two thousand seats to Wrigley Field and a large commercial facility adjacent to the ballpark on Clark Street (Spielman 2001). In late 2000, Illinois General Assembly action allowed the Chicago Bears to finally conclude their oft-stalled drive to find a new home, although in this instance their "new home" turned out to be a thoroughly reconstructed (to the tune of $600 million) Soldier Field (Long and Holt 2000). Both of these proposals generated a host of objections. In the case of the Wrigley Field expansion, old concerns over traffic, litter, and rowdiness resurfaced; the Cubs also jousted with Sheffield and Waveland avenue "roofdeck" owners, who are viewed by the franchise as poachers of their prized sports product (Donato 2001). The Soldier Field renovation raised powerful objections regarding the project's cost and its physical impact on the historic Soldier Field facade (Kamin 2001).

As it turned out, both the Cubs and the Bears substantially won what they desired. Nonetheless, the debates associated with these controversies and the history of recent sports facilities development unequivocally signal one key reality embedded in the life of contemporary Chicago. Although the city remains an important transportation and manufacturing hub, the "Hog Butcher to the World" is long gone. Both from an objective economic standpoint, as well as from the perspective of the city's civic leadership, a primary engine driving economic growth in contemporary Chicago is tourism and entertainment, with professional sports representing a core component of the local consumer economy. Stadium projects loom large on the city's civic agenda because the city's political and business leadership assumes that without aggressive sports marketing and up-to-date sports facilities, Chicago's economic fortunes would decline substantially. Furthermore, Chicago's sports franchise owners have entered the inner sanctum of the city's political and civic elite, able to marshal substantial institutional support for lavish projects, as the rebuilding of Soldier Field attests.

For decades, Chicago has been a "sporting town," hosting heavyweight boxing championships and college "all-star" football games long before the American sports boom of the 1960s. But the sheer scale of the three projects we have discussed signaled a change, one with a mixed legacy. Historically, Chicago has been a city whose identity was forged by its neighborhoods, typified by small-scale domestic construction, shop-lined commercial thoroughfares, and well-used public spaces. As every astute commentator on American cities since Jane Jacobs has noted, the neighborhood environment of cities is built on subtle, often quite fragile networks of human interaction—casual socializing, pedestrian traffic, storefront business activity, and the like.

In the interest of finding space to present "big sports," Chicago in recent years has proceeded with stadium development projects that have not been especially heedful of these lessons. On the one hand, neighborhood consultation in preparation to mounting major sports projects has been fitful. On the other hand, the physical magnitude of new projects such as Comiskey Park and the United Center, or for that matter the recent "renovation" of Soldier Field, threatens to overwhelm the adjoining physical spaces and social networks that are characteristic of neighborhood-oriented Chicago. At this point, the city's sports infrastructure would appear to be nearly "built out" for the coming generation. In the future, it will be well for the city's leaders to recognize that big projects—even big sports projects in sports-loving Chicago—can come at a very high price. Future sports complexes that threaten the city's rich collection of near-downtown residential neighborhoods may extract a price not worth paying.

Notes

Assistance for this work was provided by a grant from the National Endowment for the Humanities (NEH). Costas Spirou participated in a 2002 NEH Seminar entitled "Sport, Society and Modern American Culture," co-sponsored by Northeastern Illinois University and the Chicago Historical Society.

Bibliography

Bess, P. 1989. *City Baseball Magic: Plain Talk and Uncommon Sense about Cities and Baseball Parks.* Madison, Wis.: Minneapolis Review of Baseball.

Bukowski, D., M. O'Connell, and J. Aranza. 1987. *Comiskey Park: A Landmark Proposal.* Chicago: Save Our Sox (publisher).

City of Chicago, Department of Economic Development. April 1986. "The Impact of a Major League Baseball Team on the Local Economy." Municipal Reference, Harold Washington Library.

City of Chicago, Department of Economic Development. June 1,1988. "Lake View/Uptown Neighborhood Protection and Improvement Plan." Municipal Reference, Harold Washington Library.

Donato, M. 2001. "Wrigley Neighbors Have Say," *Chicago Tribune,* July 12.

Elie, S. J. 1986. "Joy in Wrigleyville? The Mighty Cubs Strike Out in Court," *Comm/Ent, Hastings Journal of Communications and Entertainment Law* 8: 289–300.

Fitzpatrick, T. 1986. "Reinsdorf Takes His Pitch to Addison," *Chicago Sun-Times,* July 11.

Gates, E. 1995. Interview conducted by Costas Spirou, August 17.

Gershman, M. 1993. *Diamonds: The Evolution of the Ballpark.* Boston: Houghton-Mifflin.

Hersh, P. 1986. "Comiskey Park Bears Skid Mark of White Flight," *Chicago Tribune,* July 13.

Hornung, M. 1988. "Sox Deal Benefits Team, May Shortchange the Public," *Crain's Chicago Business,* May 16.

Kamin, B. 2001. "The Monstrosity of the Midway," *Chicago Tribune,* June 11.

Kass, J. 1988a. "Despite Agreement, White Sox Aren't Safe at Home Just Yet," *Chicago Tribune,* July 3.

———. 1988b. "Chicago Stadium Replacement Urged," *Chicago Tribune,* September 13.

———. 1991. "Bulls, Hawks Arena Clears Early Hurdle," *Chicago Tribune,* May 21.

Krallitch, P. 1986. Letter to Jerry Reinsdorf, March 21.

Laramore, D. et al. v. Illinois Sports Facilities Authority et al. 1996. Memorandum Opinion and Order. April 1, 1996, WL 153672 (N. D. Ill.).

Laventhol and Horwath. 1985. "Economic and Fiscal Impacts from Existing Operations of the White Sox and Comiskey Park." Published by Laventhol and Horwath, Cook County, Ill., June.

Long, R., and D Holt. 2000. "Bears Win the Big One." *Chicago Tribune,* December 1.

Market Facts. 1985a. "Chicago Cubs, General Public Survey." Report prepared for the Chicago Cubs, November 4.

———. 1985b. "Chicago Cubs, Neighborhood Residents Survey." Report prepared for the Chicago Cubs, November 4.

McCarron, J. 1985. "Sox Owners Unmoved by City's Arena Concept," *Chicago Tribune,* November 26.

———. 1987. "Wirtz Supports Sports Complex Plan," *Chicago Tribune,* January 24.

———. 1988. "Stadium Moguls Go One-on-One," *Chicago Tribune,* October 16.

McCarron, J., and T. M. Burton. 1986. "Are Teams Dealing in Bluffs to up City's Ante?" *Chicago Tribune,* March 23.

McCarron, J., and D. Egler. 1986. "Mayor Covered All Bases to Swing Sox Deal," *Chicago Tribune,* December 7.

McCullom, R.1992. "The New 'West Side Story.'" Chicago: Interfaith Organizing Project (IOP).

Melaniphy and Associates. 1986. "Chicago Cubs Economic Impact Analysis." Chicago, Ill., June.

O'Connell, M. 1995. Interview, July 6, conducted by Costas Spirou.

Pearson, R., and J. McCarron. 1989. "Audit Sees Sox Deal as Sound," *Chicago Tribune,* November 7.

Presecky, W., and G. Fuentes. 1985. "Sox Dome Is No Wild Pitch," *Chicago Tribune,* November 24.

"A Puzzling Rebuff to the White Sox" (editorial). 1988. *Chicago Tribune,* May 11.

Reardon, P. 1987. "Stadium Could Fill Urban Void," *Chicago Tribune,* April 14.

———. 1991. "Stadium Agreement Has a Winning Look," *Chicago Tribune,* May 10.

Schmich, M. 1992. "Land War Turns to Mutual Respect," *Chicago Tribune,* June 24.

Spielman, F. 2001. "Bleacher Bums Get Break at Wrigley," *Chicago Sun-Times,* June 19.

Strong, J. 1988a. "Lights Pact for Wrigley Getting Dim," *Chicago Tribune,* February 8.

———. 1988b. "Cub's Pitch for Lights Passes Key Council Test," *Chicago Tribune,* February 24.

Wilson, T. 1987. "W. Siders Turn Blitz on Stadium Plan," *Chicago Tribune,* April 13.

Verdi, B. 1988. "Don't Blame the Sox for Stadium Mess," *Chicago Tribune,* May 12.

13

Chicago Sports! You Shoulda' Been There

An Exhibition

JOHN RUSSICK

On March 29, 2003, the Chicago Historical Society (renamed Chicago History Museum in 2006) opened *Chicago Sports! You Shoulda' Been There*, a 6,000-square-foot exhibition of great sports stories, memorable objects, and exciting images from Chicago's past. The opening was the result of years of work defining the concept, developing the content, and designing and constructing the display. The end result was an exhibition that explored the long, complex, and diverse history of sports to better understand important themes of urban life.

Looking at Chicago's history through its sports, we gain an understanding of the intricate social relationships at work across both time and neighborhood boundaries. Economics, politics, and demographics all provide the background for understanding sports history. And sports, in turn, help reveal the larger history of the city. Sports reflect changing attitudes about race, gender, ethnicity, class, and religion. Moreover, sports help make such abstract yet volatile social categories visible. And because

30. *Sports Bring Us Together.* This opening panel of the exhibition explains that sports reinforce many identities—civic, ethnic, gender, neighborhood— some of which may unite us, some divide us. (Courtesy of the Chicago History Museum.)

public interest in athletics is so deep, a sports exhibition, we believed, had an excellent chance of reaching a wide public. Our exhibit, we hoped, would give sports fans a greater appreciation of the broad historical significance of the subject; we also wanted the exhibit to give history-lovers an appreciation of sports as more than just fun and games.

The process by which most exhibitions are developed can be broken down into three main phases of work:

Conceptual Development
Content Development
Design Development

Conceptual development involves defining the main idea or theme and sub-themes of the exhibition. In the broadest sense, we asked, What can be learned by looking at sports history? Content development involves identifying the stories to be told and selecting the objects, images, and other media to reinforce them. Finally, in design development the vision expressed in the previous phases is turned into a three-dimensional experience for visitors to the museum.

Phase 1: Conceptual Development

Chicago is a great sports town. It supports professional teams from all of the nation's big leagues—hockey, football, soccer, basketball, and two baseball teams. The city also goes wild for its local prep and college teams. And all summer long in almost every city park, teams sponsored by local hardware stores, real estate agencies, and breweries crowd baseball diamonds, soccer fields, and volleyball courts. All of this is due to the large numbers of sports fans who support the vibrant local sports culture.

Using the broad appeal of the subject and the city's long experience with sports, we began developing what we hoped would be a thought-provoking exhibition that looked at sports as a way for individuals and communities to establish a sense of who they are and where they belong. More precisely, we proposed that sports have helped define the racial, gender, ethnic, religious, class, and civic identities of people all across Chicago. Sports unite Chicagoans but also mark the boundaries between various social groups. Establishing the core theme of sport and identity gave direction to all of our subsequent work, allowing us to jettison extraneous notions and to focus on the most important and relevant sports stories.

Clarifying themes serves three main purposes for those creating the exhibit. First, themes are tools for deciding which historical stories best illuminate a subject. Second, they are touchstones to return to over the course of an exhibition's development to confirm that the project is on track to achieve its goals and objectives. Third, themes provide a rough organizational scheme that exhibition designers, webmasters, publicists, and so on, can use to help guide their work in later phases of exhibit development.

With literally thousands of stories to choose from, our broad theme of sport and identity helped us select a group of case studies. Many of these stories packed a powerful emotional punch. For example, through our research we discovered stories of amateur boxers from South Chicago who fought both opponents in the ring and deep prejudices against working-class kids from Latino neighborhoods. Then there were tales of young women with the courage to join newly established professional baseball leagues challenging 1940s' expectations about their roles in American society. We also learned of Chicago's Japanese Americans, who, beginning in the late 1940s, developed athletic leagues that used traditional American sports to foster ethnic pride for people still shaken by their recent internment in World War II detention camps. And it was in Chicago where the great Negro National League was founded in 1920, offering African American migrants pouring into the city access to their own version of the national pastime.

While many of our strongest sports stories featured the exclusion of people and the response to that exclusion, some sports-minded groups were organized not so much to bar others as to promote confidence and pride in themselves and their communities. For example, Chicago Jews founded the Chicago Hebrew Institute in 1903 as a welcoming social experience for newly arriving Jews from Europe. The goal of the organization was to help these newcomers adapt to American society while strengthening the bonds of the Jewish community. One of the key tools for this purpose was the development of athletic programs to help assimilate the children of these immigrants.

Identity gains depth from a sense of place—who we are resonates with where we are. The stadiums where so many of the greatest sporting events took place are icons not just of sports but also of Chicago. They serve as communal spaces where Chicago's fans, teams, and athletes have come to compete and cheer together for generations. They are the great witnesses to the city's long-standing love affair with sports. While play on the field is fleeting—once the events have occurred they exist only in our memories, written accounts, photographs, and film—athletic arenas endure for decades, connecting us to each sport's history. The famous Dempsey-Tunney boxing match of 1927, with its "long count," was a great championship fight, but its image is indelible because it took place before one hundred thousand people in the new arena, Soldier Field. In the

31. *Tough Jews.* Like other ethnic groups, Jews took advantage of the growing availability of sports in the twentieth century. Learning to play, going
to games, buying consumer sporting goods, and rooting for the home team
were routes to becoming American. (Courtesy of the Chicago History
Museum.)

fabled story of Babe Ruth's called shot in the 1932 World Series, Wrigley
Field itself is a central character.

We hoped that by grouping stories into fabled venues such as Wrigley,
Comiskey Park, and Chicago Stadium, visitors would be able to reach
back to their own memories and revisit their experiences with a new
perspective. The emphasis on these venues in the exhibition provided a
structure for the entire project and became a favorite component of the
exhibition for many visitors.

Another idea that we strove to include was how innovation and entre-
preneurship (both key components of Chicago's self-image) are reflected
in our sports legacy. This proved to be an easy task. Chicago hosted the
first-ever "subway series" in 1906; Roller Derby was founded in Chicago in 1935, and Abe Saperstein started the Harlem Globetrotters not

in New York but Chicago. The Special Olympics began here in 1968, and the Wilson sporting goods company started in Chicago by turning waste products from slaughterhouses into tennis racquets and footballs. Major League Baseball's first all-star game took place here in 1933, and the Negro leagues held theirs in the Windy City every year.

Finally, we wanted to make certain that in the midst of these great stories, objects, and images, we were able to display the central character-istics of sports—action and excitement. Visitors needed to see a variety of sports being played by all sorts of people from different generations. We began planning for the development of two films that included historic and contemporary footage of Chicago athletes and teams.

By the end of 2001, we had a fully developed concept. Now we needed to select the stories that exemplified the themes, locate and obtain objects and images, and create a design that offered an engaging and educational experience for passionate sports fans and novices alike.

Phase 2: Content Development

The best history exhibitions feature two things—memorable stories and meaningful objects. Objects connect visitors to people and events from the past; stories use drama and emotion to tie the visitors to the objects and support the exhibition's premise. In the case of *Chicago Sports! You Shoulda' Been There*, we chose stories first, then selected materials to support them. This meant that there was a lot of work finding objects and images once the exhibit narrative was roughed-out.

About fifteen months before the exhibition opened, we began to set-tle on several powerful stories from Chicago's sporting past that would resonate with visitors of different backgrounds, ages, and interests. Each of these stories needed to support the "sports as identity" theme. Taken together, they needed to represent a century of change across a range of sporting experiences. Each story would have to be "visual" in the sense that objects and images along with a few lines of text would allow visitors to understand its meaning. If no materials could be found, the story would be cut and replaced by another one. This process would have to be nearly completed before we could proceed to the design development phase.

The original document that fleshed out the exhibit concept high-lighted a number of sports stories as examples of key themes. It quickly became clear, however, that we needed to discipline our choices. We kept drifting toward an impossible inclusiveness; after a few months, our files were bursting with research on checkers, cockfighting, and horseshoes. We had many more stories under consideration than we could possibly find room to include.

We ultimately selected some great stories, but it wasn't without compromise. First, we chose to look at only twentieth-century sports. We also decided that we simply could not cover the evolution of sporting experiences for every identity group. For example, we decided to look at the changing role of women in sports at four key points—athletic programs at Jane Addams's Hull-House; male/female skating teams in early Roller Derby; the founding of the All-American Girls Professional Baseball League; and the passage of Title IX of the Education Acts and the spectacular girls basketball teams that Title IX nurtured. We could, of course, have told other stories, but these had strong narrative lines, and good images and objects to display. These stories also covered a wide swath of time, concerned a range of players and spectators, and were all clearly important.

Another key issue to resolve during this time was how to organize the content of the exhibit. Working out an organizing scheme was necessary

32. *Hull-House.* Beginning late in the nineteenth century, Jane Addams's Hull-House pioneered in sponsoring playground sports for men, women, and children. (Courtesy of the Chicago History Museum.)

before we could proceed with object and image selection, film production, and label writing. After attempting some of the more obvious schemes, including displaying stories by type of sport (baseball stories, football stories, etc.), or by sub-theme (civic identity, racial identity, gender identity, etc.), or even by straight chronology, we decided to organize the entire exhibition by venue, dividing it into six sections, each a representation of a stadium. This decision required hard choices, but it offered some unexpected and interesting connections between various sports.

Organizing the exhibition space by venue forced us to grapple with design and content issues simultaneously. We decided to include four main professional sports venues in Chicago—Comiskey Park (renamed U.S. Cellular Field just weeks before the exhibit opened), Wrigley Field, Soldier Field, and the United Center—although in the case of Comiskey Park and the United Center we were equally invoking their predecessors, old Comiskey Park and Chicago Stadium. Amateur and school-based sports stories, however, would not easily fit into those four venues. So in addition to the four famous venues, we added two fictive ones, one to represent school sports and the other for neighborhood sports.

We also decided to emphasize the histories of the stadiums themselves, so for each venue we developed a list of secondary stories to enhance visitors' appreciation of the role the stadiums played in sports history. This approach resulted in the development of timelines for each venue, including notable games, record-breaking events, important athletes, and some unique objects and images. By the spring of 2002, after several consultations with our academic advisors and countless working meetings with our in-house team of historians and designers, we had twenty-two sports stories selected. Now, with roughly one year remaining before the exhibition was scheduled to open, we began pulling together the objects and images to help connect visitors to the stories.

The Chicago Historical Society has a massive collection of objects, documents, prints, and photographs (roughly twenty million items). However, materials related to the city's sporting culture were not, until quite recently, a high priority for the CHS. While we were able to find many great objects in our collections, we needed to look elsewhere for much of what would be included in the exhibition. In the end, we borrowed roughly two-thirds of the three-dimensional objects on display in the exhibit. We searched for materials from other sports and history museums, professional and amateur sports collectors, local high schools and colleges, local and national news outlets, team and stadium owners, active and retired sports figures, and from the local professional teams. At the end of the content development phase, we had identified over two thousand potential objects and images.

Our objects search had one goal: find the best items to support the stories. In the case of the 1919 Black Sox scandal, we wanted something from the trial and something from the players. We found the sworn testimony of "Shoeless" Joe Jackson in our archives and we borrowed his bat from a professional collector. For the story of the Golden Gloves, we wanted to find the gear of a real Golden Gloves champ. We borrowed the robe, shoes, gloves, and championship trophy from Frank Corona, a local boxing hero in the early 1970s. We wanted materials from the Negro League's annual all-star game, held every year at Comiskey Park from 1933 through 1953. We obtained images from a historian of the black baseball leagues and an original Chicago American Giants jersey (the local Negro League team) from the National Baseball Hall of Fame. And for the 1990s Bulls and the Super Bowl Bears, we shot for the moon. After months of negotiations, we borrowed the 1986 Lombardi trophy from the Bears and all six NBA trophies from the Bulls.

At this same time we started the production of two films to be featured in the exhibit. These films would be our only opportunity to show sports in action. The first film explored the importance of place and memory in Chicago sports history and featured the professional sports venues included in the exhibit. Here we were able to link some of our stories to the arenas where they took place and provide a broader context for each story. The second film explored the role sports played in the lives of four Chicago-area athletes. By mixing historical film footage and contemporary interviews with a current golden gloves boxer from South Chicago, a one-time Negro League baseball player, a former member of the All-American Girls Professional Baseball League, and a past world champion Roller Derby skater, this film provided visitors with an opportunity to meet Chicagoans whose lives were changed by sport.

As we made headway in selecting the stories, objects, images, and film subjects, the designers began turning these components into a coherent physical experience for visitors. Once the design concept was finalized, our last major hurdle was to write and edit all of the label copy, our primary communication tool.

Phase 3: Design Development

In its final form, the exhibition included over 270 objects, over 500 photographs (the vast majority from CHS) and more than 5,000 words of label copy. It had 28 exhibit cases (some stories had more than one case), and two theaters, each showing films produced exclusively for CHS in collaboration with The History Channel. The exhibit space consisted of two nearly identical, square galleries linked by a 70-foot-long bridge.

33. *Black Sox.* The "Black Sox" scandal of 1919, in which eight White Sox players were accused of throwing the World Series, once again reinforced Chicago's image as a corrupt town where everything was for sale. (Courtesy of the Chicago History Museum.)

34. *Da Bears.* . . When Chicagoans refer to the Super Bowl, they often mean not the annual event, but the game that took place at the end of the 1985 season and showcased the likes of Walter Payton and William "Refrigerator" Perry. (Courtesy of the Chicago History Museum.)

Visitors were encouraged to enter the southern gallery first then stroll to the northern gallery via the bridge.

The first step in the design process was to develop a bubble plan, a type of exhibition floor plan that uses large shapes to indicate the area dedicated to each exhibit section, each theater, and each exhibit case. After months of shifting cases and venues on the bubble plan to find the right arrangement, the exhibit team settled on a final floor plan.

It was an open plan with no partition walls. The scheme relied heavily on the perimeter walls to carry signage and a rigid color scheme to identify the venues. Each gallery also had a discreet horseshoe-shaped theater space cordoned off by floor-to-ceiling fabric banners. The films themselves were projected onto the permanent perimeter walls. The galleries were organized as follows:

Gallery 1

Main Visitor Entrance

Section 1—Neighborhood Sports (4 case studies)
- Golden Gloves (1 case)
- At play in the streets (1 case)
- Jane Addams's Hull-House (1 case)
- Spalding and other Chicago sporting goods manufacturers (1 case)

Section 2—Soldier Field (4 case studies)
- 1985 Super Bowl Champion Chicago Bears (2 cases)
- 1998 Major League Soccer Champion Chicago Fire (1 case)
- 1927 Dempsey-Tunney Long Count boxing match (1 case)
- Special Olympics (1 case)

Section 3—Comiskey Park (5 case studies)
- White Sox owner, Bill Veeck (1 case)
- 1919 Black Sox scandal (1 case)
- Negro League's East-West All-Star Game (1 case)
- Roller Derby (2 cases)
- Joe Louis and Jack Johnson (1 case)

Theater 1: Theme—Chicago's great sports venues

Bridge to gallery 2

Gallery 2

Section 4—Wrigley Field (4 case studies)
- Cubs/Sox Rivalry (1 case)
- Early NFL, George Halas, and the Chicago Bears (3 cases)
- All-American Girls Professional Baseball League (1 case)
- 1969 Chicago Cubs (1 case)

Section 5—Chicago Stadium/United Center (2 case studies)
- Blackhawks of the 1960s (1 case)
- Bulls dynasty of the 1990s (3 cases)

Section 6—School Sports (3 case studies)
- University of Chicago and Amos Alonzo Stagg (1 case)
- DuSable High School Basketball team, 1954 (1 case)
- Title IX and Marshall High School Basketball (1 case)

Theater 2: Theme—Athletes reflect on how sports changed their lives

Main Visitor Exit

After settling on the floor plan, we began developing the individual case layouts, an overall color scheme for the gallery, the design of the theaters, the content for the stadium timelines, the secondary stories for the two amateur venues, the first draft of main label copy, and the design of all the graphic panels in the exhibition. Meanwhile, we were obtaining permission to use historic film footage and still imagery from a variety of sources around the country, and confirming the loan of roughly 180 objects from outside sources.

In most instances there were many more objects and images available for a single case display than we could use. The process of deciding which materials made the most effective display was a long and complex one, involving regular dialogue between content developer and exhibit designer. The critical task for the developer was to keep measuring what the visitors will see or read when they peer into each case against what they should know about the subject by the time they walk away. The designers had to be responsive to these concerns while still creating an attractive exhibit case.

Objects are just one part of this equation. Case layouts present a host of challenges for exhibition designers. Mounts have to be designed to hold many of the objects and images selected and sized to leave room for descriptive captions and credit lines. Label copy must be accommodated inside the case and space must be left near all of the objects for identification labels. Cases need to be balanced—not too crowded, not too sparse. The design must also allow for effective lighting, which can only be judged after the case has been installed.

For some exhibit cases, designers made decisions largely based on practical considerations. For instance, the Chicago Stadium/United Center section had three cases dedicated to the Bulls of the 1990s. This material was spread out to allow a lot of people to get as close as possible to Michael Jordan's uniform, Scottie Pippen's jersey, and Dennis Rodman's shoes without crowding one another. It was also necessary to give the Bulls' six NBA championship trophies their own case to make the greatest impact. Most visitors found these golden, glowing objects easily and were thrilled that they got to see them up close. On the day the exhibit opened, one teenaged boy spotted the trophies, dropped to his knees, and crossed himself.

With the Bulls' story, we wanted to convey to visitors that the team changed the city's self-image. We were no longer the sport worlds' lovable losers with once-a-generation championships. The 1990s Bulls, with their six world titles, made Chicago a powerhouse. Michael Jordan replaced Al Capone as the city's most famous personality, emblematic of a larger change in the city's image from a dangerous town of stockyards and mobsters to a modern urban playground. This relatively complex message was communicated explicitly in the label copy, which was prominently displayed next to the first Bulls' case and more subtly in the display of Bulls' promotional material and memorabilia found within the cases.

The majority of the cases in the exhibit explored legendary sports stories that we felt had wider implications for Chicagoans than just a win-

35. . . . *and Da Bulls.* The six Bulls championship trophies from the Michael Jordan era were the most popular objects in the exhibit. (Courtesy of the Chicago History Museum.)

ning or losing season. For example, after the 1919 Black Sox (America's most notorious sports scandal, which helped define Chicago's image as a town where the fix was always in), our most famous baseball club was the 1969 Cubs. This was arguably the city's best baseball team in the second half of the twentieth century, a collection of seasoned veterans with a desire to get back into the record books after a thirty-four year absence from the Series and over sixty years since a championship. One hundred and fifty-five days after grabbing and holding first place, the team fell behind the "amazing" Mets in a heartbreaking September collapse.

To capture the 1969 Cubs, we included jerseys from some of the team's premier players, a copy of the *Chicago Tribune*'s sports section with a shot of the infamous black cat that walked in front of the Cubs dugout during a late-season game against the Mets at Shea Stadium, and Don Young's baseball mitt (Young dropped two balls in one game against the Mets weeks before the Cubs slipped from first place, and he is still seen as one of the players who cost the team the championship). We observed many older visitors study this case, sigh heavily, and walk on.

In the Comiskey Park section we featured Joe Louis's championship bout against James J. Braddock. But to tell Louis's story, we felt we needed to discuss another Chicagoan, Jack Johnson. Joe Louis's 1937 title was testament not only to hard training and ring craft, but also to Louis's ability to negotiate the social pitfalls that lay before any African American fighter seeking the title after the infamous career of Jack Johnson, the world's first black boxing champ. Johnson won the title in 1908, but he was unwilling to subject himself to the racist codes that governed daily life for blacks in early twentieth-century America. He lived lavishly in Chicago, drove fine cars, wore elegant clothing, and consorted with white women, breaking the great racial taboo of the early twentieth century. Eventually, he was forced out of boxing and an unwritten ban on black contenders was enforced until Joe Louis subverted the inequity through determination and an unassailable character.

This was a difficult case to design. We had several great objects and images from Joe Louis's career, including a pair of his boxing gloves, but we had no significant objects that belonged to Johnson, only a few photos, some books, and a program from his fight against Jim Jeffries, the "Great White Hope." However, the juxtaposition of the two men and the eras in which they lived and fought were the key to the story, for together they tell a monumental tale of race in America. The soda bottles, pomade tins, and comic books that featured Joe Louis's face, name, and signature represented his success at beginning to change the way African Americans were perceived in America.

In the Soldier Field section we told the story of the city's newest professional team, the Chicago Fire of Major League Soccer. Here the message was diversity—the changing face of Chicago sports, the sports fan, and the city itself. In the fall of 1998, the Fire brought home the MLS championship trophy. In the exhibit case we displayed this trophy, along with the jersey and championship ring of one of the club's key players, Frank Klopas, as well as a large color image of the victory celebration.

36. *Immortals.* The first African American Heavyweight Boxing Champions, Jack Johnson (who held the title from 1908 to 1915) and the great Joe Louis (champion from the late 1930s through the 1940s) resided in Chicago. (Courtesy of the Chicago History Museum.)

We also focused the visitor's attention on the fact that the Fire broadcast their games in three languages, English, Polish, and Spanish. Trilingual broadcasts reflect not only Chicago's changing demographics, but also the fact that immigrants no longer simply embrace traditional American sports. Today they are able to support the spread of the sports that they grew up with and in the process, reshape the face of what is considered American sport.

Many of the stories in the exhibition were unfamiliar to our visitors, even though they were as rich with meaning and drama as the 1990s Bulls' dynasty, the Cubs failure in 1969, or Joe Louis's triumph at Comiskey Park in 1937. Here, we needed to make the imagery strong and the displays dynamic to encourage people to take the time to investigate them. For example, the Golden Gloves case, the very first case in the exhibition, examined the story of Frank Corona, a local boxing champion, but a relative unknown outside his neighborhood. Corona came up through a South Chicago boxing club located in the basement of Our Lady of Guadalupe Church in a working-class Latino neighborhood. The club was sponsored by the local police precinct, and Chicago cops were fixtures at the club's training bouts and tournaments. After winning the Barney Ross trophy, named for the international boxing champion and neighborhood hero, Corona himself went on to become a Chicago policeman. Visitors saw Corona's robe, shoes, and gloves displayed on a mannequin. Immediately to the left of the figure was a photograph of Corona in the ring wearing the same gear and holding the Barney Ross trophy, and in front of the photograph, the trophy itself.

Corona's story is about finding identity, not just as a boxer, but as a Latino supported by the neighborhood Catholic Church in a blue-collar community in the waning years of the local steel industry. The story is also part of the legacy of the Golden Gloves, and of the Second City's long-term rivalry with the nation's first, New York. Beginning in 1934, the *Chicago Tribune* sponsored the annual Golden Gloves tournament; the best Chicago clubs fought the best New York City clubs for national bragging rights.

The final section of the exhibition (school sports) held two cases that explored the triumph of talent over discrimination. In 1954, the very year that Thurgood Marshall argued the case of *Brown v. Board of Education* before the Supreme Court, DuSable High School's all-black basketball team, the Panthers, went downstate to compete for the Illinois State championship. Although they lost in the finals by six points, the impact of their achievement is still widely recognized in Chicago. At the height of the Bulls' reign in the 1990s, one local reporter reflected that the vibe in the city around the Bulls reminded him of the citywide excitement

37. *DuSable High School.* In 1954, the DuSable Panthers headed down-state for the championship game against Mt. Vernon. The first all-black team to play for the title, DuSable lost but changed the game forever. (Courtesy of the Chicago History Museum.)

generated by the Panthers during the 1954 season. We deliberately kept the case spare to call attention to DuSable's second-place trophy, which features a little statue of a phenotypically white basketball player stretching upward with a ball at his fingertips.

Just a few feet away from the DuSable case and within view of the Bulls' materials was a case brimming with championship trophies. Here the triumph of the Marshall High School Lady Commandos under the leadership of Coach Dorothy Gaters was on display. Gaters formed the predominantly African American basketball club in 1974, two years after the passage of Title IX of the Education Acts. Over the next decades, the Lady Commandos posted an amazing 766 wins and 84 losses, winning 22 public league titles and 7 state championships.

An examination of one hundred years of Chicago sports history reveals a city transformed. Today, all-girls basketball teams, major league baseball teams with interracial and international rosters, and African American boxing champions are the norm. But sports do not simply reflect change, they help bring it about. Sports have provided a means of personal expression and social connection for generations of Chicago athletes and fans. With their broad appeal, sports help to create cohesive communities out of the diverse populations that call Chicago home. Paradoxically, sports can unite the whole city, blurring the lines of neighborhood and ethnic groups. People from across town—black, white, and Latino; Jewish, Christian, and Muslim; men and women; rich and poor—with little else in common, come together to cheer for the city's teams. When the games are great and the stakes high, rooting for the Bulls or the Bears or the Blackhawks feels like the very essence of being a Chicagoan.

Epilogue
Where Hope Goes to Die

ELLIOTT J. GORN

I became a Cubs fan about fifteen years ago; threw away old loyalties and joined the Wrigley faithful. I have been wondering why ever since. I kept a journal for a little while during the 2002 season, in which I found myself slipping into a dialogue (diatribe?) with the team, the fans, the city. Passion, of course, is what being a sports fan is all about, caring deeply precisely because it doesn't matter. No doubt these passages reveal a steady progression toward madness. So be it. As a Cubs fan, there is just one thing to say: "Wait 'til next year."

Look, it's four in the morning, and here I am writing about the Cubs. They lost last night to Florida I assume—they were down 10–1 last I looked. I caught the score while at the home of a seriously disturbed collector of Cubs paraphernalia in a northern suburb, looking for objects to display in this cursed exhibit on Chicago sports. The man's house was stuffed with headlines, tickets, pictures, baseballs, gloves, bats, spikes, all of it stacked on floors, hung on walls, piled on tables, room after room of stuff—a baseball shrine.

The man kept calling himself crazy, and I agree—madness was just around the bend. But was he mad like a schizophrenic, or mad like a seer, a poet, a prophet? Change the details a bit and his compulsion looked a little like religious devotion. He happens to be Jewish and I happen to be Jewish, but maybe not. Bear with me.

Has it ever been remarked that the word "pennant" comes from the same root as penance? The latter is from Old French, the former from early-modern Welsh. Close enough. Here in Chicago, the connection is unmistakable.

During the first two decades of the twentieth century, the Cubs arguably were the best team in baseball. They won their first World Series in 1906 and their last in 1908, and took the national league pennant (that word again) five times in those twenty years. They were even pretty good for the next twenty-five years, never winning the championship, but getting to the Series in 1929, 1932, 1935, 1938, and 1945. Then began six decades (and counting) of angst, disappointment, bitterness. They have not returned to the Series since the end of World War II. And they have not been to postseason play in consecutive years since 1907–8.

As we all know, knowledge of history is the Rosetta Stone that unlocks the hieroglyphic jumble of our lives. As the Cubs stopped winning championships, Chicagoans did penance. Literally. During the late nineteenth century the city doubled in population every decade. The demographic explosion continued until World War I cut off the flow of newcomers, then the United States government bolted the doors shut with draconian immigration laws in the 1920s. But before then, massive numbers of immigrants poured into and built the city.

By the 1920s, Chicago had become—remains—the most Catholic city in America. Irish, Germans, Italians, Poles, Bohemians. (Slavs and their descendants still come to Chicago, peoples whose histories are dark and bloodstained, nations for which existence itself was tenuous.) Sure, there were plenty of Jews and Orthodox, and some Muslims, Hindus, and Buddhists too. Protestants were here from the city's founding, their numbers reinforced by waves of African American migration between the 1910s and 1960s. But even today, outside the loop's skyscrapers and the high-rises along Lake Shore Drive, the steeples of magnificent Catholic churches dominate the prairie horizon, and parish life still exercises an outsized influence on the city's neighborhoods.

Could any more evidence possibly be needed? Being a Cub fan is worship by other means. The liturgical drama on which Chicagoans were raised—betrayal, martyrdom, resurrection (someday, someday)—is played out, eighty-one times per year at Wrigley Field.

Forgive me Father for I have sinned. What did I do? I don't exactly know. Left the city of my youth, betrayed my childhood team (the Dodgers) and the faith of my fathers (their superhero in cleats was one of us, number 32, Sandy Koufax). I was covetous, lecherous, deceitful—still am. Whatever it was I thought or did, I am doing penance for it now.

Vanity, vanity, all is vanity. Man is born to suffer. I am a Cubs fan.

• • •

Philip Dacey wrote in his great poem, "Mystery Baseball,"

> Pitchers stay busy
> getting signs.
> They are everywhere.

The signs are everywhere for fans, too—that promising reliever acquired in a trade, that young outfielder who showed he had all the tools in last September's call-up. More arcane signs, too—the great Cubs pitcher from the early twentieth century, Mordecai "Three Finger" Brown literally had just three fingers on one hand—two missing. But the new Cubs closer, Antonio Alfonseca has six on each hand—double-threes. This can't be a mere coincidence. The signs are everywhere, and they bode a return to the days of glory.

• • •

Mayor Daley needs to consider banning children from Wrigley. Watching this stuff will destroy their faith, turn them against their city, even against America. Hearing the "Star-Spangled Banner," then watching the Cubs play makes Wrigley into a breeding ground for radicals, communists, terrorists. Little ones will look at their parents after a game and say, "It's just like Santa Claus, right? The Cubs will never win, will they? There is no God, is there?"

• • •

Another magnificent effort today. Leading the Phillies 2–1. In comes Kyle Farnsworth to pitch the eighth, then Alfonseca to close it out and get the save in the ninth. But Farnsworth walks Burrell. Rolen smashes a drive to left, catchable, but Alou lets it bounce off his glove. Men on second and third, one out. Farnsworth walks Lee intentionally to pitch to the light-hitting Perez. A line drive to right, and Sammy, being Sammy, tries to catch it. He did this two weeks ago against the Mets. Rather than cut off the ball and allow just one run to score, he goes all out, misses completely, the ball rolls to the wall, and the winning run comes home.

• • •

Why do I do this to myself? Wrigley field is to blame. It's everything a ballpark should be. It feels intimate; its seating capacity of forty thousand is like the new generation of retro-stadiums—Jacobs Field in Cleveland, Camden Yard in Baltimore, etc.—with their fake old-timeiness. But Wrigley is the real thing. You pay your money, walk in, and sit down in 1915. Of course, the field dimensions of Wrigley are *not* small, a fact Cubs management seems unable to grasp. In fact, the field is large—sort of. The power alleys are short, 368 feet, but the center field fence is the industry standard 400 feet, and the left and right field foul-poles are 355 and 353 feet away, very, very far out. Nor is Wrigley the home-run park most fans imagine—total home-run production over the years is dead average. When the wind blows out (which is less than half the season) it is a power hitters park, but when it blows in you've got to play little ball. I called the general manager's office to argue this point but they put me on hold. Next time I'll use e-mail.

Such subtleties of the game are lost on the neo-yuppie scum and out-of-towners (note how few people keep a score card during the games at Wrigley) who stuff the grandstands and themselves. And of course the team owner, the soulless Tribune Corporation, is only interested in the bottom line, and will do whatever is necessary to keep those butts in the seats. Since a winning team is superfluous to the spectacle of Sammy Sosa crushing the ball, no one has to work hard at fundamentals—taking a base on balls, hitting the cut-off man, executing the squeeze play, decoying the runner—the little things that win ballgames. And since Sammy is totally narcissistic anyway, it all works out. Unless you hope to see a real baseball game—sharp defense, smart base-running, batters working the count, that sort of thing.

• • •

I went to the game with my friend John Powell last night. By the fifth inning I was overwhelmed in the same way that, a century ago, wealthy Americans on their grand tours of Europe used to be overwhelmed by the richness of art and architecture; you know, sighing, weeping, fainting. I waxed poetic, exclaimed how beautiful it all was, just a magnificent urban scene. Powell looked at me pityingly. He's a real Chicagoan, not a newcomer like me; he knows not to invest in this bunch of losers. Sometimes he calls the Cubs "your imaginary little friends."

• • •

Another buddy, Alex, was in town yesterday, called to set up a time for lunch. I said, "Why don't we dine al fresco—get a hotdog at the ballpark?" A horrific performance by the Cubs. Still, there we were on a nice warm weekday afternoon, in that great three-hour flow of talk that ranges over lefty-righty match-ups, the shortstops of our youth, marriage, children divorce, friends and assholes, wind direction, who is the best right fielder in town (Ordonez), the duplicity of team owners, and so on. I talk about how I love going to Wrigley. Walking over from my apartment and entering the stadium evokes all those goofy yet power-ful idyllic feelings about baseball—green fields, men in boys' uniforms, the love of pure play, the joy of undefiled competition. The very idea of day games is pleasurable—here we are, sitting in the ballpark, blowing off work. Speaking of blowing things off, the Cubs blow the game in the eighth with three bone-headed plays, rookie stuff at best, all committed by veteran—some might say geriatric—players.

The irony, of course, is that the Tribune Corporation cynically mar-kets this to us. Why try to give the fans good baseball when an easier and more lucrative sell is the spectacle of the ballpark itself? The broadcasters hawk tickets to upcoming games, and on TV we see drunken fans singing "Take Me Out to the Ballgame," women in skimpy clothes (the cameras spend more time on cleavage than infield play), Sammy's mighty cut at the ball (for a third strike with two on and two out). No doubt about it, Wrigley is a scene, a forty-thousand-seat bar. Not many people debating the hit-and-run here; they're too busy calling their friends on their cell phones to tell them they are at Wrigley. The Tribune figured this out long ago, realized that there is no need to field a good team. So why do I keep returning? Good question.

• • •

A little history:

The Chicago White Stockings—the team that became the Cubs—was founded in 1870, just one year before the Great Chicago Fire. These two disasters were unrelated.

Actually, the White Stockings began auspiciously. In their inaugural year, they defeated America's first professional baseball club, the great Cincinnati Red Stockings. By the mid-1870s, the incomparable Albert Spalding pitched for and managed the White Stockings, and one of base-ball's great hitters, Adrian "Cap" Anson, came over from Philadelphia. Spalding went on to become a sporting goods magnate, whose firm mo-nopolized much of the industry. Anson led the White Stockings to repeated championships, but he also spearheaded professional baseball's drive to eliminate black players, an interdiction that lasted until Jackie Robinson reintegrated the game in 1947. Perhaps it was Spalding's sharp business practices and Anson's racism that cursed the ball club in future years.

At the end of the 1800s, the team changed its name, appropriately enough, to the Orphans, but in 1902 they became the Cubs (the new American League franchise then adapted the old name and became the

J. S. Thompson & Co., Printers, Times Building, 88 Fifth Avenue, Chicago.

38. *Champions.* Professional baseball began gloriously in Chicago. The White Stockings, renamed the Cubs at the beginning of the twentieth century, were National League Champions in 1876. (Courtesy of the Chicago History Museum.)

White Sox). The Cubs prospered during the early years of the twentieth century. With sparkling defense from the double-play combination of Tinker-to-Evers-to-Chance and outstanding pitching from the likes of "Three Finger" Brown, the Cubs won the World Series for the first time in 1906, and for the last time in 1908. This is an odds-defying feat, for a statistically average team would have won four more titles before the end of the twentieth century. (The White Sox record, it should be noted, is nearly as dismal, arguably the second worst in all of baseball, the 2005 championship not withstanding. It is a measure of how far we have declined that Chicago was arguably America's greatest baseball town between 1900 and 1920.)

In 1915, the Cubs moved from the old West Side Ballpark to a new home, Weeghman Park (originally built in 1914 for the Chicago Whales of the Federal League, which lasted only two years) on the corner of Addison and Clark. Five years later, chewing gum manufacturer and team owner William Wrigley renamed the yard Wrigley Field. While no longer a baseball powerhouse, the Cubs continued to contend for several years, winning their last National League Championship in 1945, fielding future Hall of Famers Hack Wilson, Rogers Hornsby, and Gabby Hartnet,

39. *Cubbies.* The 1907 Cubs, awaiting a train in a Chicago station. The following year, the team won its last championship. (Courtesy of the Chicago History Museum.)

and being led by such luminaries as Joe McCarthy and William Veeck. Wrigley Field witnessed some great moments in these years, such as Babe Ruth's "called shot," when—allegedly—he pointed to the centerfield bleachers in the third game of the 1932 World Series, then deposited the next pitch there, and Hartnett's "Homer in the Gloamin'," in which the Cubs catcher managed, in the gathering darkness, to drive a ball into the stands and give the team a victory that all but clinched the 1938 national league pennant.

Since 1945, the Cubs have been baseball's doormat. Only the team of the late 1960s—featuring Ron Santo, Ernie Banks, Billie Williams, and Ferguson Jenkins—can be called a great one. Perhaps the most poignant year in Cubs history was 1969. The team had not won the championship in over sixty years, and had not been to the World Series in almost a quarter of a century. Managed by Leo Durocher, the Cubbies led the league from April through August, and held a thirteen-game lead with just thirty left to play. The "bleacher bums" who cheered everyday from

40. *Wrigley Field.* The newly built Weeghman Park, circa 1915, home of the Federal League's Chicago Whales. The Federal League folded the next year, the Cubs moved in, and in 1926, Cubs Park was renamed in honor of its owner, William Wrigley Jr. (Courtesy of the Chicago History Museum.)

the outfield stands were emblematic of how Chicagoans gave their hearts to this club. The Cubs did not exactly collapse, but they played under .500 ball, while the New York Mets—a franchise just a few years old, previously the game's laughingstock but now fielding a remarkable pitching staff—won almost all of their games. The summer of 1969 was the winter of Cub fans' discontent.

Since then—in a variation of Karl Marx's observation that history repeats itself, first as tragedy, then as farce—the Cubs have given their fans farce after farce after farce. Sure, the Cubbies fielded a handful of respectable squads, and they even made the play-offs a few times. But they have not had an outstanding team for decades. Not since my grandfather's day have other ball clubs come to Wrigley with fear in their hearts.

• • •

Last night was one for the ages. The boys are playing in St. Louis, rubber game of a three-game set. Good pitching match-up, Matt Clement against Matt Morris. Clement is dominant, great breaking-ball, and he's getting it over the plate. Cardinals are thoroughly off balance for five innings. Meanwhile the heart of the Cubs order breaks through early. Almost identical first and third innings—walk to Sosa with two outs, nice contact hitting by McGriff, then smashes deep into the right and left field gaps by Alou. Cory Patterson ices it, driving in McGriff and Alou with a lovely homer into the right field power alley. Six-to-nothing Cubs, and that is the way it stays until the sixth inning.

The rest is a comedy of errors. Clement gives up a single to Edmonds to start the sixth, followed by a perfect double-play ball to Gonzalez. But wait, that's not Gonzalez playing shortstop. Since the Cubs never pay attention to defense (the strategy, apparently, is that fans pay to see offense, not defense), Mark Bellhorn is at short, and Delino DeShields (who earlier in the season was cut by the lowly Baltimore Orioles) at second. Neither of these guys is much defensively. So instead of short-hopping an easy grounder, the tentative Bellhorn waits for it to come to him, makes a hurried throw to DeShields, who is playing on the wrong side of the bag, and the ball goes floating into right field. First and third, nobody out. Now, inexplicably, the Cubs manager pulls Clement—who to that point had thrown just eighty pitches and allowed only two hits—and puts in Jeff Faserro, a lefty to face a lefty. But Faserro can't get anyone out this season. Three runs score before Kyle Farnsworth comes in and stops the bleeding.

By the ninth inning, the Cubs have actually gotten two more runs, and Farnsworth's ninety-eight-mile-per-hour heater is blowing the Cardinals away. A five-run lead should hold, even for this inept bunch. And the Cubs have not one but two closers, Flash Gordon and Antonio Alfonseca. Without going into details, the Cards score six runs in the ninth, capped by a walk-off three-run dinger by Edgar Renteria. Cubs lose 10–9.

This is baseball at its ugliest—stupid base-running mistakes, failures to execute bunts, infielders out of position. But most amazing is the lack of intelligent criticism in the newspapers and on radio of all of this. In baseball, God dwells in the details—it's doing the little things right that mark the difference between .600 teams and .400 teams, between champions and goats. Which raises the key question: Why do I care so much?

• • •

Sammy Sosa is one of the greatest hitters in the game today. I would trade him for a bullpen catcher. Of course he would be a powerful presence on a championship team. But we're not a championship team. Now here is the contradiction. If you have an ignorant fan base, people who are content to just see a big homer or two, to root for their favorites, believe the false promises of management that "we are turning the corner," you can keep filling a shrine like Wrigley. And when these people realize bad baseball isn't much fun, there will be plenty more behind them, not knowledgeable fans, but folks out for a pleasant afternoon, people on vacation from Iowa and Kansas, or coming in from the suburbs for a day with the kids. That's okay—unless you believe that baseball is one of the only places left where dedication, finely honed skills, craft, fierce will, teamwork, in short, doing things right—still matters, and that being a fan means knowing the difference. It's all about pride, not the pride of blind devotion (the Cubs get plenty of that), but pride in craft. There are a lot of reasons that White Sox fans hate Cub fans, but not the least is the sense the Cubs never have to earn respect on the field.

• • •

Another bitter defeat, 6–5 to the lowly San Diego Padres. Twenty-seventh time in one hundred games the Cubs have had the lead and lost the game. Where did that phrase "loveable losers" come from? There is nothing loveable here. Pathetic losers, contemptible losers. Just plain losers. This team doesn't need steroids, it needs anti-depressants. Team? There is no team, just a collection of one-tool athletes. The Cubs had three home runs last night; three home runs and only five total runs. This game isn't really so complex. Get on base no matter how: hit, walk, bunt, homer; whatever it takes. On-base percentage is the best predictor of team success in the long run—that and on-base percentage allowed by the pitching staff.

And another thing—who are these old guys? Because Wrigley is so changeable—some days a power park, some days a little ball park—the team concept should center on athleticism. With such distant foul poles, corner outfielders must be able to cover lots of territory and have strong arms. Because the wind often blows in, many games are close, so defense up the middle is critical, as is the ability to manufacture runs. This means, unfortunately, that the Cubs have to do the opposite of management's instinct. They need athletic, multi-talented ballplayers, not these over-the-hill dinosaurs, whose names can draw a crowd. Statistically, player ability peaks at about age twenty-seven. Among position players, the team the Cubs fielded last night has one guy under twenty-seven, one exactly twenty-seven, and the rest older, considerably older.

• • •

More ineptitude. A four-run lead in the second evaporates before nine innings are over. Hope germinates in the bottom of the tenth—Cubs have runners at the corners, no outs. Strike out, strike out, pop out; game still tied. Top of the eleventh, the Padres touch-up Farnsworth for two home runs. Cubs fail to respond in their half of the inning.

On the radio, announcer Ron Santo keeps telling us that this is the best Cubs team he has seen in years; he just can't understand why they are not winning. Did it ever occur to him that maybe he's wrong; that after five months of wretched baseball (including the preseason), it might be time to reevaluate. Let's see—worst offense in all of baseball (measured by batting average and on-base percentage), among the worst defenses (measured by errors), one of the most porous bullpens (measure it any way you like); doesn't sound like a team of great promise to me. Can't blame the cold weather any more (besides, isn't it cold for both teams in April)? Can't lay it on injuries—actually, the team is very healthy—physically, anyway. They just flat-out stink.

Or consider Skip Caray's remark on television that the Cubs have to start winning to get back into this race. Excuse me? Fifteen games behind St. Louis with two-thirds of the season gone. They have been out of this race for three months now. Though I guess they were even with all the other clubs on opening day.

I've listened to lots of baseball announcers over the years, but I have never heard ones with such disregard for the fans' intelligence. Do they really think that we will remain loyal regardless of what happens on the field? That no matter how malodorous a product the Tribune Corporation gives us, no matter how incompetent the Cubs organization, no matter how mediocre the players, that we will still turn on our televisions, listen to our radios, show up at the ballpark. Do they really think we are that stupid?

Hold that thought; it's gametime.

• • •

Went to the game yesterday with friends. Spent the whole time talking about how pathetic this team is. One guy, Danny Greene, is a third-generation Cubs fan—grandfather, father, and son, not one of them have ever seen their team win a World Series. He is totally disgusted. "Give them up," I say. "I can't, it's in my blood," he replies. Then Danny adds something really interesting. He and his wife are going up to the woods in Michigan for a week, and he is really excited about it: "No newspapers, no Internet, no television, no radio—no Cubs." In other words, he can't stop himself. Now this is not a character issue; Danny is a solid guy. No, this is about fate, tragedy, sin. Being a Cubs fan is some sort of moral burden, one that he can't put down. At least not for more than a week. Danny's greatest fear is that the Cubs finally will end up in the World Series—and lose to the White Sox. He is pretty sure he'll have to shoot himself. (A footnote: Danny now has a son, Solomon, four generations of losers, and counting.)

As it turned out, the game wasn't bad. The Cubs built a small lead, then, in late innings, the bullpen did what it does best—by the end of the seventh, after another fine start by Kerry Wood, the Padres led by four runs. But in the eighth, Bellhorn comes through with a three-run homer. Still, these are the Cubs—no heart—and now in the ninth, down by a run, the Padres' closer, Trevor Hoffman, one of the best in the game, takes the mound. With two outs, Roosevelt Brown cracks a single, and Fred McGriff, pinch hitting today, does the same. Delino DeShields comes in to run for McGriff (paraphrasing the late *LA Times* sports columnist Jim Murray, people leave train wrecks faster than McGriff runs). Shortstop Alex Gonzalez, batting all of .230, lines a double into right, DeShields flies around the bases behind Brown, and slides in just under the tag for the victory.

It is one of those rare times at Wrigley when you remember how wonderful this game can be—three hours building up to just one moment. This is what the great teams do, play opportunistic baseball, put together a few good plays, and when you look up at the scoreboard, you're ahead, or maybe you've even won. The way the Cubs celebrated on the field, you'd think they just clinched the division.

· · ·

A man named Dick Brown sells me a dozen pair of Cubs tickets each year out of his season passes. A scholar and formerly the head of Research and Education at Chicago's great Newberry Library, Dick has been a Cubs fan for over sixty years. Of course, he is really Satan. I should have known. There was the tell-tale whiff of brimstone the first time he came around offering tickets. Under his hat, I am sure, are the horns, and inside his shoes the cloven hooves. But in the words of a great Chicago blues, "Too late, / Too late, / Too late."

· · ·

Epilogue to the Epilogue: And then came the wholly unexpected 2003 season, magical, wonderful, Dusty Baker and his boys levitating into October. Who ever thought the Cubbies could pound the Braves then dominate the Marlins! Up three games to two, our best pitcher on the mound with a two-run lead, five outs to go and the hometown crowd roaring the team toward the World Series. Maybe the old cycle had turned once again, the laws of physics giving way to a new age of miracles, faith surging forth as the end of days approached. But sometime before the eighth inning, the spirit of the goat entered poor Steve Bartman's body, forcing him to lean out and try to catch that ball, otherwise headed for Moises Alou's outstretched glove. It had to end as it did, we all know that. This drama was written long before the world began; we merely play our assigned roles. Fate. Destiny. Acceptance. That's the key—acceptance. If only it were so simple. Two months later, on Christmas day, I walked by Wrigley Field, cold and beautiful in the winter sun. Looking east on Waveland, the scoreboard was as green as summer, and the grandstands stood ready to hold the new season's promise. In the frigid afternoon sunlight, the old ballpark and I were poised once again between October's pain and spring training's hope.

Contributors

PETER T. ALTER is curator at the Chicago History Museum. He has published articles in the *Journal of American Ethnic History, Serbian Studies,* and *Journal of the Illinois State Historical Society.*

ROBIN F. BACHIN is Charlton W. Tebeau Associate Professor of History and Director of American Studies at the University of Miami. She is author of *Building the South Side: Urban Space and Civic Culture in Chicago, 1890–1919,* and creator of the digital archive "Travel, Tourism and Urban Growth in Greater Miami."

LARRY BENNETT is a professor of political science at DePaul University, Chicago. He is coauthor, with Costas Spirou, of *It's Hardly Sportin': Stadiums, Neighborhoods, and the New Chicago.*

LINDA J. BORISH is an associate professor of history at Western Michigan University. She is author of numerous articles on women, health and sport, and coauthor of *Sports in American History: From Colonization to Globalization* (with Gerald Gems and Gertrud Pfister).

GERALD R. GEMS is a professor of health and physical education at North Central College in Naperville, Illinois. He is author of *Windy City Wars, The Athletic Crusade: Sport and American Cultural Imperialism,* and coauthor of *Sports in American History.*

ELLIOTT J. GORN is a professor of history and chair of American civilization at Brown University. He is author of *The Manly Art: Bare Knuckle Prize Fighting in America*; with Warren Goldstein, of *A Brief History of American Sports*; and editor of *Muhammad Ali: The People's Champ*. He is writing a book about John Dillinger.

RICHARD IAN KIMBALL is author of *Sports in Zion: Mormon Recreation, 1890–1940*. He is an associate professor of history at Brigham Young University.

GABE LOGAN completed his dissertation, "Lace Up the Boots, Full Tilt Ahead: Recreation, Immigration, and Labor on Chicago's Soccer Fields, 1890–1939," at Northern Illinois University. He is an assistant professor of history at Northern Michigan University.

DANIEL A. NATHAN is an associate professor of American studies at Skidmore College. Nathan has published articles in *Aethlon*, *American Quarterly* and the *Journal of Sport History*. He is author of *Saying It's So: A Cultural History of the Black Sox Scandal*.

TIMOTHY B. NEARY is an assistant professor of history at Salve Regina University in Newport, Rhode Island. He received his Ph.D. from Loyola University in Chicago. He is author of numerous articles.

STEVEN A. RIESS is Bernard Brommel Research Professor of history at Northeastern Illinois University. He is author of numerous books, including *Touching Base: Professional Baseball and American Culture in the Progressive Era*; *City Games: The Evolution of American Society and the Rise of Sports*; and *Sport in Industrial America, 1850–1920*.

JOHN RUSSICK is curator at the Chicago History Museum. Past exhibits include "Chicago Sports! You Shoulda Been There"; "Leopold and Loeb: The 'Perfect' Crime"; and "Fashion, Flappers, 'n All That Jazz." He has published articles in *The Exhibitionist*, *Public History News*, and the *Chicago History Magazine*, and edited *Historic Photos of Chicago Crime*.

TIMOTHY SPEARS teaches American Studies at Middlebury College, where he also serves as dean. He is author of *Chicago Dreaming: Midwesterners and the City, 1871–1919*, and *One Hundred Years on the Road: The Traveling Salesman in American Culture*. He is working on a family history of Ivy League football.

COSTAS SPIROU is a professor of social science at National-Louis University, Chicago. He is coauthor, with Larry Bennett, of *It's Hardly Sportin': Stadiums, Neighborhoods, and the New Chicago.*

LOÏC WACQUANT is a professor of sociology at the Earl Warren Legal Institute at the University of California, Berkeley. He is author of *Body and Soul: Notebooks of an Apprentice Boxer.*

INDEX

Sport and Society

Making the American Team: Sport, Culture, and the Olympic Experience
  Mark Dyreson
Viva Baseball! Latin Major Leaguers and Their Special Hunger
  Samuel O. Regalado
Touching Base: Professional Baseball and American Culture in the
  Progressive Era (rev. ed.) *Steven A. Riess*
Red Grange and the Rise of Modern Football *John M. Carroll*
Golf and the American Country Club *Richard J. Moss*
Extra Innings: Writing on Baseball *Richard Peterson*
Global Games *Maarten Van Bottenburg*
The Sporting World of the Modern South *Edited by Patrick B. Miller*
The End of Baseball as We Knew It: The Players Union, 1960–81
  Charles P. Korr
Rocky Marciano: The Rock of His Times *Russell Sullivan*
Saying It's So: A Cultural History of the Black Sox Scandal *Daniel A. Nathan*
The Nazi Olympics: Sport, Politics, and Appeasement in the 1930s *Edited by
  Arnd Krüger and William Murray*
The Unlevel Playing Field: A Documentary History of the African American
  Experience in Sport *David K. Wiggins and Patrick B. Miller*
Sports in Zion: Mormon Recreation, 1890–1940 *Richard Ian Kimball*
Sweet William: The Life of Billy Conn *Andrew O'Toole*
Sports in Chicago *Edited by Elliot J. Gorn*

Reprint Editions

The Nazi Olympics *Richard D. Mandell*
Sports in the Western World (2d ed.) *William J. Baker*
Jesse Owens: An American Life *William J. Baker*

The University of Illinois Press
is a founding member of the
Association of American University Presses.

Composed in 9.5/12.5 Trump Mediaeval
with Eurostile display
by Jim Proefrock
at the University of Illinois Press
Designed by Dennis Roberts
Manufactured by Sheridan Books, Inc.

University of Illinois Press
1325 South Oak Street
Champaign, IL 61820-6903
www.press.uillinois.edu